OXFORD MID-CENTURY STUDIES

The Oxford Mid-Century Studies series publishes monographs in several disciplinary and creative areas in order to create a thick description of culture in the thirty-year period around the Second World War. With a focus on the 1930s through the 1960s, the series concentrates on fiction, poetry, film, photography, theatre, as well as art, architecture, design, and other media. The mid-century is an age of shifting groups and movements, from existentialism through abstract expressionism to confessional, serial, electronic, and pop art styles. The series charts such intellectual movements, even as it aids and abets the very best scholarly thinking about the power of art in a world under new techno-political compulsions, whether nuclear-apocalyptic, Cold War-propagandized, transnational, neo-imperial, super-powered, or postcolonial.

Series editors
Allan Hepburn, McGill University
Adam Piette, University of Sheffield
Lyndsey Stonebridge, University of Birmingham

The Promise of Welfare in the Postwar British and Anglophone Novel

States of Repair

KELLY M. RICH

OXFORD
UNIVERSITY PRESS

Great Clarendon Street, Oxford, OX2 6DP,
United Kingdom

Oxford University Press is a department of the University of Oxford.
It furthers the University's objective of excellence in research, scholarship,
and education by publishing worldwide. Oxford is a registered trade mark of
Oxford University Press in the UK and in certain other countries

© Kelly M. Rich 2023

The moral rights of the author have been asserted

All rights reserved. No part of this publication may be reproduced, stored in
a retrieval system, or transmitted, in any form or by any means, without the
prior permission in writing of Oxford University Press, or as expressly permitted
by law, by licence or under terms agreed with the appropriate reprographics
rights organization. Enquiries concerning reproduction outside the scope of the
above should be sent to the Rights Department, Oxford University Press, at the
address above

You must not circulate this work in any other form
and you must impose this same condition on any acquirer

Published in the United States of America by Oxford University Press
198 Madison Avenue, New York, NY 10016, United States of America

British Library Cataloguing in Publication Data
Data available

Library of Congress Control Number: 2023935115

ISBN 978–0–19–289343–7

DOI: 10.1093/oso/9780192893437.001.0001

Printed and bound by
CPI Group (UK) Ltd, Croydon, CR0 4YY

Cover image: Abram Games, "Your Britain – Fight for It Now (Housing)" (1942).
Army Bureau of Current Affairs.
© Imperial War Museum (Art.IWM PST 2909).

Links to third party websites are provided by Oxford in good faith and
for information only. Oxford disclaims any responsibility for the materials
contained in any third party website referenced in this work.

For Alan and Rowan

Contents

List of Figures, with Captions and Credits   vii
Acknowledgments   viii

Introduction: States of Repair   1

PART I: CRADLE

1. A Room of One's Own?: Postwar Modernism and the Reconstructive Imagination   41

2. "Nowhere's Safe": Angry Young Women and Communal Betrayal   73

3. Unhomely Empire: Seeking Hospitality in Windrush Britain   101

Interlude: Failed Utopias, or, the Beginning of the End   136

PART II: GRAVE

4. Empty Places: Unpropertied Intimacy and Queer History   153

5. Oasis Societies: Global Welfare and the Romance of Care   182

6. Institutional Life: Infrastructural Interiority as Postwar Feeling   203

Coda: A Hostile Environment   232

Bibliography   248
Index   265

List of Figures, with Captions and Credits

1. *Keep Calm and Carry On* (1939). Ministry of Information. © Crown Copyright. 8
2. Fred Taylor, *Rehabilitation: It Takes Time* (1945). © Transport for London. Reproduced courtesy of the London Transport Museum collection. 9
3. Patrick Abercrombie and John Forshaw, *County of London Plan* (1943). London County Council. © Crown Copyright. 20
4. Ernő Goldfinger, "Aerial view of rows of houses" (1944). © RIBA Collections. 22
5. "The Look In," *County of London Plan*. 23
6. Furnished rooms from *Britain Can Make It No. 12* (1946). Board of Trade. © Crown Copyright. 24
7. Bill Brandt, "Elizabeth Bowen" (1946). *Lilliput*. © Bill Brandt Archive. Reproduced courtesy of Bill Brandt Archive Ltd. 42
8. "Millions of Mean Houses Still Exist," *Planning for Reconstruction* (1943). Anonymous. © Architectural Press. 58
9. Still from *A Diary for Timothy* (1946). Crown Film Unit/Ministry of Information. © Crown Copyright. 72
10. Cover of *Picture Post*'s special issue, "A Plan for Britain" (1941). Reproduced courtesy of Getty Images. 102
11. *TOGETHER* (1939). Ministry of Information. © Imperial War Museum (Art. IWM PST 3158). 103
12. *Racial Prejudice* (1958). © Keystone Features. Reproduced courtesy of Getty Images. 130

Acknowledgments

Were it not for the care of teachers, colleagues, mentors, family, and friends, this book would never have come to be. Much of it originated at the University of Pennsylvania, whose graduate English program taught me how to be a person in this profession. I was fortunate indeed in my committee. Heather Love had a way of continually turning the project on its head, revealing its possible iterations and stakes. Jim English provided critical ballast, bringing my lacunae into view. Paul Saint-Amour fostered and modelled impeccable scholarship with heart and serious play. And Jed Esty sustained my work from the ground up with an unfailing warmth and confidence. Thanks to Monika Bhagat-Kennedy, Thomas Dichter, Mandy Edwards, Nava EtShalom, Jessica Hurley, Laura Finch, Lydia Yaitsky Kertz, Jungha Kim, Grace Lavery, Cliff Mak, Alice McGrath, Kalyan Nadiminti, Ana Schwartz, and Philip Tsang for making those years time well spent.

The Harvard English Department has proven a remarkable source of academic life. I have benefitted immensely from conversations with colleagues including Homi Bhabha, Glenda Carpio, Amanda Claybaugh, Teju Cole, Phil Fisher, Ju Yon Kim, Deidre Lynch, Derek Miller, Peter Sacks, Elaine Scarry, Laura van den Berg, Andrew Warren, Nicholas Watson, Leah Whittington, and Anna Wilson, as well as those across and through the university, including Angela Allan, Jordan Brower, Genevieve Clutario, David Damrosch, Annabel Kim, and Margaret Rhee. Beth Blum provided a bridge and camaraderie for which I will be ever grateful. The departmental staff make Barker feel like home, particularly Lauren Bimmler. Zhe Geng's last-minute assistance with the manuscript was much appreciated. And to my students: you have taught me so much. Thank you for bringing us back to the table.

This project has been furthered by various sources of institutional support, including the Institute for the Recruitment of Teachers, Penn's School of Arts and Sciences, the Mellon/ACLS, and Harvard's Faculty of Arts and Sciences. A manuscript workshop with Matt Hart, Peter Kalliney, and Ravit Reichman was integral to the development of this book: hearing its tenets refracted through three brilliant interlocutors was nothing short of a gift. I was also grateful to call Wellesley College's Newhouse Center for the

Humanities home for a semester, where I delighted in the fellowship of Elizabeth Graver, John Plotz, J. Keith Vincent, and Eve Zimmerman. Over the years, I have been inspired by the example and company of Janice Ho, Chris Holmes, Wendy Lee, Yoon Sun Lee, Melanie Micir, Nicole Rizzuto, Aarthi Vadde, Rebecca Walkowitz, and Susan Zieger. Two pairs deserve special recognition. To Jenny Hyest and Mimi Winick, and that picnic bench in Brighton: your abiding friendship has been a miracle, something more than a miracle to me. And to Gina Patnaik and Juno Richards, my kin: you make this way of life inhabitable and good—but let us continue, always, to retreat.

The life of a book is long and winding. I have been enormously fortunate that its landing point has been the Mid-Century Studies series at Oxford University Press, whose co-editors Allan Hepburn, Adam Piette, and Lyndsey Stonebridge have provided much-welcome guidance and support. I've been likewise fortunate in the press's anonymous reviewers, whose keen insights and queries have made this a better book. Special thanks to Allan for his mentorship and continued support. Versions of chapters have appeared in *ELH* and *Modern Fiction Studies*; I am grateful to Johns Hopkins University Press for the permission to reprint them here: Copyright © 2015 The Purdue Research Foundation. *MFS: Modern Fiction Studies*, Volume 61, Issue 4, Winter 2015, pages 631–651. Published with permission by Johns Hopkins University Press. Copyright © 2016 Johns Hopkins University Press. *ELH*, Volume 83, Issue 4, Winter 2016, pages 1185–1209. Published with permission by Johns Hopkins University Press.

Finally, I'd like to thank my parents, Brenda and John Rich, for their unwavering belief in me and support of my education; as well as my sister Ali, for all the fun. Carole Newlands and Jack Niles have provided much hospitality and kindness over the years. Jeanne Griffin, Annie Olinick, Marta Sierra, Moira Killoran, and Carina Vocisano-Bruel have helped me keep an even keel throughout these writing years, while care from Shannon Hennessy, Paloma Ruiz, and Paxton Wanink have made this writing doable. Mandy Vincent is the friend without whom I would be utterly unmoored. Lucy kept me company as the going got rough. And lastly, to Alan Niles: thank you for making it all possible, and that much better. This book is dedicated to him and to our daughter Rowan Haeyun, whose welfare I promise to tend to all of my days.

Introduction

States of Repair

What happened in 1945 to make it the origin of the contemporary? Marked by the unprecedented wounds of the Second World War, that year called and still calls into being the need for new forms for understanding and representing human experience.[1] History, art, design, architecture, and literature have all taken 1945 as a candidate for the origin of the contemporary. Yet 1945 inaugurates the contemporary not just for elite aesthetic discourses, but also for popular conceptions of who we are. Take, for instance, Google Earth's "Historical Imagery" tool, unveiled in 2009, which allows users to move through time as well as through space. For the interface, historical time largely means that of the Second World War, with London's 1945 featured as key to understanding "the reality of everyday life back then—bombed buildings, deprivations, militarization, and the normal appearance of what where [sic] then secret facilities."[2] What lesson is imparted when toggling between 1945 and our contemporary moment? Why is the message of 1945 especially legible through images of wartime destruction, particularly of the built environment? And what might explain the enduring cultural preoccupation with this threshold between the Second World War and its postwar, which still manages to keep so many in its thrall?

For British and Anglophone literatures, one familiar answer is to be found in the mythology of the Blitz, which plays an outsized role in the cultural imagination around the Second World War, and continues to fuel cultural production from feature films to TV series, genre and literary fiction, video games and documentaries. Its story goes something like this: as the "island fortress" standing alone against the European Nazi invasion, wartime Britain not only occupied an exceptional position among its

---

[1] Most famously, Adorno's intimation of "no poetry after Auschwitz." Theodor Adorno, *Prisms*, trans. Samuel and Shierry Weber (Cambridge: MIT Press, 1983), 34.
[2] Michael T. Jones, "History in the Unmaking," October 21, 2010, https://maps.googleblog.com/2010/10/history-in-unmaking.html.

The Promise of Welfare in the Postwar British and Anglophone Novel. Kelly M. Rich, Oxford University Press.
© Kelly M. Rich (2023). DOI: 10.1093/oso/9780192893437.003.0001

European neighbors, but also experienced total war, an exceptional form of warfare. Total war meant a collapse or conflation of the boundaries between combatants and civilians, foreign and domestic affairs, military events and everyday Home Front efforts. This experience was made possible by wartime logic and language around the public good, which catalyzed the British population into the militarized machine that would eventually win the war. As propaganda at the time reminded people, their eating habits, travel plans, and conversations were part of an intricate social web whose cause and effect went beyond their immediate scope of vision. The Second World War thus became the "people's war," one that, as Angus Calder put it, made Britain's people "protagonists in their own history in a fashion never known before."[3]

Without discounting the enduring mythology of Britain's wartime togetherness, this book offers a different metric for the cultural weight of Britain's Second World War: its promise of postwar reconstruction and the only partially realized welfare state that was its result. Literary histories of Britain's Second World War tend to consign the postwar as a coda to their work, focusing on wartime violence and state influence over literary and cultural production.[4] Yet the imagination of peace was a driving engine of war culture, with its own forms of promotion, conscription, and propaganda. During the war, the state's renewed commitment to social welfare became especially pronounced as the thing worth fighting for, not just for few, but

---

[3] Calder, *The People's War: Britain 1939–1945* (London: Jonathan Cape, 1969), 17.

[4] See, for instance, Patrick Deer's conclusion "The Boom Ends" in *Culture in Camouflage: War, Empire, and British Literature* (Oxford: Oxford University Press, 2009); Jenny Hartley's "Post-war Post-script" in *Millions Like Us: British Women's Fiction of the Second World War* (London: Virago, 1997); Marina MacKay's coda in *Modernism and World War II* (Cambridge: Cambridge University Press, 2007); and Wendy Webster's concluding section "Aftermath" in *Mixing It: Diversity in World War Two Britain* (Oxford: Oxford University Press, 2018). Notable exceptions can be found in Mark Rawlinson's chapter on "War Aims and Outcomes" in *British Writing of the Second World War* (Oxford: Oxford University Press, 2000), Valerie Holman's chapter on "Publishing for Peace (1944–1945)" in *Print for Victory: Book Publishing in England, 1939–1945* (London: The British Library, 2008); and most recently, Part III of Beryl Pong's *British Literature and Culture in Second World War Time: For the Duration* (Oxford: Oxford University Press, 2020), on "The Temporality of Ruins." Even scholars of the war's contemporary reach equate its legacy to the unprecedented wounding technologies of total war, for obvious reasons having to do with the nature of memory and trauma, such as Marianna Torgovnick's concept of the "war complex," or the "the difficulty of confronting the fact of mass, sometimes simultaneous, death caused by human volition under state or other political auspices," *The War Complex: World War II in Our Time* (Chicago: University of Chicago Press, 2008), 2; and Victoria Stewart's focus on military practices of secrecy as the war's cultural legacy in *The Second World War in Contemporary British Fiction: Secret Histories* (Edinburgh: Edinburgh University Press, 2011).

for all. As one of the most salient cultural legacies to emerge from the Second World War, this reconstructive ethos captures what Jose Harris describes as midcentury's "elusive but important change in perceptions of the mutual relationship between society and the state."[5] Welfare provisions lost some of their associated stigma and became re-centered as a national cause: a wished-for transformation into a more coherent and secure society. The project of this book, then, is to track the cultural impress left by postwar reconstruction. How does literary production communicate the value and character of the welfare state? How does it do so differently than the already highly symbolic discourses of postwar reconstruction? And, above all, why does literature keep returning to this transitional moment in order to make sense of the twentieth and now twenty-first century world?

This book argues that literature, especially the novel, keeps returning to 1945 to reanimate its transformative social potential as well as its darker failures. Midcentury writers such as Elizabeth Bowen, Muriel Spark, and Samuel Selvon used the militarized Home Front to present postwar Britain as a zone of lost privacy and new collective logics. As the century progressed, influential novelists including Alan Hollinghurst, Michael Ondaatje, Kazuo Ishiguro, and Ali Smith all looked backward to 1945; their novels register an unfulfilled nostalgia for a Britain that never was, as well as the need to come to terms with welfare's decaying remains. This book focuses on novels by these writers and draws on the works of other contemporaries to describe an enduring pattern of postwar and contemporary literature. These works index Britain's obsession with rebuilding the postwar world in terms of both physical and social structures, testing the logic of repairing structural ills through reforms to private life. Their recursive reinstatement of 1945 models several forms of attachment to a permanent transition away from war, a process that is not just unfinished but also, perhaps, unfinishable. While reconstruction produced models, surveys, and diagrams of how people ought to live together after the war, postwar novels test these promises, adapting the logic of reconstruction to present crucial counternarratives to Britain's postwar consensus. As the following chapters describe, novels continue to query, condemn, mourn, and celebrate the reparative potential of the postwar imagination, well beyond its midcentury origin.

When it comes to social welfare services, this book focuses on housing and representations of dwelling-spaces as privileged proxies for the welfare

---

[5] Jose Harris, "Society and the State in Twentieth-Century Britain," in *The Cambridge Social History of Britain* (Cambridge: Cambridge University Press, 1990), 3: 96.

state. Above all, postwar reconstruction promised that in rebuilding people's Blitzed and broken homes, Britain might create a better society. This book turns to the novel as a cultural form particularly well adapted to describing and interrogating these postwar investments. As a genre associated with the project of representing social totality, the British novel has long worked out problems of social connection, generating spaces that reflect tensions between the individual and the collective, the private and the public. This book suggests the midcentury novel adapts to new historical opportunities in intimate life and the built environment. Reconfiguring its traditional interest in private life, the postwar novel explores what it means to inhabit administered forms of personal intimacy. Through girls' hostels, swimming-pool libraries, makeshift sanatoria, and clone boarding schools, the postwar welfare ethos proposes alternative configurations of postwar institutions of care. In different ways, traditional novel genres including the country house novel, the novel of manners, the novel of consciousness, the social problem novel, the colonial adventure novel, and the science-fiction novel each adapt and modernize in relation to these new opportunities of institutional care.

To bring this aesthetic shift more fully into view, this book employs a comparative postwar approach, drawing on the conventional association between literary modernism and the First World War to understand the changing stakes of literature after the Second World War. Modernism's relationship to the First World War has often been characterized as a turn to linguistic experiment in response to state failures on the battlefield and in public reason.[6] In comparison to the clumsy, bureaucratic, jingoistic wartime state, modernism offered progressive, even radical political stances and aesthetic forms, particularly in its turn to the individual and literary interiority. The end of the Second World War, however, provoked a different approach, requiring new artistic negotiation with

---

[6] According to critics such as Paul Fussell, Vincent Sherry, and Sarah Cole, the First World War generated a modernist ethos characterized by "modern memory," in which optimistic hope yielded to ironic catastrophe (Fussell); a turn against liberalism that transformed literary reasoning (Sherry); or formal solutions to the problems of representing violence, which often centered on the body in pain (Cole). See Paul Fussell's *The Great War and Modern Memory* (Oxford: Oxford University Press, 2000), Vincent Sherry's *The Great War and the Language of Modernism* (Oxford: Oxford University Press, 2004), and Sarah Cole's *At the Violet Hour: Modernism and Violence in England and Ireland* (Oxford: Oxford University Press, 2012). As MacKay suggests, modernism's "abiding preoccupations with 'the private domain and the landscape of the mind' potentially explain the time-honoured identification of modernism with the Great War: modernist inwardness versus shattering public failure" (8). A notable dissenting voice amongst these critics and their focus on modernity is Jay Winter's *Sites of Memory, Sites of Mourning* (Cambridge: Cambridge University Press, 2014), which argues that post-WWI sites of mourning were comforting art forms insofar as they invoked memories of the past, whether romantic values, traditional elements, or the sacred.

state visions of collective justice. Literary critics have turned to new formations of citizenship, postcolonial nationhood, war crimes, and human rights as crucial to understanding midcentury culture.[7] This book suggests the welfare state as another institutional formation at the center of midcentury culture, providing a language for its reformulations of belonging, personhood, and rights.

Perhaps the greatest insight of this comparative approach is that postwar repair is always untimely. Postwar reconstruction has always been a fictive discourse: plans for peacetime made amidst the uncertain time of war. By projecting forms of repair at the sites of wartime damage, visions of the postwar made good not only on the destruction and suffering of war, but also on historical structures of social and economic inequality. Yet post-1945 reconstruction was especially untimely. Fueled by the widespread sense of guilt over Britain's reconstructive failures after the First World War, Britain's second postwar reconstruction offered the hope of finally delivering upon Lloyd George's promise of "homes fit for heroes."[8] This belatedness, even fungibility, is precisely why postwar reconstruction is such a compelling engine of literary creation, able to withstand creative substitution and imaginative application. From colonialism to class relations, the novels surveyed in this project bring other histories to bear on this moment, offering different injuries as the objects of repair. In doing so, they radically open the British welfare state imagination, making space for other types of intimate claims, social arrangements, and political viabilities. As literature bears out, this strange, proleptic postwar imagination has proven seemingly inexhaustible; it continues to summon a range of authors to make sense of its promises and failures.

---

[7] For discussions of postwar criminal trials and their imprint on cultural production, see Ravit Reichman's distinction between (interwar) literary and (postwar) legal modernism in *The Affective Life of Law: Legal Modernism and the Literary Imagination* (Stanford: Stanford University Press, 2009) and Lyndsey Stonebridge's *The Juridical Imagination: Writing After Nuremberg* (Edinburgh: Edinburgh University Press, 2011). For citizenship and rights in relation to midcentury British literature, see *Around 1945: Literature, Citizenship, Rights*, ed. Allan Hepburn (Montreal & Kingston: McGill Queen's University Press, 2016), as well as Hepburn's "Righting Queer Rights: Angus Wilson and the Jurisdiction of the Novel," *Critical Quarterly* 56.4 (2014), 83–96. For human rights in relation to world literature, see Joseph Slaughter's *Human Rights, Inc.: The World Novel, Narrative Form, and International Law* (New York: Fordham University Press, 2007) and Elizabeth Anker's *Fictions of Dignity: Embodying Human Rights in World Literature* (Ithaca: Cornell University Press, 2012).

[8] See Deborah Cohen's argument in *The War Come Home: Disabled Veterans in Britain and Germany, 1914–1939* (Berkeley: University of California Press, 2001), whose comparison of the treatment of veterans in Britain and Germany after the First World War shows the postwar's lasting effects on public conceptions of welfare services and the role of the state.

The scope of this project thus challenges literary periodization that characterizes "postwar" British literature as a distinct period, ending in the 1970s or earlier. It also moves beyond classic treatments of welfare state culture, which survey such topics as social realism, mass culture, left-wing and working-class literatures; as well as sociological approaches that target mid-century shifts in literacy, education, and the renewed institutionalization of literature as a public good.[9] This book offers a different approach, one that attends to the continued resurfacing of Britain's postwar in every subsequent era. Taking a long view of postwar British literature, it argues that the postwar has played a crucial role in determining what stories can be told about Britain's contemporaneity, by British, immigrant, and Anglophone writers alike. Through this account, the contemporary emerges as an ever-moving target. It is both restless and peculiarly static, defined in its relation to the postwar even as the stakes of its relation to that past keep getting redefined. The challenge, then, of defining Britain's postwar period is not one of better periodization: of finding a more exact Year Zero than 1945, or of dividing the postwar period into more discrete units. Instead, it requires understanding that we live with a necessarily intimate but also incomplete sense of the postwar and its multiple temporalities. These valences of the "postwar"—a term that we are no closer to achieving today than we were in 1945—continue to haunt the stories we tell, and to shape the novels that define our national pasts and our global present.

This gravitational pull of reconstruction might seem melancholic, trapping us in a never-ending loop. If, as Adam Piette provocatively suggests, the Second World War "spiritually exhausted British culture and transformed it into something approaching a theatre of dead mannequins," this account of the postwar imagination might be equally insidious: a theatre of zombie mannequins, periodically re-animated by the energy surrounding the transition from warfare to welfare.[10] After all, if you start from the explicitly messianic assurance of a reconstructive New Jerusalem—combined

---

[9] For earlier works in cultural studies, see Richard Hoggart's *The Uses of Literacy* (New Brunswick: Transaction Publishers, 1998) and Raymond Williams's *The Long Revolution* (Cardigan: Parthian, 2011). Alan Sinfield's landmark *Literature, Politics and Culture in Postwar Britain* (New York: Continuum, 2004) is a benchmark for assessing the period in relation to Britain's postwar settlement and its social changes. More recently, Asha Rogers's *State-Sponsored Literature: Britain and Cultural Diversity after 1945* (Oxford: Oxford University Press, 2020) returns to postwar state expansion in the cultural field, studying how literature became charged with demonstrating and producing a democratic multiculturalism.

[10] Adam Piette, *Imagination at War: British Fiction and Poetry, 1939–1945* (New York: Papermac, 1995), 2.

with a history that only delivers poor constructions, even destructions, of its vision—what else can you do but keep rewriting its original promise? Yet while the novels described in this book derive their force from disenchantment with forms of institutionalized or collective care, they speak equally, if not more urgently, to the continued desire for welfarist social repair, refusing to surrender to a paranoid vision of the world. Though they acknowledge that we have not yet achieved the equitable, coherent citizenry imagined by the welfare state, they are not content to stop there. Instead, they reanimate the welfare ethos and rewrite forms of state repair, asking what role state institutions might play in creating a more just society today.

Literatures of Reconstruction: Reading the Postwar at Midcentury

To understand the holding power of Britain's postwar promises, we need to revisit the materials of postwar reconstruction and their projected visions of the future. Doing so will also help disentangle the symbolic valences of Britain's postwar period from those of its wartime mythology, showing that the "People's Peace" requires different categories of analysis than that of the "People's War."[11] Compare, for instance, "Keep Calm and Carry On (Figure 1), one of the most widespread and familiar examples of the war's popular reach, to the lesser-known "Rehabilitation: It Takes Time" (Figure 2).

Designed in 1939, "Keep Calm" was part of a triad of Ministry of Information posters meant to boost civilian morale. In comparison, "Rehabilitation," produced for London Transport in 1945, might seem to lack luster. The contrast between the two is evident: the bright red of emergency against the muted tones of rebuilding; the language of command versus an explanation of inevitability ("23 railway stations, 15 bus garages and 12 trolleybus and tram depots had direct hits or suffered severe damage from enemy action. Replacements and repairs are in hand—but IT TAKES TIME").[12] These

---

[11] See, for instance, Gill Plain's *Literature of the 1940s: War, Postwar and "Peace"* (Edinburgh: Edinburgh University Press, 2013), whose structuring categories emphasize the transitional nature of this period.

[12] This poster was commissioned by London Transport after the war's end, and not before (see the description at the London Transport Museum's website, https://www.ltmuseum. co.uk/collections/stories/war/seeing-it-through-10-london-transport-posters-second-world-war). Even if it were, it would still fall under the aegis of postwar reconstruction and what I'm calling Britain's "postwar imagination": a discourse that originated well before war's end.

visual differences may account for why "Rehabilitation" is not yet part of the Second World War's cultural lexicon. Unlike the endlessly parodied "Keep Calm," "Rehabilitation" leaves us in the time of postwar reconstruction, waiting for our train to come.

Postwar reconstruction begins with the 1942 Beveridge Report, the blueprint for the modern welfare state. Postwar novels have returned to rewrite its manual for repair ever since. The Report had its origins in June 1941, when Minister Arthur Greenwood, chair of the Committee on Reconstruction, announced the need for an interdepartmental committee to undertake a comprehensive survey of existing social services. To chair the committee, Greenwood asked Sir William Beveridge, civil servant and expert on unemployment insurance. The resulting document, "Social Security and Its Allied Services," was presented to parliament on November 20,

Figure 1 *Keep Calm and Carry On* (1939).
Ministry of Information.
© Crown Copyright.

INTRODUCTION: STATES OF REPAIR 9

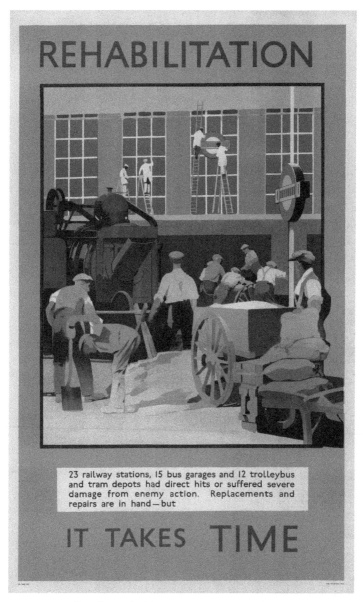

Figure 2 Fred Taylor, *Rehabilitation: It Takes Time* (1945).
© Transport for London. Reproduced courtesy of the London Transport Museum collection.

1942, and published as a White Paper two weeks later. A compelling literary document in its own right, the Report deployed inspiring rhetoric and figures of speech. Echoing Franklin D. Roosevelt's Four Freedoms, as well as the Atlantic Charter's eight war aims, the Report conjured the "Five Giants on the Road to Reconstruction"—Want, Disease, Ignorance, Squalor, and Idleness—with their corresponding welfare aims of social security, health, education, housing, and employment.

The Report had a galvanizing effect on the British population, who, having withstood two years of intense bombing, welcomed a vision of postwar peace in the midst of wartime precarity.[13] Selling at least 635,000 copies, this 300-page document produced "the most significant queues of the war" outside His Majesty's Stationery Office, as if this new vision put into words what Britain had been fighting for all along.[14] A poll conducted by the British Institute of Public Opinion found that 19 out of 20 adults had heard of the Report only two weeks after its publication, with the majority approving its proposals.[15] The Report also enjoyed a remarkable textual afterlife. Its key elements were reconfigured for different audiences through summaries, memoranda, pamphlets, postcards, and conferences, from groups including the Communist Party, the National Council for Women, the Young Women's Christian Association, the Social Security League, *Left* magazine, the Trade Union Congress and other workers' societies, the League of Nations Union, and others. It was even air-dropped into Germany and France by the Royal Air Force, which distributed "millions of leaflets extolling the principles of the Beveridge Report, as Britain's master contribution to a better world."[16]

As Beveridge proclaimed, "A revolutionary moment in the world's history is a time for revolutions, not patching."[17] Writing in the midst of the changes

---

[13] We see this as early as January 4, 1941, with the publication of *Picture Post*'s special issue, "A Plan for Britain," ed. Tom Hopkinson, Vol. 10. no. 1 (London, Hulton Press, Ltd, 1941). With essays by Maxwell Fry, Julian Huxley, and J.B. Priestley on social issues ranging from employment, social security, city planning, health, and education, the editors of the issue characterized their plan for a new Britain as "not something outside the war, or something *after* the war. It is an essential part of our war aims. It is, indeed, our most positive war aim. The new Britain is the country we are fighting for" (4).

[14] Valerie Holman, *Print for Victory: Book Publishing in England, 1939-1945* (London: British Library, 2008), 194.

[15] Interestingly, one of its questions was: "Do you think that if the Report is adopted it will make people still keener to fight the war?," to which 46% answered yes, 27% no, and the remaining 27% were unsure. "The Beveridge Report and the Public," British Institute of Public Opinion (London: H. Clarke & Co. Ltd, 1942), 15.

[16] Kenneth Morgan, *Britain Since 1945: The People's Peace*, 3rd ed. (Oxford: Oxford University Press, 2001), 37.

[17] William Beveridge, *Social Insurance and Allied Services* (London: His Majesty's Stationery Office, 1942), 6.

that followed, Richard Titmuss similarly evaluated his own time in terms of an epochal shift, proposing that "the pressures for a high standard of welfare and a deeper comprehension of social justice steadily gained in strength" over the course of the war.[18] Britain's postwar consensus brought Labour and Conservative together on a variety of social issues to create the modern welfare state, effected through a concentrated series of policies including the 1944 Education or "Butler" Act; the 1945 Family Allowances Act; the 1946 National Insurance Act and 1948 National Assistance Act, which abolished the previous Poor Law system; and the 1946 National Health Service Act.

Yet not all commentators agreed that these transformations were so swift or complete. George Orwell expressed continued disappointment with the Labour Government, commenting in 1946 that "in the social set-up there is no symptom by which one could infer that we are not living under a Conservative government."[19] Historians have since qualified the degree to which 1945 represented a sea-change, noting that the degree of redistribution achieved was limited in scope, and earlier political and social structures were "dented but by no means dismantled."[20] Moreover, these modern British welfare infrastructures did not emerge *ex nihilo* from the pressure chamber of war. Many midcentury policies were continuations of interwar developments in education, health, and income distribution: a period informed by economic upheavals such as the General Strike and the

[18] Richard Titmuss, *Problems of Social Policy* (London: HMSO, 1950), 508. Notable reiterations of this narrative include Paul Addison's *The Road to 1945: British Politics and the Second World War* (London: Cape, 1975) and most recently, Ken Loach's documentary *The Spirit of '45* (2013). Though Titmuss notes that "developments in the scope and character of the welfare services did not happen in any planned or ordered sequence; nor were they always a matter of deliberate intent," the anaphora that follows underscores his work's overall logic of revolution: "Some were pressed forward because of the needs of the war machine for more men and more work. Some took place almost by accident. Some were the results of recognition of needs hither to hidden by ignorance of social conditions. Some came about because war 'exposed weaknesses ruthlessly and brutally ... which called for revolutionary changes in the economic and social life of the country'" (507).

[19] George Orwell, "London Letter to *Partisan Review*," (Early May? 1946), in *The Collected Essays, Journalism and Letters of George Orwell*, ed. Sonia Orwell and Ian Angus, Vol. 4 (London: Secker & Warburg, 1968), 186.

[20] See, for instance, Rodney Lowe, "The Second World War: Consensus and the Foundation of the British Welfare State," *Twentieth Century British History* 1.2 (1990), 152–182; Steven Fielding, "What Did 'The People' Want?: The Meaning of the 1945 General Election," *The Historical Journal* 35.3 (September 1992), 623–639; also James Cronin, *The Politics of State Expansion: War, State and Society in Twentieth-Century Britain* (New York: Routledge, 1991). See Jose Harris, "War and Social History: Britain and the Home Front during the Second World War," *Contemporary European History* 1.1 (March 1992), 26; see also Pat Thane, *Foundations of the Welfare State*, 2nd ed. (New York: Routledge, 1996), 246–247. The degree of consensus has also been questioned, as welfare's electoral popularity may not have directly correlated with a public embrace of reconstruction's political ethos: Addison's postscript, for instance, characterizes it as a "Whitehall" consensus.

Great Recession, as well as by the residual postwar energies after the Great War.[21] The social transformations of the postwar thus must be understood in terms of multiple temporalities, and seen as historical process, rather than a static structure originating in any particular moment.

While drawing on historical accounts of these changes, this book moves its analysis in a different direction: toward the ameliorative appeal of Britain's postwar imagination, a seemingly inexhaustible wellspring of cultural production. Given the familiarity of the wartime "myth" of the Blitz, a reconsideration of the postwar myth of reconstruction is due—which in its literary form, I propose, should not be considered myth at all. For myth, as Barthes reminds us, "does away with all dialectics," providing a convenient distraction from feeling historical weight and nuance.[22] But as literature bears out, the postwar is by nature a more diffuse category than war: it presents a moving target of contemporary unity rather than its solution. The story this book tells about the postwar is likewise characterized by dialectical movement between welfare's promises and expectations, realities and residues. Unlike Blitz mythology, called upon by both Left and Right as a simple image of British unity (making a notable return during the Falklands War through Margaret Thatcher's "Churchillism"), the postwar imagination retains ideals of what the welfare state could do, even more capacious than that created after the war.[23] In their repeated activation of this postwar imagination, postwar novels keep dreams of a hospitable and pluralistic Britain open for consideration, even if only in their impossibility.

---

[21] See Thane, *Foundations*, 213–229. Looking further back further, welfare's political formation can trace its origins to the Liberal governments between 1906 and 1914, which in turn drew on discourses, policies, and forms of assistance established during the 1870s; longer trajectories of welfarist thinking could begin with the Poor Law reforms of the 1830s, or even to the advent of the Elizabethan Poor Laws. For notable long histories of the welfare state, see Derek Fraser, *The Evolution of the British Welfare State: A History of Social Policy since the Industrial Revolution*, 2nd ed. (London: Macmillan, 1984), 233; George Boyer, *The Winding Road to the Welfare State: Economic Insecurity and Social Welfare Policy in Britain* (Princeton and Oxford: Princeton University Press, 2018); and Bernard Harris's *The Origins of the British Welfare State: Society, State and Social Welfare in England and Wales, 1800-1945* (New York: Palgrave Macmillan, 2004). And longer trajectories of welfarist thinking could begin with the Poor Law reforms of the 1830s, or even to the advent of the Elizabethan Poor Laws.

[22] Roland Barthes's, *Mythologies*, trans. Annette Lavers (New York: Hill and Wang, 1972), 143.

[23] This would lead Angus Calder to note that the effect of the Myth was ultimately conservative: "For the Left it would encapsulate a moment of retrenchment as a moment of rebirth; a moment of ideological conservatism as a moment of revolution. Because the Blitz was held to have had near revolutionary consequences, to have somehow produced a 'welfare state,' the Myth would divert attention from the continuing need for radical change in British society. The Left would think that in 1940 it had captured History. In fact, it had been captured by it." *The Myth of the Blitz* (London: Cape, 1991), 15.

The Beveridge Report's most provocative claim lies in its description of social insurance as "a new type of human institution": a newness signaled by the modifier *social*, which "implies both that it is compulsory and that men stand together with their fellows."[24] With this claim, Beveridge joins a line of thinkers who saw a new form of sociality emerging from the nexus of warfare and welfare. Key participants in this postwar conversation included Titmuss, professor of Social Administration at The London School of Economics and champion of social services for what they could provide beyond market mechanisms; sociologist T.H. Marshall, whose lectures "Citizenship and Social Class" correlated the rise of the twentieth-century welfare state with the institutionalization of social rights; British Cultural Studies pioneers Richard Hoggart, Raymond Williams, and Stuart Hall, whose works and institutional program-building opened up the previously rarefied realm of culture to all; and theorist Hannah Arendt, whose concept of political life required a new care for the world and all its inhabitants. Though an admittedly diverse list, what holds these thinkers in common is their commitment to opening up what counts as society: who belongs; who can participate; who is representative. For this postwar moment, what was at stake was nothing less than how to live together, better. It was this project that would animate literary writings for decades to come.

One defining characteristic of this welfare sociality was a new awareness of collective responsibility. *Picture Post*'s 1941 special issue "A Plan for Britain" offers an early formulation of this new understanding of collective sociality even before the Beveridge Report. Admitting that "we have been forced into a knowledge of our dependence on each other," the editors recast wartime precarity as the "common ground" that would underwrite postwar reconstruction.[25] The Beveridge Report likewise drew on this new togetherness, defining "social insurance" as meaning "both that it is compulsory and that men stand together with their fellows," in order to convince the public of the social function of pooling risk.[26] As the war drew on, this new collective responsibility expanded "in a wider circle, drawing in more people and broadening the obligations to protect those in need."[27] This broadening of scope beyond the self-interested individual to the group is a guiding principle of welfare state liberalism, and is taken up in various ways by the literatures of reconstruction. As the above examples suggest, this new

---

[24] Beveridge, *Social Insurance*, 13.
[25] "Foreword," *Picture Post*, 4.
[26] Beveridge, *Social Insurance*, 13.
[27] Titmuss, *Problems*, 517.

collectivity took some convincing, especially when posed as an aim of peace instead of an inevitability of war.

Literary scholars have addressed the representational challenges of the welfare state through such concepts as the common good, public works, the actuarial, and the family.[28] This book follows the emphasis on interdependence found throughout literatures of reconstruction to focus on *care*, a word intimately associated with the work of welfare and social services.[29] The study of care, and particularly "care ethics," has its roots in the 1980s feminist philosophy of Sara Ruddick, Carol Gilligan, and Nel Noddings, all of whom sought an alternative to more traditional definitions of morality, justice, and rights. The concept then found traction in feminist political theory in the 1990s through the work of Virginia Held, Joan Tronto, and Fiona Robinson. While some works of literary criticism have addressed the relationship between care, welfare, and literature, its mid-twentieth century iterations have yet to be fully appreciated: particularly, as we'll see in the next section, in relationship to the imagined work of postwar domesticity.[30] For this project, I am interested in the political dimensions of care

---

[28] Bruce Robbins has suggested that to read for welfare means to read for the common good: that "profound shift in moral sensibility that is both a cause and an effect of that rise (of the welfare state)." *Upward Mobility and the Common Good: Toward a Literary History of the Welfare State* (Princeton: Princeton University Press, 2007), 235. Michael Rubenstein suggests an attention to what he calls "public works," infrastructures of development such as electricity and water whose "complicated admixture of the state and the market" was part of the road that led to the welfare state. *Public Works: Infrastructure, Irish Modernism, and the Postcolonial* (Notre Dame: Notre Dame University Press, 2010), 4. Michael Szalay is interested in the New Deal's investment in "actuarial models of governance that revolved around the statistical construction of population groups," which "led to a literature of liberal interdependence, as writers looked to reconcile at times conflicting impulses towards individual agency and collective affiliation." *New Deal Modernism: American Literature and the Invention of the Welfare State* (Durham: Duke University Press, 2000), 2–3. And Susan Edmunds shows how American modernist domestic fiction interrogates the sentimental and racialized logic of "family values" that underwrote the New Deal and the rise of the U.S. welfare state. *Grotesque Relations: Modernist Domestic Fiction and the U.S. Welfare State* (Oxford: Oxford University Press, 2008).

[29] As Daniel Engster notes, "care ethics is closely aligned with the traditional purpose of welfare states: helping individuals to meet significant needs that they cannot reasonably meet on their own." *Justice, Care and the Welfare State* (Oxford: Oxford University Press, 2015), 15.

[30] Two accounts bookending the mid-twentieth century come to mind. The first is Talia Schaffer's study of what she calls "care communities," or "ad-hoc, flexible, small communities of caregivers, usually composed of voluntary connections and including perhaps three to ten people" that gather around characters in need, in the Victorian novel. *Communities of Care: The Social Ethics of Victorian Fiction* (Princeton: Princeton University Press, 2021), 61. Apropos of the welfare state, Schaffer's historical focus is on works between the 1840s and 1860s, a period that saw a shift to professional medical care as the norm rather than these small communities. Moving forward, Arne de Boever proposes the contemporary novel as a "as a form of life-writing, a kind of aesthetic care of the self and of others," informed by Derrida's theory of the

as they overlap but also remain distinct from liberal politics, particularly in the privileging of interpersonal relationships and interdependence over the autonomy of the sovereign individual. As a political philosophy, the concept of care urges us to think relationally and responsively, attuned to our interdependence on each other; the interrelation between the private and the public; and the importance of context and emotion, all of which influence the readings that follow.[31]

If one of the classic definitions of care is "everything that we do to maintain, continue, and repair our 'world' so that we can live in it as well as possible," I suggest that it is the promise of *repair*, not just maintenance nor continuity, that impels literature to return to this pivotal midcentury moment.[32] Though reconstruction fell short of being truly revolutionary, it nevertheless sought to rebuild the postwar world not only in terms of restoration, but also in relation to the utopian possibilities of social change and moral development. This impulse would become part of the foundation of Britain's postwar future. However, the glimpses of repair offered by literature are not strong or stable forms of repair, or what we might think of as reparation. Reparations, particularly in the legal sense, suggest a closed action consisting of material, often financial reparation accompanied by an expression of legalized affect such as apology, regret, guilt. On the contrary, the literary repair the postwar novel models—a repeated return to the transition from warfare to welfare—indicates an open-ended process whose duration is uncertain, and whose materials are not contained by financial and legally affective means.[33] It may be that the reparative mechanism of this

pharmakon as curative and poisonous, as well as Agamben's work on the state of exception and bare life. *Narrative Care: Biopolitics and the Novel* (New York and London: Bloomsbury Academic, 2013), 8.

[31] For a useful schematic of care's contribution to political theory, see the introduction to *Care Ethics and Political Theory*, ed. Daniel Engster and Maurice Hamington (Oxford: Oxford University Press, 2015). One might think here too of Michel Foucault's "care of the self," the focus of his later work in the history of sexuality. Drawing on the Greek concept of *epimelei heautou*, Foucault seeks to re-establish the centrality of care over the injunction to "know yourself," or *gnōthi seautou*, which has taken primacy in the history of Western philosophy. This care is neither narcissism nor melancholy, but rather gave rise to systems of strict moralities, and can be seen as the precondition of ethics, and by extension, public life. See *The Hermeneutics of the Subject: Lectures at the Collège de France, 1981–82*, trans. Graham Burchell (New York: Palgrave Macmillan, 2005).

[32] Berenice Fisher and Joan Tronto. "Toward a Feminist Theory of Caring," in *Circles of Care: Work and Identity in Women's Lives*, ed. Emily K. Abel and Margaret K. Nelson (Albany: State University of New York Press, 1990), 40.

[33] My differentiation between these two terms echoes Anne Anlin Cheng's conceptualization of grief and grievance, with grievance being the "social and legal articulation of grief... incapable of addressing those aspects of grief that speak in a different language." *The Melancholy of Race* (Oxford: Oxford University Press, 2001), x.

literary history depends on the repair remaining incomplete and unfinished: a condition that enables novels to continue preserving and transposing the potential of post-1945 for their present moment.

This account of literary history resonates with our discipline's recent "reparative turn," first articulated as such by Eve Kosofsky Sedgwick in affiliation with the work of Melanie Klein. From "distant reading" to "surface reading," object-oriented ontology to actor network theory to "weak theory," literary theorists today question our longstanding practice of what Paul Ricoeur has called the "hermeneutics of suspicion": a form of paranoid reading, based on existing interpretive codes, that knows in advance what it is going to find. While the work that follows is not squarely in a reparative mode, I believe welfare's midcentury development has something to teach us about the hermeneutics of suspicion through its constitutive tension between state violence and state care. To start, the term "welfare state" only emerged in opposition to warfare, first used in Britain to critique the "warfare states" of other country's totalitarian governments, particularly Germany, before gaining its current denotation in the late 1940s through widespread academic and popular use.[34]

More trenchant, however, was the way the welfare state set itself up as both a reward for citizens' wartime efforts and their enabling of state violence, as well as an assurance that they would never feel precarious again. This substitution of postwar material security for the traumatizing experiences of war is of course preposterous. To see the welfare state as a reparation of the war machine underscores its non-symmetry. One cannot evoke the promise of care or assurance of security "from the cradle to the grave" without invoking the vast losses of the Second World War. Yet this lack of symmetry and indeed, fictionality of reparation is a condition endemic to repair, which works squarely in the realm of the "as if." In this way, repair itself is an eminently literary concept. It is not an instance or finite event of reparation, but rather a labor to be borne, one that demands perhaps infinite work,

---

[34] Rodney Lowe, *The Welfare State in Britain from 1945*, 3rd ed. (New York: Palgrave, 2005), 13. Though the OED dates the first usage of the term to 1894, I'm interested in the more precise genealogy resonant with the welfare state's modern formation. Historian Asa Briggs provides the postwar inception story, noting, "From Britain the phrase made its way round the world." "The Welfare State in Historical Perspective," *European Journal of Sociology* 2.2 (1961), 221. See also Raymond Williams's *Keywords*, revised edition (New York: Oxford University Press, 1985), which notes that the "Welfare State, in distinction from the *Warfare State*, was first named in 1939" (333).

INTRODUCTION: STATES OF REPAIR   17

and which proves a durable characteristic, even central problematic for the literature of this long postwar.

Warfare, then, is a critical supplement to the welfare state, a shadowy counterpart it cannot shake. Even Beveridge wanted to play a larger role in the war, imagining himself commanding Britain's war-making rather than designing its peace: as the story goes, when he finally accepted the job of chairing the interdepartmental committee, he did so "with tears, not of joy but of bitter disappointment."[35] This book's approach, however, moves away from Beveridge's enthrallment with war and settling for peace. Determining to what extent welfare is, to recall Carl von Clausewitz, "war by other means," is not the aim of this project. That would risk seeing the war everywhere, without bounds or terminus: a critical instinct that is challenged here.[36] Instead, *States of Repair* joins recent work on literature and the state that acknowledge the challenge of studying literary representations of state structures, and the Janus-faced tendency to see the state as either a dystopia of totalitarian control or a utopia of large-scale care.[37] To read the welfare state's potentiality as well as its shortcomings requires resetting or at tempering the critical instinct to take the state negatively, which, in the vein of Michel Foucault and Giorgio Agamben, would emphasize its capacity to wield power, even in its most productive sense. Rather, this book approaches wartime visions of social repair on their own terms: as attempts to achieve something like a break in the circuit rather than a continuation of perpetual war. However much the welfare state's origins might be bound up in war, this project is motivated by the possibility that there is something worth excavating in its midcentury birth pangs—something, that is, of the original

---

[35] Nicholas Timmins, *The Five Giants: A Biography of the Welfare State, Revised Edition* (London: HarperCollins Publishers, 2001), 11. This might explain the Report's militaristic language, which raised the projects of peace to the level of war: "Freedom from want cannot be forced on a democracy or given to a democracy. It must be won by them" (172).

[36] Michel Foucault, *"Society Must Be Defended": Lectures at the Collège de France, 1975–6*, trans. David Macey (New York: Picador, 2003), 16; and Carl von Clausewitz, *On War*, trans. Michael Howard and Peter Paret (Princeton: Princeton University Press, 1989), 87.

[37] See Matthew Hart and Jim Hansen's "Contemporary Literature and the State," which seeks to "challenge the seeming necessity of the opposition between monolithic state and individual artist," or the paranoid logic that can only descry or affirm the work of the state (*Contemporary Literature* 49, no. 4 (2008), 493). See also Robbins's "Orange Juice and Agent Orange," *Occasion: Interdisciplinary Studies in the Humanities* 2 (December 20, 2010), https://arcade.stanford.edu/occasion/orange-juice-and-agent-orange, Rubenstein's *Public Works*, 7–10, and Amanda Claybaugh's "Government is Good," *The Minnesota Review* 2008, no. 70 (2008), 161–166 for pithy overviews of this aspect of literary criticism and the state.

excitement, commitment, and imaginative energy that went into postwar reconstruction.

Architectures of Care: Domestic Space, Institutional Life

This book turns to the home as the *sine qua non* of postwar repair: the primary site of regeneration of the relationship between self and society, private and public life, individual and state institutions.[38] During a time when spectacular damage was being done to the homes on the Home Front, and when people were thrown together in ways never before experienced, the questions of what Britain would look like after the war loomed large in the popular imagination. The new welfare state raised difficult new questions about the nature of housing, including: What happens when the ideals of private property collide with ideas of public good? What happens when the home is both the space of individual freedom, and a place of social organization? How does housing capture the aspirations of modernity while also retaining tradition? What kind of private, everyday life would people enjoy in the comfort of their own homes? And what kind of social relations would such rebuilding foster? In other words, what happens when infrastructures of collective living threaten to displace older structures of private life?

This book joins the critical tradition of investigating novelistic representations of domestic space.[39] Like others, I read the home space as offering acute commentary on the relations between private and public life, excavated through examinations of narration, character, and interiority. As the lived

---

[38] As Peter Kalliney writes, "[I]t would be difficult to overstate the importance of the family home as a trope for capturing the social atmosphere of the 1950s." *Cities of Affluence and Anger: A Literary Geography of Modern Englishness* (Charlottesville, University of Virginia Press, 2006), 115. Though as historian Clare Langhamer reminds us, the modern domesticity of the postwar home was in many ways a continuation of 1930s aspirations. "The Meanings of Home in Postwar Britain," *Journal of Contemporary History* 40.2 (April 2005), 341–362.

[39] Works on twentieth-century architecture and literature include Victoria Rosner's *Modernism and the Architecture of Private Life* (New York: Columbia University Press, 2005), Matthew Taunton's *Fictions of the City: Class, Culture, and Mass Housing in London and Paris* (New York: Palgrave Macmillan, 2009), Laura Colombino's *Spatial Politics in Contemporary London Literature: Writing Architecture and the Body* (New York: Routledge, 2013), and most closely related, Ashley Maher's *Reconstructing Modernism: British Literature, Modern Architecture, and the State* (Oxford: Oxford University Press, 2020) and Paula Derdiger's *Reconstruction Fiction: Housing and Realist Literature in Postwar Britain* (Columbus: The Ohio State University Press, 2020).

INTRODUCTION: STATES OF REPAIR   19

modality of the welfare state, housing was the most visible giant on the road to reconstruction. It was also one of the most controversial welfare infrastructures, what historian Rodney Lowe characterizes as "the extreme instance of irrationality among all the social services."[40] From the start, housing was the "Achilles' heel" of the Beveridge Report and its attempt to provide benefits based on subsistence needs rather than means, given the wide variations of rent due to region and class.[41] It then continued to prove what Ulf Torgersen has called the "wobbly pillar" of the welfare state, due in part to Britain's mixed landscape of private and public housing. Indeed, Thatcher's welfare restructuring began, and was most successful, in this area.[42]

This focus on the enduring association between housing and the dreams of British social reconstruction adds to the spatial lexicon of Britain's Second World War, whose better-known sites include the bombsite, the blackout, and the shelter, among others.[43] What distinguishes these spaces of reconstruction, however, is their charge of pure potentiality: a promise, however preposterous, to make amends for structures of inequality and histories of violence. In response, the postwar novel demonstrates that even the best-laid plans of collective living and built space are not enough to safeguard against injury, whether in the form of intimate treachery or systemic violence. Still, these works find energy and promise in the logic of reconstruction, and offer experiments in domesticity that test, and ultimately transform, their midcentury pedagogies of national community.

Reconstruction literatures offered vaunted rhetoric, grandiose language, and instructions, outlines, and descriptions that were aspirational in nature, exceeding what realistically could be done. Many of these accounts took a birds-eye view, encouraging readers to look from above. Asking readers to imagine life at this scale introduced an uneasy slippage between aerial shots as both a technology of war-making as well as reconstruction. John Forshaw

---

[40] Lowe, *Welfare State in Britain*, 259.
[41] Jose Harris, *William Beveridge: A Biography* (Oxford: Oxford University Press, 1997), 389.
[42] Ulf Torgersen, "Housing: the Wobbly Pillar under the Welfare State," *Scandinavian Housing and Planning Research* Vol. 4 (1987), 116–126. Housing scholars have since embraced this metaphor in evaluations of the British housing market, particularly after "Right to Buy": see, for instance, Peter Malpass's discussion in "Housing and the New Welfare State: Wobbly Pillar or Cornerstone?" *Housing Studies* 23.1 (January 2008), 3.
[43] For studies of wartime spaces, particularly the ruin, see Leo Mellor's *Reading the Ruins: Modernism, Bombsites and British Culture* (Cambridge: Cambridge University Press, 2011) and Part III of Pong's *For the Duration*.

and Patrick Abercrombie's 1943 *County of London Plan*, perhaps the second-most canonical work of postwar reconstruction after the Beveridge Report, relied on this panoramic view.[44] Their work relied on stylized maps such as that shown in Figure 3:

Figure 3 Patrick Abercrombie and John Forshaw, *County of London Plan* (1943). London County Council.
© Crown Copyright.

To emphasize the reader's role in reconstruction, some representations of postwar planning superimposed figures of people on the image in question. These uses of photomontage call attention to the indelible relationship between the individual and their environment, and the belief that reconstruction would create stronger social bonds as well as convenient residential life. For instance, the booklet accompanying "Rebuilding Britain,"

---

[44] Patrick Abercrombie and John Forshaw, *County of London Plan*, London County Council (London: Macmillan and Company Ltd, 1943). As Peter J. Larkham and Keith D. Lilley have shown, this text is one of the most-cited texts amongst standard histories of planning. *Planning the "City of Tomorrow," British reconstruction planning, 1939–1952: an annotated bibliography* (North Yorkshire: Inch's Books, 2010), 1.

a 1943 exhibition at the National Gallery organized by the Royal Institute of British Architects, featured a cover image of two soldiers overlaid on an aerial view of London, their backs to the viewer as if looking out upon the ruined city, wondering what is next.[45] And in the 1944 exhibition "Planning Your Neighbourhood: for home, for work, for play," presented to the Army Bureau of Current Affairs, architect Ernő Goldfinger envisioned a redesigned Shoreditch that would improve upon the previously dense urban area, correcting its "jumble of houses and jumble of people" so as not to lose "the advantage of neighbourliness" (Figure 4).

Equally crucial to these views from without were those from within. Reconstruction encouraged people to imagine themselves living within these new dwellings. It invited the public into the physical structures of welfare state infrastructure, asking them to imagine sleek blocks of flats, modern schools and health centers, and cities built along perfectly planned blueprints. From the *County of London*'s peek into the working-class home (Figure 5), to the pull-out centerfolds detailing "the house that women want" in 1944 *The Daily Mail Book of Post-War Homes*, to the Furnished Rooms section of the 1946 *Britain Can Make It* exhibition (Figure 6), the reconstructive imagination depended on looking in, projecting oneself into interior space, and above all, making a judgment as to whether its design afforded a good fit to the inhabitants' daily routines and desires.[46]

Adopting an "as above, so below" mentality, this reconstructive imagination cultivated a sense that the British public could apprehend the interrelations of a social totality, from its largest-scale ideals and aspirations to the register of everyday life. The family living happily and productively in their perfectly working, ideally fitting home provided a microcosm for the harmonious order of the local community, which in turn mapped to the level of the nation.

Such a vision of public-private interpenetration echoed that which was called upon during the war, reminding people that the way they lived their private lives had direct ramifications for public well-being, and that

---

[45] Royal Institute of British Architects, *Rebuilding Britain* (London: Percy Lund, Humphries and Co. Ltd, 1943).

[46] Millicent Pleydell-Bouverie, *Daily Mail Book of Post-War Homes* (London: Daily Mail, 1944). The centerfolds, facing pages 24 and 56, unfold into large, color-printed floor plans of the ideal home based on a "nation-wide consensus of (women's) opinion" (22). The pictures were meant as a substitute for seeing the real thing in Britain's annual "Daily Mail Ideal Home Exhibition," which was suspended during wartime: as the author notes, "as war conditions make such things impossible you are invited to make your inspection through the following pages" (22).

Figure 4 Ernő Goldfinger, "Aerial view of rows of houses" (1944). © RIBA Collections.

the success of their labor mapped onto the victory of their nation. To secure one level of social life offered a pattern through which to secure

Figure 5 "The Look In," *County of London Plan*.

all. These projections of rebuilding and social organization were thus what Jameson calls "symbolic acts": resolving social contradictions that could not be resolved by other means. They offered solutions to existing social inequalities that adhered to housing, variously flattening or shaming their subjects; appealing to traditional gender roles while also promising better, more modern experiences for them; and above all, imagining a frictionless relationship between individual life and social totality. Yet they also revealed conflicts about what postwar Britain might look like, from decisions between distinctively British and international architecture styles, to

Figure 6 Furnished rooms from *Britain Can Make It No. 12* (1946). Board of Trade.
© Crown Copyright.

uncertainties over what kinds of lives were (or were not) accounted for in these designs.

Novels follow and transform this reconstructive discourse in several ways. They bring strangers into situations in which they jostle each other in often uncomfortable ways, under forms of cohabitation, neighborliness, and other types of sharing space and resources. They portray what happens when we are forced to live together in new forms of intimacy and dependency, positioning ourselves as sharing risk as well as wealth. Roland Barthes's 1976–77 lectures *How to Live Together: Novelistic Simulations of Some Everyday Spaces* provide a touchstone for grasping these problematics. These lectures are particularly interested in how the individual navigates the experience of "Living Together," a unit of sociality locating between the couple or family and the crowd, commune, or convent. Structuring his talks around the concept of "idiorrhythmy," or the rhythm of individual life within a group setting, Barthes circles the possibility of "something like solitude with regular interruptions: the paradox, the contradiction, the aporia of bringing distances together—the utopia of a socialism of distance."[47] Yet for all this

---

[47] Roland Barthes, *How to Live Together: Novelistic Simulations of Some Everyday Spaces* (New York: Columbia UP, 2013), 6. Barthes's prime examples are Thomas Mann's *The Magic*

INTRODUCTION: STATES OF REPAIR   25

theorizing of togetherness, Barthes's ideal remains solitude, or independence from the social. Reading his lectures, one is left unsure as to what, if anything, is to be gained from putting oneself in proximity to others. For a treatise on living together, the work is in the end coolly abstract.[48] In contrast, postwar novels dwell on the uncomfortable claims characters make on each other by virtue of their proximity. For Samuel Selvon's Moses in *The Lonely Londoners*, for instance, his status as an early immigrant forces him into the unofficial role of employment bureau and housing officer, helping fellow Windrush arrivals feel not so lonely. Such situations of unfamiliarity and estrangement test the very premise of the modern welfare state, that of care not only for one's neighbor, but also for one's stranger.

The housing sites studied in this book depart from those traditionally associated with the welfare state and their typical categories of analysis, such as the working-class home and the nuclear family, leftist, socialist, or proletarian literatures, and realist narrative techniques.[49] Taking a cue once again from postwar reconstruction, Britain's postwar housing policies envisioned people living together in a balanced social mix that reflected the make-up of the nation. Health Minister Aneurin Bevan spoke to this ideal in his defense of what would become the 1949 Housing Act, describing housing as the "living tapestry of a mixed community, which entailed severing the long association of planned housing as a solution for the working classes."[50] Following these aspirations, this book focuses on the particular awareness fostered by reconstruction: one that alerts people to their interconnectedness, collective responsibility, and heterogeneity. As Bevan described, "If we are

---

Mountain, about life in a sanatorium, and Émile Zola's *Pot Luck*, about a bourgeois apartment building, with Daniel Defoe's *Robinson Crusoe* and André Gide's *The Confined Woman* as counterexamples of isolated life.

[48] This abstract quality is underscored by Barthes's idiosyncratic, academic use of Greek and odd avoidance of the word μετοίκιον (metoikion) to describe living together. Formed from the word "meta" (change) and "oikos" (dwelling, or house), the μετοίκιον was a system of managing immigration to Athens, being a tax leveed on "metics": foreign residents (and their descendants) or ex-slaves who lived in the city-state, but were not citizens.

[49] See, for instance, Kalliney's discussion of the Angry Young Men and the welfare state in *Cities of Affluence*, Alison Ravetz's *Council Housing and Culture: The History of a Social Experiment* (New York: Routledge, 2001), or Nicola Wilson's *Home in British Working-Class Fiction* (Farnham: Ashgate, 2015).

[50] Aneurin Bevan, "Housing Bill," Hansard. House of Commons Debate, 16 March 1949, vol 462, col. 2121–231, https://api.parliament.uk/historic-hansard/commons/1949/mar/16/housing-bill. Spearheaded by urban planner Ebenezer Howard, the Garden City movement advocated self-contained, satellite communities branching off from urban centers. While a few Garden Cities were built before 1945 (Letchworth and Welwyn), the idea took off after the Second World War through the New Towns Act of 1946 and the Town and Country Planning Act of 1947, as well as through the New Towns Act of 1965. These ideals were unevenly achieved, with the postwar New Towns attracting a largely working-class population rather than the mix of middle- and working classes originally imagined: a segregation later compounded by racial and ethnic divides.

to enable citizens to lead a full life, if they are each to be aware of the problems of their neighbours, then they should be all drawn from the different sections of the community."[51] This awareness is neither pleasant nor easy. Instead, it is something like a civic duty, paramount to modern life.

The novels studied here also test the social structure of the domestic home through their imaginations of quasi-administered living spaces. Clone boarding schools, an abandoned Italian villa turned into a makeshift hospital, and a basement apartment functioning as an employment office: these experiments in collective domesticity open up the unit of the family home, exploring the other forms of social connection and community insisted upon—but relatively less explored by—the discourses of postwar reconstruction. In doing so, they test how private life changes in relation to new forms of welfare infrastructure, with its interest in distributing public good in the name of the common good. These administered arrangements contain echoes of other disciplinary institutions such as the hospital, prison, gym, school, and camp: what sociologist Erving Goffman calls the "total institution," or "a place of residence and work where a large number of like-situated individuals, cut off from the wider society for an appreciable period of time, together lead an enclosed, formally administered round of life."[52] Yet the social logic of each space extends past the purely institutional in search of meaningful collectivity, one predicated on voluntary, intersubjective connection between a diverse group of people. Even the most instrumentalized fictional world, that of Kazuo Ishiguro's *Never Let Me Go* (2005), refuses to abandon reconstruction's fantasies of care: a testament to the long reach of Britain's postwar.

These settings provide conditions that borrow from the ideals of postwar reconstruction. Postwar novels offer institutional spaces as proxies for the welfare state, shared sites of living where strangers produce a stronger social fabric for the nation. For instance, Muriel Spark's description of a ladies' boarding house in *The Girls of Slender Means* (1963) opens with an almost parodic declaration of these social ideals: "Long ago in 1945 all the nice people were poor, allowing for exceptions."[53] Yet the postwar novel's institutional spaces also depart from midcentury projections of wish-fulfillment and social repair, offering their own versions of social organization and

---

[51] Bevan, *Housing Bill*.
[52] Erving Goffman, *Asylums* (Garden City: Anchor Books, 1961), xiii.
[53] Muriel Spark, *The Girls of Slender Means* (New York: New Directions Pub., 1998), 7.

simulations of everyday life: the "exceptions" that are the subject of Spark's novel. Though some postwar novels take a directly oppositional stance to postwar ideals—the thwarted rebellion of Orwell's *1984* (1949), or the nostalgic retreat of Evelyn Waugh's *Brideshead Revisited* (1945)—this book has a different focus. The novels addressed here do not ultimately seek to escape the state, though they at times they gesture toward what that might look like, however fleeting. Instead, their plots continue to test whether the social organization of space has the potential to produce meaningful forms of interpersonal connection across divides of class, race, gender, age, and culture. These operations draw on, while they also critique, the community imagined by the welfare state.

In turning to the rhythms of domestic and institutional spaces, I take inspiration from Michel de Certeau's classic study *The Practice of Everyday Life* (1980), which considers how subjects operate within totalizing systems in mobile and even idiosyncratic ways despite the systems' disciplinary effects. Though influenced by Foucault, De Certeau was less interested in revealing the workings and transmutation of power, seeking instead "to bring to light the clandestine forms taken by the dispersed, tactical, and makeshift creativity of groups or individuals already caught in the nets of 'discipline.'"[54] Again, this does not mean seeking a theory of revolution, rebellion, or even resistance in a strong or paranoid manner: what De Certeau calls "strategy," or actions undertaken by "a subject of will and power" who can be "isolated from an 'environment'" and therefore generate actions against, or exterior, to the systems they inhabit.[55] Instead, De Certeau is interested in the "tactical," which insinuates itself into the other's place, fragmentarily, without taking it over in its entirety, without being able to keep it at a distance."[56] This is the realm of the weak and the everyday: of those who must operate by *bricolage,* bringing together heterogenous elements as best they can to live their lives. It is also, I propose, the mechanism of the literary tradition documented by this book: one in which novels reinscribe to midcentury promises of welfare for their own purposes. Unable and unwilling to apply reconstruction's original mandates to their contemporary moment, they creatively transform them, manipulating their texts and traditions to produce their own language, their own postwar aesthetics.

[54] Michel de Certeau, *The Practice of Everyday Life*, 2nd ed., trans. Steven F. Rendall (Berkeley and Los Angeles: University of California Press, 1988), xiv.
[55] *Ibid.*, xix.
[56] *Ibid.*

This concept of reinscription is also an apt way to describe the work of postwar literature in relation to its predecessor, literary modernism. Here again a comparative postwar approach proves useful, helping to distinguish the literary affordances of housing after the Second World War.[57] Modernist artists, especially the Bloomsbury coterie, envisioned the home as a space for social experiment against traditional mores of kinship, gender, and sexuality of the Victorian household. The preoccupation with these private spaces shaped what we now celebrate as a hallmark of literary modernism—the idea of interiority and its imaginative capacities—which stood in stark contradistinction to state failures on the battlefield and in post-1918 reconstruction. Indeed, it is this fusing of private space and personhood that allows modernist literature to dramatize what Lionel Trilling called the "liberal imagination": the belief that, in the midst of life's extreme complexity, individuals can still reconcile their private and public selves without recourse to political or religious dogma, relying instead on a sense of morality, private sentiment, and aesthetic appreciation.[58]

As an aesthetic solution to social problems, then, modernist literature connected narrative form and ethics, imagining radical interpersonal connection and the possibility of communal life. The individual, signaled stylistically by interior depth, had the rare possibility to transcend social differences and, as E.M. Forster puts it, "Only connect." Despite these insights, the possibility of political or social change in modernist literature often stayed critically *in potentia*, signaled through a deployment of irony. As we witness characters attempting to "only connect," we also know that such relationships are not enough to effect social change, as revealed in the "not yet, not there" separating Forster's Aziz and Fielding in *A Passage to India* (1924), the fading of Gabriel's identity at the end of James Joyce's "The Dead" (1914), or, as discussed in Chapter 2, the divide between Septimus and Clarissa in Virginia Woolf's *Mrs. Dalloway* (1925). This modernist deferral is critically open-ended as to the fate of this liberal imagination, undecided as to whether connection should remain a negative possibility, or whether future

---

[57] I am particularly indebted to Victoria Rosner's work, whose approach to literary interiors and narrative interiority provided a rich model for how to read the role of the built environment in literary history.

[58] See Daniel Born's reading of *Howards End* and its tension between "real life" and "realty" Born, "Private Gardens, Public Swamps: *Howards End* and the Revaluation of Liberal Guilt," *NOVEL* (Winter 1992), 142.

generations should rebuild the world in such a way as to privilege these interpersonal relationships. With the advent of the Second World War, these distant possibilities threatened to become new realities through promises and practices of democratization, even and especially through the reorganization of home life and private inhabitation. I thus read the period after the Second World War as catalyzing a need to rethink modernist interiority. As I show, rethinking does not mean severing the modernist and postwar novel. Instead, it suggests a relationship that might be thought of as its own form of literary reconstruction, an updating or renovation that also preserves traces of former fictional infrastructures. As we'll see, postwar literature reorganized the private chambers that recur in classic literary modernism, moving from a room of one's own to experiments in living together. The site for transformation or empowerment is organized around certain kinds of semi-public, semi-communal spaces. These are proxy communities for that of the welfare state, rather than the modernist *locus classicus* of the individual and her exceptional personhood.

This book describes crossings between architecture and aesthetics such as Bowen's emphasis on the exterior street and interior life, which dramatizes class difference and the inevitable failure of solidarity; Spark's interest in the haunting space of the ruin; and Selvon's focus on neighborliness as a symbolic working-through of social problems faced by the Windrush generation. Though these novels are the closest inheritors of literary modernism, similar mappings of architectures of care resonate throughout later, more contemporary literature. The second half of the book thus studies Hollinghurst's clubs and gyms, which allow for more mobile intimacies than the family home; Ondaatje's Italian villa, which models an international community in miniature; and Ishiguro's cloning structures, which test the humanizing abilities of infrastructure. For these books, inhabited space is the metonym for welfare social relations. The stories they tell are of perpetually reorganized repair, featuring characters whose interiority and insight are framed against collective rather than individual norms and values.

Book Overview: The Long Reach of Britain's Postwar

To take postwar reconstruction as a category of analysis requires rethinking what counts as "war's time," or in this case, "postwar's time." Taking up Mary Dudziak's challenge, "What kind of time is a 'wartime'?," this project suggests that Britain's postwar time requires a creative reconsideration.[59] Indeed, the "time" of the postwar was always already in flux, its most vivid imaginings beginning before the war's official end. To take the postwar as an origin point thus means continually redefining the future based on wartime promises, what Brian Larkin calls the "promise of infrastructure," or "reflexive points where the present state and future possibilities of government and society are held up for public assessment."[60] This peculiar temporal fold meant that social reconstruction would never quite catch up with itself: a gap different in kind than the inevitable lags involved with politics and bureaucratic institutions.

This postwar condition is vividly invoked in Hannah Arendt's *Between Past and Future* (1961), which itself draws on a parable from Kafka's "Notes from the year 1920." Kafka's tale recounts the situation of a traveler beset by two antagonists: the past, which presses him from behind, and the future, which stops him from advancing. Once caught, the traveler wishes for a way to "jump out of the fighting line and be promoted, on account of his experience in fighting, to the position of umpire," exerting some sort of force to access another viewpoint on the scene.[61] Before the war, Arendt argues, it was possible to achieve this viewpoint through recourse to the Western philosophical tradition. However, as that explanatory power was broken by the rise of totalitarianism, we are all Kafka's traveler, seeking to renew the "original spirit which has so sadly evaporated from the very key words of political language—such as freedom and justice, authority and reason, responsibility and virtue, power and glory."[62] As we have seen, postwar Britain offered a threshold moment for rethinking the concept of welfare: one whose fullest dimensions were never

---

[59] Mary Dudziak, *War Time: An Idea, Its History, Its Consequences* (Oxford: Oxford University Press, 2012), 3. Claire Seiler offers a powerful characterization of postwar temporality as a form of suspension, able to "hold open a whole host of proximities to 'history' and 'the recent war' and also to indicate or allow for varying degrees of anticipation, experience, and recollection of violence, often without explicitly naming the war." *Midcentury Suspension: Literature and Feeling in the Wake of World War II* (New York: Columbia University Press, 2020), 227.

[60] Brian Larkin, "Promising Forms: The Political Aesthetics of Infrastructure," *The Promise of Infrastructure*, ed. Nikhil Anand, Akhil Gupta, and Hannah Appel (Durham: Duke University Press, 2018), 177.

[61] Hannah Arendt, *Between Past and Future: Eight Exercises in Political Thought* (New York: Penguin Books, 1977), 7. In her notes, Arendt notes her English translation follows that of Willa and Edwin Muir "except in a few places where a more literal translation was needed for my purposes" (276). Arendt's translation emphasizes the man's experience as a confrontation of sorts, substituting the words "battle" and "fight" where the Muirs use "struggle."

[62] *Ibid.*, 14.

reached, remaining as suggestion, horizon, or even absence in the materials of reconstruction. The novels we encounter here attempt to settle this gap, making elaborate, moving bids to gain perspective on these forces from the ground on which they stand, reconciling past promises with the felt urgencies of their contemporary situation. Whether this takes the form of satiric mythology, penitent biography writing, or racial repatriation, authors transform the burden and potential of post-1945 to their own creative ends.

In this book's approach, "postwar" or "post-1945" turns out not to be a period in the traditional sense. It is not a container, line, nor boundary dividing the late twentieth century, though it often finds itself in conversation or even competition with them. Nor is it an aesthetic category that cuts through historicism, despite its signature investment in novelistic representations of domestic life. Instead, the "post" of postwar Britain names a temporal orientation, characterized by a peculiar amalgam of belatedness, modernity, and contemporaneity. On the one hand, it shows an untimely desire for modernity, which as scholars have shown, is a concept informed by various, often conflictual chronotopes. Welfare's modernity was both a brave new world and a revolution long in the making. It was sworn in the name of the dead, the living, and those to come. And it was promised as a reward for fighting and winning the war, precisely when victory was far from a fait accompli. Postwar texts are also obsessed with their "postness," which they process as belatedness, an unchanging present, haunting and intergenerational debt, unfinished labor, or counterfactual history. Yet this belatedness is not purely melancholic. Nor is it nostalgic, whether a conservative nostalgia for heritage Britain or a radical nostalgia for the unrealized socialist revolution. Rather, the work of the postwar novel is to perpetually update what reconstruction might mean in our time. Its various returns to 1945 help reanimate specific political problems for their reader and interrogate the ideas of society or welfare that we have inherited.

This historical push and pull informs the structure of this book. In organizing these discussions under the two parts "Cradle" (Chapters 1–3) and "Grave" (Chapters 4–6), I draw on the famous description of the British welfare state as providing security "from the cradle to the grave."[63] Here,

---

[63] Though associated with the Beveridge Report, this phrase wasn't used in the actual report itself. Instead, it was introduced in Winston Churchill's March 21, 1943 broadcast on postwar reconstruction and what he called Britain's Four Year's Plan: "Here is a real opportunity for what I once called 'bringing the magic of averages to the rescue of the millions'. Therefore, you must rank me and my colleagues as strong partisans of national compulsory insurance for all

however, I use this phrase not to describe an individual's lifespan, but rather the lifespan of the welfare state itself, from its wartime conception and postwar development to its Thatcherite demise. The book's two halves also follow the periodizing power of 1945 in two directions: backward to the movement of literary modernism, and forwards to the ever-expanding contemporary. The first half of the book demonstrates how the power of post-45 must be thought in relation to literary modernism, further modeling one of its primary methods of reading this history: a comparative postwar approach. In this study, I depart from the recent trend of folding studies of midcentury into the discourse of late modernism, a period marked by a growing awareness of Britain's diminution, its loss of Empire, and declining global power.[64] My study of postwar domesticity is influenced by this conversation, and reads the growing interest in social welfare to the period's return to and revaluation of the idea of British Isles as homeland. However, I am less concerned with the "ends" of modernism than with the midcentury rewriting of the home, which might be considered its own form of modernism. I follow this revision of domestic space as a kind of break with the past, attending to its implication in the expression and experience of everyday life.[65] The works in this section privilege metropolitan London as the primary site of social experience, a legacy of both modernist practice and the discourse of postwar reconstruction.

With the receding of the immediate postwar period, and the transition from the rise of the welfare state to its Thatcherite dismantlement and neoliberal iterations, the events of 1945 have come to demand to be told in a different light. As 1945 has increasingly been consigned from immediate memory to distant history, contemporary authors have thematized this distance within their own work, preserving its transformative potential in

---

classes for all purposes from the cradle to the grave." *The War Speeches of Winston Churchill*, Vol. 2 (London: Cassel, 1965), 425–437. This phrase goes back much earlier than Churchill's invocation, popular in the nineteenth century and an update of the popular Early modern poetic rhyme of "womb" and "tomb." What's new here, I believe, is the association of the phrase with state care, rather than with religious or philosophical contexts.

[64] See, for instance, Jed Esty's *A Shrinking Island: Modernism and National Culture in England* (Princeton: Princeton University Press, 2003); MacKay's *Modernism and World War II*; and Thomas Davis's *The Extinct Scene: Late Modernism and Everyday Life* (New York: Columbia University Press, 2015).

[65] On a different note, the postwar saw the renewal of architectural modernism, a style that finally broke its way into a previously resistant England, and which influenced many housing projects and interior design during the period of reconstruction. See Elizabeth Darling's *Reforming Britain: Narratives of Modernity before Reconstruction* (London: Routledge, 2007) for an account of this.

INTRODUCTION: STATES OF REPAIR   33

narrative form. With this distance also comes greater geographical experimentation: after a focus on post-Blitz London lodgings in Part I, I consider other forms of care and spaces of collective living away from Britain's capital city. This focus on 1945 draws together periods often treated as distinct: "postwar" British literature and "contemporary" British and Anglophone literature. Bringing these fields together in this way allows this book to reconsider the relationship of "postwar" and "postcolonial" in literary studies: a tension that, as I suggest in Chapter 3, is symptomatic of the racial imaginary of postwar reconstruction. Britain's 1945 draws a line of continuity between these different periodizing and geographical signifiers, showing that the contemporary is suffused with postwar problematics, and that other geopolitical histories of violence inform the very concept of British identity.

Chapter 1, "A Room of One's Own?: Postwar Modernism and the Reconstructive Imagination," begins Part I amidst the ruins of the British Home Front, and frames postwar literature in relation to literary modernism's belief in individual connection as a radical social force. Bloomsbury's ethos of "only connect" falls flat after 1945, at odds with new ideas of collective justice and living together. Yet fiction of the immediate postwar shows a deep skepticism of social welfare. Authors such as George Orwell, Graham Greene, and Elizabeth Bowen were unable to write convincing accounts of this postwar society; they produce novels whose formal failures and ungainly treatment of the working class anticipate the challenges of reconstruction. I focus on Bowen's novel *The Heat of the Day* (1949) as inaugurating a critical skepticism about the wartime promises of postwar repair. Among her contemporaries, Bowen offers the most robust critique of how we might emerge from the shadow of war, attending to the lived experience of social change rather than falling prey to nostalgic yearning, dystopian pessimism, or apocalyptic fulfillment. *The Heat of the Day* collapses the relationships afforded by modernist treatments of interpersonal intimacy, questioning the possibility of connection with regard to its invasive, uncertain time. Yet this is also where Bowen meets her limit, unable to imagine a concrete social reality without these older models of individual connection. What is left, I argue, is a deeply troubled novel, whose formal failures and unsympathetic treatment of the working class points to the limits of the reconstructive imagination.

Chapter 2, "'Nowhere's Safe': Angry Young Women and Communal Betrayal" examines a counterliterature to that of the Angry Young Men: that of Angry Young Women, whose focus on group dynamics models a very different engagement with the promises of the welfare state than the male Angries' claustrophobic domesticity. In particular, I read Muriel Spark's *The Girls of Slender Means* (1963) as a case study in alternative forms of welfare, one that challenges both the burgeoning mythology of the "People's War" and the reparative logic of postwar reconstruction. Set in a girls' wartime hostel, Spark's novel idealizes her lodgers' communal life, only to spectacularly reveal their inherent selfishness and savagery. While the novel positions its readers to find meaning in the ruins of the club, I argue, it eventually repudiates this solace, refusing to transform state violence into an occasion for redemption. The chapter closes with a consideration of Hilary Mantel's 1995 *An Experiment in Love*, which I read as a direct rewriting of *The Girls of Slender Means*. Though Mantel's rendition of girlish intimacy is just as bleak as Spark's, Mantel ultimately re-enchants welfare's social potential, a statement of belief that flies in the face of welfare's Thatcherite demolition, reflecting another iteration of postwar mythology.

Chapter 3, "Unhomely Empire: Seeking Hospitality in Windrush Britain" addresses another challenge to Britain's plans for social welfare: midcentury decolonization movements and mass immigration to the UK. It begins by bringing the study of the postwar squarely in relation to another key term—the postcolonial—arguing that the rise of Britain's welfare state cannot be read without reference to its decline as a global superpower. Until recently, these two terms have tended to describe completely different datasets, with the "post" of the postwar rarely equating to the "post" of the postcolonial. While this division has been due to chronology and disciplinary formation, it can also be read as symptomatic of the racial imaginary of British reconstruction, which projected a largely white, insular postwar nation that had little relation to its colonies overseas. This chapter seeks to correct this tendency, turning to Windrush literary production as a critical testing-ground where wartime visions of reconstruction met postwar social realities, manifested in the unevenly felt experiences of making Britain home for colonial migrants turned "Citizens of the United Kingdom and Colonies." Specifically, it tracks the dream of communal domesticity that saturates the work of author Samuel Selvon, from the Sunday basement meetings in *The Lonely Londoners* (1956), the foray into collective home ownership in *The Housing Lark* (1965), and the disastrous experience of playing landlord in *Moses Ascending* (1975). I then track how this legacy continues to inform contemporary literary production in works such as different as Andrea Levy's *Small Island* (2004) and Zadie Smith's *NW* (2012), reminding readers of the powerful backward eddy that is Britain's postwar imagination.

INTRODUCTION: STATES OF REPAIR   35

Marking the hinge between Part I and Part II is a short Interlude, entitled "Failed Utopias, or, the Beginning of the End." This section marks a crucial inflection point in British welfare state history and its cultural representations: namely, the transition from welfare's "classic phase" of 1945–1975 to its neoliberal restructuring in the late 1970s and beyond. As an intermediary between the book's two halves (Part I's "Cradle" to Part II's "Grave,") this section describes how the stakes of Britain's "postwar" shift across this divide, both historically and aesthetically. In particular, the Interlude tracks welfare's consolidation to residualization through the rise and fall of public housing, using remarks by Clement Attlee and Margaret Thatcher to capture the changing ethos of housing as a social service. It then turns to Buchi Emecheta's *In the Ditch* (1974) and J.G. Ballard's *High-Rise* (1975) as works that use the modern architecture of public housing as a way to metonymize the persistent utopian and dystopian undercurrents of the British welfare state.

Chapter 4, "Empty Places: Unpropertied Intimacy and Queer History" begins by considering a phenomenon that I call "the novel of the century," or a subset of contemporary novels whose plots span the length of the twentieth century, projecting something like historical totality as they move briskly through time. This genre has a remarkable coherence in large part due to its figuration of midcentury, and specifically the Second World War, as its conceptual limit-point, the event that requires revisiting and reworking in order to get right (for example, Kate Atkinson's *Life After Life*, Ian McEwan's *Atonement*, Martin Amis's *Time's Arrow*). The chapter examines Alan Hollinghurst's *The Swimming-Pool Library* (1988), which encrypts the postwar period as its hidden source of narrative trauma, and reflects upon the intensified, institutionalized homophobia in the 1950s and 1960s. Doing so reveals the exclusionary power of postwar reconstruction, whose plans formed around the heterosexual nuclear family. Rather than use the family home as the standard for narrative social security, Hollinghurst turns away from propertied domesticity to embrace mobile practices of queer intimacy. Yet his work also relies on the spatialized, welfarist logic of postwar reconstruction to imagine a better life for queer people, turning to spaces such as gyms, bathrooms, prisons, and colonial outposts that facilitate alternative forms of community and caretaking. These sites in turn offer a different orientation to historical trauma, working against a reparative mandate while suggesting a relationship to history that maintains queerness's promise and precarity. The chapter closes with a consideration of Hollinghurst's most recent work, *The Sparsholt Affair*

(2018), which directly engages with the Second World War and postwar reconstruction by beginning during the Blitz and following the life of David Sparsholt, an architect whose personal and business life are embroiled in scandal.

Chapter 5, "Oasis Societies and Enchanted Care," considers a historiographic challenge to the visions of postwar Britain that emerged in the 1980s and flourished in the 1990s: the contemporary heritage industry, as well as the related cultural phenomenon of imperial nostalgia. These reactionary discourses vied with postwar reconstruction's modernizing tendencies, particularly when it came to the family home, by reinvesting in the institution of the country house and romanticizing its forms of sociality. This chapter turns to Michael Ondaatje's *The English Patient* (1992) as a text that stages the battle between the heritage industry and reconstruction, precisely in the name of postwar repair. While the novel outwardly embraces heritage and imperial nostalgic tropes, the novel ultimately undoes them, offering instead an experiment in multicultural living together and the newfound intimacies produced therein. This, then, is the real romance of *The English Patient*: a transnational welfare without the state, based on mutual, domestic care. Unlike the other novels considered in this book, which fall properly (though ambivalently) under the category of "British" literature, Ondaatje's work is considered part of the global Anglophone canon. Yet as its title suggests, its concerns center around the fate of postwar Englishness, and as such, I include it as an exceptional case marking just how far the concerns described in this book extend into contemporary fiction. Ondaatje's earnest treatment of wartime sociality and its enchantments is just as relevant for this study. Though his miniature community is shattered by the news of Hiroshima, which breaks the spell of uncolonized space and scatters the villa's inhabitants, Ondaatje's novel still asks us to invest in the possibility of a welfarist domestic space. While critics tend to characterize this quality as "bad form," I read it instead as a cultural legacy of Britain's 1945, one that offers its own take on the British heritage industry. The chapter concludes with a reading of *Warlight* (2018), Ondaatje's disappointing return to the Second World War, the narrative of which ultimately discounts its socially transformative potential.

Chapter 6, "Institutional Life: Infrastructural Interiority as Postwar Feeling" reads Kazuo Ishiguro's *Never Let Me Go* (2005) as a counterfactual allegory of postwar Britain. The novel challenges the reader to contend not only with its characters' statistical structures of feeling, but also with the ways institutional space shapes their aggregate individualism—a cold vision of the welfare state's endgame and the risks of a reconstructive ethos. Yet even in this world of complete instrumentalization, *Never Let Me Go* cannot abandon the spatial fantasies of care so characteristic of Britain's postwar imagination. Unlike Ishiguro's other works, whose epiphanies are motivated by a form of historical consciousness-raising, this sense of history is not available to the clone protagonist Kathy. Instead, her postwar crisis and epiphany is mediated through her abiding relationship with her environment, from empty English country highways to the fantasy of Norfolk as the site of England's lost-and-found.

Finally, the Coda, "A Hostile Environment," reflects on the book's contemporary moment, a time when discussions of the need for welfare have intensified due to the catastrophic combination of atrophied welfare states, the European refugee crisis, and the Home Office's introduction of "hostile environment" policies. Instead of studying representations of housing and quasi-administrated domestic life, this section considers a structure often hidden from view: the Immigration Removal Centre, used to hold and remove those seeking entry to Britain. Analyzing representations of these centres in the work of Abdulrazak Gurnah, Caryl Phillips, and Ali Smith, the Coda brings human rights concerns to bear on domestic welfare, connecting these structures of inhospitality to postwar dreams of social life. From this, it is clear that Britain's postwar has yet to relinquish its hold on us, and that it continues to update its midcentury mandate along new and necessary lines.

PART I
CRADLE

1
A Room of One's Own?
Postwar Modernism and the Reconstructive Imagination

In 1946, photographer Bill Brandt published a series entitled "An Odd Lot: A Gallery of Literary Portraits" for *Lilliput* magazine, featuring a who's who of literati including E.M. Forster, Ivy Compton-Burnett, Robert Graves, Evelyn Waugh, Graham Greene, and Elizabeth Bowen. In an echo of his documentary work *The English at Home* (1936), which underscored England's socioeconomic disparities through scenes of domestic life, Brandt captured the authors' likenesses in largely interior settings. In Bowen's case, Brandt chose to situate her beside a large window in her London home, as we see in Figure 7.

Lost in thought, Bowen, facing away from the window, looks pensively beyond the frame of the photograph. The book on her lap suggests an allegorical reading of the portrait of the artist, her literary sensibilities caught between the private and the public, individual and social life. The image presents a perfect likeness of Bowen as the intermediary she was. As the accompanying description by critic Alan Pryce-Jones suggests, Bowen "carried on where Forster left off, using the new world of ever-rising uncertainty as her background, but always keeping in touch with the subtle realities of private life as it is lived behind the decorous façades shown to the street."[1] Indeed, among her contemporaries, Bowen was the preeminent inheritor of a modernist literary sensibility, described by biographer Victoria Glendinning as "what happened after Bloomsbury; she is the link which connects Virginia Woolf with Iris Murdoch and Muriel Spark."[2] This chapter turns to Bowen as offering an especially nuanced engagement with how modernism registers the deformations of war. Her midcentury work stands torn

---

[1] Bill Brandt and Alan Pryce-Jones, "An Odd Lot," *Lilliput* 25, no. 5 (November 1949), 49–56.
[2] Victoria Glendinning, *Elizabeth Bowen: Portrait of a Writer* (New York: Alfred A. Knopf, Inc., 1977), xv. Bowen was also an admirer of Spark's, and convinced Knopf they should publish her in America (Glendinning, *Elizabeth Bowen*, 273).

The Promise of Welfare in the Postwar British and Anglophone Novel. Kelly M. Rich, Oxford University Press.
© Kelly M. Rich (2023). DOI: 10.1093/oso/9780192893437.003.0002

Figure 7 Bill Brandt, "Elizabeth Bowen" (1946). *Lilliput.*
© Bill Brandt Archive. Reproduced courtesy of Bill Brandt Archive Ltd.

between modernist principles and what she understands as the new sociality of war: a communal consciousness, united under the threat of the Blitz; a democratized Britain, brought to fruition through postwar welfare; and an administered population, whose private life is infiltrated by the state. How, then, does Bowen negotiate these contradictions in her prose? What exactly does she see from her position at the window?

Bowen was of a generation that participated in the British war machine to an unprecedented degree. By the Second World War, the British propaganda machine—which originated in the First World War and accelerated during the interwar period—reached its fullest development, conscripting authors specifically for their writerly abilities.[3] Despite the deeply critical, pacifist stances that characterized many artists' reactions to the First World War, several midcentury writers made what Marina MacKay characterizes as "the guilty compromise" of supporting the Second.[4] George Orwell, for instance, issued broadcasts with the BBC's Eastern Service; Evelyn Waugh served in Marine and commando units; Henry Green fought fires in the Auxilary Fire Service; and Graham Greene worked for MI6 in Sierra Leone. Bowen was of this generation, doing her part by reporting on Ireland for the Ministry of Information.[5] Even the older E.M. Forster did his bit through his popular broadcasts for the BBC, which championed liberalism and tolerance, as well as providing the script to Humphrey Jenning's propaganda film *A Diary for Timothy*, which I will return to in the conclusion to this chapter. War service had a discernible influence on these authors' wartime and immediate postwar fictions, providing key sites of engagement in Bowen's *The Heat of the Day* and short story collection *The Demon Lover*; Orwell's *1984* and wartime composition "The Lion and the Unicorn"; Waugh's *Brideshead Revisited* and *The Sword of Honor* trilogy; Green's *Caught, Loving,* and *Back*; and Greene's *Ministry of Fear, The Heart of the Matter,* and *The End of the Affair*. But again, none of these authors were quite as committed to the aesthetic legacies of modernism as Bowen, and in particular, to the nexus of domestic and private life in the postwar novel.

For as Brandt's portrait suggests, the changing idea of the home was very much on Bowen's mind during and after the war, in part due to the trauma of wartime destruction, which inaugurated new forms of social, material, and psychic insecurity through its destruction of everyday life. These transformations are lucidly captured in a January 5, 1941 letter to Virginia Woolf, in which Bowen expresses her dismay over the destruction of Woolf's apartment at 37 Mecklenburgh Square.[6] Bowen had visited Woolf the previous

[3] See Mark Wollaeger, *Modernism, Media, and Propaganda: British Narrative From 1900 to 1945* (Princeton: Princeton University Press, 2006), xvi.
[4] Marina MacKay, *Modernism and World War II* (Cambridge: Cambridge University Press, 2007), 10.
[5] See also Bowen's expression of "a sort of despair about my own generation—the people the same age as the century, I mean—we don't really suffer much but we get all sealed up." Elizabeth Bowen to Virginia Woolf, 5 January 1941, Monks House Papers, University of Sussex Special Collections.
[6] Virginia came up from Rodmell every week to Bloomsbury to survey the damage. See Hermione Lee, *Virginia Woolf* (New York: Alfred A. Knopf, 1996), 728–731. Bowen's own London residence, No. 2 Clarence Terrace, was to be bombed just a year later.

July, and it was in reference to that visit that she asked: "When your flat went did that mean all the things in it too? All my life I have said, 'Whatever happens there will always be tables and chairs' - and what a mistake."[7] With bombs raining down across Britain, Bowen's words registered a new need to come to terms with the obliteration of solid everyday things, especially domestic objects whose existence was taken for granted. Midcentury authors indexed Britain's transformation into a militarized Home Front precisely through this destruction of the home. While other critics have analyzed the importance of damage and ruination to late modernist and wartime literatures, this project is interested in another formal registration of the period's instability: namely, the comparison of older models of domestic life with new institutionalized settings.[8] Think of Orwell's Ministry of Love versus Winston and Julia's clandestine, surveilled room above the antiquities shop; Waugh's military camps versus Ryder's recollections of a lost Brideshead; and the dislocations of Greene's sanatoriums and hotels. These new social spaces show the unsettling effect of war on the home, as well as the perceived effects of postwar sociality on the fate of individual privacy and autonomy.

In Bowen's case, this rescripting of literary interiors was further inflected through her modernist sensibilities, to modernism, particularly the type of relationship that modernism figured between domestic space and the production of the sympathetic individual. As Victoria Rosner reminds us, the aesthetic we know as modernist interiority was indelibly shaped by authors' engagement with the affordances of architectural interiors.[9] Despite her close relationship to Woolf, Bowen attributed her literary obsession with space to Forster, whom she once named as her greatest novelistic influence. Describing the power of what she called Forster's "place-feeling" on her own work, she notes:

---

[7] Bowen to Woolf, 5 January 1941. Bowen's last letters to Woolf introduce diverging interest in interior spaces, as Bowen begins to write about her rooms in Dublin where she worked as a spy, and of the interiors of various London War Offices. See especially the letter dated July 1, 1940.

[8] See, for instance, Leo Mellor's *Reading the Ruins: Modernism, Bombsites and British Culture* (Cambridge: Cambridge University Press, 2011); Beryl Pong's *British Literature and Culture in the Second World Wartime: for the Duration* (Oxford: Oxford University Press, 2020); and Paul Saint-Amour's *Tense Future: Modernism, Total War, Encyclopedic Form* (Oxford: Oxford University Press, 2015).

[9] Victoria Rosner, *Modernism and the Architecture of Private Life* (New York: Columbia University Press, 2005), 2.

Intense sense of locality, and deference if not subjection to its power could in itself make distinguishable, did nothing else, the Forster atmosphere. My own tendency to attribute significance to places, or to be mesmerised by them even for no knowable reason, then haunted by them, became warranted by its larger reflection in E.M. Forster. Formerly I had feared it might be a malady.[10]

Woolf, for her own part, believed Forster's deference to environment a malady. Though Forster was one of the "new" novelists named in her 1924 essay "Mr. Bennett and Mrs. Brown," Woolf found he still cared too much about realism as well as symbolism; about the novel of ideas as well as the novel of impressions; and above all, about the overbearing effect of the public on the private, or material environment on character.[11] While Bowen provides a middle ground between these older modernists, her *oeuvre* is veritably infected by the "Forster atmosphere," charting the effects of setting and especially domestic space on characters' personal development. These relationships often fall into one of two categories. First, there are novels centered around aristocratic Big Houses, contrasting their protagonist's *Bildung* with the other inhabitants' moral lassitude, ghosts of lovers past, and the imminent decay of Anglo-Irish life (*The Last September, A World of Love*.) Then there are stories without a domestic center, leaving the main character to come of age haphazardly amidst temporary housing, relatives' apartments, vacation rentals, hotels, and schools (*The Death of the Heart, Eva Trout, The House in Paris*). For Bowen's characters, the home environment matters as much as the people who live there, their characters being as much the product of windows, bedrooms, and dining-rooms as they are of lovers, friends, and relations. Indeed, one gets the sense that characters actually *could* grow up correctly if only they had the right surroundings: the very gambit of postwar reconstruction.

Bowen's literary treatment of domestic space changed remarkably during the Second World War. Gone were the interiors of modernist interiority in postwar novels: those rooms that created space for individual thought and creativity, and whose boundaries marked borders between public and private lives. Instead, the homes of the Home Front were stripped open, both

---

[10] Bowen, "A Passage to E.M. Forster," *Aspects of E.M. Forster*, ed. Oliver Stallybrass (London: Edward Arnold Publishers, 1969), 5.

[11] For an overview of Woolf's and Forster's relationship, see Mark Goldman, "Virginia Woolf and E.M. Forster: A Critical Dialogue," *Texas Studies in Literature and Language* 7:4 (Winter 1996), 387–400.

by unprecedented physical damage and by state management. In Bowen's short fiction, the home is destroyed ("Oh, Madam..."), haunted ("The Demon Lover"), darkly fantastic ("Mysterious Kôr"), or, at best, a myopic shelter from the realities of war ("Sunday Afternoon"). For these stories, domesticity affords no peace, functioning mainly to produce an unsettling uncanniness. Bowen attributed the stories' experimentalism to wartime's new collective consciousness, which she described in the postscript as "flying particles of something enormous and inchoate that had been going on. They were sparks from experience—an experience not necessarily my own."[12] Wartime was thus uniquely generative for Bowen's literary style, allying her more with Woolf's experimental "art of fiction" than that of the liberal Forster.

What would prove more challenging, in fact, was what came after war: the new realities of postwar reconstruction, and the evacuation of what Bowen again calls "atmosphere" in her 1950 essay "The Bend Back":

> Where is the eye to linger, where is fancy to dwell? No associations, no memories have had time to gather around the new soaring blocks of flats, the mushroom housing-estates. And, will they ever do so?—where shall they find a foothold? Nothing rustles, nothing casts a feathery shadow: there is something frightening about the very unhauntedness of "functional" rooms. Atmosphere has been conditioned out of the air. Nor even, among all this oppressiveness of brick and concrete, do we feel secure—all this, in a split second, could become nothing. Nor, stacked and crowded upon one another in our living and moving, do we feel in contact: personal isolation has increased.[13]

Bowen's horror over the loss of atmosphere is as palpable as that expressed over Woolf's apartment, if not more so. Instead of producing a secured citizenry and sense of community, reconstruction for Bowen signaled the very destruction of society, one that was possibly irredeemable. In the essay, she notes how this state of affairs was also registered by novelists' nostalgic "bend back" to childhood or other historical eras: "Are we to take it that our own time has been, from the point of view of its inhabitants,

---

[12] Bowen, "Postscript By the Author," *The Demon Lover and Other Stories*, 2nd ed. (London: Jonathan Cape, 1952), 216–217. This generic working-through is also registered in her aphoristic "Notes on Writing a Novel," published in *Orion* in 1945, which compared to her pieces about *The Demon Lover*, reads more like a sketch or draft of an essay than a fully developed piece of writing.
[13] Bowen, "The Bend Back," in *The Mulberry Tree: Writings of Elizabeth Bowen* (London: Virago Press, 1986), 54–60.

irreparably injured—that it shows some loss of vital deficiency?"[14] She must have thought so, as her later postwar novels *A World of Love* (1955) and *The Little Girls* (1963) indulge in their own backward turn. Revolving around hidden relics from the First World War, they encrypt the interwar period as the only history worth remembering, returning to the more familiar milieu of Bowen's earlier *oeuvre*. But her 1949 *The Heat of the Day*—a novel begun in wartime, abandoned, and finished after the war—offers a different story. Through it, we see a writer trying to re-engage readers with their own time, however difficult that may be.

This chapter tracks the ways *The Heat of the Day* engages the reconstructive imagination, and the tension it manifests between the tenets of literary modernism and the demands of the postwar period. It reads *The Heat of the Day* as unable to imagine a concrete reality that exists without older models of sociality and their accompanying domestic atmospheres. Though the novel engages the psychological merging of consciousness during war and the uncaring equality of bombs, in the end, neither is taken seriously as a vehicle for social change. This is why I ultimately approach *The Heat of the Day* not as a late modernist, wartime, or midcentury novel, but rather as a postwar novel troubled by the potential of postwar sociality. Bowen's unease results in a palpable drag on the novel's forward momentum, especially in its final chapters, which take place after the narrative climax. Devolving into a series of nested endings, the novel offers a series of worries over how the postwar period will remember the war, and spirals into side plots addressing who will inherit England: the mass-interpellated working-class or naïve upper-class youth. *The Heat of the Day* is thus haunted by its non-productive recursivity, a quality that will continue to inform postwar literary production. While the novel returns to the Second World War as a site of meaningful plenitude, it eventually leaves its reader with nothing but dead ends and non-starters for the postwar period. In doing so, it inaugurates a new tradition for the postwar British novel, in which novelists return to the midcentury to illustrate its failed potential, testifying to a Britain trapped by its postwar promises.

Spaces of Disconnect in *The Heat of the Day*

The Heat of the Day provides a telling case study for Bowen's wartime writing due to its form. While her short stories may have been generated by the

---

[14] Bowen, "Bend Back," 55.

wartime collective consciousness, Bowen felt this new sociality could not sustain the genre of the novel: as she noted in the postscript to the US edition of *The Demon Lover*, "A novel must have form; and, for the form's sake, one is always having to make relentless exclusions."[15] This emphasis on novel form surfaces again in letters between Bowen, Graham Greene, and V.S. Pritchett, who like other artists and intellectuals, were contemplating the role of the writer in the postwar period. Given the urgency and popularity of this subject, their exchange was later broadcast on the BBC Third Programme, published in the *Partisan Review*, and reprinted as a longer book. In the radio version, Bowen emphasized that it was the responsibility of the artist, particularly the novelist, to "impose shape" on fiction, transforming what would otherwise be its "mass" of characters into an intelligible "society."[16] Through this shaping, Bowen suggested, an author can suggest meaning and direction for the lives of her readers. She returned to this concept in "The Bend Back," which concludes that the writer should "re-instate the idea of life as livable, lovable."[17]

The question is, then, whether *The Heat of the Day* manages to balance the innovative demands of wartime with the formal demands of the novel. Although *The Heat of the Day* channels the exhilarating collectivity that makes *The Demon Lover* so innovative, especially in its opening portrait of wartime London, Bowen struggles to adapt the deformations of domestic interiors for the novel form by linking them with the drama of individual development. Indeed, for all her avowals of novelistic constraint, it is shocking how few "relentless exclusions" there are in *The Heat of the Day*. It is a novel that cannot make up its mind. Part thriller, romance, and domestic fiction, it moves in fits and starts amidst recognizable generic forms. Set in London between 1942 and 1944, *The Heat of the Day* centers around the upper-class Stella Rodney, her lover Robert, later revealed to be a German spy, and Harrison, a British counterspy. Harrison is in the midst of blackmailing Stella, promising Robert's immunity in exchange for a sexual relationship. And though these intertwined love and espionage plots are the main focus of *The Heat of the Day*, the novel also entertains other minor storylines, including the inheritance plots surrounding Stella's son Roderick and Mount Morris, Robert's family and their Irish Big House, Holme Dene;

---

[15] Bowen, "Postscript," 217.
[16] Graham Greene, Elizabeth Bowen, and V.S. Pritchett, "The Artist in Society," *From the Third Programme: A Ten-Years' Anthology*, ed. John Morris (London: Nonesuch Press, 1956), 101.
[17] Bowen, "Bend Back," 55.

and the coming-of-age story of Louie Lewis, a working-class girl whose husband is away in the army. As this summary might suggest, the plot is difficult, even convoluted. Even the novel's syntax is convoluted, full of double negatives and strange invocations of the passive voice, which critics have read as capturing the effect of living under the strain of war.[18]

Despite its difficulties, *The Heat of the Day* has achieved pride of place in literary criticism, especially given recent interest in the previously undertheorized middle of the twentieth century. Given her chronology and literary preoccupations, Bowen has been read as a late modernist, her work marked by a growing awareness of Britain's diminution, loss of Empire, and declining global power.[19] Bowen has also become a go-to author for critics focusing on literature of the Second World War, used as an example of the phantasmagoric and dramatization of wartime surveillance.[20] She also has been claimed in the name of midcentury, whether on behalf of particular years ("around 1945"), decades (the 1940s), or more broadly, the self-aware middleness Claire Seiler calls "midcentury suspension."[21] My reading of *The Heat of the Day* is indebted to all of these terms. In this

---

[18] See, for instance, Anna Teekell's excellent analysis of double negatives, which she reads as symbolic of its "espionage-based epistemology: it is the grammar of Stella's refusal to believe Harrison's story, and her refusal to disbelieve it as well." "Elizabeth Bowen and Language at War," *New Hibernia Review* 15:3 (Autumn 2011), 63. See also Heather Bryant Jordan's reading of the novel's passive voice as evoking "the torpor and convolutions of the war years." *How Will the Heart Endure: Elizabeth Bowen and the Landscape of War* (Ann Arbor: University of Michigan Press, 1992), 164.

[19] See, for instance, Thomas Davis's reading of Bowen's wartime short stories as exemplary of what he calls late modernism's "outward turn," or focus on everyday life as a way to register changes in the world-system. In particular, Bowen's use of the Anglo-Irish gothic helps make legible insecurity about Britain's changing place in the world, noting this genre, which was "initially suited for a dying settler colonial class is uniquely, if counterintuitively, appropriate for a bombed imperial metropole." Davis, *The Extinct Scene: Late Modernism and Everyday Life* (New York: Columbia University Press, 2016), 174.

[20] See Patrick Deer, *Culture in Camouflage: War, Empire, and Modern British Literature* (Oxford: Oxford University Press, 2009), 168–191; Jenny Hartley, *Millions Like Us: British Women's Fiction of the Second World War* (London: Virago, 1997), 95–105; Mellor, Leo Mellor, *Reading the Ruins: Modernism, Bombsites and British Culture* (Cambridge: Cambridge University Press, 2011), 157–165; Adam Piette, *Imagination at War: British Fiction and Poetry, 1939–1945* (London: Papermac, 1995), 4; and Mark Rawlinson, *British Writing of the Second World War* (Oxford: Clarendon, 2000), 99–103. Bowen scholars also focus on her wartime production in a manner delimited to wartime itself—studying the impact of the war on women and the home (Kristine Miller), the wartime uncanny and ghostly phenomena (Petra Rau, Lee Rumbarger), or the war's new social occasioning of espionage and treachery (Lee) or the undoing of the individual (Neil Corcoran).

[21] See Chapter 3 of Claire Seiler's *Midcentury Suspension*, which pairs Bowen with Samuel Beckett as contemporaries in historical waiting: in particular, Seiler reads *The Heat of the Day* and *Waiting for Godot* as characterized by "a distinctly midcentury historicity neither extricable from nor reducible to the war that both works are, in varying ways, 'about' and whose temporal bounds they trouble." *Midcentury Suspension: Literature and Feeling in the Wake of*

chapter, however, I offer another approach to the novel's narrative and stylistic complexities, attributing its difficulty to its status as a postwar novel, what I call *postwar modernism*.[22] As we will see, studying the midcentury transition between wartime and postwar means being invested not only in narratives of decline and endings, but also in reconstruction and beginnings, and the inextricable relationship between the two. It means asking how the modernist injunction of "make it new" turned into "make it *anew*," an ethos that carried a distinct social and political reparative charge. And as the next chapters on Muriel Spark and Samuel Selvon bear out, it means asking how the immediate postwar's version of "making it new" revised—indeed, reconstructed—literary modernism in light of contemporary concerns.

In *The Heat of the Day*, the most notable episodes of reading the social into the architectural happen at the borders of private rooms, which prove all too permeable to intrusion and observation. The mutually inflecting domestic and political energies of the novel come to a head during the narrative climax, when Robert finally admits to Stella that he is, in fact, a spy. This scene takes place in Stella's rented flat, a space made doubly precarious by enforced blackout conditions as well as by Harrison's surveillance. Under these conditions, the windows of Stella's flat gain heightened significance, becoming imbued with their own language. These apertures risk revealing too much of the secret life within, emphasized by the impersonal "multiplication of [Harrison's] personality, all round the house."[23] Yet this is no valuation of the life within. Instead, the room becomes a claustrophobic, apolitical space, heightening Bowen's previous description of the couple as

---

World War II (New York: Columbia University Press, 2020), 146. While Seiler reads this middleness as reflecting the uncertainty of living in a war without known end, the temporality I want to capture is more dynamic, constantly shuttling back and forth between the promises of the war and their failures in the present—the sense, in other words, of never arriving at one's destination.

[22] My reading of Bowen's postwar modernism also diverges from that of Allan Hepburn and Lyndsey Stonebridge, who attribute the holding power of the postwar for Bowen to the uncertain judicial landscape of postwar Europe, and the need to determine culpability and the rights of the displaced person in the wake of war. While such legal mechanisms do require re-reading backward, I see a more properly proleptic temporality that originates from the crucible of war: one that is demanded by wartime imaginings of postwar repair. In other words, while postwar judicial imagination was an exercise in creative retrospect, trying to make sense of what happened, the postwar reconstructive imagination was one of creative projection. See Allan Hepburn, "Trials and Errors: *The Heat of the Day* and Postwar Culpability," *Intermodernism: Literary Culture in Mid-Twentieth-Century Britain*, ed. Kristin Bluemel (Edinburgh: Edinburgh University Press, 2009), and Chapter 5 in Lyndsey Stonebridge, *The Judicial Imagination: Writing After Nuremberg* (Edinburgh: Edinburgh University Press, 2011), which is largely about Bowen's final work, *Eva Trout*.

[23] Bowen, *The Heat of the Day* (New York: Anchor Books, 2002), 311.

a "hermetic world, which, like the ideal book about nothing, stayed itself on itself by its inner force"—an uncanny echo of Winston Smith's reading of "the book" in Orwell's *1984*, which tells him what he already knows.[24] Robert speaks directly to this hermeticism when he asks Stella: "You have been my country ... are you and I to be what we've known we are for nothing, nothing outside this room?"[25] This question contains echoes of a modernist ethical impulse that seeks a synthesis between private sentiment and public feeling, dramatized by the boundaries of domesticity. In this instance, the desire for connection also paves the way for political detachment, and, eventually, treason.

For once confided in, Stella is caught in a double-bind: while to empathize would be treasonous, to refuse Robert would carry its own intimate treachery. In a burst of sympathetic connection, she suddenly aligns with Robert's way of thinking. The moment then reaches epiphanic proportions when she tries to imagine life without Robert, turning a photograph of his around to face the wall: "The ice broke; she had to hold on to the chimneypiece while she steadied her body against the beating of her heart... She tried to say 'Robert!' but had no voice. She looked at the door: it was incredible that anyone loved so much should be still behind it."[26] As if by magic, Robert opens the door, and they fall into each other's arms. The narration then turns away from the couple, as if to give them privacy:

> If there were any step in the street of sleeping houses, it was impossible it should now be heard by the two blotted out. To anyone silently posted down there in the street, the ranks of windows reflecting the paling sky would have all looked the same; it was in this room that an eyelid came down over the world.[27]

This iteration signals the dangerous endgame of only connecting in a room of their own. In pledging allegiance to the individual over other forms of collectivity, these characters have not only engaged in wartime treason, but they have also, paradoxically, erased any defining features of their characters. Bowen effects this stylistically by erasing the specificity of people and places, flattening the social world so that there seems no difference between observer and observed, betrayer and betrayed.

[24] *Ibid.*, 97.
[25] *Ibid.*, 307.
[26] *Ibid.*, 312.
[27] *Ibid.*, 312–313.

This scene heralds a breaking point with Stella, who, until this point, had been the most sympathetic character in the novel. The rest of *The Heat of the Day* is spent grappling with who, exactly, will replace Stella as the reader's avatar and ethical model for how to live in the postwar world. Bowen tests this responsibility on the younger generation by focusing on Louie, a working-class girl, and Roderick, Stella's son and a soldier who is to inherit their family home. Through the actions of these secondary characters, the reader witnesses two very different crises over what to make of the central wartime drama in the novel, and, more generally, the historical legacy of the war for the postwar period. Bowen's treatment of Louie and Roderick evinces an ambivalence toward, even distaste for, burgeoning social democratization during the war. (Their very names—Louie Lewis and Roderick Rodney—signal a lack of faith in their characters, the repetition of given and surname suggesting no personal depth.) In particular, Bowen's revulsion toward Louie reveals the limits of her novelistic social imagination. But it is also symptomatic of the midcentury novel writ large, caught in between residual and emergent literary forms of social connection: modernist individualism versus postwar collectivity. Bowen is not the only novelist with a modernist hangover: try as it might, the postwar British novel cannot let go of the humanizing power of interiority, and keeps returning to this midcentury moment as a frame for this problem.

Bowen writes Louie Lewis with a hand that is strikingly, even unconscionably, heavy. Introducing her character as lacking self-consciousness, Bowen describes Louie's main object to be "to feel that she, Louie, *was*, and in the main she did not look back too willingly at what might have been said or done by her in pursuit of that."[28] This pursuit is accompanied by a marked lack of historical perspective, as "Louie had, with regard to time, an infant lack of stereoscopic vision; she saw then and now on the same plane; they were the same."[29] Both shortcomings find synthesis in Louie's abiding love for the newspaper, which Marina MacKay describes as "almost a direct instantiation of Benedict Anderson's theory of newspapers and nationalism."[30] Compared to Stella, then, Louie seems incapable of being an individual, a flat character lacking her counterpart's rounded interiority. Yet this massification also enables various types of connective possibilities, providing Louie with a comforting nationalism imagined as kinship: "War now

---

[28] Ibid., 13.
[29] Ibid., 15.
[30] MacKay, "'Is Your Journey Really Necessary?': Going Nowhere in Late Modernist London," *PMLA* 124.5 (October 2009), 1607.

made us one big family...She was re-instated; once again round her were the everlasting arms."[31] This feeling recalls the ferment of wartime democratization, the *jouissance* of being in it together characteristic of the Second World War. There was of course some irony to this new fellow-feeling: after all, it took a war to create it. Bowen's turns of phrase underscore this irony, acknowledging Louie's newfound sensibility as yet another form of wartime conscription, imbued with quasi-religious communality.

For Bowen, wartime social ferment provides a way to test the viability of modernist connection, especially across Louie's and Stella's class differences. The working-class Louie recalls Leonard Bast of E.M. Forster's *Howards End* as the novel's experimental subject with the most to gain and also the most to lose. Indeed, we might read them as literary recipients of modernist social welfare, one whose upward mobility relies more on individual connection than individual contribution. This experiment begins after the women's two plot lines finally and improbably converge in a restaurant, after which Louie walks Stella home. When Louie returns to her own flat, she has a form of sympathetic shock contemplating the "effect of her [Stella's] person":

> Louie felt herself entered by what was foreign. She exclaimed in thought, "Oh no, I wouldn't be her!" at the moment when she most nearly was. Think, now, what the air was charged with night and day—ununderstandable languages, music you did not care for, sickness, germs! You did not know what you might not be tuning in to, you could not say what you might not be picking up—affected, infected you were at every turn. Receiver, conductor, carrier—which was Louie, what was she doomed to be? She asked herself, but without words. She felt what she had not felt before—was it, even, she herself who was feeling?[32]

This moment reverses the polarity of modernist social welfare, whose meaning flows from the Helen Schlegels and Clarissa Dalloways of the world to the Leonard Basts and Septimus Smiths. Instead, Bowen gives access to the mind of the working-class character. What we find is surprising. Instead of receiving the comforts of the masses, Louie "dwell(s) on Stella with mistrust and addiction, dread and desire."[33] This ambivalence stems from the gap between the two women's social stations: as much as she might imaginatively

---

[31] Bowen, *Heat*, 169.
[32] Ibid., 278.
[33] Ibid.

tune into Stella's being, Louie could never actually be her.[34] This dissymmetry awakens in Louie a sense of her own status as "receiver, conductor, carrier" of other people, a feeling she describes to her roommate Connie as "like being crowded to death—more and more of it all getting into me."[35] While modernist fiction raises this sensitivity as a privileged and desirable feeling, in this case it signals an uncomfortable precarity, as Louie has no choice but to receive and obey other people's inclinations. Indeed, her thoughts culminate with her transformation into an automaton, dissociated from herself ("now her lips seemed bidden: 'A soul astray,' they repeated with awe, aloud"[36]). This form of connection might even be worse than Louie's conscription into wartime nationalism, making her into an unwilling host of other people's dramas.

Bowen gives one more twist to this situation when Louie decides to visit Stella. Gazing at the posh row of flats, Louie feels "outwitted" by the architecture of the houses that "seemed to cheat and mock her," noting that "to enter Weymouth Street was to quail at the unspeakingness of its expensive length." Yet as she stands before this strange line of homes, Louie still hopes to connect, only connect. Listening to "the sunless toneless reverberation, from planes of distance, of the victory bells," Louie imagines, "*That* could but being heard—from behind which window out of this host of windows?—by Mrs. Rodney. Louie stood still to listen again, in company."[37] In this touching moment, Louie tries to memorialize this connection, only to have it interrupted by someone else's memory: Robert's fall from the rooftops as he fled from Stella's apartment. Though Louie is ignorant of the recent event, the experience nevertheless comes upon her like some Benjaminian flash, putting her yet again in the position of receiver, conductor, or carrier of other people's drama and trauma:

> But then instantaneously she was struck, pierced, driven forward into a stumbling run by anguish—*an* anguish, striking out of the air. She looked round her vainly, blindly, for her assailant. Flee?—no, she was clutched, compelled, forbidden to leave the spot. She remained pacing to and fro, to and fro, like a last searcher for somebody said to be still alive, till the bells stopped.[38]

[34] See Kristine A. Miller's comparison of Stella and Louie's war work and class, in "'Even a Shelter's Not Safe': The Blitz on Homes in Elizabeth Bowen's Wartime Writing," *Twentieth Century Literature* 45, no. 2 (1999), 145–146.
[35] Bowen, *Heat*, 275.
[36] Ibid., 279.
[37] Ibid., 328–329.
[38] Ibid.

In effect, Louie relives the violence of Robert's fall, her psychic anguish of bearing witness to the event doubling its physical force. While the directionality and agency of the violence is unclear, what is certain is that she cannot leave, and that she is charged with a responsibility to care for the trauma. Like Louie's previous epiphany, this haunting raises the question of the unequal labor involved in working through an event you have not experienced: a dubious inheritance she will share with Roderick as he contemplates the fallout of his mother's drama. When Louie finally learns of Robert's death later in the novel, she "received, in an unbearable flash, the import of that street in which *she* had that morning stood."[39] Bowen again registers betrayal through architectural vocabulary: "There was nobody to admire: there *was* no alternative. No unextinguished watch-light remained, after all, burning in any window, however far away."[40] Stella's own fall from grace leads not only to Louie's own relaxation of respectability—and ultimately, to an illegitimate pregnancy—but also to a return to seeking comfort in massification. Now that individual connection is rendered undesirable, Louie reverts to the passive security of being one of many, returning her interiority once more to the complacency of the crowd. Whatever sensitivity she might have had is irrevocably lost, culminating with her callous reaction to the death of her husband, which re-legitimizes her pregnancy. Favoring her role as an "orderly mother" rather than mourning her husband represents the worst form of social complacency, and disqualifies her once and for all as a viable model for postwar personhood.

Viewing Reconstruction

While for Bowen, Stella's apartment is represented as an exceptional site that sparks Louie's psychic drama, the working-class home is represented as a vast, mind-numbing wasteland of the London suburbs. In this regard, she echoes the discourse of postwar reconstruction and its anxiety over the working-class home. The literature of reconstruction was not without its judgment. Indeed, its logic often relied on an underlying distaste for the working class, not only for their homes, but also, implicitly, for their general behavior. They were the substrate population of postwar improvement schemes, to be managed through mass clearances of the slums and re-housing in garden cities and high-density high-rises.

[39] *Ibid.*, 344.
[40] *Ibid.*, 346.

This concept of bettering society through improving working-class housing had a genealogy extending at least as far back as nineteenth-century Poor Law reforms. The moral, evaluative gaze at the working-class home was taken up in a range of influential publications, from social reformist Edwin Chadwick's *Report on the Sanitary Condition of the Labouring Population of Great Britain* (1842), journalist Henry Mayhew's series *London Labour and the London Poor* (1849–1850), clergyman Thomas Beames's *The Rookeries of London* (1850), and architect George Godwin's *London Shadows: A Glance at the "Homes" of the Thousands* (1854), among others. While written in the spirit of social reform and at times, charity, the accounts were also often highly condemning, using binaries of good and bad housing to make their pedagogical point. Legislation of the time also developed ways to judge which homes were "unfit for human habitation," from the 1846 Nuisances Removal and Disease Prevention Act to the 1868 Torrens Act and 1875 Cross Act, culminating in the 1890 Housing of the Working Class Act, which began providing local authorities the means of clearing and redeveloping certain urban areas. Reformist impulses were also captured in fiction of the time, particularly the social-problem or "condition of England" novels by Charles Dickens, Elizabeth Gaskell, and Benjamin Disraeli.[41] After the First World War, Lloyd George picked up where Disraeli's reformist policies left off, with his "Homes Fit for Heroes" campaign initiating a drive for council housing, while re-iterating the logic of "fit" and "unfit" homes. Though the Housing Acts of 1930 and 1936 again encouraged slum clearances and areas of redevelopment, increasing the numbers of homes deemed unsuitable for inhabitation. Yet it was not until the period after the Second World War that their destruction began in mass quantities, with a staggering 1.48 million houses and more than 3.66 million people effected in the period between 1955 and 1985, compared to an estimated 321,444 houses demolished in interwar slum clearances.[42]

In deeming houses "unfit," the reconstructive imagination displayed an inherent logic that stigmatized the working class. Though some publications such as *Picture Post* showed sensitivity to such forms of condemnation, avoiding class-based attributions in favor of a more general unit of the

---

[41] Nicola Wilson addresses the spectacle of the working-class home in *Home in British Working-Class Fiction*, tracking the home's representation from an "observed space" to a site "taken for granted – often in fact non-narrated" in postwar literature (Burlington: Ashgate, 2015), 7. While she attributes this sea-change to sociological shifts in readership and material culture as well as aesthetic changes in narratology and media, she does not situate it in relation to the discourse of reconstruction and the welfare state.

[42] Jim Yelling, "The Incidence of Slum Clearance in England and Wales, 1955–1985," *Urban History* 27:2 (2000), 234–235.

"people" or "society," many did not. Whether implicit or explicit, the reasoning behind reconstruction depended on transformation, or a "before and after," by counterbalancing bad working-class homes with the good ones to come. This narrative causality is evident in one of the most canonical works of reconstruction, Abercrombie and Forshaw's *The County of London Plan* (1943). Though the report claimed that housing, "whether considered as individual dwellings or in the broader, community sense, directly affects every citizen, young and old," its frontispiece featured a quotation from Prime Minister Winston Churchill from early in the Blitz: "Most painful is the number of small houses inhabited by working folk which has been destroyed ... We will rebuild them, more to our credit than some of them were before. London, Liverpool, Manchester, Birmingham may have much more to suffer, but they will rise from their ruins, more healthy and, I hope, more beautiful."[43] This avowal offered a strong reading of the intended beneficiaries of rebuilding, as did the plates accompanying the Plan's chapter on housing, which began its visual pedagogy of improvement with a "look in" to a dark, claustrophobic home (see Figure 5, Introduction), before offering future thoughts on what "the outlook" would be.

This evaluative look was also evident in occasional publications such as the Royal Institute for British Architects' booklet *Rebuilding Britain*, which proclaimed that the working-class home as "little better than an open-air prison, and besides being unhealthy, thwarts the opportunity for a full and happy life."[44] And in a series of small books published by the Architectural Press, working-class neighborhoods are characterized as nothing but "abandoned factories and wasted land, busy factories and wasted lives": areas in which "Millions of Mean Houses Still Exist" (Figure 8).[45] These "the slummy homes of Britain" were seen as needed to be made "friendly and loveable" again—language that Bowen also used in her essay "The Bend Back."[46]

Bowen's *The Heat of the Day* startlingly recapitulates this reconstructive judgment, when she affords us a portrait of life inside the working-class home as viewed from a train. Inside, she finds a bleak picture of working-class life, almost sociological in its family typology:

---

[43] John Henry Forshaw and Patrick Abercrombie, *County of London Plan* (London: Macmillan and Co. Limited, 1943).
[44] Royal Institute of British Architects, *Rebuilding Britain*, 16.
[45] Anonymous, *Planning for Reconstruction* (London: The Architectural Press, 1943), 10 and 6–7.
[46] Anonymous, *Towards a New Britain* (London: The Architectural Press, 1944), 5–6.

Figure 8 "Millions of Mean Houses Still Exist," *Planning for Reconstruction* (1943). Anonymous.
© Architectural Press.

Prominent sculleries, with bent-forward heads of women back at the sink again after Sunday dinner, and recessive living-rooms in which the breadwinner armchair-slumbered, legs out, hand across the eyes, displayed themselves; upstairs, at looking-glasses in windows, girls got themselves ready to go out with boys. One old unneeded woman, relegated all day to where she slept and would die, prised apart lace curtains to take a look at the train, as through calculating whether it might not be able to escape this time. Children turned out to play went through with the mime of it, dragging objects or pushing one another up and down short paths where vegetables had not been able to be sown. It was striking how listlessly, shiftlessly and frankly life in these houses—and what else was life but this?—exposed itself to the eyes in the passing or halting trains: eyes to be taken, one could only suppose, to be blinded by other preoccupations.[47]

This judgment shows Bowen's cards most frankly, even more than her dismissive treatment of Louie Lewis. For she seems to say: even if you are granted a view inside these homes, you will learn nothing, be given no epiphany. You will only learn the desolation of everyday life, which no one can escape. (Even children's play is a simulacrum, situated symbolically in infertile ground.) By the time she reaches the question—"and what

[47] Bowen, *Heat*, 330.

else was life but this?"—the reader is primed for anything else, grateful that the novel will not continue in this vein. Bowen's view does not lead to any moment of insight: indeed, it expressly refuses it. Still, it creates a restlessness around the site of the family home, whose architecture allows for this domestic travesty with its prominent sculleries, recessive living-rooms, and lace-curtained tombs for the unneeded elderly. These excesses were precisely the targets of postwar reconstruction, which promised to counter the outmoded family home with modern kitchens and labor-saving appliances, open floor plans, natural light, and separate dwellings for old people, all situated in a more neighborhood-friendly, networked array of living spaces.[48]

While this abstraction to the collective recalls Bowen's earlier descriptions of wartime London, focalized through the war-besieged population, it also reflects a paradigm shift within the novel. Gone is the excitement and romance of war: in its place is a de-mythologized England, with vistas of disrepair not attributable to the violence of war. Her style engages a different form of modernist aesthetics: the documentary ethos of the 1930s, as pioneered in film, photography, non-fiction, and the organization Mass Observation. In particular, works such as J.B. Priestley's *English Journey* (1934), Bill Brandt's *The English at Home* (1936), and George Orwell's *Road to Wigan Pier* (1937) all turned to the home as a key site for exposing the need for social, political, and material reform. Bowen's language also resonates with that of postwar British cultural studies and sociology, itself influenced by the documentary aesthetic of the 1930s. British cultural studies opened up the concept of "culture" from its narrow definition as high art, meant for the upper- and upper-middle classes, to what Raymond Williams would call "a whole way of life."[49] As with 1930s documentary culture, postwar cultural studies often focused on the home as a *locus classicus* that helped define working-class culture, as exemplified in Richard Hoggart's *The Uses of Literacy* (1954), which carefully described the setting and patterns of "their

---

[48] See the Ministry of Health's *Housing Manual*, both 1944 and 1949 editions, as well as the 1949 and 1952 supplements, which detailed special accommodation needs from the elderly, apprentices, students, single workers, and the disabled—showing how normative the plans for housing really were (London: His Majesty's Stationery Office, 1944, 1949, and 1952). See also the wealth of *Mass Observation* reports on the family home, particularly *An Enquiry into People's Homes*, which studied what kinds of housing people wanted after the war (London: Advertising Service Guild, 1943).

[49] Raymond Williams, *Culture and Society: 1780–1950* (New York: Columbia University Press, 1983), xvi.

own recognisable styles of housing."[50] As Hoggart suggests, the importance of working-class domesticity was due in part to the very real threat of institutional life offered through the Poor Law: "Working-class people have always hated the thought of 'ending up in the work'ouse' for several good reasons, and of these the deepest is the sense of the inalienable quality of home life."[51] *The Uses of Literacy* was in this way deeply nostalgic, an elegiac attempt to document a prewar, pre-reconstruction way of life. So, too, was the bestselling *Family and Kinship in East London* (1957), an influential work of sociology by Michael Young and Peter Willmott, two of the founders of the Institute of Community Studies. Based on research done in 1953–1955, the study documented East Londoners' move out of the inner city to Dagenham, a new housing estate in Essex. In their work, Young and Willmott lamented what they saw as the destruction of older, organically formed communities by statist postwar reconstruction, which as Joe Moran describes, "fe[d] into a nascent public mood which remained hopeful about postwar reconstruction but was increasingly suspicious of the technocratic, centralized approach of the welfare state that was engineering it."[52]

Bowen's view from the train, however, contains neither the ideals of working-class nostalgia and democratizing culture, nor the interwar and postwar impulse for reform, nor an intellectual project born from personal defiance. Indeed, her novel lacks any sense of the planning imagination: that is, any sense of a happily ever after. This is reflected in the conclusion to this train episode: "It was not to be taken into account that from any one train there should be looking any one pair of eyes which had no other preoccupation, no other resort, nothing; eyes themselves exposed forever to what they saw, subjected to whatever chose to be seen."[53] Completely dissolving any hint of agency, this sentence reduces Stella's subjectivity into one of radical passivity. As usual, Bowen's complicated syntax reveals a facet of her own social ambivalence. The sentence's final clause suggests her version of authorial hell and the fate of the postwar author: to be nothing but a pair of eyes, gazing in presumable horror at the world. While this reminds the reader of the reforming work to be done, it also underscores an aversion to the fate of the general populace, whom Bowen imagines as types, or through the limited consciousness of her working-class characters. Perhaps this tendency, recapitulated in the literatures of reconstruction, is why years

---

[50] Richard Hoggart, *The Uses of Literacy* (New Brunswick: Transaction Publishers, 1998), 6.
[51] *Ibid.*, 18.
[52] Joe Moran, "Imagining the Street in Post-War Britain," *Urban History* 39:1 (2012), 172.
[53] Bowen, *Heat*, 330.

later, Carolyn Steedman would begin her landmark *Landscape for a Good Woman* (1986) by fiercely contesting this condemning gaze, recalling a welfare visit to her childhood home: "We both watched the dumpy retreating figure of the health visitor through the curtainless window. The woman had said: 'This house isn't fit for a baby.' [...] And I? I will do everything and anything until the end of my days to stop anyone ever talking to me like that woman talked to my mother."[54] As in Bowen's novel, an optical logic signals the power dynamics of being judged. Steedman pointedly reverses this gaze's directionality, reclaiming agency by allowing her and her sister to watch the health worker leave their home.

The working-class home is not the only site that augurs the social future of postwar Britain. The other option for postwar personhood is Stella's son Roderick Rodney, whose symbolic role lies in his potential to inherit his family estate, Mount Morris. The fate of the Big House was very much on Bowen's mind during the war, a preoccupation evident not only in *The Heat of the Day* but also in *Bowen's Court*, a memoir of her family estate, of which she was the first female heir as well as its last. Bowen composed *Bowen's Court* around 1939–1941, finally publishing it in 1944. Beginning with her eighteenth-century ancestor Henry Bowen through nine subsequent generations, *Bowen's Court* assembles a genealogy held together by the Big House, which "stamps its own character on all ways of living."[55] Just when it seems this form of domesticity has the capacity to sustain itself, Bowen raises the catastrophe of her present moment in the Afterword, reminding the reader of the threat to this way of life. Written in Christmastime of December 1941, *Bowen's Court* ends with Bowen sitting in her London apartment, looking out the window at Regent's Park while meditating: "I have written (as though it were everlasting) about a home at a time when all homes are threatened and hundreds of thousands of them are being destroyed. I have taken the attachment of people to places as being generic to human life, at a time when the attachment is to be dreaded, as a possible source of too much pain."[56] These words expressly recall Bowen's personal turmoil of being attached to both wartime London and neutral Ireland. As Bowen points out, neutrality allowed the Irish to remain attached to their places, in stark contrast to Britain's status as the "island fortress." Despite this controversy, Bowen still acknowledged how much she cared for Bowen's Court. She called it the "one

---

[54] Carolyn Steedman, *Landscape for a Good Woman: A Story of Two Lives* (New Brunswick: Rutgers University Press, 1987), 2.
[55] Bowen, *Bowen's Court* (New York: Alfred A. Knopf, 1942), 449.
[56] Ibid., 454.

private image—one peaceful scene" that sustained her during war.[57] She was also canny enough to recognize that this peaceful image could only have been forged by war: "War has made me this image out of a house built of anxious history."[58] This leads to her following prophetic meditation:

> It will be more difficult when the war is over to keep in view this absolute of peace. It will be likely to be obscured by minor achievements and false promises. We must be on our guard when peace, practicably coming, loses poetic status again. The peace of the image can never be realized: staying human, as we must stay human, we shall still fumble and blunder—but along better roads? We shall not really see a new heaven and a new earth. But we did once see peace, in the heart of war-time. That is the peace to remember, seek and ensue.[59]

Bowen's prediction came true. Postwar Britain was inexorably shaped by its wartime imagination of peace. Architects, state propaganda, popular magazines all produced similar images of peacetime Britain, whose symbolic power was most often concentrated in depictions of the home. Reconstruction, when it did come, was often perceived as only achieving the "minor achievements and false promises" Bowen warns about, quickly losing its poetry. The syntax of Bowen's writing underscores this quotidian achievement, undercutting its lyrical musings on the human with an ungainly infrastructural query ("—but along better roads?"). This ambivalence about the postwar's concrete reality, along with the wish to remember a wartime peace, reveals the inherent conservatism of Bowen's idealism. Straddling a prewar and postwar world, *Bowen's Court* concludes mired in a wartime apotheosis, with no foreseeable way out. Bowen sold the property in 1959 to Cornelius O'Keefe, who wanted it for the land and its timber. Unsurprisingly, Bowen could not accept this repurposing: instead, she "persuaded herself that he meant, however, to live in and care for the house."[60] That not being the case, she was relieved the house was ultimately demolished, calling it "a clean end. Bowen's Court never lived to be a ruin."[61]

Many shared Bowen's desire to preserve the Big House and its way of life through documentation, description, and artistic reproduction. After all, the other side of postwar reconstruction is that of historic preservation. This

---

[57] *Ibid.*, 457.
[58] *Ibid.*
[59] *Ibid.*
[60] Glendinning, *Elizabeth Bowen*, 257.
[61] Quoted in Glendinning, *Elizabeth Bowen*, 258.

A ROOM OF ONE'S OWN?: POSTWAR MODERNISM   63

tension is captured in the difference between "rebuilding" and "recording," the latter of which reflected a conservatism and desire to keep the *status quo*. For instance, one of the forerunners of English Heritage, the National Buildings Record, was set up in 1940, as a scheme meant to document buildings of national importance through photography or other artistic renderings.[62] Another major endeavor was the "Recording Britain" project (1940–1943), which was spearheaded by Kenneth Clark, organized by the Ministry of Labour's Committee for the Employment of Artists in Wartime, and financed by the Pilgrim Trust. The scheme—a welfare-like endeavor modeled in part on American federal programs—commissioned established and upcoming artists to produce watercolors of the Home Front, rather than war fronts or industrial sites. Artists including John Piper, Charles Knight, Kenneth Rowntree, Barbara Jones, Enid Marx, and Michael Rothenstein contributed more than 1500 portraits and drawings. Though the original idea was to capture the changing landscape of Britain, the resulting volume emphasized heritage, continuity, and tradition, with portraits mainly of landscapes and historic buildings such as churches and castles. Focusing on rural life in favor of urban settings, the effect of the watercolors was mythical, almost elegiac, depicting a culture whose farms, mills, and villages were under threat of disappearance. The "Britain" of "Recording Britain" also largely meant England, with only a handful of Welsh subjects and none from Northern Ireland; Scotland had its own project, "Recording Scotland," begun in 1942. The works from "Recording Britain" were then displayed across the country in various venues. They were displayed at the National Gallery during the war, and toured the country under names such as "Art on a Rural Tour," "Lovely Britain," and "Beautiful Britain," as part of the British Institute for Adult Education's "Art for the People" series.[63]

The question, of course, was which people. Despite the populist bent of "Art for the People," Tom Jones, secretary of Pilgrim Trust, refused to display the paintings in British Restaurants; similar refusals were made to publish cheap versions of the book for a popular audience.[64] As Gill Saunders

---

[62] The National Buildings Record was an independent body from the Royal Commission on the Historical Monuments of England, established in 1908, until their merger in 1963, and eventually, their 1999 merger with English Heritage. See Valerie Holman, *Print for Victory: Book Publishing in England, 1939–1945* (London: British Library, 2008), 206–207. Allan Hepburn details parallel and intersecting preservation efforts undertaken by the Church of England in the name of its bombed churches and cathedrals: see *A Grain of Faith: Religion in Mid-Century Britain* (Oxford: Oxford University Press, 2018), 31–33.

[63] David Mellor, "'Recording Britain': A History and Outline," *Recording Britain: A Pictorial Domesday of Pre-War Britain*, ed. David Mellor, Gill Saunders, and Patrick Wright (London: David & Charles, 1990), 19.

[64] Ibid., 20.

suggests, "Recording Britain" "belonged to a predominantly middle-class intellectual milieu for whom the economic benefits of development were outweighed by the loss of beauty and amenity."[65] Thus the difference between recording and rebuilding turned out to be profound. Their politics and aesthetics are diametrically opposed: *recording* geared toward nostalgic preservation that inevitably preserved prewar class structure; *rebuilding* toward new forms of architecture that would match, and even create, radical social change after the war.

The Heat of the Day does not place much faith in the next generation to preserve the Big House way of life, nor even to record it. For most of the novel, Roderick's character is largely that of a nonperson, figured as a hapless youth who lacks the capacity to reflect on matters of war and peace. Yet a shift occurs at the end, as Roderick surveys Mount Morris, the family Big House of his future inheritance. The year is now 1944, the narrator having accelerated two years forward from 1942 through historically punctuated paragraphs ("1942, still with no Second Front, ran out...Cryptic were new 1943 block calendars. February, the Germans capitulated at Stalingrad; March, the Eighth Army broke through the Mareth Line...")[66] These matter-of-fact timelines forecast the imminent end of the war, not only to the reader, but also, seemingly, to the characters. By the time we reach 1944, Roderick, feeling a new sense of purpose, has begun to view Mount Morris through the lens of his forthcoming inheritance. Echoing the planning imagination of the time, he says to Donovan, the property's caretaker: "Mount Morris has got to be my living. To start with, I'll have to learn—go to one or another of those agricultural set-ups for two, three, four years. Everything's got to be done scientifically these days; one can't just go fluffing along as an amateur."[67] His language reflects the professional energy underwriting postwar reconstruction, and the new planning discourses that transformed the art of domesticity into a science. In the end, however, Mount Morris's fate remains unclear. That the decaying estate can be thus transformed is cast into doubt by Donovan's reminiscence over the property's previous owner, Mr. Morris, who also loved to dabble in improvement schemes that were never followed through: "'There was nothing to show in the end of it all,' said Donovan.

---

[65] Gill Saunders, "Introduction," in *Recording Britain: A Pictorial Domesday of Pre-War Britain*, ed. David Mellor, Gill Saunders, and Patrick Wright (London: David & Charles in association with the Victoria and Albert Museum, 1990), 7.
[66] Bowen, *Heat*, 347.
[67] Ibid., 353.

'However, the master had a great time with ideas.'"[68] This may be taken as a prediction for the postwar world: big on wartime ideas, but with little to show afterward.

Yet there is another reason why the future of Mount Morris hangs in the balance: the possibility of its heir perishing in the war. Bowen never discloses Roderick's fate, leaving it open-ended at the novel's close. This was a cause of anxiety for some readers including Rosamond Lehmann, who upon reading *The Heat of the Day*, wrote Bowen to ask "whether Roderick is at Mount Morris now."[69] This uncertainty leaves the reader to inherit and make sense of the war: a fate that mirrors that of the characters in the novel, particularly Roderick. For as Roderick sleeps in the old master's bedroom, reflecting upon the possibility of his own death, he finds himself instead caught in a web of the dead's demands: "that what worked most on the world, on him, were the unapprehendable inner wills of the dead. Death could not estimate what it left behind it."[70] The final chapters of *The Heat of the Day* thus ask the reader how to come to something further than this; that is, how to think one's history beyond the war, and how to make one's own postwar world inhabitable in ways other than reanimating or housing the ghosts from the past. As I will argue in subsequent chapters, this charge turns out to be an impossible task, reflected in literature's unceasing return to the Second World War as a source of meaning.

Bowen, for her part, anticipates this literary labor in *The Heat of the Day* by thematizing it through Roderick's troubled sense of "being posterity." What begins as a personal meditation turns into a didactic speech on the role of art and history:

"I wish I were God," he said. "Instead of which I am so awfully young—that's my disadvantage. The only hope would have been my having happened to say some inspired thing, but now there hasn't been that I shall be no good for about another fifty years—because all I can do now is try and work this out, which could easily take my lifetime; and by that time you'd be dead. I couldn't bear to think of you waiting on and on and on for something, something that in a flash would give what Robert did and what happened enormous meaning like there is in a play of Shakespeare's—but, must you? If there's something that *is* to be said, won't it say itself? Or

---

[68] *Ibid.*, 354.
[69] See Hepburn, "Trials and Errors," 135.
[70] Bowen, *Heat*, 353.

mayn't you come to imagine it has been said, even without your knowing what exactly it was?... Or are you telling me, then asking me, because I *am* young, and so ought to later into time? You want me to be posterity? But then, Robert's dying of what he did will not always be there, won't last like a book or a picture: by the time one is able to understand it it will be gone, it just won't be there to be judged. Because, I suppose art is the only thing that can go on mattering once it has stopped hurting?..."[71]

This twisting, vexed language reflects Roderick's ambivalence over his role as postwar recorder and interpreter, first through its convoluted verbs, and then through the escalating series of questions about the nature of his responsibility. Roderick finds little solace to this project of "being posterity": a labor injurious both to him and to his mother, who risks waiting indefinitely for her son to grant her a flash of meaning. Though art emerges as a potential source of recuperation, even this idea is questionable—what begins as a statement turns interrogative, left for the reader to decide. The prospect of infinite labor facing Roderick offers yet another element distinguishing Bowen from her modernist predecessors. In their valuation of epiphanic sympathy, modernists figured connection as a near-instantaneous forging of insight. For Bowen, however, the postwar artist faces a lifetime of attempting to make sense of the past, a form of responsibility without end as seen in this belabored monologue in search of epiphanic insight.[72] While the characters of *The Heat of the Day* are cognizant of this need, its potential for success is uncertain. The best possible result is an infinite cycle of working through other people's problems, a Sisyphean form of labor. This model of relationship to the past is ultimately a non-exit from the dead ends of wartime trauma. How desirable, then, is such an inheritance?

"London's Creeping"

I want to conclude this chapter with a final study of Bowen's postwar modernism, and its uncanny relationship to the work of E.M. Forster. As mentioned earlier, Bowen named Forster as her chief literary influence. The influence of *Howards End* (1910) can be felt particularly strongly in

---

[71] *Ibid.*, 337.
[72] While other postwar novelists such as Waugh, Orwell, and Beckett agree upon the importance of this work, Waugh cheapens this labor by turning immediately to nostalgia, Orwell refuses its viability, and even Beckett (of "I can't go on, I'll go on") stays in the more abstract register of the infinite.

The Heat of the Day. Both works grapple with how to translate private sentiment into public feeling, and how to imagine connection across class lines. For both, such rifts prove too vast to cross, resulting in novelistic solutions resting on uneasy and rather contrived social syntheses, whether through the inheritance of Howards End by the bastard son of Leonard Bast and Helen Schlegel, or by Louie Lewis's newly legitimized illegitimate child upon the death of her husband, Tom. The apparent unease of these social syntheses reflects the authors' abiding ambivalence about democratization. Both inhabit a cultural elitism deriving from their self-conscious affiliation with dying social institutions (Forster and the Victorian liberal intellectual; Bowen and the Anglo-Irish aristocracy). But perhaps the most conspicuous kinship is in their writing of place, what Bowen called Forster's "place-feeling." *Howards End* takes the family home as a metonym for England itself, a substitution that begs the question, "Who shall inherit England?"[73] Forster's novel circles around the liberal paradox of how to reconcile the life of the spirit with the material reality of property. This paradox results in what Daniel Born has called that "most comprehensive picture of liberal guilt in this century," played out through dramas of domestic space.[74] Strikingly, both *Howards End* and *The Heat of the Day* conclude with a retreat from London, as we see in Forster's ending:

> From the garden came laughter. "Here they are at last!" exclaimed Henry, disengaging himself with a smile. Helen rushed into the gloom, holding Tom by one hand and carrying her baby on the other. There were shouts of infectious joy. "The field's cut!" Helen cried excitedly—"the big meadow! We've seen to the very end, and it'll be such a crop of hay as never!"[75]
>
> Across the canal the hills rose, bare, above the other bank's reflected oak trees. No other soul passed; not a sheep, even, was cropping anywhere nearby. A minute or two ago our homecoming bombers, invisibly high up, had droned over: the baby had not stirred—every day she saw him growing more like Tom. But now there began another sound—she turned and looked up into the air behind her. She gathered Tom quickly out of the pram and held him up, hoping he too might see, and perhaps remember. Three swans were flying a straight flight. They passed overhead, disappearing in the direction of the West.[76]

---

[73] Lionel Trilling, *E.M. Forster* (New York: New Directions, 1964), 118.
[74] Daniel Born, "Private Gardens, Public Swamps," 141.
[75] E.M. Forster, *Howards End* (New York: Penguin, 2000), 293.
[76] Bowen, *Heat*, 372.

Like Bowen's, Forster's ending takes place outside the home, and rejoices in its natural setting (growing crops, flying swans). It also centers on an illegitimate child, whose futurity is enigmatically, even spiritually linked to this vision of a restorative nature. This sense of potential repair also comes from the marked transitions away from a source of past harm (Henry's betrayal of his late wife's final wishes; the homecoming bombers) to a scene of present natural bounty and resolved social conflict. This, in turn, raises the question of whether readers can accept these final gestures of novelistic reconciliation, particularly under the modernist injunction to "only connect."[77]

Yet there is trouble in paradise, not only in light of the personal abysses that had to be traversed and betrayals effected to arrive at these social syntheses (Margaret's shiver, the death of Louie's husband), but also in light of their domestic structures. For just at the moment that the Schlegels feel they have achieved proper spiritual possession of Howards End, we are reminded of the wider threat to the Big House's rural idyll: London's expansion into the country, signaled by a red rust at the edge of the meadows ("All the same, London's creeping").[78] This suburban encroachment sits uneasily with the reader, particularly after the Schlegel's hard-won inheritance of Howards End. But the result is more than just a threat to liberal, home-owning ideals. Indeed, it is an elemental revulsion to this urban architecture that can only be envisioned in apocalyptic terms. It is impossible to the pastoral joy of "such a crop of hay as never!" without remembering that it is competing with a vision of rust and decay, or, in Forster's mind, global meltdown ("And London is only part of something else, I'm afraid. Life's going to be melted down, all over the world").[79] While Bowen shares Forster's patrician yet mildly apocalyptic distaste for London suburbia, *The Heat of the Day* throws these questions into greater relief. By the 1940s, global meltdown seemed more and more the reality, whether at home through the London Blitz, or abroad through the atomic bombings of Hiroshima and Nagasaki. The question posed by *The Heat of the Day* is thus not Trilling's formulation of "Who shall inherit England," but rather: "What, exactly, will this England

---

[77] For a good reading of this along the lines of Forster's belief in art and culture, see Leslie White, who reads *Howards End* in light of his later writings such as *Two Cheers for Democracy*, arguing that Forster ultimately desired "not a marriage but a salutary disconnection of disparate sensibilities" in order for the Schlegels and their beliefs not to be subsumed by the imperialistic, rational Wilcoxes. "Vital Disconnection in *Howards End*," *Twentieth-Century Literature* 51.1 (Spring 2005), 44.
[78] Forster, *Howards End*, 289.
[79] Ibid., 290.

look like? Will there be anything left to inherit?" As we have seen, the answer she leaves us with is largely unsatisfactory, with the Big House, middle-class flat, and working-class home disqualified as uninhabitable. While the Westward-flying swans may revivify some hope in a reconstructed Europe, as Allan Hepburn suggests, the future is ultimately uncertain, left in the tiny hands of Louie's baby Tom.[80]

Leaving the future in the hands of a child is not an uncommon trope, especially for literatures of reconstruction. But these novelistic endings produce an uncanny resonance when read alongside the 1946 documentary *A Diary for Timothy*. The film brought together an unlikely pair in director Humphrey Jennings and writer E.M. Forster, whose respective modernist aesthetics and representations of the social might at first seem at odds. Forster's Edwardian modernism was a far cry from Jennings's documentary filmmaking, particularly Jennings's early works, which experimented with surrealism, using juxtaposition and montage to reveal the incongruities of everyday life. Yet by the time 1944 rolled around, Forster and Jennings were in many ways a perfect match, having each shifted more toward the political center in their war work. As Thomas Davis reminds us, while avant-garde in its aesthetic, the documentary movement helped secure politically liberal norms, particularly in its late modernist phase, which was generally more amenable to consensus than earlier instantiations.[81] *A Diary for Timothy* reflects a shared commitment to liberal humanism, as well as their investment in "only connecting" on a communal level.

Film, of course, was a critical genre for indexing the aspirations of postwar reconstruction, from the ruins of Britain to the actual building involved.[82] Though these films all promoted rebuilding, there was no singular approach: audiences were introduced to the stakes and work of rebuilding from a variety of social, economic, political, and occupational perspectives. One of the earliest, *Builders* (1942), directed by Pat Jackson and produced by the Crown Film Unit, was meant to increase Home Front morale, especially of those tasked with rebuilding the ruins of the Blitz. Others were expressly political, such as Kay Mander's *Homes for the*

---

[80] See Hepburn's reading of the swans flying to the West: "The West was guarantor of the reconstruction of Europe. From the West—Western Europe, the US—came the moral and financial resources to reconstruct war-ravaged Central and Eastern Europe" ("Trials and Errors," 135–136).

[81] Davis, *Extinct Scene*, 11.

[82] See James Chapman, *A New History of British Documentary* (New York: Palgrave Macmillan, 2015), 138–144.

People (1945), made for the Labour campaign for the 1945 election and sponsored by the *Daily Herald*, and which highlighted women's perspectives on reconstruction. Many films focused on specific towns' postwar planning, such as *A City Reborn* (1945) on Coventry, scripted by Dylan Thomas; Jill Craigie's *The Way We Live* (1946), on the rebuilding of Plymouth; *A City Speaks* (1947), commissioned by the City of Manchester Corporation; and Kay Mander's *A Plan to Work On* (1948), on Dunfermline. Others were more commercially or industrially inflected, such as *Britain Can Make It* (12 installments throughout 1946); Terry Bishop's *Five Towns* (1948) on the Staffordshire Potteries region and their reconstruction challenges, or builder John Laing & Son's *Building Homes* (1950), which detailed the company's new "Easiform" construction system (followed by the 1955 *Easiform*, featuring happy families in completed homes).[83]

Among its contemporaries, the documentary *Diary for Timothy* is notable for its sensitivity and poeticism, due in large part to Jennings's directorial eye and Forster's narrative style. The film centers on one Timothy Jenkins, born September 5, 1944, and tracks his infant milestones alongside key events of the Second World War. Compellingly voiced by Michael Redgrave, the unseen omniscient narrator speaks directly to Timothy, using a "you" that slips conveniently between character and audience ("All the same, you're in danger. You're in danger, Tim"). The effect is unsettling, at once tender and accusatory, ominous and consoling ("You didn't know anything about this, of course. How could you? But you were part of the war even before you were born"). The film also has a supporting cast of characters—Peter the RAF pilot, Geronwy the coal miner, Allan the farmer, and Bill the train driver—real people who, the viewer is reminded, are fighting for Timothy. Like the end of *Howards End* and *The Heat of the Day*, *A Diary for Timothy* symbolically concentrates the postwar future in the figure of an infant boy. The difference, though, lies in its moral charge of reconciliation, and sense of what is owed to the working class. The Forster of *Timothy* is more radical than that of *Howards End*, made so in the wake of war and with the prospect of postwar reconstruction. *A Diary for Timothy* re-enchants the creeping red rust of London suburbia with recuperative value by figuring it as potentially livable and lovable if rebuilt correctly.

---

[83] Reconstruction also played an important role in postwar cinema, such as Roberto Rossellini's War Trilogy—*Rome Open City* (1945), *Paisan* (1946), and *Germany Year Zero* (1948)—and later, films such as Robert Aldrich's *Ten Seconds to Hell* (1959) and Alain Resnais's *Hiroshima, Mon Amour* (1959), among others.

This democratic spirit is evident in Forster's own misgivings about the project. After attending a rough cut of the film accompanied by Jennings's commentary, he wrote that "quite contrary to the intentions of the producers—the film comes out with a social slant and suggests that the world Britain ought to be kept right for this one class of baby and not got right for babies in general."[84] It is difficult to know how this misgiving influenced Forster's final script, as Jennings's original commentary has not survived. But a few clues emerge: Timothy is often hailed as one of many, "you and the other babies," which does some pluralizing work. More pointedly, he is also introduced as "one of the lucky ones," born in a comfortable nursing home near Oxford with a family to take care of him: "If you had been born in war-time Holland or Poland or a Liverpool or Glasgow slum," the narrator notes, "this would be a very different picture." As Marina MacKay notes, this moment is an "encouragingly radical vein" in a work that is for the most part "heart-sinkingly sentimental."[85] But perhaps the most moving and socially radical comparison happens later in the film, through the miner Geronwy's interior monologue. Geronwy muses, "One afternoon, I was sitting thinking about the past." It then it cuts to an image of a young boy looking out over a row of houses (Figure 9), as adult Geronwy's voice continues in voice-over: "The last war, the unemployed, broken homes, scattered families. And then I thought, has all this really got to happen again?"

This moment is remarkable. It is the only representation of internal thought in the film, and it is not linked to the narrator's address to Timothy. As such, the addressee here is especially ambiguous, going further to implicate the audience than ever before. This recalling of the past war is not characterized by the fierce determination or cynical despair of the film's earlier references to the Second World War, which draw a hard line between success and failure. Instead, it turns to an interrogative mode, leavened by spontaneity. Its primary subject, perhaps a young Geronwy, displaces Timothy's comfortable, middle-class childhood as representative of all others. It also opens up the possibility that *this* postwar might be different than the period after the First World War, making good not only for children

---

[84] *Selected Letters of E.M. Forster*, Vol. 2: 1921–1970, ed. P.N. Furbank and Mary Lago (Cambridge: Belknap Press, 1985), 212.
[85] MacKay, *Modernism and World War II*, 35. MacKay also reads the juxtaposition of Peter's wound and Geronwy's wounding as "a surprisingly brave parallel between total war and the ordinary condition of the working class that would be made many years later by Jennings's Mass-Observation collaborator Tom Harrisson when he suggested that the celebrated stoicism of the Blitzed urban poor was an ironic consequence of their appalling pre-Welfare-State conditions" (35).

Figure 9 Still from *A Diary for Timothy* (1946). Crown Film Unit/Ministry of Information.
© Crown Copyright.

in Timothy's generation, but also for those of the past. Though the film returns to Michael Redgrave's omniscient narrator, it maintains its reference to Geronwy's interior monologue ("You heard what Geronwy was thinking. Unemployment after the war, and then another war, and then more unemployment. Will it be like that again?") In doing so, this moment ends on a note of "only connecting," not just through the collective sociality of the welfare state, but also on a highly improbable individual connection.

2
"Nowhere's Safe"
Angry Young Women and Communal Betrayal

The previous chapter described authors' reactions to war as a contemporary phenomenon, or writing concurrent with the war. Bowen, Greene, Green, and Waugh offer key texts for literary criticism of the Second World War, their works a testament to the experience of living with the war—more so, even, than living through it. Theirs is a literature of wounds to both bodies and buildings, as well as of the immediate emotions produced by war's social upheavals, including anxiety, pleasure, fear, and boredom. Yet the temporality of the Second World War was informed as much by the violence of war as by its eventual repair, with postwar reconstruction emerging as a palpable, inspiring war aim. As in Elizabeth Bowen's case, grappling with the immediacy of war also meant a deep unease with the imagined future to come, one whose rebuilding, modernization, and even democratization would erase those characteristics that made the home inhabitable, not to mention knowable. Her depiction of domestic life was largely motivated by the fear that postwar reconstruction would actually deliver on its promises.

This chapter jumps forward in time to the year 1963, almost two decades after the official end of the Second World War. Following extended years of wartime austerity, Britain finally began to experience a boom of prosperity in the late 1950s, with wages up, unemployment down, and living standards generally on the rise. As Conservative Prime Minister, Harold MacMillan, put it in his 1957 "never had it so good" speech:

> Let's be frank about it; most of our people have never had it so good. Go around the country, go to the industrial towns, go to the farms, and you will see a state of prosperity such as we have never had in my lifetime—nor indeed ever in the history of this country. What is worrying some of us is "Is it too good to be true?" or perhaps I should say "Is it too good to last?"[1]

---

[1] Harold Macmillan, Speech, 1957, BBC News, http://news.bbc.co.uk/onthisday/hi/dates/stories/july/20/newsid_3728000/3728225.stm.

The Promise of Welfare in the Postwar British and Anglophone Novel. Kelly M. Rich, Oxford University Press.
© Kelly M. Rich (2023). DOI: 10.1093/oso/9780192893437.003.0003

This age of affluence was registered in rising standards of comfort and leisure in the home, with washing machines, refrigerators, cars, and TVs providing markers of financial success. Yet as the 1961 Parker Morris report *Homes for Today and Tomorrow* suggested, public housing still needed to change accordingly, with floor plans and amenities reconfigured for Britain's widening consumer class.[2] For while Britons "never had it so good," they also never had it quite as good as what was promised to them during the war, at least when it came to housing. While a high number of high-quality, single-family dwellings were constructed under the Attlee government, particularly through the construction of New Towns and other suburbs, it still was not enough given the housing shortage. The Conservative Party's 1951 win was due in part to its promise to build 300,000 homes a year.[3] Frustrated by slow growth and unrealistic plans, building began to embrace other visions of domesticity, including that of the high-rise, whose popularity began in the mid-1950s and continued into the late 1960s, a housing initiative that I address in this book's Interlude.[4] Affluence also raised other concerns beyond MacMillan's fear of whether it was "too good to last," with emergent anxieties surrounding such real and imagined social shifts as the decline of the political left, the destruction of working-class tradition, the rise of youth delinquency, and Britain's Americanization.[5] Challenges to MacMillan's conception of "good" also came from beyond, as Britain's postwar period was characterized by continuing violence through counterinsurgency campaigns in countries including Kenya, Malaya, Egypt, Cyprus, and

---

[2] See Alistair Kefford's suggestion that the Report signaled a move from the social individual of postwar welfare provisions and the collapse of that individual into what he calls a "citizen-consumer" in the 1950s, prefiguring the break between postwar social democracy and neoliberalism conventionally situated in Britain's 1970s. "Housing the Citizen-Consumer in Post-war Britain: The Parker Morris Report, Affluence and the Even Briefer Life of Social Democracy," *Twentieth-Century British History* 29.2 (2018), 225–258.

[3] Matthew Taunton, *Fictions of the City: Class, Culture and Mass Housing in London and Paris* (London: Palgrave Macmillan, 2009), 143.

[4] See Nicholas Timmins, *The Five Giants: A Biography of the Welfare State*, new ed. (London: Harper Collins Publishers, 2001), 185.

[5] See *The Age of Affluence, 1951–1964*, ed. V. Bogdanor and R. Skidelsky (London: Macmillan, 1970), as well as John Kenneth Galbraith's *The Affluent Society* (Boston: Houghton Mifflin, 1998), which, though about the United States of America, speaks to the United Kingdom's rising affluence as well (though its calls for more public expenditure are perhaps more urgent in the US context than the UK at the time). On youth, delinquency, and affluence, see Mark Abrams's *The Teenage Consumer* (London: London Press Exchange, 1959), and Kate Bradley's "Becoming Delinquent in the Post-War Welfare State: England and Wales, 1945-1965," in *Juvenile Delinquency and the Limits of Western Influence, 1850-2000*, ed. Heather Ellis (Palgrave, 2014), 227–247 for an overview of this issue.

Northern Ireland at the end of Britain's empire, as well as the increasing nuclear chill of the Cold War.

Literary criticism routinely juxtaposes postwar affluence with the literature of the Angry Young Men.[6] Exploding onto the literary scene in the mid-1950s, their works included Kingsley Amis's debut novel *Lucky Jim* (1954), John Osborne's play *Look Back in Anger* (1956), and John Sillitoe's *Saturday Night and Sunday Morning* (1958), and were associated with the English "Movement" poetry of Philip Larkin, Thom Gunn, and John Wain. The Angries signaled a profound, unanswerable discontent with the political and economic effects of postwar consensus, a masculine-stylized affect that Peter Kalliney describes as "a complex negotiation of an unstable gender position—in which both exaggerated heterosexuality and the domestic responsibilities implied by marriage and a family are highly esteemed—and the continuing existence of undiminished class anger under conditions of material prosperity."[7] The resentment simmering in their works is a distinctly postwar structure of feeling, associated with lower-middle-class and working-class youth who were supposed to inherit the visions of rebuilding Britain (i.e., the Geronwys, and not the Timothys, of last chapter's "A Diary for Timothy"). Thus, it is Arthur Seaton, not his father, who provides the voice of Sillitoe's *Saturday Night and Sunday Morning*, musing: "The difference between before the war and after the war didn't bear thinking about. War was a marvellous thing in some ways, when you thought about how happy it had made so many people in England."[8] Or as Jimmy Porter describes in *Look Back in Anger*, "There aren't any good, brave causes left," only the numbing anticipations of everyday life in which everything remains the same.[9]

---

[6] See, for instance, Alan Sinfield's reading of the Movement's misogyny as "part of the attempt to repudiate the perceived ethos of the literary establishment." *Literature, Politics and Culture in Postwar Britain* (London: Athlone Press, 1997), 81. Jim English diagnoses the "campus novel" as "symptomatic of particularly fundamental and persistent contradictions in the postwar social order and in England's attempted rethinking of the national community." *Comic Transactions: Literature, Humor, and the Politics of Community in Twentieth-Century Britain* (Ithaca: Cornell University Press, 1994), 133.
[7] Kalliney, *Cities of Affluence and Anger: A Literary Geography of Modern Englishness* (Charlottesville, University of Virginia Press, 2006), 30.
[8] Alan Sillitoe, *Saturday Night and Sunday Morning* (New York: Vintage International, 2010), 22. Indeed, the Angries' oppositional energy and anger can be tracked in dystopian fiction of the time as well, with works such as William Golding's *Lord of the Flies* and Graham Greene's short story *The Destructors* (both 1954) and Anthony Burgess's *A Clockwork Orange* (1962) offering their own versions of angry young men.
[9] John Osborne, *Look Back in Anger* (New York: Penguin, 1982), 84.

Like earlier wartime literature, the works of the Angry Young Men took the space of the family home as the battleground and stage for critique. However, they swapped the spectacle of ruined, surveilled domesticity for claustrophobic, often misogynistic renderings of family life. Their melodramas revolve around the family home, as exemplified by the one-room Midlands flat that constitutes the setting of *Look Back in Anger*. These homes are decidedly not Englishmen's castles, fit for heroes. Instead, they are unsympathetic, confining, maddening spaces. Their evident repugnance recalls the evaluative gaze of Bowen's Stella Rodney, as in *Saturday Night and Sunday Morning*:

> July, August, and summer skies lay over the city, above rows of houses in the western suburbs, backyards burned by the sun with running tar-sores whose antiseptic smell blended with that of dustbins overdue for emptying, drying paint even drier on front doors, rusting knockers and letter-boxes, and withering flowers on windowsills, a summer blue sky up to which smoke from factory-chimneys coiled blackly.[10]

This unsparing representation is often characterized as "kitchen-sink" realism: a style associated with the Angries' gritty, unsentimental engagement with domestic life, as well as their antipathies to the modernist interest in cosmopolitanism and avant-gardism. Yet even among these unsparing descriptions, there is a surprising idealization of domesticity as a respite from the outside world, whether Jimmy and Alison's play-acting of animal homes in *Look Back in Anger*, or Arthur's projections of doing family life "right" if he ever gets the chance (which, by the end of the novel, he does). While these works address the war's mythic consolidation into the "People's War" and deconstruct the plenitude projected by the postwar imagination, they cannot let go of domestic life as the object and agent of repair.

In this chapter, I argue that Muriel Spark can be considered an "angry young woman" occupying a distinctive place in these considerations of postwar literature and the social forms activated in and around the Second World War, particularly those at the nexus of welfare, housing, and living together. Critics typically address Spark's work within a trajectory

---

[10] Sillitoe, *Saturday Night*, 136.

of modernism to postmodernism, in relation to her own fraught national and religious identities, or in reference to her fiction's political context.[11] But where might Spark be placed within a history of social forms? What does she have to teach us about rebuilding Britain, especially through her restructuring of the novel? And how does she do so without recourse to either wartime sentimentalization, masculine class anger, or dystopian critique, three options that have received considerably more critical attention, yet remain strangely silent on the realities of the postwar world?

Rather than place faith in war's transformative power or, conversely, invite a recapturing non-institutionalized space, Spark insists her readers take stock of how they live now. Her fiction studies what types of social intimacy are left for those in domestic spaces that, like those of the postwar welfare state, are administered but not completely totalitarian. Though savage and satirical, Spark does not give up on the idea of society. Indeed, her novels offer insight into diverse social worlds, letting an ethic of cohabitation displace the more recognizable dynamics of familial domesticity. From the schools of *The Prime of Miss Jean Brodie* (1961) and final novel *The Finishing School* (2004), to the boarding-houses of *The Girls of Slender Means* (1963) and *A Far Cry from Kensington* (1988), from the nursing home in *Memento Mori* (1959) to the abbey of *The Abbess of Crewe* (1974), Spark focuses on the problems of communal living, what I am identifying as a hallmark of the midcentury transition from warfare to welfare. Her work offers a female alternative to the Angry Young Men and their domestic melodramas. It also marks a significant departure from "Angry Young Women" such as Shelagh Delaney and Lynne Reid Banks, whose respective *A Taste of Honey* (play 1958, film 1961) and *The L-Shaped Room* (novel 1960, film 1962) likewise revolve around the nuclear family, foregrounding the experience of women and the crisis of illegitimate pregnancy.

While the jewel of Muriel Spark's oeuvre is, at least within literary criticism, *The Prime of Miss Jean Brodie*—a novel deeply engaged with the spectacle of fascist authority—I contend that *The Girls of Slender Means* has more to teach us about the forces at play in the Second World War and its warping of domestic life. Recounting the fate of "The May of Teck Club," a hostel in wartime London existing "for the Pecuniary Convenience and

---

[11] See, for instance, the recent cluster of essays occasioned by Spark's 2018 centenary in *Textual Practice*, or David Herman's "'A Salutary Scar': Muriel Spark's Desegregated Art in the Twenty-First Century," *Modern Fiction Studies* 54.3 (Fall 2008), 473–486.

Social Protection of Ladies of Slender Means," the novel follows a group of girls as they negotiate the pressure to stay beautiful, graceful, and poised during the lean times of total war.[12] Turning its focus away from what Judy Suh calls Brodie's "familiar attractions of fascism" and toward the mechanisms of collectivity, *The Girls of Slender Means* raises the less glamorous but still critical problem of what it means to live together under a welfarist ideology, sharing resources, power, and space.[13] Rather than read Spark's critique of welfare consensus through either Catholicism (versus the secular welfare state) or a focus on the corporeal (versus welfare capitalism and economic psychology), this chapter takes the question of how to live together as itself Spark's fundamental concern—that is, how to make sense of the ideals of community and fellow-feeling attached to the transition between warfare and welfare.[14]

Despite her focus on communal living, Spark is not only interested in the social aggregate and its representations. Rather than Orwell's boot stamping in a face forever, her novels give space to autonomy and individual decision, allowing for surprising betrayals and lingering injuries, keenly felt. For this reason, Spark's work bears an intimate relation to literary modernism, not just through its negation (such as the Angries' turn to "kitchen-sink realism"), but through its complex interrogations of the radical potential and limitations of individual connection. Seeking to address a newly postwar world, modernists turned to narrative interiority in the traumatic wake of the First World War as a way to make space for epiphanic moments of sympathy between individuals. This chapter will show how Spark's unusual formal demands borrow from and then upend this modernist narrative architecture, using Virginia Woolf's novel *Mrs. Dalloway* (1925) to expose Spark's narrative innovations. As I will show, Spark destroys physical structures of domesticity, revealing its brand of sympathy to be inaccessible as a postwar structure of feeling. This stylistic work characterizes Spark's contribution to postwar literature, a literary reconstructive logic that

---

[12] Muriel Spark, *The Girls of Slender Means*, New Directions Classics (New York: New Directions Pub., 1998), 9).
[13] Judy Suh, "The Familiar Attractions of Fascism in Muriel Spark's *The Prime of Miss Jean Brodie*," *Journal of Modern Literature* 30:2 (2007), 86–102.
[14] See MacKay's reading of the influence of Catholicism on *The Girls of Slender Means*, which suggests that Spark's "savage ironising of comforting national mythology can be explained and domesticated by the religious principles underlying her scepticism about a secular version of the New Jerusalem." *Modernism and World War II* (Cambridge: Cambridge University Press, 2007), 145. See also Michael Gardiner's suggestion that Spark's work reminds us of the personal and corporeal elements that underlie the various rationalizations made in the name of the public good. "Spark versus *Homo economicus*," *Textual Practice* 32.9 (2018), 1513–1528.

critiques the historiographic reconstruction of Britain's Second World War. I then conclude this chapter by turning to Hilary Mantel's *Experiment in Love* (1995) as an adaptation of Spark's novel, which renovates its source for a generation faced with the ruins of the postwar welfare state.

Windows and Sympathy

As its title indicates, *The Girls of Slender Means* plays with the nexus between deprivation and deprivatization, a warfare-to-welfare logic that began with the Beveridge Report and ended with postwar consensus. Set in 1945 between V-E and V-J Day, and against the backdrop of Labour's ascent to power, the novel raises the question as to whether a society forged by war would likewise band together under the causes of social welfare. It does so by combining its characters' limited financial means and wartime austerity measures, which are savagely satirized by Spark. The girls pervert the original meaning of state rationing by creating their own systems of control: in the May of Teck Club, deprivation is noble not as a patriotic gesture but as a dieting tool. The title of the novel recalls the dreaded means tests of earlier welfare systems, often a humiliation to those in need of state assistance, a reality famously documented in George Orwell's *The Road to Wigan Pier* (1937). Acknowledging popular objection to means tests, the new welfare state defined itself against them by using an egalitarian logic of contribution-based benefits for all, rather than free allowances for some.[15] At the May of Teck Club, the diverse inhabitants pay a small fee for room and board. The Club thus functions as a literary test case for the warfare-to-welfare state, both in its microcosmic likeness and its difference as a quasi-domestic, gendered alternative.

As I suggested earlier, the opening to *The Girls of Slender Means* signals a wide critique of 1945 Britain and the unifying implications of postwar consensus. It accomplishes this critique by pairing a focus on space with a focus on art:

> Long ago in 1945 all the nice people in England were poor, allowing for exceptions. The streets of the cities were lined with buildings in bad repair or no repair at all, bomb-sites in which decay had been drilled out,

---

[15] Sir William Beveridge, *Social Insurance and Allied Services*, 11–12. See also Virginia Noble, *Inside the Welfare State: Foundations of Policy and Practice in Post-War Britain* (New York: Routledge, 2009), 2.

leaving only the cavity. Some bomb-ripped buildings looked like the ruins of ancient castles until, at a closer view, the wallpapers of various quite normal rooms would be visible, room above room, exposed, as on a stage, with one wall missing; sometimes a lavatory chain would dangle over nothing from a fourth- or fifth-floor ceiling; most of all the staircases survived, like a new art-form, leading up and up to an unspecified destination that made unusual demands on the mind's eye. All the nice people were poor; at least, that was a general axiom, the best of the rich being poor in spirit.[16]

Unlike the pedagogical function of reconstructive discourses, these denuded buildings do not evoke a modernity worth fighting for, or even a vision of the rebuilding to come. Instead, Spark, turning this logic on its head, questions the productivity of wartime damage. It does this in part by employing a fairy-tale tone that satirizes the romance of the war in a manner both familiar and discomfiting. But it also achieves this critique through a remarkable juxtaposition between social axioms and physical ruins, depicting a wartime landscape devoid of human life prior to the reader's encounter with the girls of slender means. By doing so, Spark's opening unsettles the longstanding association of the Second World War as the People's War.[17] Furthermore, the passage begs the question of what new art-form the war would occasion, its series of analogies reaching for an apt style of representation to fit the strangeness of the scene.

In following these spatial cues of the opening passage, this chapter proposes that *The Girls of Slender Means* most saliently registers the transition from warfare to welfare through its attention to built space and its characters' inhabitation of the May of Teck Club. Reading the Club's physical architecture alongside its social structures allows us to see the novel's skeptical engagement with Britain's postwar fantasy of repair, one that imagined that reconstruction—the gleaming schools, health centers, and housing flats of wartime propaganda—would result in new forms of social equality.

Additionally, this chapter seeks to build on the analyses offered in Chapter 1 of the sources of Elizabeth Bowen's postwar modernism, arguing that Spark presents a more ambiguous case of literary inheritance.

---

[16] Spark, *Girls*, 7.
[17] A phrase coined by Angus Calder's *The People's War: Britain 1939-1945* (London: Jonathan Cape, 1969). Calder would later write the self-corrective *The Myth of the Blitz* (1991), which, as Julian Symons points out, still never quite manages to shake the mythos associated with the Second World War. "The brief possibility of a different history," *London Review of Books*, 12 September 1991, http://www.lrb.co.uk/v13/n17/julian-symons/the-brief-possibility-of-a-different-kind-of-history.

While Chapter 1 took Bowen as revisiting her own version of E.M. Forster's "place-feeling," this chapter reads Spark in counterpoint to Virginia Woolf, to see how Spark updates Woolf's literary encounter between public and private during wartime.[18] For both writers, fiction and life writings are inextricable from one another, as evidenced by the close relationships between Woolf's post-First World War trilogy *Jacob's Room, Mrs. Dalloway,* and *To the Lighthouse,* as well as her wartime memoir *A Sketch of the Past*; and what might be read as Spark's postwar triad *The Prime of Miss Jean Brodie, The Girls of Slender Means,* and *The Mandelbaum Gate,* as well as her autobiographical *Curriculum Vitae.* In each of these texts, domestic space provides a powerful index of what effect war has on individual and psychic interior life.

In particular, both Woolf and Spark rely on the architectural form of the window to stage their narrative revelations, which *The Girls of Slender Means* calls directly into focus:

> Windows were important in that year of final reckoning; they told at a glance whether a house was inhabited or not; and in the course of the past years they had accumulated much meaning, having been the main danger-zone between domestic life and the war going on outside: everyone had said, when the sirens sounded, "Mind the windows. Keep away from the windows. Watch out for the glass."[19]

Laura Marcus and Victoria Rosner have established a useful baseline against which Spark's fenestral language comes into relief. Marcus locates the window-trope as a critical legacy of literary modernism and its treatment of temporality, suggesting that Woolf uses the window to mark "the relationship between past and present, or the ways in which the present becomes the past."[20] For Rosner's study of modernist interiority and its relationship to the rich material histories of modernist interior design, the window functions variously as frame, threshold, and marker of interior and exterior.[21]

---

[18] Virginia Woolf, of course, provides the paragon modernist example, for as Victoria Rosner avers, "No other major novelist of the period was so preoccupied with the critique of Victorian domesticity or so explicit about the relationship of literary modernism to the changing nature of private life." *Modernism and the Architecture of Private Life* (New York: Columbia University Press, 2005), 15.
[19] Spark, *Girls,* 8.
[20] Laura Marcus, "The Legacies of Modernism," *The Cambridge Companion to the Modernist Novel,* ed. Morag Shiach (Cambridge: Cambridge University Press, 2014), 95.
[21] Rosner, *Modernism,* 164.

Spark's windows, however, register a different set of boundaries: the physical, damaging intrusion of the state into the private home, a war no longer going on outside. Through a reading of Woolf's *Mrs. Dalloway*, a novel that provides a model of how domestic life engages with thresholds, we can see how *The Girls of Slender Means* presents an acute turn away from the modernist model of psychological and material interiority, especially in relation to wartime violence.

In an iconic scene, *Mrs. Dalloway* uses the window-threshold to stage Clarissa's private epiphany at the end of the novel, as she meditates on the death of Septimus Smith.[22] The source for this epiphany is an earlier scene describing how the shell-shocked veteran threw himself out his Bloomsbury lodging-house window rather than face another meeting with the ultra-rational Doctor Holmes. Clarissa's return to this moment provides one of literary modernism's most famous epiphanies: an imagined connection to this perfect stranger, felt through bodily echo, vicarious projection, empathetic assertions of similarity, and comparative self-critique. Woolf then ends the scene with Clarissa's following revelation:

> But what an extraordinary night! She felt somehow very like him—the young man who had killed himself. She felt glad that he had done it; thrown it away. The clock was striking. The leaden circles dissolved in the air. He made her feel the beauty; made her feel the fun. But she must go back. She must assemble. She must find Sally and Peter. And she came in from the little room.[23]

This moment was crucially altered in the British edition of *Mrs. Dalloway*, which omits what is arguably its cruelest line: "He made her feel the beauty; made her feel the fun."[24] Though presented in different forms, in both, Clarissa's epiphany relies on a moment of radical sympathy, one that conjures the connective possibilities between two strangers. Yet the scene also

---

[22] This moment is also critically triangulated by the appearance of the old lady in the opposite room, who, like Septimus, we have encountered earlier in the narrative. Clarissa is taken by the woman, watching her as she gets ready for bed. We might read this as a vision of her future self, a quieter spectacle of death in the midst of the party. However, the figure of the old lady does not offer the same quotient of epiphanic transformation as Septimus, instead generating an observational, even descriptive mode ("It was fascinating, with people still laughing and shouting in the drawing-room, to watch that old woman, quite quietly, going to bed"). Virginia Woolf, *Mrs. Dalloway* (New York: Harcourt, Inc., 1981), 185.
[23] Woolf, *Dalloway*, 186.
[24] Molly Hoff, *Virginia Woolf's Mrs. Dalloway: Invisible Presences* (Clemson: Clemson University Digital Press, 2009), 235.

falls short of complete connection, as Clarissa returns back to her party, back to life, refusing to recapitulate Septimus's deadly fall. This distinction is further enhanced if we attend to each character's relation to their home spaces and the architecture of their respective interiorities. While Septimus's room entraps him, Clarissa's room is eminently habitable, affording her space for private, individual contemplation. While domestic objects present themselves as possible suicide tools for Septimus, for Clarissa, they are a source of care, even pleasure.[25] And while Septimus's movements are forward and top-down, escaping from the ministrations of his doctor by throwing himself out from the window, Clarissa's are a sideways escape into a little adjoining room. We might read this domestic architecture as the very means of her epiphany, catalyzing her imaginative reach out to this stranger as well as her return to her party, two very different forms of hospitality.[26] *Mrs. Dalloway* thus addresses the postwar social fragmentation between civilians and veterans by creating a room of one's own, a critical space-making gesture that cordons off the violence as though sequestering some problem guest. Though the exterior trauma of war interrupts the private, interior home space, Clarissa's epiphany suggests that anything can be domesticated and made interior, possibly even redemptively so, through acts of individual apprehension and sympathy.[27] That this assimilation takes place at such a distance from the original event, and that it mediates a moment of violence, only reinforces its epiphanic structure and connective, transformative power.

If the First World War was integral to the development of a central tenet of literary modernism—the connective possibilities of modernist interiority contra the violent failures of the state—then the violence of the Second World War with its unprecedented Home Front required a reconsideration of the very boundaries between public and private, military and civilian

---

[25] "No pleasure could equal, she thought, straightening the chairs, pushing in one book on the shelf, this having done with the triumphs of youth, lost in the process of living, to find it, with a shock of delight, as the sun rose, as the day sank." Woolf, *Dalloway*, 185.

[26] This is not to say, of course, that this is Woolf's celebration of the enabling effects of domesticity: as others have suggested, we can read this scene as a precipitate of Clarissa's claustrophobia, whether a flight from the stifling boundaries of the home, or inversely, a flight into interiority contra the terror of an urban environment. See Anthony Vidler, "Bodies in Space/Subjects in the City," *differences* 5:3 (1993), and Rosner, *Modernism*, 149–150. It also is a moment of some irony, signaling the potential for radical social connection between two disparate individuals through its very lack. Indeed, Clarissa's feeling of gladness is an ironic sign of critique on Woolf's part, as she does not equip her protagonist with the means to see the cruelty of her feelings.

[27] Think also of the bracketed war in *To the Lighthouse*'s "Time Passes," or the fraught inheritance of Jacob's shoes in *Jacob's Room*.

life. With the tableau of stripped buildings that opens *The Girls of Slender Means*, Spark immediately signals the lack of any stable interiority, whether structural or psychic. Likewise, her focus on a group of girls, rather than the singular Mrs. Dalloway, provides an emphasis on group experience, institutionalized through the May of Teck Club. As with the Brodie set, a handful of these girls come into focus: Selina, the most slender and savage; Joanna, a rector's daughter and Selina's pious, morally upright foil; and Jane, a plump, bookish girl, a version of Sandy Stranger in *The Prime of Miss Jean Brodie*. Compared to *Brodie*, *The Girls of Slender Means* analogizes social differentiation using institutional space. Devoting a considerable amount of time to a blueprint of the Club, the novel maps its architectural organization onto the social status of the girls. From the first floor's young, schoolgirl virgins, the second-floor staff and temporary members, the third-floor old maids, and the fourth floor's sophisticated coterie, the novel makes it difficult to imagine any roundedness in these characters, any side rooms affording interior epiphanies.

These changes to the structure of the novel blast open a modernist architecture of interiority and connection. Instead of relying on intersubjective grounds for the novel's climax (i.e., the imagined connection between Septimus and Clarissa), *The Girls of Slender Means* relies on infrastructural elements: a lavatory window, whose bars admit the passage of only the thinnest girls in its own slender means test; a taffeta Schiaparelli dress, the Club's one object of luxury that circulates for special occasions, and which also only fits the slimmest of girls; and the "Two Sentences" from Selina's correspondence "Poise Course," which the top-floor girls respectfully listen to every morning and evening ("Poise is perfect balance, an equanimity of body and mind, complete composure whatever the social scene. Elegant dress, immaculate grooming, and perfect deportment all contribute to the attainment of self-confidence"[28]). These shared elements combine in the most horrific of ways at the end of the novel, when a bomb explodes belatedly in the garden and causes the May of Teck Club to catch fire. The top-floor girls, trapped by the fire, cannot escape except through a lavatory window leading onto an adjacent roof. Dramatically, this is the very window the girls had used to test their slimness, and which only some can succeed in squeezing through. The elegant Selina, of course, is able to slide through to safety. Yet as her fellow housemates wait in fear and anticipation, Selina

---

[28] Spark, *Girls*, 50.

returns through the lavatory window and moves back into the smoke and din. Her progress is tracked by an outside observer, Nicholas Farringdon:

> She was carrying something fairly long and limp and evidently light in weight, enfolding it carefully in her arms. He thought it was a body. She pushed her way through the girls coughing delicately from the first waves of smoke that had reached her in the passage. The others stared, shivering only with their prolonged apprehension, for they had no curiosity about what she had been rescuing or what she was carrying. She climbed up on the lavatory seat and slid through the window, skilfully and quickly pulling her object behind her. Nicholas held up his hand to catch her. When she landed on the roof-top she said, "Is it safe out here?" and at the same time was inspecting the condition of her salvaged item.
>
> Poise is perfect balance. It was the Schiaparelli dress. The coat-hanger dangled from the dress like a headless neck and shoulders.
>
> "Is it safe out here?" said Selina.
>
> "Nowhere's safe," said Nicholas.[29]

In a sort of delayed decoding, the narrator obscures the object Selina carries until the very end. The description of the object moves from the neutral "something fairly long and limp and evidently light in weight," to the ominous "He thought it was a body"; then to the hopeful "What she had been rescuing or what she was carrying."[30] Even when she reaches the rooftop, though Nicholas can surely see the dress, it still registers as an indeterminate object: the fact that it is not identified speaking to his inability to process its significance. It takes a strong narrative intrusion to finally name the object for what it is: the Schiaparelli dress. Though the multiple namings of the object are reminiscent of the various permutations of Clarissa's modernist epiphany, they do not afford space for flights of sympathetic imagination, but rather lead to a singular, horrifying revelation. There is no little side room to retreat to as in *Mrs. Dalloway*, and no returning to the party. Spark reverses the epistemology of the window so that the danger is within the domestic structure, and safety seems to be in the world outside. With no division between domestic life and state violence, the May of Teck Club implodes and sinks into its center. Joanna is killed in the debacle. But Selina's decision to return for the dress gives this catastrophe its true horror.

[29] *Ibid.*, 125.
[30] *Ibid.*

Her action makes the window a two-directional portal between danger and safety, adding another layer of porosity and precarity so that, as Nicholas's final line suggests, "Nowhere's safe."

Girl Society

The fire not only ruins the May of Teck Club, but also reveals its sociality to be rotten—and perhaps to have been rotten all along. This revelation is arrived at through the eyes of Nicholas, a mediocre writer, dubious anarchist, and intelligence worker who is infatuated with several of the girls of slender means. In a way, it is he who most believes the novel's opening line, "All the nice people in England were poor," a myth finally broken with the retrieval of the Schiaparelli dress. For upon meeting the girls, he began to craft a "poetic image" (65) of the Club as a "miniature expression of a free society ... held together by the graceful attributes of a common poverty."[31] Just as Septimus does for Clarissa, the girls make Nicholas feel the beauty and the fun, especially in comparison to his work "winding-up" the business of war: "Winding-up was arduous, it involved the shuffling of papers and people from office to office; particularly it involved considerable shuffling between the British and American Intelligence pockets in London. He had a bleak furnished room at Fulham. He was bored."[32] For him, the work of stopping the war machine required a new preoccupation, one that could furnish him with a new reality. While the girls have no such pretensions or fascination with their own lives, Nicholas insists on reading them as a microcosm of an ideal community.

Gender shapes both Nicholas's fantasy of this ideal community and its "freedom" itself, which is granted through the girls' unmarried status and lack of surrounding family. Rather than focusing on the family as the basic unit of sociality, Spark trains her gaze on the group, and more specifically, on unmarried women. This attention presents a marked difference from welfare policy, which institutionalized the family, made up of male breadwinners and female dependents, as its natural unit. This categorical relation between state and family had been in the making well before the Second World War, and, in certain ways, was strengthened by emerging welfare provisions

[31] Ibid., 84–85.
[32] Ibid., 60.

as well as pro-natalist discourses of the 1940s.[33] The Second World War unsettled this sexual division of labor to a degree, as the number of women entering the workforce rose due to wartime production needs and peacetime labor shortages. The new socioeconomic status attached to this work helped shift traditional gender roles and mores, though there was still strong social disapproval of working married women with children and other limitations to women's full participation in the workforce.[34] The developing discourse of postwar sociology helped identify these changing experiences, in works such as Ferdynand Zweig's *Women's Life and Labour* (1952), Alva Myrdal and Viola Klein's *Women's Two Roles: Home and Work* (1956), Judith Hubback's *Wives Who Went to College* (1957), and Pearl Jephcott's *Married Women Working* (1962).[35] But as these titles suggest, much of this cultural conversation centered on the problem of married women and their relation to paid work, rather than girls or those who remained unmarried.

Spark, in contrast, turns to a new analytic category: a group of women and their desires outside the controlling frameworks of the nuclear family, at least as far as they can be. In *The Girls of Slender Means*, this means a group of mostly young women, with a few spinsters thrown in for good measure. Though Spark was also interested in elderly group sociality, particularly in *Memento Mori* (1959), it is the girls' youth that provides the defining focus in this novel.[36] In the tradition of the *Bildungsroman*, youth functions as a metaphor for social change, or as Franco Moretti puts it, as the "symbolic concentrate of the systemic uncertainties and tensions of a culture."[37] Spark signals such a concern by beginning narrative action on the day after V-E Day, when "everyone began to consider where they personally stood in the new order of things."[38] Like Nicholas, readers are invited to view the May of Teck Club as an allegory for nascent social change: what it would

---

[33] On the development of the British model of family welfare, see Susan Pedersen's study *Family, Dependence, and the Origins of the Welfare State, 1914-1945* (Cambridge University Press, 1993).
[34] See Helen McCarthy's chapter on gender equality in the volume *Unequal Britain: Equalities in Britain since 1945*, ed. Pat Thane (London: Continuum, 2010), 105–124.
[35] For a more nuanced account of these postwar sociologists, see McCarthy's "Social Science and Married Women's Employment in Post-War Britain," *Past and Present* 233.1 (November 2016), 269–305.
[36] See Hope Howell Hodgkins' "Stylish Spinsters: Spark, Pym, and the Postwar Comedy of the Object," *Modern Fiction Studies* 54.3 (Fall 2008), 523–543, as well as Allan Hepburn's "*Memento Mori* and Gerontography," *Textual Practice* 32.9 (2018), 1495–1511.
[37] Franco Moretti, *The Way of the World: The Bildungsroman in European Culture* (London: Verso, 2000), 185.
[38] Spark, *Girls*, 17.

look like; how it would act; what would hold it together. For if the girls' male acquaintances were planning "vivid enterprises for the exploitation of peace," what, then, would their version of peacetime be?

This focus on girls also recall the importance of youth as a potent social and cultural category in postwar Britain: both as a problem to be studied as well as a key optic for understanding the period.[39] While the social category of youth was not historically new, its midcentury iterations were novel and visible enough to garner labels, media attention, legislation, and institutional study, particularly in the development of British cultural studies. Mods, Teddy boys (and to some degree, girls), Skinheads: all fell under the heading of "Youth Culture," which was studied as much for its relation to the dominant culture as its transgressive charge. This culture was able to emerge due to new patterns of affluence, which gave rise to the teenage consumer and youth-oriented spaces of leisure, as well as the rise of mass media. Spark's girls index these emerging postwar categories and contexts. Signs of girl subculture proliferate in *The Girls of Slender Means*, including midcentury self-help manuals such as Selina's "Poise Course," or Jane Wright's later career as a gossip columnist whose work serves as a frame tale.[40] The novel's schematic tendencies also invite a sociological reading of the Club and its rules as a closed system. If a focus on girls was largely missing in the annals of cultural studies and broader world of postwar sociology—an attention that would only begin to be rectified in the early 1980s—Spark's work can be read as a playful corrective to this history, though it ultimately dismisses any apparent coherence and predictability of the Club's observable rules.[41]

Though it draws on these 1960s intellectual concerns, 1945 is still the organizing and untimely origin point for Spark's novel. Unlike Elizabeth Bowen's contemporaries, whose fictions "bend back" in time in a nostalgic or

---

[39] See Stuart Hall and Tony Jefferson, eds., *Resistance Through Rituals: Youth Subcultures in Post-War Britain*, 2nd ed. (London: Routledge, 2006).

[40] Thus, Marina MacKay's recent reading of *The Girls of Slender Means* in light of midcentury self-help manuals, particularly those addressed to young women. While at their best these manuals encouraged self-reliance and achievable happiness, others, employed a more toxic gendered form of self-advancement. One such example is Margery Wilson's *The Woman You Want to Be*, a possible source of Selina's "poise" course in *The Girls of Slender Means*, which MacKay characterizes as one of the "oppressive productions...about female self-stylization." "Muriel Spark and Self-Help," *Textual Practice* 32.9 (2018), 1568. Indeed, one could say that self-help led Selina to help only herself.

[41] This lack of attention to women in early cultural studies is exemplified by the seminal collection *Resistance Through Rituals: Youth Subcultures in Post-War Britain*; a notable exception in the early postwar years was the work of Pearl Jephcott, and in the mid-1970s, Angela McRobbie, who along with Jenny Garber, wrote the only chapter focused on women in *Resistance Through Rituals*.

otherwise recuperative way, Spark returns to 1945 to question the founding myth of postwar consensus. This narrowly defined setting is unlike other works by Spark's contemporaries that center on groups of young women, such as Mary McCarthy's *The Group* (also published 1963, film 1966) or Jacqueline Susann's *The Valley of the Dolls* (published 1966, film 1967), which rely on their characters' development over time for the source of their drama. For instance, *The Group* follows a group of Vassar alumnae from their graduation in 1933 to one of their funerals in 1940, while casting a backward glance at sexual conservatism. (The novel also opens with a marriage.) In contrast, Spark firmly locates narrative action between V-E and V-J Day, a historical snapshot that allows for a broader, synchronous cross-section of the May of Teck Club. In turn, this retrospective vision allows the novel to study the more proximate ties that bind the girls together such as shared spaces, habits, and historical events such as the General Election, rather than the expected landmarks of female life and its progression of courtship, marriage, and childbirth.

This is not to say that the girls are unconcerned with male desire or heteronormative timelines: indeed, the Club's "vital themes" are love and money, with love coming first, helped by money.[42] Yet men are ancillary to the social drama and organization of the club. They cannot compete with the group's respect and envy for Selina's "Two Sentences"; their pride in Joanna's elocution lessons; the collective obsession with the skylight window. And, tellingly, the narrative crisis takes the form of theft of a communal object, rather than, say, the illegitimate pregnancies that preoccupy "Angry Young Women" Shelagh Delaney and Lynne Reid Banks. Even Doris Lessing, whose life strangely aligns with Spark's (even if her work does not), was more concerned in *The Golden Notebook* (1962) with whether women could ever be freed from patriarchal social forces, and especially how sexual desire, not to mention love, factors into that calculus.[43]

But what, exactly, holds Spark's girls together? In other words, if Spark moves away from family romance and domestic brutalities, what kind of social romance takes its place? Certainly not friendship, which Hilary Mantel will address as she revisits *The Girls of Slender Means* in *An Experiment in*

---

[42] Spark, *Girls*, 26.
[43] See Spark, *Curriculum Vitae: A Volume of Autobiography*: "I had nobody to talk to. Some miles away — but too many miles, as I know now — lived Doris Lessing, then a young girl like me, still in her teens. How I would have loved to have someone like Doris to talk to. She was a Rhodesian by upbringing, and I am sure she already had a distinguished mind. But I didn't meet Doris till many years later" (*New Directions*, 2011: 120).

Love. Spark's Catholicism is perhaps insinuated in the novel's demonstration of the fallacy and folly of secular values. Even more clearly, when Selina's theft reveals the true nature of the Club to Nicholas, he reacts by converting to Catholicism. His private epiphany, whatever it is, remains a negative one: as he later concludes in his personal notebooks, "A vision of evil may be as effective to conversion as a vision of good."[44] To recall Woolf again, where Septimus makes Clarissa feel the beauty, fun, and new sympathetic openness precipitated by the news of his death, Nicholas's belief in the Girls crumbles, as the house he built up in his mind comes figuratively and literally tumbling down. Rather than suggest the potentiality of interpersonal connection, this postwar revelation is experienced as a painful break, a crisis of connection in ruins. But again, what is destroyed is an outsider's vision. The girls themselves carry no such pretentions, revealing the ultimately mythic dimension of a community made sympathetic by common poverty.

The "New Art-Form" of Reconstruction

So much for all the nice people of the Second World War. Unsurprisingly, the novel leaves all these nice people behind in its concluding, much more devastating treatment of good and evil. Yet even Nicholas's conversion does not fully address the novel's opening challenge of finding a new art-form within the ruins of the Blitz. A comparison to modernism and the First World War can only take us so far; while it helps give insight to changing mores of human character and interpersonal connection, it is unable to account for the more proximate, infrastructural damages that shape *The Girls of Slender Means*. The novel, too, is not satisfied to end with Selina's betrayal. Instead, it concludes with a series of nested endings, a protracted coda that includes the ascent of the Labour government, London's celebration of V-J day, and a final nod to the recurring present-day frame narrative. Among these, Spark's gesture of mourning and remembrance in a return to the club is particularly poignant. Until this point, the novel has challenged the mythos of wartime Britain and the ennobling effects of violence by participating in a form of historiographic reconstruction. In the final pages, however, it makes a marked turn to the previous, and only vaguely foreshadowed, possibilities of physical reconstruction.

---

[44] Spark, *Girls*, 140.

As recent studies have shown, British late modernism reflects a marked inward turn, perceptible in the rising discourses of home anthropology as described by Jed Esty, and self-critical national historiography as described by Marina MacKay. Postwar reconstruction, I propose, offers yet another version of this inward turn, perhaps even its endgame. In the quest to plan a postwar Britain, the literature of domestic reconstruction toggled between a desire for conservation and radical transformation, a dialectic that influenced the formation of the postwar welfare state. Yet both possibilities shared an acknowledgment of the vast damage incurred by wartime Britain, which, as Spark herself indicates, required new interpretive and representational demands. This aestheticization of violence sits uneasily with the reality of wartime damage, especially as injury was the catalyst of political change. If, as Mark Rawlinson explains, "Material events of military conflict, notably lethal wounding, require symbolization and discursive mediation if war is to function as an instrument of political policy," then we should be equally cognizant of the politics of postwar repair, which rely on tableaux of ruined buildings in order to underscore the need for reconstruction—more so, even, than bodies in pain.[45] Indeed, the absence of the wounded body seems a prerequisite to postwar reconstruction, as it is difficult to move forward when reminded of the claims of the dead. To a certain degree, *The Girls of Slender Means* challenges this forward movement by reinserting the wounded body back into the landscape, puncturing the generic optimism of "long ago in 1945" with the particular horrors of Joanna's death.[46] Yet this scene is ultimately superseded by an attention to the remains of the Club, and the signification of their ruinous spatiality.

When Spark brings us to the site of the Club, she does so not through its former inhabitants, but through Nicholas and Joanna's father, the rector. Rather than using the narrator's sardonic voice to set the scene, Spark presents this ruin-gazing as a moment of potential revelation for the two men. Until this point, these characters have circled awkwardly around the subject of Joanna: an awkwardness exacerbated by the fact that Nicholas lost her recorded recitation of "The Wreck of the Deutschland," the only material testament left of her existence.[47] Without this last evidentiary trace

---

[45] Mark Rawlinson, *British Writing of the Second World War* (Oxford: Clarendon, 2000), 4.
[46] Spark, *Girls*, 7.
[47] Lyndsey Stonebridge's reading of *The Girls of Slender Means* underscores the pivotal role the voice plays in the girls' group psychology. To Stonebridge, even if Nicholas was able to retrieve Joanna's voice, Spark's novel ultimately suggests he would not be able to hear it: he is

of Joanna, Nicholas and her father return to the ruined Club, not just for closure but also, it seems, for empathetic traction. This contemplation of ruins presents a version of Woolf's sideways, modernist room, giving the two men a chance to reflect upon Joanna's death, and setting up a potential moment of real connection. On arrival to the site, they find this tableau:

> They came to the site of the May of Teck Club. It looked now like one of the familiar ruins of the neighbourhood, as if it had been shattered years ago by a bomb-attack, or months ago by a guided missile. The paving stones of the porch lay crookedly leading nowhere. The pillars lay like Roman remains. A side wall at the back of the house stood raggedly at half its former height. Greggie's garden was a heap of masonry with a few flowers and rare plants sprouting from it. The pink and white tiles of the hall lay in various aspects of long neglect, and from a lower part of the ragged side wall a piece of brown drawing-room wall-paper furled more raggedly.[48]

This description of ruin harkens back to the opening description of the Club. In this repetition, however, the ruins are no longer generic, but familiar: instead of the staircases to nowhere, there are the particular paving stones of the porch; instead of the "wallpapers of various quite normal rooms," there is the brown drawing-room wall-paper, whose color was fiercely detested by the Girls.[49] Spark personalizes the postwar landscape of damage, making its details diegetically resonant and forcing us to confront our own attachment to the May of Teck Club. Notably, she also largely omits the narrator's metafictional commentary that was woven through the opening: rather than characterize ruin-gazing as viewing a stage or a new art-form, her description is flatter, barer. Is this damage now mere damage, without the figurative pretensions of artistry and the enchantments of violence? Or does *The Girls of Slender Means* now figure as the new art-form, performing its novel literariness through our reading of it? Furthermore, if the novel's climax taught us that a vision of evil is equally persuasive as one of good, what, if anything, is the vision of ruins supposed to catalyze in us?

One answer to these questions can be found in the characters' own response to the ruins of the May of Teck, which laces their spare observations

---

too busy imposing his own ideal of the Club onto its actual inhabitants. "Hearing Them Speak: Voices in Wilfred Bion, Muriel Spark and Penelope Fitzgerald," *Textual Practice* 19 (2005), 458.
[48] Spark, *Girls*, 137.
[49] Ibid., 7.

with a line from one of Joanna's favorite poems, John Drinkwater's 1917 "Moonlit Apples":

> Joanna's father stood holding his wide black hat.
> At the top of the house the apples are laid in rows,
> The rector said to Nicholas. "There's really nothing to see."
> "Like my tape-recording," said Nicholas.
> "Yes, it's all gone, all elsewhere."[50]

This remnant of the Club offers a different form of Spark's negative epiphany: an emptiness, or refusal of transformation. The rector's impersonal, exaggerated language suggests the wider ramifications of this disappearance. Rather than a personalized loss of the individual Joanna, his words reflect the impossibility of the Club itself, as well as the idealism Nicholas attached to its sociality. Perhaps the only consolation Spark gives us is that unlike Clarissa Dalloway's feeling of gladness at Septimus's suicide, such affirmation is impossible in *The Girls of Slender Means*. Instead, these ruins of war resist being made interior or domesticated, letting ruins, as it were, be ruins.

This exchange provides a stark challenge to those seeking meaning in ruins, whether it be consolation, sublimity, catharsis, or a catalyst of mourning. Indeed, as the rector suggests, this conclusion challenges the impulse to represent the ruins at all. By suggesting there is nothing left to see, Joanna's father offers a commentary on Britain's wartime self-mythologizing, and the transformation of the Second World War into Britain's "People's War." *The Girls of Slender Means* uses the ruins of the Club to access this historiographic national consciousness, only to conclude that it may be kenomatic, the mythology of the People's War founded on an emptiness. Unlike Selina's dramatic betrayal, this moment reads more like a disappointment, a muted iteration of the previous fiery spectacle. The characters find an uneasy peace in this emptiness, relieved of the burden to find redemption or retrospective plenitude in the ruins.

An even more obvious variation of Spark's refusal of war's revelatory power can be found in her later novel *The Hothouse by the East River*, published in 1973. Set in postwar New York, the novel follows the disturbing and dreamlike lives of its two main characters, which, as the novel reveals, were killed by a V2 bomb years ago in 1944 wartime London. Yet the protagonists

---

[50] *Ibid.*, 137.

cannot accept this fact until their home space is physically destroyed to make way for a new block of apartments:

> They stand outside their apartment block, looking at the scaffolding. The upper stories are already gone and the lower part is a shell. A demolition truck waits for the new day's shift to begin. The morning breeze from the East River is already spreading the dust.
> Elsa stands in the morning light reading the billboard. It announces the new block of apartments to be built on the site of the old.
> "Now we can have some peace," says Elsa.[51]

Peace for the dead, perhaps, but also peace for the living: both *The Hothouse by the East River* and *The Girls of Slender Means* express a wariness of the uncanny, vivifying power that the war holds for both its characters and its readers. Spark's works critique the reparative logic of social reconstruction as well as the historiographic reconstruction of the Second World War as Britain's finest hour. The myth may have outstayed its welcome; continuing it is like occupying a building already slotted for destruction. Indeed, it may be the very overvaluation of war that is war's unfinished business, and the source of cultural unrest.

Despite her literary skewering of the Second World War and its mythical hold, Muriel Spark's autobiography *Curriculum Vitae* fully participates in a rosy-tinted revaluation of the war. Like many authors, Spark actively did her part for wartime Britain, finding work in a black propaganda unit headed by Sefton Delmar. Yet she belonged to a generation younger than authors such as Orwell, Bowen, Waugh, and Greene, and, unlike them, she had not yet established her place on the literary scene. As a younger, working middle-class woman just starting out in the world, Spark lacked cultural (and actual) capital. As *Curriculum Vitae* shows, she thought of the war as both an escape from a stifling marriage and as a way to gain much-desired life experience. In her chapters on the war, Spark speaks fondly of her experience at the Helena Club, a lodging-house for "Ladies from Good Families of Modest Means who are Obliged to Pursue an Occupation in London."[52] While recognizably the origin of the fictional May of Teck, Spark has only the kindest things to say about the Helena Club. She calls it "absolutely charming" and ruled by "a presiding angel," Mrs. G.S. Taylor (who wrote affectionately to Spark

---

[51] Spark, *The Hothouse by the East River* (New York: Penguin Books, 1977), loc. 1813–1817 of 1904, Kindle.
[52] Spark, *Curriculum Vitae*, 143.

upon reading the novel).⁵³ Spark's autobiography challenges the reader of *The Girls of Slender Means*, combining the resiliency and luck of youth with the familiar trappings of the People's War, in an affective register nearly irreconcilable with her novel. This is not to say, of course, that one should have the same expectations for autobiography as for fiction. As a genre, autobiography has a different categorical imperative, announced at the opening of Spark's *Curriculum Vitae* as "to put the record straight."⁵⁴ But in thinking of other novelists' autobiographical work (Woolf's *Moments of Being*, Nabokov's *Speak, Memory*) or in relation to the undeniable authorial personal Spark leaves on her fiction, it might be disappointing how little Spark's autobiography resonates with her literary work.

There is one important overlap between the two Clubs, however: the strange, almost inconceivable fact of their complete physical demise. Yet while the May of Teck was destroyed by a bomb, the Helena Club's demise was due rather to a postwar "course of total reconstruction, probably to make a hotel."⁵⁵ Spark is clearly shaken by this transformation, noting: "I had stayed so often in that club in Lancaster Gate, it seemed incredible that it was no more."⁵⁶ This incredulity is one of the few signs Spark gives as to the losses of her Second World War past, a marked inversion point where her cheerful "keep calm and carry on" manner gives way to a colder reality. While this moment does not take recourse to the black humor or total devastation that characterizes Spark's fiction, the Helena Club's destruction nevertheless signals the need for a new style of representation, one that she refuses to engage in the space of her autobiography. We might read Spark's fiction as taking on this task, as the new art-form that, like Joanna, finds the right words for the event. Indeed, returning to the language of the novel's secondary epiphany, we find it is not entirely negative. Though Joanna's father characterizes the ruins as nothing to see, he also notes that while it is all gone,

---

⁵³ *Ibid.*, 144.
⁵⁴ *Ibid.*, 11.
⁵⁵ *Ibid.*, 145. Today, the club exists as residential, luxury flats complete with gym, spa, and swimming pool. See http://idoxpa.westminster.gov.uk/online-applications/propertyDetails.do?activeTab=summary&keyVal=LITPKERP0ZM00.
⁵⁶ *Ibid.* Another notable autobiographical account of wartime home spaces is her essay "The Poet's House," first broadcasted on the BBC Home Service on July 7th, 1960, recounting a night spent in Louis MacNiece's house during the war. Like *Curriculum Vitae*, it contains none of the satirical flash or devastating wit of her fiction. Indeed, Spark offered this anecdote as an answer as to why she became a writer: "I think I must have felt that by some sympathetic magic I could draw from the poet's possessions some essence which would enable me to get down to my writing," with the house becoming "a symbol of what I was to attempt to make of my life." "The Poet's House," *The Informed Air: Essays*, ed. Penelope Jardine (New York: New Directions, 2014), 23.

it is also all elsewhere. This should give us pause, for where else might it be, along with Joanna, the other girls, the Club, and their perceived idealism? Spark's answer can be found in the floating poetic fragment that interrupts the language of the empty epiphany, a line from John Drinkwater's "Moonlit Apples" that Joanna used in her recitations: "At the top of the house the apples are laid in rows."[57] The entire novel is overlaid with these fractured poeticisms, some directly attributed to Joanna's elocution lessons, while others are purely literary utterances unattached to character (or even, it seems, narrator). This particular line, of course, is no random choice. Like Joanna's habit of choosing "the words for the right day," it recalls and even metaphorizes the May of Teck Club, gently reconstructing the prior trauma of the rooftop into a quiet domestic scene, reconstituting the girls as moonlit apples in neat, orderly rows. The line's reparative force is especially clear as it cuts off right before the line, "And the skylight lets the moonlight in," excising any mention of the fatal attic aperture.[58] The poem also provides a remarkable contrast to Nicholas's lost recording of Joanna reciting "The Wreck of the Deutschland," not only in content, but more hauntingly, in form. Joanna, the individual, finds remembrance or replacement in the work of the novel, which remembers her through a fragmentary, yet reconstructive, gesture. As this poetic interruption demonstrates, while material structures may crumble and fade away, the space of literature can house epiphanic moments, crystallizing them through figurative language that is mobile, iterable, and translatable. *The Girls of Slender Means* stretches these loci of wartime damage, taking the long view of ruins repaired, reconstructed, and repurposed. It takes into account the archaeology of structures that we have come to inhabit, and whose histories subtend the spaces of everyday life.

Coda: Hilary Mantel's *An Experiment in Love*

Though mostly overlooked in the literary and critical canon, *The Girls of Slender Means* has enjoyed a degree of popularity, testified by its adaptations as a radio play (1965), a three-episode mini-series for BBC TV (1975), and, most recently, a theatrical version by Judith Adams (2009). Each adaptation has had to negotiate the novel's alternating viewpoints and historical vantage points: the radio play, for instance, presents *The Girls of Slender Means* as Nicholas's autobiography, doing away with an omniscient narrator and

---

[57] Spark, *Girls*, 137.
[58] Ibid., 128.

relying instead on him; the television drama tints BBC stock footage of the Blitz in sepia to underscore the storybook "long ago in 1945."[59] However, the most compelling transformation of Spark's *The Girls of Slender Means* is not its translation to stage, screen, or sound. Instead, it can be found in Hilary Mantel's 1995 novel *An Experiment in Love*, a direct rewriting of Spark's novel and an uncannily faithful extension of it for the next generation of girls. In an interview in 1998, Mantel notes her affinities with Spark, but also distances herself from Spark's Catholicism, which "influences entirely the way she (Spark) views the world."[60] Yet theological and institutional forms of Catholicism undoubtedly animate Mantel's *oeuvre*, whether in her examination of Thomas Cromwell in the Wolf Hall Trilogy, or in her memoir *Giving Up the Ghost*, which describes her Catholic upbringing as teaching her two things: bladder control and "that I had got almost everything terribly wrong."[61] Yet Mantel is still haunted by faith and its trappings, which her work bears out through other means, including the semi-autobiographical *An Experiment in Love*. Thus when the protagonist of *An Experiment in Love* concludes that "we haven't the class for Girls of Slender Means," this should be taken less as an eschewal of Spark than as a form of affirmation.[62]

Focusing on a group of young women in Tonbridge Hall, a residence hall in a London university, *An Experiment in Love* details the color of the girls' everyday lives, the austere discomforts of their communal living-situation, and the minute oscillations between betrayal and care that characterize female sociality. Like the perverse relationship introduced between slenderness and wartime rationing in *The Girls of Slender Means*, Mantel's novel focuses on the girls' eating habits and what is allotted to them by the state, playing with "want" as both desire and lack. Her protagonist Carmel McBain develops an anorexia intimately bound to her position as a working-class scholarship girl, as pride, discipline, and shame profoundly shape what she allows herself to eat, on top of what little she can afford to. While these resemblances are general, the most obvious rewriting of Spark's novel occurs in the novel's climax, in which the residence hall goes up in flames; a girl dies a terrible death as the others watch, huddled in safety outside; and a precious fox-fur coat is salvaged by Karina, Carmel's childhood friend

---

[59] "BBC radio script by Christopher Holme, with letter, 1965, of Christopher Holme," Acc. 10989/97, Muriel Spark Archive, National Library of Scotland. Also: "BBC television rehearsal script by Ken Taylor, 1975," Acc. 10989/98-100, Muriel Spark Archive, National Library of Scotland.
[60] Rosario Arias and Hilary Mantel, "An Interview with Hilary Mantel," *Atlantis*, 20.2 (1998), 282, http://www.jstor.org/stable/41055527.
[61] Hilary Mantel, *Giving Up the Ghost* (New York: Picador, 2003), 60.
[62] Mantel, *An Experiment in Love* (New York: Picador, 1995), 18.

and enemy. Even the mechanisms of this epiphany are familiar. The fox-fur is once again revealed by delayed decoding ("She was holding something over her arm; it was a strange draping softness, something limp and slaughtered. My hand crept out to it: Lynette's fox fur"[63]); the death is staged at the window ("Outlined against a window, I saw a single figure; a silhouette, a blackness against red. It was Lynette. I knew her at once: I would have known her anywhere"[64]).

Not only does Hilary Mantel rewrite *The Girls of Slender Means*, but more importantly she extends Spark's work beyond its time, translating and updating it for the next generation of readers. While *The Girls of Slender Means* was positioned to destroy the myth of wartime sociality that underwrote the formation of the postwar welfare state, *An Experiment in Love* was positioned to mourn its demise, situated after the end of the Thatcher era and its dismantlement of welfare programs. Like Spark, Mantel is canny about her literary historiography, setting her work as a retrospective on an origin story. Just as the narrative action of *The Girls of Slender Means* looks back to the 1945 ascent of Labour, *An Experiment in Love* looks back to the 1970 ascent of the Tories, capturing a naïve time with the plenitude of perspective.[65] As Mantel recounts in the opening pages:

> It was the year after Chappaquiddick, the year Julia and I first went away from home. All spring I had dreamt about the disaster, and remembered the dreams when I woke: the lung tissue and water, the floating hair and sucking cold. In London that summer the temperatures shot into the mid-eighties, but at home the weather was as usual: rain most days, misty dawns over our dirty canal and cool damp evenings on the lawns of country pubs where we went with our boyfriends: sex later in the clammy, dewy dark. In June there was an election, and the Tories got in. It wasn't my fault; I wasn't old enough to vote.[66]

Like Spark's opening onto 1945, these lines orient us not only in a specific time and place, but also in a specific social sensibility. However, unlike the satirical "nice people of England,"[67] Mantel immediately begins with

---

[63] Ibid., 245.
[64] Ibid., 242.
[65] Thatcher herself even makes a cameo appearance near the end of the novel as Secretary of State, being "the Guest" at Tonbridge Hall's Guest Night banquet: unsurprisingly, the girls twitter at her, and she is described as wearing a dress "of the shape that is called ageless, and of a length that is called safe," with hair in curves "like unbaked sausage rolls" (Mantel, *Experiment*, 216).
[66] Mantel, *Experiment*, 2.
[67] Spark, *Girls*, 7.

a collective, girlish "we": one that, by the late 1960s, is both in charge of their sexuality but also rather uneasy about it. This girlishness also has an uneasy relationship to politics: not only is it too young to vote, and therefore politically passive, but as the Chappaquiddick reference suggests, it is also intensely precarious, even disposable. If Senator Ted Kennedy could shake off the death of his colleague Mary Jo Kopechne, so too, the reference suggests, might government drop its duty of care for young women, leaving them behind to drown in their own quiet disasters.[68] In a way similar to Carolyn Kay Steedman's *Landscape for a Good Woman* (1987), *An Experiment in Love* seeks to give voice to those subjects excluded, sometimes violently so, from being given an account in official politics and culture.[69] It is a deeply sociological book, one that takes the material formation of societies seriously, even of girls of slender means.

Of course, Mantel's novel does not merely mourn welfare ideology, just as Spark's novel does not merely indict it. *An Experiment in Love* shows the uneven effects of welfare, as felt by the protagonist in relation to both her working-class family and her various classmates as she becomes upwardly mobile. The novel continues to reveal these class-based fault-lines, so strikingly incongruent to Britain's self-narrative of rising postwar equality. Indeed, in her reminiscence about her scholarship days, Carmel directly associates her new schoolmates' affluence with the early postwar period: "When I think of the early lives of these girls—of Julianne, let us say—I think of starched sun-bonnets, Beatrix Potter, of mossy garden paths, regular bedtime, regular bowels: I see them frozen for ever in that unreclaimable oasis between the war and the 1960s, between the end of rationing and the beginning of the end."[70] One way to gloss the title of the novel, then, is to read it as a reference to the welfare state itself, being an experiment in love that—as the novel bears out—does not turn out to be a striking success. These class divides ultimately lead to the tragedy of the novel, Karina's theft of the precious fox-fur coat. What is more, we learn that Karina locked her roommate Lynette in their room, leaving Lynette to perish while she escaped to safety. This escalation of violence inverts the aims of postwar reconstruction, with

---

[68] Mary Jo Kopechne was part of her own girl posse: the "boiler-room girls," a group of young women helping with Robert F. Kennedy's 1968 presidential campaign. See "Who's Who at the Kennedy Inquest," *TIME*, September 5, 1969, http://content.time.com/time/magazine/article/0,9171,901341-4,00.html.

[69] Steedman's work is particularly relevant here, especially regarding Mantel's characters and their constant negotiation with envy for material things, which Steedman locates as a central, legitimate structure of feeling for working-class women. *Landscape for a Good Woman: A Story of Two Lives* (New Brunswick: Rutgers University Press, 1987).

[70] Mantel, *Experiment*, 124.

the divisive energies of welfare and its aspirations actually destroying social cohesiveness.

Yet unlike *The Girls of Slender Means*, this violence does not provide the negative epiphanic spark of the novel. Instead, the climax of the novel occurs in a moment of radical connection between Carmel and Karina. Just as the enormity of Karina's crime dawns on Carmel, a wind rises and pastes Karina's nightdress to her body, revealing a pregnant belly about five to six months developed. This sight catalyzes a flashback to an earlier scene where Carmel viciously kicked Karina's baby doll, an event that turned their easy, innocent friendship into one riven by jealousy, comparison, and ambivalence. In turn, this remembrance leads Carmel to decide not to give Karina away, a complicit and perverse act of repair. The novel ends with the two girls linking hands and running away from the dormitory fire, a moment of almost inconceivable defiance, alliance, and tenderness. *An Experiment in Love* thus gives one more turn to Spark's negative postwar epiphany, moving along a dialectic of care and harm, connection and disconnection. It proposes that, while welfare might be a failed experiment in one particular kind of love—the "all the nice people" postwar thesis of warfare to welfare—it might also create other forms of love, unanticipated by its initial planners as well as its detractors. As Carmel queries, "It struck me that perhaps Tonbridge Hall was drawing us together: who is my neighbour?"[71] *An Experiment in Love* is thus both an inhabitant and a neighbor of Spark's *The Girls of Slender Means*, dwelling within its novelistic infrastructure while also carrying out a duty of literary care for the questions and problems created therein. "Social theorists may talk of the death of the social," suggests James Vernon, "yet we still inhabit its increasingly shabby infrastructure."[72] Spark and Mantel testify to this continuance. Though Spark's criticism of 1945 may eviscerate wartime nationalism and the mythology of postwar repair, it does not leave us with nothing to see. Instead, it creates a literary space that future novelists can inhabit, and that we all, to some degree, have inherited.

---

[71] *Ibid.*, 201.
[72] James Vernon, *Hunger: A Modern History* (Cambridge: Harvard University Press 2007), 276. He elaborates: "[The] material world provided by postwar social democratic welfare states, just as in Britain the new hospitals and schools of the welfare state were frequently housed in the old workhouses." "Hunger, the Social, and States of Welfare in Modern Imperial Britain," *Occasion* v.2 (December 20, 2010), 7–8.

3
Unhomely Empire
Seeking Hospitality in Windrush Britain

On January 4, 1941, the magazine *Picture Post* issued what is arguably the first major publication to address postwar reconstruction, almost two years before Sir William Beveridge's *Social Insurance and Allied Services*, the November 1942 government report typically identified as the origin text of the British welfare state. Run as a special number entitled "A Plan for Britain," the magazine consisted of a series of short pieces dealing with unemployment, social security, education, health, and housing—in short, Beveridge's "Five Evils" *avant la lettre*. Though the magazine offered several visions of reconstruction, its starkest version was its choice of cover (Figure 10), which showcased six white children cascading down a playground slide, naked save for their shoes and socks.

This image makes a striking contrast this with the "TOGETHER" war propaganda poster, where representatives from across the Commonwealth march together under the Union Jack (Figure 11). If, as Michel Foucault reminds us, biopolitics inverts the sovereign order of "Let live and make die" to "Let die and make live," these two images make this logic painstakingly clear: colored bodies are to be sacrificed in service of the Empire, while white bodies are to be reproduced for its future. This tension is further crystallized in *Picture Post*, which describes its contents as outlining "a fairer, pleasanter, happier, more beautiful Britain than our own—but one based fairly and squarely on the Britain we have now."[1] Taking this syntax seriously, the dash in this sentence marks a troubling contradiction, one that both acknowledges and then erases the presence of colonial history and racial difference. A more beautiful Britain, it implies, not only will be white, but more insidiously, will have always been.[2]

---

[1] "Foreword," *Picture Post*, January 4, 1941, 4.
[2] See also the October 30, 1954 issue *Picture Post*, which asks: "Would You Let Your Daughter Marry a Negro?," discussed in Thomas Davis's *The Extinct Scene: Late Modernism and Everyday Life* (New York: Columbia University Press, 2016), 208–211.

The Promise of Welfare in the Postwar British and Anglophone Novel. Kelly M. Rich, Oxford University Press.
© Kelly M. Rich (2023). DOI: 10.1093/oso/9780192893437.003.0004

102 STATES OF REPAIR

Figure 10 Cover of *Picture Post*'s special issue, "A Plan for Britain" (1941). Reproduced courtesy of Getty Images.

Yet Britain was diversified during the Second World War as never before, due to the influx of refugees, immigrants, soldiers, war workers and

UNHOMELY EMPIRE: HOSPITALITY IN WINDRUSH BRITAIN   103

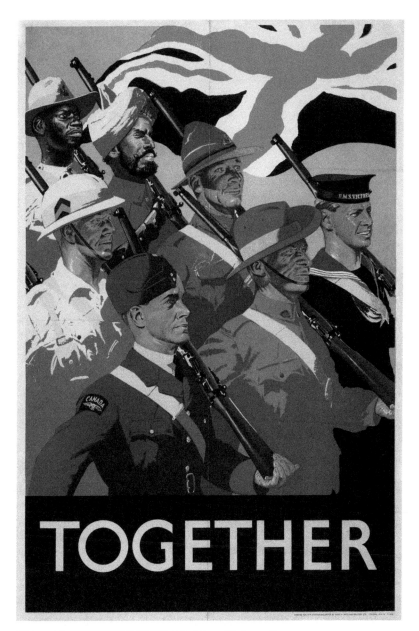

Figure 11 *TOGETHER* (1939). Ministry of Information.
© Imperial War Museum (Art. IWM PST 3158).

volunteers, and prisoners of war.[3] Though Britain's victory depended on the image of tolerant, liberal empire, brothers-in-arms soon turned back to foreigners after the war.[4] As *Picture Post* demonstrated, postwar Britain depended on an insular, even amnesiac vision of nationhood. Stuart Hall characterizes this selective remembrance as "the *Dad's Army* version of the national story," diagnosing this amnesia as a kind of misapprehension.[5] Though much scholarly work has been done to challenge the presumed "people" of the "People's War" along lines of gender, race, nationality, and class, the war continues to be coded as white despite the globality of the Second World War and the contributions of Britain's Empire.[6]

This chapter suggests that this racial and ethnic rescripting was likewise borne out by the discourse of British reconstruction, in which there was no imaginative place for others, whether Jamaican or Polish, Czech or Irish, Canadian or Indian. This whitewashed version of reconstruction would soon be dramatically tested by the MV *Empire Windrush*, a ship whose arrival on June 22, 1948 brought one of the first large groups of immigrants from the West Indies to the British Isles. Though by no means the beginning of Black colonial presence in the UK, this event heralded major demographic change, marking the advent of "the Windrush generation."[7] This chapter focuses on those Windrush years of 1948–1962, a period that began with the ship's arrival, and which ended with the independence of Jamaica and Trinidad and Tobago, the end of the West Indies Federation, and the Nottingham and Notting Hill "race riots," or rather, acts of anti-Black violence perpetrated by white gangs.[8] It is a relatively small window,

---

[3] Wendy Webster characterizes this wartime demography as Britain's "big proposition," a term she borrows from the 1945 documentary *The True Glory* to signal how new, even experimental this racial, national, and ethnic diversity felt across the UK. *Mixing It: Diversity in World War Two Britain* (Oxford: Oxford University Press, 2018), 7.
[4] Ibid., 16.
[5] Hall, *Familiar Stranger*, 178.
[6] See especially Sonya Rose's *Which People's War? National Identity and Citizenship in Britain 1939–1945* (Oxford: Oxford University Press, 2003), and Webster's *Mixing It*.
[7] On this point, see Marc Matera's *Black London: The Imperial Metropolis and Decolonization in the Twentieth Century* (Berkeley and Los Angeles: University of California Press, 2015); Peter Fryer's *Staying Power: The History of Black People in Britain* (London and New York: Pluto Press, 2010); and Stuart Hall's *Familiar Stranger: A Life between Two Islands* (Durham and London: Duke University Press, 2017).
[8] See *Beyond Windrush, Rethinking Postwar Anglophone Caribbean Literature*, ed. J. Dillon Brown and Leah Reade Rosenberg (Jackson: University Press of Mississippi, 2015), 3; Virginia Noble's focus on 1948–1965 in *Inside the Welfare State: Foundations of Policy and Practice in Post-War Britain* (New York: Routledge, 2009), 7; Jordanna Bailkin's "core" of 1958–1962 in *Afterlife of Empire* (Berkeley and Los Angeles: University of California Press, 2012). James Procter's edited collection *Writing Black Britain* (Manchester: Manchester University Press, 2000) has a slightly different periodization, choosing "1948 to the late 1960s" to encompass the first phase of Black British history. To the editors, the 1970s and early 1980s marked a new phase, one characterized by criminalization and more official policing of Black communities.

bookended by two British Nationality Acts that opened and then restricted rights of entry to the UK, restrictions that would only increase in the subsequent years (with Acts in 1968, 1971, and most aggressively, 1981). It is also, as I discuss, a period of increased contestation over the concepts of domesticity and neighborliness: that is, the very project of living together in the dual wakes of the Second World War and movements toward decolonization. With the influx of immigrants, especially to metropolitan areas such as London, Birmingham, and Nottingham, Britain became more aware of its "colour problem," with welfare services such as housing, education, and employment being highly contested sites for racial equality and national belonging.

Recent scholarship has critiqued the holding power of "Windrush" as a limiting category of analysis, observing how "institutional and critical biases have decisively shaped the characterization of this period, pruning out much of its diversity and interest in favor of a simplified account of regional-national literary triumph."[9] When scholars invoke the Windrush generation, it tends to be gendered (male); sexualized (heterosexual); genre-specific (the novel); and geographically restricted (British empire-focused). Its historiography as an expressly postwar phenomenon can also be limiting when such periodization obscures the long durée of colonialism. Despite these potential calcifications, I find it useful to retain the name of "Windrush," especially in studying the legacies and holding power of midcentury Britain and the transition from warfare to welfare. In tracking the nature of the "postness" of post-1945, this moment's cultural production gives us a particularly fraught vocabulary for understanding the imaginative power of reconstruction and the symbolic power of living spaces. Writers including Samuel Selvon, George Lamming, V.S. Naipaul, Roger Mais, Andrew Salkey, Beryl Gilroy, James Berry, and Kamau Brathwaite focus on the welfare of immigrants in the metropole: their disappointment with the ruins of postwar London and its austerity blues; the sociality of council estates; and the racism that keeps them outside the trajectories of upward mobility. Their works offer a critique of welfare Britain as it is actually lived, contesting

---

[9] *Beyond Windrush*, 4. Especially useful in this collection is Alison Donnell's discussion of Caribbean women writers, which shows that the timeline and geography of Windrush is not so clean-cut—much work was done before Windrush in the UK, and during Windrush back in the West Indies. See also Donnell's *Twentieth-Century Caribbean Literature: Critical Moments in Anglophone Literary History* (London: Routledge, 2006). There is also a growing body of criticism on pre-Windrush "Black Britain": see, for instance, Matera's *Black London* and Kennetta Hammond Perry's *London Is the Place for Me: Black Britons, Citizenship and the Politics of Race* (Oxford: Oxford University Press, 2016). For an earlier, general account, see Peter Fryer's *Staying Power: The History of Black People in Britain* (London: Pluto Press, 1984), and David Olusoga, *Black and British: A Forgotten History* (London: Macmillan, 2016).

its wartime "togetherness" and postwar promises of social reconstruction. Yet they also participate in a welfarist logic, offering characters who serve as proxies or agents of the welfare state, or who seek to build alternative communities within welfare's system of rules and regulations.

In the first part of this chapter, I address the uneasy relationship between "postwar" and "postcolonial." I do so through a consideration of literary studies' disciplinary formation as well as by a reading of the arrival of *Empire Windrush* that highlights this moment's potent nexus of these two terms. Although I use the word "postcolonial" throughout the chapter, in acknowledgment of its usage and legacy in literary studies, I also employ the terms "postimperial," "late colonial," and even "early postcolonial" to describe particular geopolitical and historical moments with more precision. The works this chapter describes were written during a transitional moment when the British West Indies were still colonies, in the process of decolonization and determining what their postcolonial, potentially pan-West-Indies identity might look like. In addition, the London location of the texts I discuss is more properly imperial than colonial, though as the poet Louise Bennett put it, the Windrush generation could also be seen as "colonizing in reverse" ("Wat a devilment a Englan! / Dem face war an brave de worse, / But me wonderin how dem gwine stan / Colonizin in reverse").[10]

The second part of this chapter then turns to literary works that expressly deal with the Black British experience of trying to make London home, as it is registered through complex relationships between people and living spaces including interiors such as the bedroom, living room, and basement apartment, as well as in liminal places such as the street and train station.[11] As in the previous chapters, London continues to provide a privileged site for which to analyze the cultural imaginary of postwar reconstruction, as imperial metropolis, cultural center, and in this chapter, for its historic association with internationalism, avant-gardism, and anti-colonial political movements. This chapter will focus on the work of Samuel Selvon, whose *oeuvre* registers the evolution of this experience, moving from the moment of arrival to later forms of social activism. I begin with the novel that has

---

[10] Louise Bennett, "Colonization in Reverse," http://louisebennett.com/colonization-in-reverse/.

[11] Here, I build on James Procter's useful study of what he calls "dwelling places" in Black British literature from the 1950s to the 1990s, which include many of those named here, as well as cafes, suburbia, and the place of the North or region in Black British cultures. Procter, *Dwelling Places: Postwar Black British Writing* (Manchester: Manchester University Press, 2003). See also John McLeod, *Postcolonial London: Rewriting the Metropolis* (London: Routledge, 2004).

garnered the most attention of all his works, *The Lonely Londoners* (1956), which I read alongside the lesser-known *The Housing Lark* (1965) in order to address what I see as Selvon's literary politics of place and participation in the discourse of postwar reconstruction. I then track how this concept of place develops in the sequel *Moses Ascending* (1975), especially as a transition point to a post-Windrush generation. If *The Lonely Londoners* and *The Housing Lark* hold out hope that domestic living spaces can still be enchanted places—that is, places of potential social and political transformation, if only you can get them right—*Moses Ascending* sardonically punctures that dream, with its thoroughly disenchanted treatment of home ownership.

In a final section, this chapter concludes by addressing recent iterations of Windrush literature, showing how their preoccupations with inhabitation and living together continue to shape contemporary literature. In particular, I read Zadie Smith's *NW* (2012) as a noteworthy inheritor of Windrush, one that combines a modernist sensibility with an interest in London's postwar tower blocks and the lives of their postcolonial inhabitants. Although most critics classify *NW* as Smith's Joycean novel, I argue it can also be read in relation to Selvon's *The Lonely Londoners* through its concern over how to build community in the face of racial antagonism and alienation. By reading *NW* as an inheritor of this postwar and postcolonial literary tradition, we can get a more precise view of the belated uses of modernist form, which extend the purview of Windrush historiography into our contemporary moment.

Postwar Windrush

Inspired by Kwame Anthony Appiah's influential essay on whether the "post" of postmodernism is the "post" of the postcolonial, this chapter asks whether the "post" of postwar British literature is the same as the "post" of postcolonial literature.[12] How do we put these terms in relation? To what extent are these histories coeval, and where do they come apart? In literary

---

[12] See Kwame Anthony Appiah's "Is the Post-in Postmodernism the Post-in Postcolonial?" *Critical Inquiry* 17.2 (Winter 1991), 336–357, as well as Shu-mei Shih's "Is the *Post*-in Postsocialism the *Post*-in Posthumanism?" *Social Text* 30.1 (Spring 2012), 27–50. These studies share a desire to bring a more historical energy back into the conversation—that is, to go back to the historically articulated roots of modernism and colonialism, and humanism and socialism, to understand what we gain (and what we stand to lose) by considering their relationship in a world where they have been seemingly superseded. They do so to recapture the political energy

108 STATES OF REPAIR

studies, at least, they have tended to exist at a skewed angle to each other. "Postwar" often denotes a specific time period, adhering to literature of the 1950s and early 1960s, before postmodernism and/or "contemporary" British literature. "Postcolonial," on the other hand, carries a theoretical charge as well as denotes a body of literature, emerging as a school of thought in the 1980s through Anglo-American universities and postcolonial criticism. In comparison, the term "postwar" can be seen as risking a certain parochialism both in subject matter and style, recapitulating the "shrinking island" syndrome discussed in Jed Esty's and Marina MacKay's studies of late modernism.[13] Happily, there has been increased merging of these datasets in literary scholarship, not only in what titles or authors "count" under either term, but also, more importantly, in the thick, mutual relationship between them.[14]

Still, these field formations suggest taking a closer look at why a certain conservatism, parochialism, and whiteness continues to be associated with the term "postwar." This relationship might be attributed to the specific whiteness of postwar reconstruction, a trope that continues to haunt British cultural production. Paul Gilroy calls this racial attachment to the whiteness of the Second World War a "postcolonial melancholia," arguing that, since 1945, "the life of the nation has been dominated by an inability even to face, never mind actually mourn, the profound change in circumstances and moods that followed the end of the empire and consequent loss of imperial prestige."[15] This structure of feeling goes well beyond grief. The national

of their favored term (for Appiah, postcolonial; for Shih, postsocial) *for the present moment*—a very Benjaminian gesture.

[13] As Bill Schwarz notes, "It has now become commonplace to describe a certain sector of the postwar English novel, often resolutely English and upper—or middle-class in its preoccupations, as parochial." *The End of Empire and the English Novel Since 1945*, ed. Rachael Gilmour and Bill Schwarz (Manchester: Manchester University Press, 2011), 3. And while Lyndsey Stonebridge and MacKay favor the term "mid-century" over "postwar" in their collection *British Fiction After Modernism: The Novel at Midcentury*, they still characterize this period as "critically awkward," one where "mid-century writers became more domestic and domesticated." *British Fiction After Modernism: The Novel at Mid-Century*, ed. Marina MacKay and Lyndsey Stonebridge (New York: Palgrave Macmillan, 2007), 1.

[14] See, for instance, the collections *End of Empire and the English Novel since 1945* and *British Literature in Transition*; the overviews in Graham MacPhee's *Postwar Literature and Postcolonial Studies* (Edinburgh: Edinburgh University Press, 2011) and Dominic Head's *Cambridge Introduction to Modern British Fiction* (Cambridge: Cambridge University Press, 2002); and most recently, and as an excellent example of the new scholarship on the "postwar," see Asha Rogers's *State-Sponsored Literature: Britain and Cultural Diversity after 1945* (Oxford: Oxford University Press, 2020).

[15] Paul Gilroy, *Postcolonial Melancholia* (New York: Columbia University Press, 2005), 90.

consciousness would rather return to (indeed, *cling to*) the identification of 1945 as a clean-cut storyline of good (British) and bad (Nazi Germany) than entertain the possibility of another narrative: that is, 1945 as marking a changing imperial history. And so, Gilroy argues, any explanation of contemporary British nationalism must take account of this melancholic relationship between colonizer and colonized, an account that:

> ...must also be able to acknowledge that exceptionally powerful feelings of comfort and compensation are produced by the prospect of even a partial restoration of the country's long-vanished homogeneity. Repairing that aching loss is usually signified by the recovery or preservation of endangered whiteness—and the exhilarating triumph over chaos and strangeness which that victory entails.[16]

These words precisely describe the wished-for repair of postwar reconstruction: a form of comfort and compensation that comes from the prospect of restoring a white, homogenous Britain, especially in the face of its wartime annihilation.

In light of this racial nostalgia, re-establishing the relationship between the terms "postwar" and "postcolonial" should go far beyond bringing non-synchronous terms into an easy synchrony. Instead, we need to find a different way of talking about them, one that emphasizes their intimacy while still recalling their racial power dynamics. Postcolonial scholars have long advocated such a rewriting of narratives and categories: as Homi Bhabha reminds us, "The Western metropole must confront its postcolonial history, told by its influx of postwar migrants and refugees, as an indigenous or native narrative *internal to its national identity*."[17] In light of the historic tendency to divide the postwar and the postcolonial, as well as the current global migration crises, the need to read these two terms together has become more urgent than ever. As Britain and Europe fight over who, exactly, properly belongs within their borders, it is important to recall the immediate history of these debates, in all its complexity and diversity.

Postwar building required learning how to newly live together, a struggle that manifested through a language of hostility and hospitality: or as Derrida puts it, "hostipitality," a reminder that the condition of hospitality or the host is the ability to exercise hostility through limiting how, exactly, one

---

[16] *Ibid.*, 88.
[17] Homi Bhabha, *The Location of Culture* (London: Routledge, 2004), 9.

can become a guest.[18] In the specific case of the Windrush generation, the hostility that immigrants experienced surfaced visibly and violently in the recent 2018 "Windrush scandal," in which it was revealed that as many as eighty-three people were wrongly deported from the UK. These deportations and threats to legal, political, and social rights were due to Theresa May's 2010 "hostile environment" policy, whose aim she described as "to create, here in Britain, a really hostile environment for illegal immigrants."[19] As the Windrush generation had the legal right to enter the UK under the 1948 British Nationality Act, and were then granted the right to remain if they entered the UK from a Commonwealth country before 1973, many were unable to prove legal residence as required by the new Home Office policy, and were thus treated as illegal immigrants.

The point here is not to prove the validity of the Windrush generation's citizenship, which would cede too much ground to the logic of deportation. Instead, I want to underscore how the concept of hostility, and its counterpart, hospitality, continue to form the paradigmatic language through which national belonging gets worked out. While these categories are often racially divided, my project seeks to knit them together through the concept of collective living, part of the recursive logic of 1945 that keeps animating literary production. This focus reiterates and revises the concept of postimperial melancholia. While cognizant of the contestation between the "we" of the postwar (white) and the "we" of the postcolonial and postimperial (non-white), this return to 1945 seeks a different first-person plural: a demilitarized version of the "TOGETHER" poster. This new collective is defined not only by its multi-nationalism, but also by what Paul Gilroy has called "conviviality," or the "processes of cohabitation and interaction that have made multiculture an ordinary feature of social life in Britain's urban areas and in postcolonial cities elsewhere."[20]

What would it mean, then, to insist upon reading the arrival of the Windrush generation into this national narrative of postwar reconstruction?

---

[18] Jacques Derrida, "Hostipitality," *Angelaki: Journal of Theoretical Humanities* 5:3 (December 2000), 3–18.

[19] Amelia Hill, "'Hostile environment': the hardline Home Office policy tearing families apart," *The Guardian*, November 28, 2017, https://www.theguardian.com/uk-news/2017/nov/28/hostile-environment-the-hardline-home-office-policy-tearing-families-apart. For an early timeline of the Windrush Scandal, see Kevin Rawlinson, "Windrush-era citizens row: timeline of key events," *The Guardian*, April 16, 2018, https://www.theguardian.com/uk-news/2018/apr/16/windrush-era-citizens-row-timeline-of-key-events.

[20] Gilroy, *Postcolonial Melancholia*, xv. Gilroy means this concept to take off from where "multiculturalism" fails, as it distances itself from "identity."

To start, it would mean imbricating the great optimism of arrival with the optimism of rebuilding Britain, and recasting the event as a move from wartime to peacetime. After all, many migrating to England had served during the Second World War in defense of the British Empire, and they were ready to share in the brave new world of post-1945. The *Windrush* ship was itself a repurposing of wartime technology: with the war over, Britain was building a New Jerusalem, borrowing heavily on a swords-to-ploughshares logic.

As Ashley Dawson notes, immigrants had traveled to Britain because they were "intent on helping to rebuild the devastated motherland, [and] saw the voyage to Britain as a continuation of their wartime sacrifice."[21] This spirit is captured on a film recording of the *Empire Windrush*, with the segment beginning: "JAMAICANS COME TO BRITAIN TO LOOK FOR WORK." The newsreel emphasizes the men's previous wartime service, presenting a narrative of continuity:

> Many are ex-servicemen who know England. They served this country well. In Jamaica they couldn't find work. Discouraged but full of hope, they sailed for Britain, citizens of the British Empire coming to the Mother Country with good intent.[22]

While the film interviews several passengers to ascertain this "good intent," the most powerful affirmation came from Trinidadian calypsonian Aldwyn Roberts who sang "London Is the Place for Me" as he disembarked from the ship.[23] Many scholars begin their discussion of the Windrush generation by citing this iconic moment, and for good reason: it manifests a powerful optimism about returning to the "Mother Country," a feeling soon to be betrayed the discrimination immigrants faced as they made a new life in the metropole.[24] Its performance also indexes a complex history of colonial power and resistance. As a calypso sung in Standard English rather than Trinidadian creole, its language and form index both the imperial history

---

[21] Ashley Dawson, *Mongrel Nation: Diasporic Culture and the Making of Postcolonial Britain* (Ann Arbor: University of Michigan Press, 2007), 2.

[22] "Pathé reporter meets—," June 24, 1948, *British Pathé*, https://www.britishpathe.com/video/pathe-reporter-meets.

[23] Lord Kitchener, "London Is the Place for Me," in *London is the Place for Me: Trinidadian Calypso in London, 1950–1956* (London: Honest Jon's Records, 2002), compact disc recording. Lyrics can be found at http://www.songlyrics.com/lord-kitchener/london-is-the-place-for-me-lyrics/.

[24] See, for example, the introduction to Dawson's *Mongrel Nation*, as well as Perry's *London Is the Place for Me*.

of British colonial education as well as subversion and adaptation to British rule.

Roberts's performing name, "Lord Kitchener," was an apt choice for this mythology of arrival. As Secretary of State during the First World War, Lord Kitchener had been the face of the infamous recruitment poster "Your Country Needs YOU," which would inspire several imitations (including the US's Uncle Sam). Before the Great War, Kitchener had made his career in several imperial campaigns, including the re-conquering of Sudan; subduing Boer fighters during the Second Boer War through scorched-earth policies and concentration camps (the first usage of that term); and serving as Commander-in-Chief of India from 1902 to 1909. Roberts's adoption Kitchener's name serves as a reminder of Britain's military and imperial history, and is perhaps even an instance of "colonization in reverse."

As immigrants like Roberts arrived in Britain, they participated in the dismantling and rebuilding of empire while also refiguring their relationships to the "mother country." They also played a crucial role in Britain's postwar reconstruction, as industries including London Transport, British Rail, British Hotels and Restaurant Association, and the National Health Service advertised for and recruited West Indian labor.[25] West Indian nurses were sought by the NHS under health minister Enoch Powell (who would later deliver the infamous "Rivers of Blood" speech, decrying what he saw as a racially tainted Britain). The government first tried to solve Britain's postwar labor problem by conscripting European Voluntary Workers (white foreign workers from Poland, Ukraine, and Latvia, many of whom were displaced by war) and then Irish immigrants. Black laborers from Britain's Commonwealth were taken as a last resort, deemed as being unfit for both work and assimilation into British society. Upon arrival, they were immediately construed as a problem rather than a much-needed solution in ways white foreign workers were deemed to be.[26]

In the domain of literary and aesthetic production, the relationship between welfare and decolonization takes shape through the concept of home. Home is a defining trope in immigrant literatures, as characters

---

[25] See Olusoga, *Black and British*, 500; Fryer, *Staying Power*, 373; and Julian Simpson, Aneez Esmail, Virinder Kalra, and Stephanie Snow, "Writing migrants back into NHS history: addressing a 'collective amnesia' and its policy implications," *Journal of the Royal Society of Medicine* 103 (2010), 392–396.

[26] See Olusoga, *Black and British*, 490–496; Kathleen Paul's *Whitewashing Britain: Race and Citizenship in the Postwar Era* (Ithaca: Cornell University Press, 1997), 83–89.

seek a place of their own in their new environments.[27] For the Windrush generation, this meant navigating their arrival in a Britain taken by rather conservative images of domesticity. From its wartime beginning to postwar realization, Britain's reconstructive imagination was coded as desiring certain kind of whiteness: that is, a British race intent on its replication and prolongation through the nuclear family, which largely excluded colonial subjects, the poor, and at times, the Irish. Colonial arrivals were seen as incapable of proper domesticity. As Wendy Webster puts it, "Differences between white and black were constructed through an opposition between an Englishness, characterized by the privacy of domestic and familial life, and 'immigrants,' who were characterized in terms of an incapacity for domestic and familial life, or domestic barbarian."[28] This racial logic was tested by the increasing numbers of immigrants, who were perceived as not fitting into the "British way of life."

This racial logic was inherent from the start of migration, a legacy of colonial paradigms of thought. In Kenneth Little's *Negroes in Britain* (1947), published as part of the International Library of Sociology and Social Reconstruction, Little observes, "The Colonial problem of yesterday is taking on a fresh shape as the racial and national problem of to-day."[29] And while Sheila Patterson's *Dark Strangers: A Sociological Study of the Absorption of a Recent West Indian Migrant Group in Brixton, South London* (1963) attempted to distinguish the recent demographic upheavals as an "immigrant situation" rather than a "colour problem," calling Britain's "antipathy to outsiders ... a cultural norm," this race-neutral line quickly erodes in her study, which showed the range of racial prejudice faced by Afro-Caribbean immigrants as they tried to make Britain home.[30] What was called the "colour problem" or "colour line" resulted in discrimination and *de facto*

---

[27] Notable secondary works on this topic include Rosemary Marangoly George, *The Politics of Home: Postcolonial Relocations and Twentieth-Century Fiction* (Cambridge: Cambridge University Press, 1996), as well as *At Home with the Empire: Metropolitan Culture and the Imperial World*, ed. Catherine Hall and Sonya Rose (Cambridge: Cambridge University Press, 2006).
[28] Webster, *Englishness and Empire, 1939–1965* (Oxford: Oxford University Press, 2007), xii. See also Pearl Jephcott's *A Troubled Area: Notes on Notting Hill, London* (London: Faber & Faber, 1964).
[29] Kenneth Little, *Negroes in Britain: A Study of Racial Relations in English Society* (London: Kegan Paul, 1948), xiii.
[30] Sheila Patterson, *Dark Strangers: A Sociological Study of the Absorption of a Recent West Indian Migrant Group in Brixton, South London* (London: Tavistock Publications Limited, 1963), 7.

segregation, even (and especially) in intimate settings of home and family. Finding adequate housing proved a particular hurdle, especially given the persistence of postwar housing shortages that created animosity and competition. Signs and advertisements declaring "No Irish, Blacks, or Dogs," "Europeans only," and "English only" suggested the categorical refusals Black people faced in their search. Black women who migrated with children faced the additional line, "So Sorry, No Coloured, No Children."[31] Would-be tenants faced additional racial discrimination from local authorities, both *de facto* and *de jure*. In Lambeth, for instance, residency requirements made newly arrived immigrants ineligible for accommodation; their applications were often screened for race; and they often took the worst types of property "because no one else would take it."[32] While one solution to housing shortages and discrimination was for West Indians to turn landlord themselves, the types of property they were able to buy, and the costs required for their investments, still resulted in overcrowded, dilapidated, and expensive living arrangements (another version of the "colour tax").

Lord Kitchener's "London Is the Place for Me" calypso anticipates this battle over living together, especially in later verses omitted for the Pathé newsreel. Delving deeper into the specific place-feeling of London, the calypso's surface earnestness starts to fray as it comments on the hospitality of the English ("To live in London you're really comfortable / Because the English people are very much sociable"). Eyebrows might also rise at the final stanza's repeated assurances of the good life in London, as well as the assertion that his home is "Hampton Court," echoing the name of Henry VIII's sixteenth-century palace. Roberts and his fellow immigrants would find a world of difference between these magnificent, palatial dreams and the reality of postwar Britain: disappointments of arrival reckoned with by later Windrush literatures.

Making Space and Making Place in Windrush Literature

Samuel Selvon's *The Lonely Londoners* (1956) chronicles the difficult, often bewildering experience of West Indian immigrants trying to make a life in 1950s London. Selvon's novel takes a collective focus, stepping away from

---

[31] See Perry, *London Is the Place for Me*, 83–85. See also Sally MacDonald and Julia Porter, *Putting on the Style: Setting Up Home in the 1950s* (London: Geffrye Museum, 1990), especially the section "Room at the Top."
[32] Patterson, *Dark Strangers*, 174.

the individual protagonist to consider a wider bandwidth of social experience. The novel alternates accounts of a handful of characters, spreading narrative attention across nine men, interleaved with breathtaking prose sections that address the collective experience of this generation. At the same time, however, the novel is focalized through the character of Moses Aloetta, who is introduced in the opening paragraph. As one of the early immigrants in the Windrush generation, Moses, the voice of experience and reason, frequently advises the new batch of arrivals to "take it easy." As such, his world-weary perspective grants Selvon license to reflect on the bigger picture, whether the signature trials and joys of the new arrival, or the larger historical arc of how things were different in Moses's day. With this narrative distance from the social world, it is no surprise that at the end of the novel, Moses emerges as a definitive author-figure ("wondering if he could ever write a book like that, what everybody would buy"), perhaps of the novel we are just finishing.[33] This implication is confirmed in *Moses Ascending*, the sequel to *The Lonely Londoners*, in which Moses declares: "There are those who will remember that if it wasn't for me, Galahad would of catch his royal arse in Brit'n. [...] I have chronicled those colourful days in another tome, and it is not my wont to hark back to what is done and finish with."[34] With this shift from third- to first-person narration, Selvon formally extends Moses's writerly station, representing Moses in the midst of writing his memoirs (he addresses his audience as "Dear Reader").

Yet there is another reason why Moses is the central character in *Lonely Londoners*: his position of guardian, advisor, even welfare officer, as he helps new arrivals seek housing and employment. When Galahad, Moses's newest ward, asks Moses how he knows so many people, Moses responds, "I didn't come to London yesterday. [...] I was among the first set of spades what come to Brit'n. And then, it ain't have so many places the boys could go to, so you bound to meet them up sooner or later."[35] Though this statement is made in relation to party spaces, a longing for communal place suffuses the novel's framework as the wished-for structure that would create good sociality and erase the loneliness of these Lonely Londoners. This desire is realized to comic and disastrous results in the sequel *Moses Ascending*, when Moses purchases an apartment-building and turns landlord. In this sense

---

[33] Samuel Selvon, *The Lonely Londoners* (New York: Longman Publishing Group, 2001), 142.
[34] Selvon, *Moses Ascending* (Oxford: Heinemann Educational Books Ltd, 1984), 44.
[35] Selvon, *Lonely Londoners*, 120.

these novels can be read as suggesting a literary welfare system, in which achieving a sense of place is tantamount to getting welfare right—a relationship that draws on and renovates postwar dreams of reconstruction. The loneliness of the Lonely Londoners, in other words, is felt as a longing for hospitality, and the forms of belonging that accompany it. Moses emerges as an alternative welfare officer precisely because these new arrivals seek the spaces and institutional arrangements that would allow for the feeling of social citizenship.

For Selvon, like Lord Kitchener, the keyword for postwar migration is *place*, announced at the opening of *The Lonely Londoners* in the description of London as a "strange place on another planet."[36] Place proves a flexible and capacious concept in Moses trilogy, including both public and private spaces, which drive different representational styles ranging from fantastic idealism to grim realism. Tracking this constellation of places produces a specifically Black London, refracted through the lens of the immigrant's experience. The most public of these places are specific, immediately known locations in London—Waterloo Station, Oxford Circus, Speaker's Corner at Marble Arch and St. Pancras's party hall—as well as non-specific locales including parks, pubs, and employment offices.

The Lonely Londoners is a pedagogical novel, instructing its readers to associate certain affective resonances with specific locations across London. In doing so, it invites what Forster called "place-feeling." Take, for example, Moses's arrival at Waterloo:

> When he get to Waterloo he hop off and went in the station, and right away in that big station he had a feeling of home-sickness that he never felt in the nine-ten years he in this country. For the old Waterloo is a place of arrival and departure, is a place where you see people crying goodbye and kissing welcome...[37]

The declaration of the last sentence stands out, calling attention to this moment as one in which some wisdom is imparted. Its transition into free indirect discourse doubles its sense of privileged narrative access, capturing Moses's interiority and the narrator's judgment. Another instance appears even within the same scene ("Still, the station is that sort of place where you have a soft feeling"), an interruption that modifies and expands the original pronouncement.[38] Selvon repeats these gestures throughout the

---

[36] Ibid., 23.
[37] Ibid., 25.
[38] Ibid., 26.

UNHOMELY EMPIRE: HOSPITALITY IN WINDRUSH BRITAIN 117

novel, turning the reading of place as an opportunity for opening rather than closing meaning, offering proliferation and possibility rather than tidy pronouncement.

Recent work on *The Lonely Londoners* highlights the metropolitan quality of Selvon's place-feeling as an aspect of his engagement with literary modernism. These approaches have extended earlier readings of the novel as an evocation of collective consciousness through the use of creole and calypso, pointing to its implication in discourses of cosmopolitanism, reverse ethnography, metropolitan postcolonial phenomenology, or experiments in vernacular.[39] Recent readings also engage the novel's urban setting to consider more liberal democratic forms of justice, measured through a more equitable relation between the city's racial populations, and achieved through participation in public discourse or public spaces.[40] To these studies of the "London" in *The Lonely Londoners*, I add a focus on private space, or how Selvon's characters seek to find a home of their own in a rather inhospitable city. For above all, "place" is associated with finding a place for themselves, a preoccupation that defines the Moses trilogy's alignment of upward mobility with property ownership. This focus on domestic space is evident in the beginning of *The Lonely Londoners*, when Moses goes to Waterloo Station to greet a fellow Trinidadian in an exhausted reiteration of the Windrush arrival. While waiting, he finds himself hounded by a newspaper reporter, who keeps demanding of Moses why "so many Jamaicans are immigrating to England." These questions stop when Moses

---

[39] For a representative example of the canonical reading, see Kenneth Ramchand's introduction to *The Lonely Londoners*. Selvon's modernist readers include J. Dillon Brown's *Migrant Modernism: Postwar London and the West Indian Novel* (Charlottesville and London: University of Virginia Press, 2013); Jed Esty's *A Shrinking Island: Modernism and National Culture in England* (Princeton: Princeton University Press, 2003); Peter Kalliney's *Cities of Affluence and Anger: A Literary Geography of Modern Englishness* (Charlottesville, University of Virginia Press, 2015) and *Commonwealth of Letters: British Literary Culture and the Emergence of Postcolonial Aesthetics* (New York: Oxford University Press, 2013), which takes a more institutional approach to late colonial and early postcolonial modernism; and Thomas Davis's *The Extinct Scene: Late Modernism and Everyday Life* (New York: Columbia University Press, 2015).

[40] For instance, Brown characterizes *The Lonely Londoners* as a work of attempted "reconciliation" or "rapprochement," insofar as it reflects a desire that West Indians be "accepted as equal contributors in the social and cultural world" (*Migrant Modernism*, 124). Janice Ho routs the possibility of social transformation through the concept of citizenship and authorship, suggesting that while postwar immigrant fictions turn to authorship's democratic potential, they at the same time challenge the possessive individualism associated with the act of authorship. See chapter 4, *Nation and Citizenship in the Twentieth-Century British Novel* (Cambridge: Cambridge University Press, 2015). And finally, Kalliney's focus on London's literary geography studies the way various public spaces produce subjects through an urban phenomenology, specifically the diversity, relaxation, and overall sociality afforded by London parks, which as quasi-democratizing spaces, give the Lonely Londoners a temporary respite from discrimination. See chapter 3, *Cities of Affluence and Anger*.

starts to give his opinion on the state of the nation: "We can't get no place to live, and we only getting the worse jobs it have..."[41] This proves too much for the reporter, who uncomfortably moves on. This moment is also a test for the reader's commitment to hear the rest of the story, and to learn what kinds of places sustain Black life—even if, as Moses puts it, they are "no places."

One of the worst no-places in the novel is the material embodiment of the official welfare state. Moses and Galahad describe a visit to a welfare office to collect Galahad's insurance or unemployment card:

> It ain't have no place in the world that exactly like a place where a lot of men get together to look for work and draw money from the Welfare State while they ain't working. Is a kind of place where hate and disgust and avarice and malice and sympathy and sorrow and pity all mix up. Is a place where everyone is your enemy and your friend.[42]

Despite its status as a collective space, this welfare office offers no connection, hospitality, or security, underscoring the existential loneliness and alienation of the "Welfare State" itself. In response, *The Lonely Londoners* seeks proxies for welfarism: places that offer alternative forms of caretaking and collectivity. Along with its portraits of individual characters, the novel offers sketches of different domestic spaces. Through experiments in hospitality and living together, it tests the degree to which London is truly the place for them.

Of course, domestic space is not always welcoming. The most private of places in the novel are apartments and homes that do not belong to any of the main characters: spaces associated with white women and the promise of sex. For a novel obsessed with place-feeling, it is telling how Selvon depicts these private interiors as inaccessible, dangerous, even prohibitive. While Black characters are afforded a glimpse within these chambers, they remain at their thresholds, eventually and forcefully thrown out. One painfully clear example of this happens to a character named Bart, whose white girlfriend tells him to "come home and meet the folks":

> The mother was friendly and she went in the kitchen to make tea, leaving Bart sitting down in the drawing room. He make himself comfortable and was just looking at a *Life* magazine when the girl father come in the room.
> "You!" the father shouted, pointing a finger at Bart, "you! What are you doing in my house? Get out! Get out this minute!"

---

[41] Selvon, *Lonely Londoners*, 28–29.
[42] Ibid., 45.

The old Bart start to stutter about he is a Latin-American but the girl father wouldn't give him chance. "Get out! Get out, I say!" The father want to throw Bart out the house, because he don't want no curly-hair children in the family.[43]

The father interprets Bart's presence as a threat to the nuclear family and its racial purity. What makes this confrontation even more injurious, however, is the hospitality that he receives before his is shown hostility. The opening sentences admit Bart to this domestic tableau, allowing him to experience the cozy specificities of kitchens, drawing-rooms, and even *Life* magazine before being ejected from the colder, more generalized spaces of the "room" and "house."

A similar moment takes place in the remarkable summer section (one long Molly Bloom-esque sentence, written in almost fugal form), detailing an encounter between a Jamaican and a white woman. The scene takes place "in Chelsea in a smart flat with all sorts of surrealistic painting on the walls and contemporary furniture in the G-plan," details only available to the Jamaican man once invited inside.[44] While each item on this string of signifiers depicts of an apartment on the cutting-edge of style, the reference to "the G-plan" bears further mention as a test case for the hospitality of modern design. A signature development of Midcentury Modern, the G-plan was a brand of non-suite furniture introduced by Gomme of High Wycombe in 1953, the year after the wartime Utility Furniture Scheme ended. After years of wartime rationing, demand for new furnishings was high, and the G-plan offered people affordable, flexible, and durable options for their modern home.[45] That Selvon mentions this brand by name shows a heightened attention to contemporary design, and suggests that the woman who owns the flat might be similarly forward-thinking. Yet this is not the case when it comes to her guest: "[I]n the heat of emotion she call the Jamaican a black bastard though she didn't mean it as an insult but as a compliment under the circumstances but the Jamaican fellar get vex and he stop and say why the hell you call me a black bastard and he thump the woman and went away."[46] This

---

[43] *Ibid.*, 65.
[44] *Ibid.*, 109.
[45] See MacDonald and Porter, *Putting on the Style*; also Judy Attfield, "Good Design by Law: Adapting Utility Furniture to Peacetime Production: Domestic Furniture in the Reconstruction Period 1946–56," in *Design and Cultural Politics in Postwar Britain: The Britain Can Make It Exhibition of 1946*, ed. Patrick Maguire and Jonathan Woodham (London and Washington: Leicester University Press, 1997), 105.
[46] Selvon, *Lonely Londoners*, 109.

domesticity is thus not a proxy for welfarism or mutual care: instead, it is a dead end.

A more complex instance of Selvon's writing of domestic space—and one of the more promising visions of living together in postwar Britain—is provided when the novel pans out to consider Harrow Road, a neighborhood shared by the traditionally British working class and the newer population of Black British immigrants. Though the passage describes the difference between these two demographics, it ultimately collapses the divide between them insofar as they occupy the same space: "Wherever in London that it have Working Class, there you will find a lot of spades."[47] Their common poverty creates "a kind of communal feeling with the Working Class and the spades, because when you poor things does level out, it don't have much up and down."[48] Though this might recall the opening of Muriel Spark's *Girls of Slender Means* ("all the nice people in England were poor"), Selvon's invocation of communal feeling is less ironic, as cohabitation carries with it a real possibility of social alliance. A different kind of postwar consensus emerges in the signs saying "Vote Labour" and "Down With The Tories" painted on the buildings' walls. While the current significance of these slogans is unreadable—do they signify hope, or failed promises?—their presence frames the passage in relation to the democratizing ethos of postwar politics.

Selvon's description of Harrow Road is also the novel's most expressly sociological moment, a miniature depiction of everyday life that evokes the nascent work of British Cultural Studies and its emphasis on culture as life as it is actually lived. As Jed Esty has noted, many of the 1950s colonial and early postcolonial writers converged with this new school of thought, "in the project of making England over into a minor culture susceptible to romantic discourses of local color and to realist protocols of ethnography."[49] In some regards, Selvon's thick description of Harrow Road characterizes it as part of the "old Brit'n" and its establishments (shops, park benches, bus queues, fish and chips shops, pubs) refracted through the "old geezers" who "who does be pottering about the Harrow Road like if they lost, a look in their eye as if the war happen unexpected and they still can't realise what happen to the old Brit'n."[50] Yet the advent of multicultural Britain also means change. Grocers sell foodstuffs like saltfish and rice, and tailors cater to

---

[47] Ibid., 73.
[48] Ibid., 75.
[49] Esty, *Shrinking Island*, 165. A key example of this reverse ethnography is, of course, E.P. Thompson's *The Making of the English Working Class* (1963).
[50] Selvon, *Lonely Londoners*, 75.

West Indian culture: "All over London have places like that now."⁵¹ While this consumerist citizenship is far from idealized, it nevertheless registers a changing urban landscape, transformed through what Michel de Certeau calls the tactics of everyday life, or the "making do" or *bricolage* of rendering a space habitable.⁵² Notably, this change is catalyzed by Tolroy's aunt, Tanty, who bends the space to suit her needs: "Like how some people live in a small village and never go to the city, so Tanty settle down in the Harrow Road Working Class area."⁵³ Tanty's role anticipates Selvon's *The Housing Lark*, whose female characters' practicality and desire finally result in the purchase of the house.

Selvon's description of Harrow Road ultimately underscores its uninhabitability. Taking a broad view, the narrative describes the deteriorating condition of the neighborhood, with "the houses around here old and grey and weatherbeaten, the walls cracking like the last days of Pompeii."⁵⁴ The neighborhood lacks basic utilities such as electricity and gas, as well as urban services such as regular street cleaning or open parks. Descriptions give an overall sense of dank and dirt, a world closing in on itself due to overcrowding and neglect. This is precisely the urban conditions protested against in literatures of reconstruction, slums that needed to be completely overhauled in order to restore space, light, and health to postwar Britain. Yet as *The Lonely Londoners* powerfully evokes, this world did not disappear with the advent of the postwar; instead, this working-class London was inherited by Britain's former colonial subjects. As with Stella Rodney's train ride in Elizabeth Bowen's *The Heat of the Day*, during which she stares disbelievingly into working-class family homes, the division between the haves and have-nots is seemingly insurmountable on the basis of place. Whereas Bowen's gaze damns the working class, Selvon's damns the upper classes: "Them rich people who does live in Belgravia and Knightsbridge and up in Hampstead and them other plush places, they would never believe what it like in grim place like Harrow Road or Notting Hill."⁵⁵

Selvon emphasizes these class divisions in yet another return to the modernist scene that looks through the window:

Up in that fully furnished flat where the window open (rent bout ten or fifteen guineas, Lord) it must be have some woman that sleep late after

---

⁵¹ Ibid., 77.
⁵² Michel de Certeau, *The Practice of Everyday Life*, trans. Steven Rendell (Berkeley and Los Angeles: University of California Press, 1988), 29.
⁵³ Selvon, *Lonely Londoners*, 80.
⁵⁴ Ibid., 73.
⁵⁵ Ibid., 74.

a night at the Savoy or Dorchester, and she was laying under the warm quilt on the Simmons mattress, and she hear the test singing. No song or rhythm, just a sort of musical noise so nobody could say that he begging. And she must be just get up and throw a tanner out the window. Could be she had a nice night and she in a good mood, or could be, after the night's sleep, she thinking about life and the sound of that voice quavering in the cold outside touch the old heart. But if she have a thought at all, it never go further than to cause the window to open and the tanner to fall down.[56]

This moment builds on earlier descriptions of domesticity as private, feminized space, complete with indicative details such as the flat's furnishings and modern mattress brand. The window scene also serves as a narrative sympathy test, predicated on and dramatized by the total division between inside and outside. As in other window scenes, the threshold offers a test of radical social connection, either by the enchantment of the privileged insider, or by the disenchantment of the excluded outsider. Selvon's version, however, refuses connection. While the woman may be touched enough to throw a coin out the window, the thought stops there, nothing more than a financial transaction. This divide is further emphasized by the labor of imagining the other, which falls largely on the man outside, the narrator, and the collective "you" of immigrants and the working class. The "must be's" and "could be's" conjecture a portrait of interior life, but one that, like others before it, is only available to the inhabitant and not the visitor.

Selvon's answer to what makes a habitable, hospitable home for the lonely Londoners finally appears in the depiction of the Sunday gatherings in Moses's basement apartment. These get-togethers solidify Moses's status as a proxy welfare officer, exceeding the offers of the welfare state in a rare instance of shelter and sociality. Moses's apartment offers a communal gathering-point: "Nearly every Sunday morning, like if they going to church, the boys liming in Moses room, coming together for a oldtalk, to find out the latest gen, what happening, when is the next fete."[57] His room collects disparate characters into one domestic and narrative space while framing their interactions and conversation. The pieces are held together by a distinct center of gravity, creating a social unit that, despite the odds, seems to be self-sustaining. And it is not just Moses holding these people together; they also sustain him, keeping him from leaving London for Trinidad.

---

[56] *Ibid.*, 75.
[57] Selvon, *Lonely Londoners*, 138.

The value of Moses's apartment is presaged earlier in the novel, through comparison to a now-closed hostel that held earlier Windrush arrivals:

> When Moses did arrive fresh in London, he look around for a place where he wouldn't have to spend much money, where he could get plenty of food, and where he could meet the boys and coast a old talk to pass the time away—for this city powerfully lonely when you on your own.
>
> It had such a place, a hostel, and you could say that in a way most of the boys graduate from there before they branch off on their own and begin to live in London. This place had some genuine fellas who really studying profession, but it also had fellas who was only marking time and waiting to see what tomorrow would bring.[58]

This hostel had prewar historical progenitors in the YMCA Indian Students' Union and Hostel, founded in 1920; the West African Students' Union (WASU) House, from 1933; and Aggrey House, from 1934, which was controversially funded by the Colonial Office. These spaces were hugely influential in facilitating political, intellectual, and social interactions in the imperial city, and were themselves highly symbolic as colonial organizations. Marc Matera, for instance, characterizes the WASU hostel as the union's "most consistent argument for self-government and colonial reform."[59] Matera and others have studied the divisive ideological dispute over Aggrey House's ties to the Colonial Office, which was scathingly rebuked by WASU's journal *Wasu* and co-founder Ladipo Solanke. Nonetheless, *The Lonely Londoners* continues to invest the hostel—or Moses's version of it—with transformative possibility. This utopian space becomes even more domestic, swapping the burden-of-proof of self-government for the language of conviviality and hospitality, testing out the postwar promises of making Britain home.

Yet what is still unresolved—and what Selvon's later novels keep returning to—is whether a similar vision can be achieved on a private level, one that would facilitate a positive sense of domestic camaraderie rather than this metropolitan anomie. Continuing the saga in *Moses Ascending* (1975) and to a lesser degree, *Moses Migrating* (1983), Selvon continues to figure home ownership as the ultimate sign of immigrant staying-power, one that eludes his characters' grasp. *Moses Ascending* literalizes Moses's upward mobility

---

[58] Ibid., 47.
[59] Matera, *Black London*, 55. See also Daniel Whittall, "Creating Black Places in Imperial London: The League of Coloured Peoples and Aggrey House, 1931–1943," *The London Journal* 36:3 (November 2011), 225–246.

by detailing his shift from "worm's eye view to bird's eye," as he moves from renting a basement apartment to living in the penthouse of his very own building.[60] He also gains his very own Man Friday in Bob, a working-class Northerner who does odd jobs around the place. As the novel progresses, Moses learns his status as landlord grants him only so much power. He finds himself unwillingly renting to a series of unsavory characters, whether the Pakistani immigrants who sacrifice sheep in the backyard and use the building as a halfway house for illegal immigrants, or more vexedly, the Black Power Movement, with whom Moses has trouble associating. The politics of community thus shift in this novel, registered by increasingly entrenched identity and racial criminalization. While Moses's private apartment was a space of informal recuperative community in *The Lonely Londoners*, *Moses Ascending* makes new demands on inhabitation: making it more politicized, riskier, and to Selvon, less rewarding. This is borne out by the trilogy's final installation, *Moses Migrating*, which sees Moses fallen from grace, having ceded his penthouse to Bob and retreated back to the basement apartment. Having finally divested from the project of making London, Moses returns to Trinidad.

These novels register the increasing hostility toward colonial immigrants of their time. Under the 1962 Commonwealth Immigrants Act, a new era of immigration politics restricted rights of entry into the United Kingdom and made provisions for deportation. The Act was followed by a 1965 government White Paper *Immigration from the Commonwealth*, which reduced employment vouchers, made more stringent rules for admitting dependents, and attached "landing conditions" to those entering.[61] In the same year, Parliament passed a Race Relations Act—the first of its kind in the UK—making racial discrimination a civil offense in "places of public resort," though this did not apply in matters of housing or employment until the 1968 Race Relations Act. Yet immigration discrimination continued with restrictions that reinforced what Kathleen Paul calls "separate spheres of nationality," including the 1968 Commonwealth Immigrants Act under Harold Wilson's Labour government (addressing, in large part, fears of an influx of Kenyan Asians), as well as the 1971 Immigration Act under Edward Heath's Conservative government (which introduced the regulatory concept of "right of abode"). As Paul puts it, this latter act distinguished between the "familial" and "political" communities of Britishness, or descendants of the

---

[60] Selvon, *Moses Ascending*, 4.
[61] See Paul, *Whitewashing Britain*, 174–175.

UNHOMELY EMPIRE: HOSPITALITY IN WINDRUSH BRITAIN 125

"truly British" (i.e., white colonizers) and those acquired through imperial conquest (i.e., all others).[62] Fears over immigration found a front man in Conservative MP Enoch Powell. In his 1968 "Rivers of blood" speech, Powell projected a national future overrun by the descendants of immigrant families, while his 1970 "The enemy within" speech figured the nation as in the midst of a racial "Battle of Britain":

> Race is billed to play a major, perhaps a decisive, part in the battle of Britain, whose enemies must have been unable to believe their good fortune as they watched the numbers of West Indians, Africans and Asians concentrated in her major cities mount toward the two million mark, and no diminution of the increase yet in sight.[63]

For Powell, immigrants replayed the invasion Britain had anticipated but never endured amidst the Blitz.

This legislative era saw a new era of identity politics that included the adoption of "Black" as a political signifier encompassing Caribbean, African, and South Asian communities. Though this category would metamorphose over time, especially by the mid-1980s, it emerged at a specific historical moment, described by James Procter as "demarcating a united front against what was becoming an increasingly explicit racialized white national community in the late 1960s," and in relation to the global Black Power Movement.[64] Official attempts to reinscribe Britain's multiracial, imperial legacies into the landscape of postwar Britain included the symbolic rebuilding of the Commonwealth Institute from 1957 to 1962, whose modern architecture was meant to counter its legacy as the Imperial Institute, as well as the 1965 Commonwealth Arts Festival.[65] Though the 1958 Notting Hill

---

[62] Ibid., 181. See also Chapter 5 of Nadine Attewell's *Better Britons: Reproduction, National Identity, and the Afterlife of Empire* (Toronto: University of Toronto Press, 2014), which examines changes to Britain's postwar immigration laws in light of what she calls Britain's "fantasy of demographic collapse," brought on by postimperial decline (171).

[63] Enoch Powell, "The Enemy Within," speech during 1970 general election campaign, Birmingham, June 13, 1970.

[64] See *Writing Black Britain*, 5.

[65] Contrast Ruth Craggs's more optimistic reading of the Institute's goal of modernization (and its role of adding "another layer to the museum landscape"), namely by making the Commonwealth visible. "The Commonweath Institute and the Commonwealth Arts Festival: Architecture, Performance, and Multiculturalism in Late Imperial London," *The London Journal* 36.3 (2011), 257. See also Mark Crinson's "Imperial Storylands: Architecture and Display at the Imperial and Commonwealth Institutes," which reads its new architecture as mere repetition or worse, disempowerment, "emphasize(d) through the persistent redundancy of its panoptic gestures." "Imperial Storylands," *Art History* 22.1 (March 1999), 120.

race contributed to the passage of the 1962 Commonwealth Immigrants Act, their violence also inspired social protest from below, and contributed to the formation of the 1959 Caribbean Carnival under the hand of Trinidadian political activist Claudia Jones, a cultural event whose legacy continues in the annual Notting Hill Carnival.

Selvon's later work addresses the empowering yet also fraught possibilities of identity politics in ways that the 1956 *The Lonely Londoners* could only anticipate. The Moses trilogy thus offers an important index of the changing language of political identity. Unlike *Moses Ascending* or *Moses Migrating*, the loneliness of *The Lonely Londoners* is not articulated in relation to race-based identity of the 1960s and 1970s. That novel's struggle for social belonging is instead located in claims and desires for hospitality, whether in the public spaces of the city or the private spaces of the home. As the trilogy continues, its protagonist remains still attached to these residual imagined forms of social belonging, unable to fully adapt to emergent identity politics that would characterize later decades.

Selvon's lesser-known 1965 novel *The Housing Lark* offers an important development of this dream of hospitality deferred. The novel follows a group of men and women who want to buy a house "instead of paying all that wicked rent."[66] In certain ways, *The Housing Lark* reads much like *The Lonely Londoners*, in terms of its vernacular, character sketches, and interest in the small group dynamic. It also forestalls the more cynical reading of landlordism and property in *Moses Ascending* by imagining the freedom and camaraderie of collective ownership—a permanent iteration of Moses's basement apartment in *The Lonely Londoners*. Its sense of collectivity also vacillates between the informal basement socializing and formalized identity politics. Instead, *The Housing Lark* is suspended *in potentia* both socially and in terms of domestic space, and as such, offers a clearer portrait of an alternative welfarist living-situation than those represented in the Moses trilogy.

From its opening lines, it is evident that *The Housing Lark* tests the reparative potential of interior space. It begins in a basement room in Brixton, with a character named Bat fantasizing about upward mobility as he contemplates the genie design of his wallpaper:

> But is no use dreaming. Is no use lying down there on your backside and watching the wallpaper, as if you expect the wall to crack open and

[66] Selvon, *The Housing Lark* (Washington, DC: Three Continents Press, 1990), 20.

money come pouring out, a nice woman, a house to live in, food, cigarettes, rum. And sometimes in this fantasy he used to rub the wall, remembering Aladdin in the wonderful lamp, just to see if a geni would come and ask him: "What you want, just tell me what you want, no matter what it is, I could get for you."

The irony of it was that the wallpaper really had a design with lamps on it, Aladdin lamps all over the room. It may be that the company know they could only get dreamers to live in a dilapidated room like that, and they put up this wallpaper to keep the fires of hope burning.[67]

Rich in symbolism, the wallpaper becomes a running leitmotif for the novel, which itself alternates between idealism and gritty realism about the characters' everyday lives. In a departure from Selvon's typically male fictional worlds, it is the female characters who actualize the housing "lark," making decisions, collecting money, and moving from a dream world into reality. In one particularly memorable episode, the character Teena lambasts the group in a dramatic monologue, lecturing: "You all can't even get serious about a thing like housing. You know the distresses we have to go through, you know the arse black people see to get a roof over their heads in this country, and yet, the way you behave is as if you haven't a worry in the world. [...] That is what you come to Brit'n to do?"[68]

In this light, house-buying is figured as a racialized political act, one that helps consolidate an expressly Black West Indian identity in the face of British anti-Black racism. Yet Selvon is unwilling to fully cede the meaning of home to that of identity politics, maintaining a certain skepticism about the forms of community that might result from racial activism and group identification. This feeling is realized in the calypsonian Harry Banjo, who rises to fame with a ballad about "the loyalty and bonds of friendship that exist among the coloured members of the community."[69] The gimmick sells not only to the white English public, but also to West Indians, who "rise in support," offering reporters "some tall tales about how Harry do good in the neighbourhood."[70] While Harry and others may have subscribed to these emerging identity politics—whether in earnest or for show—the novel ends on a note of ambivalence, denoted through the fantasy of the old genie

---

[67] Ibid., 7–8.
[68] Ibid., 145.
[69] Ibid., 152.
[70] Ibid., 152–153.

wallpaper. Returning to the old house, Bat gently tears off a piece of the Aladdin wallpaper, pocketing it to show his future housemates.

> "You don't want no stupid paper like that, man," Harry say. "We got to have contemporary designs."
> But Bat only smile and look around at the walls. You could see as if he wishing he could strip the lot and carry it go in the new house.[71]

With these final lines, Windrush's dreams of postwar migration have become newly historical. That earlier, more hopeful sensibility, conditioned and occasioned by wartime promises of hospitality, is no longer viable in this new contemporary moment. And yet, Selvon suggests, we cannot help but take a final glance at that promise, in an almost nostalgic way, wishing that we could carry it forward into the present moment. In this bittersweet ending, Selvon provides a moving valediction to the decolonizing and antiracist potential of postwar reconstruction, which animated *The Lonely Londoners* and is finally foreclosed in *The Housing Lark*. Taken together, Selvon's novels make the case for maintaining the fantasies of postwar, postimperial inhabitation—even if they were conditioned by naivete and racist structures of power, and even when they become superseded or disenchanted.

Reconstructing Windrush

This book follows the ways the postwar informs, even dictates, the contours of the contemporary. As we move away from the immediate moment of the Windrush generation, it is worth examining the way its legacy has been written and maintained, if only to ask whether the specific nexus of welfare and hospitality continues to shape the way artists, intellectuals, and the wider public think about this historical moment. Following Stuart Hall, this cultural history might also carry the name of "reconstruction," as suggested by Hall's 1984 article "Reconstruction Work," which addressed the role of collecting and preserving Windrush archival materials in shaping historical memory. Building on the recent 1981 establishment of the Black Cultural Archives in London, Hall's essay examines a range of photographs, including documentary-style images of arrival, pictures embedded in articles such as Hilde Marchant's "Thirty Thousand Colour Problems" (*Picture*

---

[71] Ibid., 154–155.

Post, June 9, 1956), and portraits from the Dyche studio, which produced formal, in-studio images of immigrants to Birmingham from the 1950s to the 1970s. But how exactly are we to read these images and reconstruct a history from them? As a pioneer of reception theory, Hall was interested in examining the ways these photographs had been produced, circulated, and received, and what they might signify in his contemporary moment. In particular, he was taken by the way they projected innocence and hope: "Why do they look so respectable? Where are the street fighters, the rude boys, the Rastas, the reggae? How are we to read what these photographs most powerfully construct: a certain form of *innocence*?"[72] Mindful of the historical, discursive ways Blackness is rendered as primitive, "not yet quite up with the fast ways of the advanced world," his article reiterates the difficult material and psychic facts of migration: the journey, cost, uncertainty, and determination needed to survive.[73] In doing so, he re-imbues a sense of personhood to these images, which are too often read as either passive objects, subject to impersonal flows of history, or as the *Picture Post* tagline suggests, "colour problems." And for Hall, returning to these images meant seeing "how persistently in these early days there was constructed, at the centre of the problem—the problem of the problem, so to speak—the core issue: *miscegenation*": an issue that, from the Nottingham race riots to *The Lonely Londoners*, was often the cause of hospitality turning into hostility.[74]

While the risks of reading these photographs as merely hopeful, innocent, or naïve are serious indeed, especially in their tendency to simplify and objectify their subjects, they nevertheless index an expectation or desire to make Britain home. Reconstructing the history of Windrush from these images means attending to the promises of postwar reconstruction itself. Hall himself seems attuned to this, not only in his choice of title ("Reconstruction Work"), but also in his reading of the iconic image of a man, suitcases in hand, staring at a sign that reads "Rooms to Let: No Coloured Men" (Figure 12).

While Hall describes this as "now over-typical and over-typified," "stop[ping] short before the deeper realities of *Racism*," the fact of its documentation nevertheless mattered a good deal to the collective consciousness: "If it had been left unsaid, the Black politics of resistance of a later period would have had only an empty, unspoken void to build on."[75] I would

[72] Hall, "Reconstruction Work," *Ten.8* 16 (1984), 4.
[73] *Ibid.*
[74] *Ibid.*, 9.
[75] *Ibid.*, 8.

Figure 12 *Racial Prejudice* (1958).
© Keystone Features. Reproduced courtesy of Getty Images.

add that it is no mere chance that Hall reads this image in particular as expressly political. It captures precisely the nexus of hospitality and hostility that Selvon attaches to the work of the welfare state and its promise of care, and serves as an immediate, if overdetermined signifier of the racial discrimination against Windrush immigrants.

The legacy of the Windrush generation has also had a clear influence contemporary literary production. As one example, Andrea Levy's *Small Island* (2004) follows four characters who navigate the Windrush moment, the plot alternating between the landmark year 1948 and sections titled, simply, "Before." The book has enjoyed considerable success: it won three prestigious prizes and was adapted as a BBC miniseries and National Theatre stage production. It garnered praise from critics including Stuart Hall as "a story of the integration of Black West Indians into domestic, feminine England, in a way that the earlier generation of writers, the Selvons and Lammings, were never able to imagine."[76] Notably, the National Theatre production, adapted by British playwright Helen Edmundson and directed by Rufus Norris, makes strategic use of archival Windrush photography and footage from the British Film Institute and British Pathé to create a sense of historical time. Its most powerful photographic citation appears at the conclusion of Act I, as Gilbert boards the *Empire Windrush* and leaves his new wife, Hortense, behind. The static image of the boat and its passengers is projected onto a backdrop, while the shadowy outlines of cast members move across and finally disappear into the photograph, as if boarding the actual ship.[77]

Despite *Small Island*'s historical focus, I suggest Zadie Smith's *NW* enjoys an even closer kinship with the concerns of Selvon's works than Levy's Windrush novel. While *Small Island* offers a relatively straightforward temporal engagement with this historical moment, sticking within the boundaries of the postwar period, *NW* carries Selvon's preoccupations into the contemporary moment, when the dream of private property has been supplanted by a housing project of five tower blocks. In particular, *NW* presents a new version of the ambivalent look backward at the end of *The Housing Lark*, carrying forward the midcentury's legacy of collective living as a potentially reparative force. Smith recapitulates Selvon's modernist tendencies stylistically well. *NW* occupies a belated position that productively destabilizes the literary traditions of both modernism and postwar Black British writing, revealing the seams of both. *NW* is clearly a modernist novel, an homage to Joyce in the same way that *On Beauty* refers back to Forster, and *White Teeth*, albeit to a lesser extent, to Rushdie. Its ambitious, experimental style has encountered some critical ambivalence. Yet the social world of *NW* presents

---

[76] Hall, "Caribbean Migration: The Windrush Generation," *Familiar Stranger: A Life Between Two Islands* (Durham and London: Duke University Press, 2017), 177–178. Hall continues: "Levy's is also a tale steeped in ambiguity, in which the metropolitan consequences of race remain dramatically uncertain. Promise and defeat are intertwined. In the same conjuncture, contrary, dissimilar and unresolved histories coexist" (178).

[77] The play's citation of this image is actually a mis-citation, as it depicts the ship's arrival at London's Tilbury Dock rather than its departure from the West Indies, as is suggested at this moment in the play.

132   STATES OF REPAIR

an even greater challenge than its stylistic pyrotechnics.[78] Much like Levy's *Small Island*, *NW* follows the lives of four individuals who grow up together in the same north-west London council estate. Unlike *Small Island*'s closed narrative system composed of four individuals and rooted in the events of 1948, *NW* is a more open world that accepts the ways in which chance structures lives. In this way, it echoes and resembles the episodic, metropolitan form of *The Lonely Londoners*.

Such a narrative structure draws on the potential of the modernist epiphany, which relies on the perversity of desire and the fortuitous, impulsive nature of interpersonal connection. The novel's form of sociality invests in the redeeming potential of individual connection that Selvon also tested and ultimately dismissed. We might read Smith's modernism as a recuperative one, one that reinvests in individuality as a meaningful substrate for social connection. This is not to say, however, that *NW* is purely optimistic, seeking to restore the world to some irreconcilable plenitude. Its Londoners are still lonely and alienated as ever, struggling for social and economic upward mobility in a world still shot through with racist micro— and macro-aggressions. Despite her privileging of individual connection, in Smith's Northwest London, chance encounters and intimacies as often lead to violent conflict as they do to moments of social cohesion.

Though Smith's novel is interested in the mechanics of connection, it is even more enthralled by the potential of hospitality. In other words, while Smith excels at dramatizing interpersonal, one-on-one interactions, the net effect of these episodes is to explore how individual acts of generosity can create—or fail to create—a sense of the commons in this corner of Northwest London. The novel's opening section, entitled "visitation," begins with one of the main characters, Leah, admitting Shar, a stranger seeking money, into her apartment. Their interaction swiftly transforms from one between supplicant and host ("the good stranger who opened the door and did not close it again"), to recognizing each other as fellow classmates with a shared history ("I know you. You went Brayton!").[79] The narrative frames them as something like old friends, though such generous interpretation fades with Shar's departure: "Already the grandeur of experience threatens to flatten into the conventional, into anecdote: only thirty pounds, only an ill

---

[78] In this, I agree with David James's reading of *NW* as an invigorating next step for Smith's literary *oeuvre*, characterized by a purposively depersonalized narrative style that allows the world to be messier, rawer, and more uncompromising than *On Beauty* or *White Teeth*. "Wounded Realism," *Contemporary Literature* 54.1 (2013), 210.

[79] Zadie Smith, *NW* (London: Penguin Group, 2012), 6.

mother, neither a murder, nor a rape. Nothing survives its telling."[80] Still, the experience has been recorded in *NW* with all its awkwardness and luminosity. As the threshold of the novel, this section's key terms of hospitality and hostility continue to inform the work's overall architecture, with subsequent sections that follow entitled "guest," "host," and "crossing," and once more, "visitation." Both characters and reader are tested over the course of the book to see whether they can learn to be more hospitable: whether a second visitation might repair the mistakes of the first.

In emphasizing the collective rather than the individual, Smith's modernism is even more closely connected to Selvon's *The Lonely Londoners* than that of Joyce, Woolf, or Forster. Like Selvon, Smith examines the ways people form community to offset social loneliness, a condition that often falls along raced, gendered, and classed lines. Echoing *The Lonely Londoners*, *NW* asks whether hospitality might be the necessary supplement to the work of the postwar welfare state. Though both evince an allergy to relying on government intervention, whether the unemployment lines of *The Lonely Londoners* or Leah's husband Michel's rant against his taxes' misuse, they are not arguments against the state or a welfare ethos per se. Both believe in the reparative potential of collective living, whether the Sunday gatherings in Moses's basement apartment or the neighborly world of *NW*'s council housing. Still, both show that the work of hospitality falls on the inhabitants themselves, a labor that is not always gratefully or gracefully undertaken.

Selvon's legacy in *NW* is most strongly felt, however, through Smith's references to 1960s and 1970s London, above all to the fictional photojournalist work *GARVEY HOUSE: A Photographic Portrait*. As Smith's Acknowledgments section suggests, this fictional work echoes photographer Colin Jones's series *The Black House* (1973–1976), which documented the hostel, Harambee, a site of collective living much like those described in *The Lonely Londoners* and *The Housing Lark*.[81] *NW*'s version is a glossy, expensive volume, describing itself as "a photographic account of a fascinating period in London's history." The book's self-presentation is read to us by the character Felix: "A mix of squat, halfway house and commune, Garvey House welcomed vulnerable young adults from the edges of…"[82] At this point, the description is interrupted. Felix's father, Lloyd, himself one of

---

[80] Ibid., 13.
[81] See Colin Jones, *The Black House* (Prestel Pub, 2006). Jones's photographs were originally commissioned for "On the Edge of the Ghetto," a *Sunday Times* article by Peter Gillman, and then shown at the Photographers' Gallery in 1977.
[82] Smith, *NW*, 92.

the "vulnerable young adults" referenced in the hardcover album, dismisses the description, saying, "Don't read me shit I already know. I don't need the man dem telling me what I already know. Who was there, me or he?"[83]

In a way, GARVEY HOUSE is NW in miniature. Both return to a council estate to provide insight into its everyday life, and by doing so, give a rich account of what it means to live together. Even for NW, a novel shot through with the materiality of local history, this album is an exceptional artifact. Unlike the long-forgotten churchyard graves, literary history of Hampstead, or tower blocks' philosophical names (Hobbes, Bentham, Locke, Russell), GARVEY HOUSE offers a direct encounter with history, a glimpse that promises a revelation about the characters' back stories. Yet as Stuart Hall's "Reconstruction Work" reminds us, there is no such unmediated reading. As Felix examines the images of his inherited past, "He could not be sure if he had a memory of this, or whether the photograph itself was creating the memory for him."[84] Still, it confirms something for him about this period of collective life and social organizing: "BLACK POWER sprayed in three-foot-high letters on the garden wall. Strange to see here, confirmed in black and white, what he had all his life assumed to be a self-serving exaggeration."[85]

Though the Garvey House episode is relatively short, its mode of encapsulating history returns at the end of the novel through another black and white photograph. This time, however, the photograph depicts the contemporary aftermath of Felix's murder:

> On a tatty sofa a Rastafarian gentleman sat holding a picture of his adult son. Beside the father sat a beautiful young woman, clutching the left hand of the father between her own. There was a depth of misery in both these faces that Natalie found she could not look at in any sustained way.[86]

Capturing Lloyd yet again in a domestic setting, the photograph is an eerie repetition of the project of GARVEY HOUSE. Smith's description here recalls the album's exposition, reminding us that, in a different time, it too could have been included as evidence in the photography album. But rather than have a character cut off the description, Smith critically opens up the viewing of the image, both through the photograph's tagline of "ALBERT ROAD

---

[83] Selvon, *Housing Lark*, 93.
[84] Smith, *NW*, 93.
[85] Ibid.
[86] Ibid., 288.

SLAYING. FAMILY PLEA FOR WITNESSES," and through its refraction through the novel's third main character, Natalie née Keisha Blake.[87] Their interplay calls attention to what it means to bear witness: both a looking and a looking away, connection and disconnection. Although Natalie looks away, this intimate scene charges us to see—or rather, imagine—what this character could not. Situated in the final "visitation" section, the plea for witness also carries the charge of hospitality. In a reversal of the novel's opening scene, however, it is not a stranger who rings the doorbell, but rather a domestic scene that opens up and appeals to the stranger. And the reader, too: at the novel's end, we are reminded that we are reading a form that encourages its readers to keep looking in a sustained way, and to find a space for its descriptions over the threshold of our own lives.

[87] *Ibid.*, 287.

Interlude

Failed Utopias, or, the Beginning of the End

This Interlude describes a crucial inflection point in British welfare state history and its cultural representations: the transition from welfare's "classic phase" of 1945–1975 to its neoliberal restructuring and residualization. Though Britain's welfare state was never completely dismantled, it underwent serious reform beginning with the Conservative premiership of Margaret Thatcher. This deconstruction relied on shifting the perception, even social imagination, of the welfare state, which as Thatcher described, "encouraged illegitimacy, facilitated the breakdown of families, and replaced incentives favouring work and self-reliance with perverse encouragement for idleness and cheating."[1] This "swing to the Right" was no mere repetition of earlier conservative ideologies, nor could it be seen solely in economic terms.[2] Indeed, as Stuart Hall put it, what was most remarkable about Thatcherism was its "translation of a theoretical *ideology* into a populist *idiom*," its moralism of "social market values" offering a powerful alternative to the welfarist philosophy of the "caring society."[3] This idiom proved durable and flexible, its values including law and order, anti-collectivism, anti-statism, self-reliance, respect for authority, and fear of national dilution by Blacks and immigrants. Undermining the social democratic ethos of postwar consensus, it offered a new consensus built on neoliberal terms—one that cast a lasting shadow not only on future politics but also on British cultural production.

---

[1] Margaret Thatcher, *The Downing Street Years* (New York: HarperCollins, 1993), 8. Thatcher attributes these ills to welfare's current practice of disseminating benefits "with little to no consideration of their effects on behaviour" (8).

[2] Stuart Hall suggests the seeds of Thatcherism emerged in response to the social movements of the 1960s, and as a form of "authoritarian populism," drew on already existing practices and ideologies. Hall, *The Hard Road to Renewal: Thatcherism and the Crisis of the Left* (London: Verso, 1988), 39–56.

[3] Ibid., 47.

For the narrative of this book, the welfare state's shift "from the cradle to the grave" shapes the project's organization into two parts. Part I addressed what we might call the "early" postwar moment of 1945 to the mid-1970s, or the classic phase of welfare state expansion. In these years, cultural and political fears were mainly concentrated on the transformation of the private into the public, including the sweeping nationalization of industries and infrastructure, the development of state-built housing, and, more broadly, the opening of previously elite realms (education, media, cultural production) to wider demographics (in terms of class, race, nationality, gender, and age). Moving forward, Part II addresses the "late" postwar period, which saw systematic challenges to the state postwar consensus built. Inverting earlier postwar transformations, the public was privatized, and the liberal state become increasingly neoliberal.[4] If, as this book has suggested, representations of living together can be taken as indices for Britain's dreams for postwar society, the severity of this political shift is exemplified by comparing statements from Prime Ministers Clement Attlee and Thatcher, the two figureheads of these "early" and "late" postwar periods. Many will recall Thatcher's line "there's no such thing as society," taken from a 1987 interview in *Women's Own* magazine, which has been taken as shorthand for her brand of individualism, neoliberalism, and rejection of older welfarist principles. In context, we can see what Thatcher envisioned instead of "society": a world where individuals and their families took primacy over one's neighbor.

> [T]hey are casting their problems on society and who is society? There is no such thing! There are individual men and women and there are families and no government can do anything except through people and people look to themselves first. It's our duty to look after ourselves and then also to look after our neighbour...[5]

Less known, but no less instructive, is Attlee's speech at the opening of West India House, the first London housing estate to be completed after the war

---

[4] These changes are what led to Gøsta Esping-Andersen to associate Britain as a "liberal, residualist" welfare state akin to the USA and Canada, rather the "social democratic" forms of welfare states as found in Sweden, Denmark, and Norway. *The Three Worlds of Welfare Capitalism* (Princeton: Princeton University Press, 1990), 53. For a delineation between the "classic" and "new" welfare state (and their associated theories), see Paul Pierson's analysis of welfare state retrenchment and its departure from the thirty years of welfare state expansion. "The New Politics of the Welfare State," *World Politics* 48, no. 2 (1996), 143–179.
[5] Thatcher, Interview for *Women's Own*, October 31, 1987, 29–30, https://www.margaretthatcher.org/document/106689.

in 1946, in which he expressed "hope that those who move into these new houses here are going to be happy; are going to be successful; are going to be good neighbours; and are going to be good citizens."[6] With this comment, Attlee invoked the new plurality brought together by public housing, echoing reconstruction's belief that housing would facilitate encounters, produce community, and ultimately, transform society for the better. Thatcher's contrasting priority of the individual and family unit over the neighbor thus signaled a key shift in what counted as the "social": a shift that is taken up in various ways by the authors addressed in the following chapters.

This changing ethos was inaugurated and enduringly effected through Thatcher's attack on public housing. While Thatcher sought a restructuring of all welfare programs, her cuts to the housing budget represented as much as three-quarters of all planned cuts in the early 1980s, making housing "the leading edge of the Conservative government's attempts to reduce and remodel the welfare state in line with 'what the country can afford.'"[7] Moreover, Thatcher's controversial "Right to Buy" policy, enshrined in the 1980 Housing Act, allowed council tenants to purchase their home at a large discount, and then to keep the profit when they sold to private landlords, which many did.[8] This policy capitalized on housing's status as the "wobbly pillar" of the welfare state, as owner-occupation had always been part of Britain's mixed landscape of private and public housing.[9] Thatcher's policies sought to topple the pillar, moving housing decisively into the role of a commodity rather than the social service envisioned by postwar reconstruction. Housing's de-elevation presaged the reforms of other nationalized services: utilities, industries, and transport systems including British Gas, British Steel, British Telecom, and British Rail.[10]

---

[6] "Pathe Front Page—Stepney 1946," May 12, 1946, *British Pathé*, https://www.britishpathe.com/video/pathe-front-page-stepney.

[7] Peter Malpass, *Housing and the Welfare State: The Development of Housing Policy in Britain* (New York: Palgrave, 2005), 104.

[8] Though Thatcher reportedly needed to be talked into the policy, the policy featured heavily in the 1979 Conservative Manifesto, and she would later credit Right to Buy as helping her win the 1979 general election. Peter Malpass and Alan Murie, *Housing Policy and Practice*, 5th ed. (Houndsmills, Basingstoke, Hampshire and London: Macmillan Press Ltd, 1999), 81.

[9] Ulf Torgersen, "Housing: the Wobbly Pillar under the Welfare State," *Scandinavian Housing and Planning Research* Vol. 4 (1987), 116–126.

[10] Lynsey Hanley provides another metaphor of this domino effect, noting that "Right to Buy was the Trojan horse of privatization: it made the paring-back of the welfare state seem attractive and reasonable, a proposition which, in turn, made those who remained reliant on the state seem weak." *Estates: An Intimate History* (London: Granta, 2007), 295.

The impact of this paradigm shift on housing was tremendous. An estimated two million council houses were sold between 1980 and 1997, with another 250,000 dwellings shifting from local authorities to housing associations in England.[11] Yet these homes were not replenished: neither by local authorities, who could not reinvest their profits into rebuilding; nor by the state, whose investment in housing plummeted; nor by the market, which contrary to Conservative projections, did not self-regulate with private builders filling the vacuum of housing. As more desirable units were purchased and not replaced, housing became a "residual" public or welfare sector.[12] "Right to Buy" revealed and exacerbated the social inequalities and exclusions resulting from welfare residualization, especially affecting the elderly, unemployed, single-parent families (largely women), and minority ethnic groups.[13] In practice, the policy reinforced, even increased, social divisions: the very antithesis of postwar reconstruction's idealization of mixed housing and the social cohesion it was thought to inspire. As Lynsey Hanley describes, "Both poverty and difference became visible: it became a matter of whether you had double glazing or mass-produced council windows; whether your front door was made of strong oak or blue-painted council wood; whether you had brass house numbers or council plastic ones."[14]

One cultural metric of this changing landscape was the character "Loadsamoney," played by comedian Harry Enfield on Channel 4's "Saturday Night Live." As a Cockney plasterer benefiting from the booming private housing market, Loadsamoney lampooned the changing social and economic landscape of Thatcherite Britain, bragging about his "journey into money" and the consumerist lifestyle it enabled. Enfield's character reached peak popularity through his hit single, "Doin' Up the House," which reached #4 on the UK Top 40. In the song, Loadsamoney obscenely flaunts his "wad" around, a perverse conflation of body and cash echoed by his other catchphrase, "I've got piles...piles of money!" Affluence is enjoyed for its own sake, as Loadsamoney boasts: "Doin' up the house is my bread and butter / Me bird's page

---

[11] Malpass and Murie, *Housing Policy*, 79. That said, while "Right to Buy" signaled the decline of council housing, it did so unevenly, as council housing enjoyed varying degrees of support across Britain (especially in Scotland) and in local areas. See Alison Ravetz, *Council Housing and Culture: The History of a Social Experiment*, Planning, History, and the Environment Series (New York: Routledge, 2001).
[12] See, for instance, the telling statistic that public sector housing completions fell from 88,590 in 1980 to only 3218 by 1995. Malpass and Murie, *Housing Policy*, 91.
[13] Malpass, *Housing and the Welfare State* (New York: Bloomsbury, 2005), 163.
[14] Hanley, *Estates*, 295.

three and me car's a nutter / Loadsamoney is a shout I utter / As I wave my wad to the geezers in the gutter."[15] This brash greed became shorthand for Thatcher's monetary policies and the mentality they created. In one now-apocryphal moment, Labour MP Neil Kinnock charged the Conservative government as creating a "loadsamoney economy," to which Thatcher replied, presumably not understanding the reference, "Well, what's wrong with that?"[16]

Part II of this book attempts to answer this question, with each chapter registering the diminished legacy of postwar consensus, or Loadsamoney's "geezers in the gutter," along different lines. If the first three chapters were about youth, reflecting the early stages of postwar consensus and the naivete of its ideals, the last three chapters are about old age, symbolizing the etiolating welfare state. Character-wise, Part I's early postwar fiction was wary about the future belonging to the young, whether Elizabeth Bowen's hapless Roderick Rodney and Louie Lewis; Muriel Spark's ruthless girls of slender means; or Samuel Selvon's new migrants from the West Indies, who depended on the older Moses to facilitate their arrival. In comparison, the fictions in Part II model different character-systems, revolving around older figures who are the "last of their kind," who are in turn taken care of by younger characters. Hence Alan Hollinghurst's young Will Beckwith, whose biography of the elder Charles Nantwich is revealed as complex reparation for postwar violence against gay men in *The Swimming-Pool Library* (1988); the caretaking required in Michael Ondaatje's *The English Patient* (1992), whose titular character raises questions of what the colonized owe their colonizer; and even Kazuo Ishiguro's Kathy H., who holds on to older ideals of welfare institutions *Never Let Me Go* (2005) despite their care being so clearly, and so devastatingly, a sham. In their look backward to Britain's postwar period, the novels of Part II clearly foreground the labor of continued attachment to promised transformation, and find themselves negotiating the

---

[15] Harry Enfield, Lyrics to "Loadsamoney (Doin' Up the House)," London: Guerilla Studios, 1988, https://genius.com/Harry-enfield-loadsamoney-doin-up-the-house-lyrics.
[16] Lorraine Mcbride, "We Created Loadsamoney, Harry Enfield Cashed In," *The Daily Telegraph* (January 31, 2016), https://www.telegraph.co.uk/finance/personalfinance/fameandfortune/12127643/Charlie-Higson-We-created-Loadsamoney-Harry-Enfield-cashed-in.html. See also Neil Kinnock's 1988 Blackpool speech, in which he notes, "It is impossible to accept that there is no connection between the fracturing of our society and the grabbing 'loadsamoney' ethic encouraged by a government that treats care as 'drooling,' compassion as 'wet.' A government led by a Prime Minister who says that 'There is no such thing as society.'" Leader's speech, Blackpool, 1988, http://www.britishpoliticalspeech.org/speech-archive.htm?speech=194.

INTERLUDE: FAILED UTOPIAS   141

increasing distance between ideal and reality in ever fiercer, more desperate ways.

This distance is also signaled by Part II's turn to historical fiction, or works that directly engage with the historiography of Britain's move from wartime to postwar period. Moving into the 1970s and beyond, the referent of the "postwar" shifts in signification: it becomes an object of nostalgia and desire as well as a symbol of proven failure. This long durée has already been modeled in the codas to Chapters 2 and 3, which considered later twentieth-century novels that returned to and rewrote earlier postwar social movements (Windrush) or texts (*Girls of Slender Means*). In Part II, the works I describe take this look backward as an impetus for formal and generic innovation, one that opens up midcentury promises beyond their original social and geographical referents. This playfulness unites Hollinghurst's encryption of midcentury as the forgotten wound of the twentieth century; Ondaatje's experiment in healing European colonial violence with an international experiment in care; and finally, Ishiguro's insistence on the felt legacy of the Second World War even in speculative form. Contrary to literary periodization that names the mid-1970s as the end of "postwar" British literature and the beginning of the "contemporary," Part II makes the case that *all* literature after 1945 is "postwar," arguing that ever-finer slicings of the twentieth century are held together by long and unevenly articulated durée of the postwar.[17] Taken together, these chapters prove that the idea of welfare was never just the compensatory effect of a state's bad conscience during wartime. Instead, the dream of the welfare state proves amorphous and adaptable, especially when evoked in the name of new forms of care.

[17] This literary history is, of course, contested, with one term often taken to subsume the other. Some critics take the postwar as a moniker to describe everything from 1945 onward. Dominic Head, for instance, insistently uses the moniker "post-war" to describe novels published from 1950 to 2000 in his *Cambridge Introduction to Modern British Fiction, 1950–2000* (Cambridge: Cambridge University Press, 2002). Earlier, but no less instructive, is Alan Sinfield's *Literature, Politics and Culture in Postwar Britain*, whose literary-historical perspective only "became feasible in the mid-1980s, when most of the book was written, as the collapse of the postwar consensus exposed the vulnerability of many customary left-liberal assumptions, while opening the way for a broader critique of the cultural apparatus." (London and New York: Continuum Press, 1997, xx). Those who claim the particularity of the "contemporary" often date it from about the mid-1970s, as in Philip Tew's *The Contemporary British Novel* (New York: Continuum, 2004; 2nd ed. 2007) and *A Concise Companion to Contemporary British Fiction*, ed. James F. English (Oxford: Blackwell, 2006). The recent 1970s volume of Bloomsbury's *Decades Series*, ed. Nick Hubble, John McLeod, and Philip Tew, cements this periodization, beginning its history of contemporary British fiction in the 1970s (London: Bloomsbury Academic, 2017). For an explanation of the need to recover the 1970s, see Mark Williams's "Selective Traditions: Refreshing the Literary History of the Seventies" in the above volume.

The End of an Era: Public Housing and Postwar Sociality

The fictional living spaces described in the preceding chapters borrow from, but do not necessarily map onto specific design trends of postwar reconstruction. In this Interlude, however, I will focus on a specific housing style that emblematized the ethos of the British welfare state: the high-density council estate. In the early days of postwar consensus, construction followed the early twentieth-century "garden city" ideal, with about two-thirds of housing built between 1945 and 1951 consisting of single-family council homes spread out in suburban "New Towns."[18] By 1951, however, building could not keep up with demand due to the volume of war damage, practices of slum clearances, and the postwar baby boom. As a result, the garden city was displaced by what Matthew Taunton characterizes as "an all-consuming obsession with building as many dwellings as possible in the shortest possible time."[19] One particular answer to this situation was the multi-story, high-density estate, particularly the tower block or highrise, whose construction was aided by the 1956 Housing Subsidy Act which offered builders extra funding for every story built above the sixth floor. The style of these buildings was especially influenced by "New Brutalism," which shaped British council housing from the mid-1950s into the 1970s. In their early stages, these structures carried a decidedly utopian cast, with their modernity representing the best that had been thought and planned. Imagined as cities in the sky, they promised an unprecedented type of urban living, and carried with them perhaps the purest democratizing impulses of postwar reconstruction.

By the late 1960s and early 1970s, however, these concrete jungles were falling decidedly out of favor. The buildings themselves seemed to give proof of their failure: some, such as Trellick Tower, were vandalized as soon as construction stopped; others imploded from within, as in the 1968 Ronan Point disaster, when a twenty-two-floor East London block partially collapsed after a gas explosion. And in 1972, the modernist housing experiment seemed at a close, with Charles Jencks citing the demolition of the Pruitt-Igoe estate in St. Louis, MI, USA as the moment when architectural modernism died.[20] That year also marked the appearance

---

[18] See Miles Glendinning and Stefan Muthesius, eds, *Tower Block: Modern Public Housing in England, Scotland, Wales, and Northern Ireland* (New Haven: Yale University Press, 1993), 2.

[19] Matthew Taunton, *Fictions of the City: Class, Culture and Mass Housing in London and Paris* (London: Palgrave Macmillan, 2009), 143.

[20] Charles Jencks, *The Language of Post-Modern Architecture* (London: Academy Editions, 1977). While Jencks names many failures of architectural modernism, an important one for

of Oscar Newman's *Defensible Space*, which blamed modernist design for anti-social and criminal behaviors in US. public housing. These principles found UK adoption through geographer Alice Coleman, whose *Utopia on Trial* (1985) critiqued council estates and espoused a "responsibilization" through private ownership in line with Thatcher's housing polemic and policy changes.[21] Thus the longstanding belief of postwar reconstruction—that the built environment, particularly public housing, could foster community and "animate a richer form of associational life"—seemed to come to an inglorious end.[22] While brutalism has become somewhat fashionable again ("too late for the less well-off; just in time for the hipsters"), its structures are still lightning rods for public debate and political commentary, from Prince Charles's 1984 "monstrous carbuncle" speech in front of the Royal Institute of British Architects to the heated discourse around the June 2017 Grenfell Tower disaster.[23]

If the housing estate metonymizes both the utopian promise and the dystopian detritus of Britain's postwar reconstruction, what lessons can we learn from its literary representation? Scholars of literary modernism have demonstrated the complex relationship between modern architecture and modern literature, noting how architecture moved from a source of literary inspiration in the 1920s to threat by the 1930s, deemed a tool of communist politics. This perceived threat only increased with modern architecture's promotion during the Second World War as a style of postwar reconstruction, a fear seen expressed by Elizabeth Bowen in Chapter 1 of

---

this book project is its unresolvable conception of the home as both a Le Corbusian "machine for living in" as well a traditional sense of "place," a contradiction crystallized in the work of Alison and Peter Smithson. Additionally, and potentially more damning, the modern architect never lived up to his role as a social utopian, instead building for monopolies and big business, international exhibitions, factories, and consumer distractions.

[21] Jane M. Jacobs and Loretta Lees, "Defensible Space on the Move: Revisiting the Urban Geography of Alice Coleman," *International Journal of Urban and Regional Research* 37.5 (September 2013), 1569. Coleman would go on to serve as an advisor to the Department of the Environment, which with Thatcher's support, created the Design Improvement Controlled Experiment to implement Coleman's ideas in council housing.

[22] Sam Wetherall, *Foundations: How the Built Environment Made Twentieth-Century Britain* (Princeton: Princeton University Press, 2020), 95.

[23] See Owen Hopkins, *Lost Futures: The Disappearing Architecture of Post-War Britain* (London: Royal Academy of Arts, 2017), 10. See also James Meek's "Where Will We Live?": "As the decades pass and the council homes of the 1950s, 1960s, and 1970s grow into the urban landscape, as their brick and concrete weathers, as they benefit from comparison with the mean little boxes being built by private housebuilders, as a mix of new management, new investment, and funds from the last Labour government have dealt with some of the backlog of repairs and design flaws, as the original intentions of architects become unexpectedly visible to a new generation, they are beginning to look like more attractive places to live." "Too Late for the Less Well-Off; Just In Time for the Hipsters," *London Review of Books* 36.1 (January 9, 2014).

this book.[24] Given the ambit of this project, I am less interested in identifying the ways modern literature shares the "modern" of modern architecture, and more in tracking how representations of collective life continue to activate the "postness" of Britain's postwar period. In the space that remains, then, this Interlude will consider two works from the 1970s that take high-density estates as their setting: J.G. Ballard's 1975 *High-Rise* and Buchi Emecheta's 1972 *In the Ditch*. Ballard's novel tests the limitations of modernist design, dramatizing what happens when welfarist architecture becomes privatized and emptied of its corresponding social ideals. Emecheta, in contrast, offers a more complex engagement with the welfare state's social promises, critiquing its failure to provide adequate services while at the same time acknowledging that there is such a thing as society, even in a problem estate. Though these two works could not be more different from each other in terms of style and project, they activate similar concerns over what it means to inhabit a planned environment, exploring the affordances and limits of collectivized, institutionalized living. Taken together, their problematizing of built space registers the period's transitional energies—both emergent and residual—as ideals of the welfare state began to detach from their original wartime conceptualization.

As a dystopian depiction of tower-block living, Ballard's *High-Rise* provides perhaps the most iconic novelistic engagement with this architecture, published during the major shift in public opinion regarding the desirability of high-rises. Over the course of the novel, the inhabitants of the high-rise slowly go mad, stratifying into classes based on floor number and waging war on each other. It is a world without exit, without mercy, without humanity. It is a world where people eat dogs, a prospect more savage than any clock striking thirteen. Riffing on Le Corbusier's famous edict, "The house is a machine for living in," Ballard's high-rise is "a huge machine designed to serve, not the collective body of tenants, but the individual resident in isolation."[25] There really is no such thing as society here: no communal

---

[24] See Victoria Rosner's *Modernism and the Architecture of Private Life* (New York: Columbia University Press, 2005), as well as Ashley Maher's *Reconstructing Modernism: British Literature, Modern Architecture, and the State* (Oxford: Oxford University Press, 2020), 37–38. Both Maher and Marina MacKay argue that architectural modernism gave rise to "anti-state" novels, particularly in the form of dystopian fiction. See Maher's longer discussions in Chapters 3 and 4 of *Reconstructing Modernism*, as well as Marina MacKay's "Anti-State Fantasy and the Fiction of the 1940s," *Literature & History* 24.2 (2015). Paula Derdiger's *Reconstruction Fiction: Housing and Realist Literature in Postwar Britain* (Columbus: The Ohio State University Press, 2020) addresses modern architecture's influence on postwar realism, as both share interests in representation as what Peter Smithson called a "direct expression of a way of life." Peter Smithson, "The New Brutalism," *Architectural Design* 25 (January 1955), 1; quoted and contextualized in Paula Derdiger, *Reconstruction Fiction*, 97–98.

[25] J.G. Ballard, *High-Rise* (New York: Liveright, 2012), 17.

INTERLUDE: FAILED UTOPIAS   145

understanding of how to look after "ourselves" without first ensuring the destruction of "our neighbor." Instead, Ballard transfers all acts of care to the auspices of the building, creating a "new social type...with minimal needs for privacy, who thrived like an advanced species of machine in the neutral atmosphere" (46). The frenzied violence that results can be read as a Dionysian response to fascistic, psychogeographical control: a feature shared by Ballard's other fictions of the period, *Crash* (1973) and *Concrete Island* (1974). Compared to Winston's failed political rebellion in *1984*, in which there is no exit from Big Brother's watchful eyes, *High-Rise* reveals the imminent failure of such controlling architectures, perverting their attempts at order.[26]

High-Rise is ultimately less telling as a fiction of reconstruction because its idiom is of war rather than the postwar. Its return to 1945 is thus limited, lacking the sense of that moment as a source of social renewal and political potential. Instead, *High-Rise* recalls architectures built expressly for war-making, with the high-rise characterized as a "concrete landscape...an architecture designed for war, on the unconscious level if no other," built like a "row of concrete bunkers."[27] As such, the building gives the inhabitants, as well as the reader, the sense that "a future that had already taken place, and was now exhausted," with Ballard comparing its violence to Dunkirk and air-raids of the Second World War.[28] This feeling is then confirmed by the novel's ending, which suggests that all this will happen again to another high-rise across the way ("Laing watched them contentedly, ready to welcome them to their new world"[29]). With this final line, which invokes repetition rather than difference, Ballard offers us warning of the dark potential of reconstruction, which builds not in the name of peace, but in the name of perpetual war.

Emecheta's *In the Ditch* offers a counterpoint to Ballard's maximally drawn portrait of a communal living, as well as to Oscar Newman's paranoid

---

[26] For a good reading along these lines, particularly the role of the body in *High-Rise*, see chapter 4 in Laura Colombino's *Spatial Politics in Contemporary London: Writing Architecture and the Body* (New York: Routledge, 2013).
[27] Ballard, *High-Rise*, 16. Indeed, Ballard has explicitly linked the cultural imagination producing the high-rise to the ruins of the Atlantic Wall and Siegfried Line, which as he notes, underwrote Britain's own turn to postwar brutalism and architectural modernism: "Whenever I came across these grim fortifications along France's Channel coast and German border, I realised I was exploring a set of concrete tombs whose dark ghosts haunted the brutalist architecture so popular in Britain in the 1950s. Out of favour now, modernism survives in every high-rise sink estate of the time, in the Barbican development and the Hayward Gallery in London, in new towns such as Cumbernauld and the ziggurat residential blocks at the University of East Anglia." J.G. Ballard, "A handful of dust," *The Guardian*, 20 March 2006.
[28] Ballard, *High-Rise*, 176.
[29] Ibid., 207.

reading of public housing as creating asocial, criminal behavior. Emecheta's fiction has played a large role in the formation of both the postcolonial and Black British literary canons, especially *Second-Class Citizen* (1974). Though her first work, *In the Ditch*, is lesser-known, it provides Emecheta's strongest statement of what it means to live together in postwar Britain, with its portrayal of a community of working-class women offering an even more complex social world than the more individuated, nuclear family of *Second-Class Citizen*. The novel's main conflict lies between protagonist Adah's desire for independence and the negative models of dependency practiced by her neighbors in the Pussy Cat Mansions, whose lives are structured by welfare state provisions such as the dole and the Mansions' Family Adviser. For Emecheta as for Ballard, the Mansions' sociality cannot be separated from its architectural organization: as Adah remarks upon first seeing the council housing, "Most of the flats were dark in sympathy with the dark atmosphere. Ah, yes, the Mansions were a unique place, a separate place individualized for 'problem families.'"[30] Yet unlike Ballard's high-rise, the Mansions are not solely a source of harm. The decrepit bicycle sheds, for instance, are transformed into a "hippy shrine" by the compound's children; the vandalized social worker's office still serves as the mothers' social meeting-ground and archive for their children's paintings.[31] Though the flats are in a state of disrepair, readers are not asked to judge them as dystopian or somehow unlivable, as though looking on in the mode of social workers evaluating their fitness.

Adah eventually finds a form of comfort, solace, and to some degree, identity with her fellow "ditch-dwellers." Their working-class sensibility reminds Adah of the community she left in Nigeria, as both have "that sense of mutual help that is ingrained in people who have known a communal rather than individualistic way of life."[32] This community is by no means unitary, fragmented along different sociopolitical and racialized lines that anticipate feminist debates over the category of "woman." The women also clearly remain supplicants to the state. Still, the novel suggests that Adah enjoyed a richer social life in the Mansions than where she ends up at its close: a beautiful, gleaming maisonette, part of a working-class estate in the middle of a middle-class neighborhood. Though on all accounts an upward move, the new flat is as isolating as any in Ballard's high-rise, swapping the communal compound for sterile hallways, and neighborly noise for silence.

---

[30] Buchi Emecheta, *In the Ditch* (London: Heinemann International Literature & Textbooks, 1994), 17.
[31] Ibid., 16.
[32] Ibid., 65.

In comparison to this new, sterile environment, Emecheta crucially grants the Pussy Cat Mansions the capacity to catalyze the novel's chief revelation. For when an elderly neighbor dies, Adah realizes that the Mansions were built on an old burying ground, and enters into an extended meditation upon the dead:

> What a terrible life for a lonely woman, thought Adah. *O God, let me die in my country when my time comes. At least there'll be people to hold my hand.* But then her thoughts went to her people who had recently died in the bush during the Biafran War. Most of them had died from snake bites, running away to save their lives. There was no safety anywhere, really. One never knew.[33]

This moment echoes the other literary epiphanies such as the old woman in *Mrs. Dalloway* or the "nowhere's safe" of *The Girls of Slender Means*, which position their protagonists to experience radical sympathy with complete strangers and acknowledge the precariousness of life. In this case, rather than test out connection with an individual stranger, Adah turns to a nation, "her people," and the dream of Biafran independence that haunts the novel as the political double of Adah's own quest for autonomy. By invoking the post-1970 of the Biafran Civil War, *In the Ditch* adds another layer of signification to Britain's postwar period: the long durée of decolonization, which calls into question the very terminology of Britain's "postwar" period. This epiphany, like others, is ultimately negative. Aligning Biafra's independence movement with the failures of the British welfare state, the novel concludes that there is no safety to be had, only the broken promises of state repair. But unlike *Mrs. Dalloway, The Girls of Slender Means,* or *High-Rise*, all of which suspend the social or political ramifications of this realization, *In the Ditch* transforms this into an occasion of acknowledgment and carrying-on, as Adah decides to leave the Mansions. As she bids farewell to the space—"Goodbye, ghosts, whoever you are, and sleep well"— the reader senses that the gesture is directed as much to these bigger dreams of working collectivity as it is to the specific historical dead.[34] As Adah moves away from private domesticity as a source of comfort toward an emergent public sphere, it seems the ghosts of the Second World War gain more company with the passing of time. Where *High-Rise*'s narrative presents a closed loop of history, its building only ever able to produce war-making, *In the*

[33] Ibid., 117.
[34] Ibid., 127.

Ditch offers the reader an important acknowledgment of the multiple long reconstructions of postwar periods, whatever their failures or futures.

Following Emecheta's lead, Part II of this book shows how the dreams of Britain's postwar period continue to provide a complex, robust engine for literary creation, haunting and haunted by different histories and geographies. Indeed, as we gain more distance from 1945, this project's comparative postwar approach becomes ever more urgent. The flexibility and iterability of the postwar as an analytic allows other timelines to bear on postwar British historiography, including those of colonization and decolonization.

In this light, we might return to this Interlude's initial example of Britain's postwar ethos: Clement Attlee's hope for "good neighbours" at the moment of London's first housing estate, West India House, in 1946. For that site was itself haunted by the ghosts of an earlier structure of collective life: the "Strangers' Home for Asiatics, Africans and South Sea Islanders," on whose site West India House was built. Founded in 1857 by various Protestant groups and funded by Maharajah Duleep Singh (along with other Indian visitors who were "distressed and even annoyed to find Indian beggars approaching them on the streets of London"), Strangers' Home provided room and board for foreign laborers in need of short-term accommodation until its closure in 1937.[35] These "strangers" primarily included sailors, or "lascars," as well as various others, such as doctors accompanying ships to the West Indies, or performers joining exhibitions and circuses.

Like other hostels near the West India Docks, the institution was multipurpose, offering room and board as well as religious instruction by Protestant missionaries. But as a home for Asians and Africans in London, there was a particular racial charge, even necessity, to providing these living quarters. In *The Asiatic in England: Sketches of Sixteen Year's Work among Orientals* (1873), Joseph Salter, missionary and religious instructor in Strangers' Home, made his opening case for the institution by invoking the corpse of an Asian lascar frozen to death, lamenting, "Poor fellow, he could have found neither help nor sympathy in this land of gold and philanthropy!"[36] An 1897

---

[35] See Antoinette Burton, *At the Heart of the Empire: Indians and the Colonial Encounter in Late-Victorian Britain* (Berkeley: University of California Press, 1998), 54. For a history of dockworkers' accommodation, which only developed in the mid-nineteenth century out of "fear of disorder more than compassion," see "The West India Docks: Offices, works and housing," *Survey of London: Volumes 43 and 44, Poplar, Blackwall and Isle of Dogs*, ed. Hermione Hobhouse (London: London County Council, 1994), 313–326, *British History Online*, http://www.british-history.ac.uk/survey-london/vols43-4/pp.313-326.

Saturday Review piece would underscore this continued need, noting that "painful experience has proved that no respectable people will take in these Oriental waifs and strays, and, if any house is opened to them, the very fact proves it to be a dangerous house": a comment that resonates with the later experiences of the Windrush generation.[37] Yet Strangers' Home was not just help and sympathy. It also served as repatriation center, as British law increasingly monitored and criminalized lascars' presence in Britain, particularly through the 1823 Merchant Shipping Act, which was only repealed in 1963.[38] For all its philanthropy, then, the Strangers' Home ensured that its guests remain just that: guests; or rather, strangers.

This imperial history haunts Attlee's ribbon-cutting. It is there in the uniform whiteness of the crowd, for whom West India House was planned and made, despite the area's diverse history and status as London's first "Chinatown." It is there in Attlee's hope that, along with being good neighbors, those moving in "are going to be good citizens," echoing Britain's longstanding association between whiteness and nationality. It is even there in the 1857 opening date of Strangers' Home, a year shared with the Indian Rebellion of 1857, which as Zadie Smith's *White Teeth* persuasively details, provides another historical "root canal" of Britain's contemporaneity. This history would continue to condition who gained admittance to the dreams of the postwar welfare state. For in the years following West India House's opening, gaining access to council housing would still prove a struggle for postwar Commonwealth migrants, who were barred from these spaces due to their race and, significantly, in the name of the very "community" they were meant to foster.[39] To admit the longer history of this "first" postwar housing block, then, is to deepen the neighborly claim made by these "Strangers" seeking admittance to their home. As we gain distance from the threshold of 1945, the fictions studied here will likewise continue to ask: *what if*? What if the aperture of 1945 had been just a bit wider, its revisions in reference to a longer past? What if postwar repair could salve deeper wounds? What if those strangers were neighbors after all?

---

[36] Joseph Salter, *The Asiatic in England: Sketches of Sixteen Year's Work among Orientals* (London: Seeley, Jackson & Halliday, 1873), 20.
[37] Anonymous, "A London Caravanserai," *Saturday Review* 47, 1232, June 7, 1897, 702.
[38] See Rozina Visram, *Asians in Britain: 400 Years of History* (London: Pluto Press, 2002), 59–60, as well as Panikos Panayi, *Migrant City: A New History of London* (New Haven: Yale University Press, 2020).
[39] See Wetherell, *Foundations*, 98–100.

PART II

GRAVE

4
Empty Places
Unpropertied Intimacy and Queer History

As this book moves forward in the twentieth century, the works it addresses approach the events of midcentury from a distance—that is, as history. This chapter examines one method of thematizing the midcentury, which I call "the century novel," a form that narrates the twentieth century by covering large swathes of its history. In giving an account of the past century, the century novel typically makes a number of punctuated stops, sectioning the narrative into specific, clearly demarcated years. Rather than alternate between a present and a specific, defining past, it moves briskly through time, projecting a sense of historical coverage as it marshals the numerous events of the twentieth century into one cohesive narrative.

Directionality of this movement varies. Some century novels relentlessly move forward in time between years that are either landmarks for characters' personal histories or for world-historical time, as in Penelope Lively's *Moon Tiger* (1987), Ian McEwan's *Atonement* (2001), and Kamila Shamsie's *Burnt Shadows* (2009). Others choose to move curiously backward, such as Martin Amis's *Time's Arrow* (1991) and Don DeLillo's *Underworld* (1997). Still others jump around the century, such as Kate Atkinson's novels *Behind the Scenes at the Museum* (1995), *Life after Life* (2013), and *A God in Ruins* (2015), Michael Cunningham's *The Hours* (1998), and Zadie Smith's *White Teeth* (2000). Though this form is indebted to the historical novel tradition, it found new purchase in the efflorescence of postmodern historiographic novels, particularly in the late 1980s and 1990s, which helps account both for the specific twentieth-century form of these *fin-de-siècle* novels as well as their popularity.[1] But what kind of conceptual work is narrative structure doing for these novels, other than help them cover the century's temporal

---

[1] Linda Hutcheon termed this genre as "historiographic metafiction," or "those well-known and popular novels that are both intensely self-reflexive and yet paradoxically also lay claim to historical events and personages." *A Poetics of Postmodernism: History, Theory, Fiction* (Routledge: New York and London, 1988), 5.

breadth? What desires for historical understanding do they offer to satisfy and in what form?

These novels' long sweeps across the twentieth century share a remarkably coherent tendency: to locate narrative conflict during the Second World War and its immediate aftermath. Despite their looseness in playing with time, they often figure the midcentury—and specifically the Second World War—as their conceptual limit-point, the encrypted trauma of their narratives that they cannot get over. In their scriptings of the twentieth century, then, these novels of the century are in a sense trying to get midcentury right.[2] For some, this work is counterfactual: in Kate Atkinson's *Life After Life*, the protagonist relives her life over and over again until, it is implied, she is able to kill Hitler. For others, the return to midcentury means including social histories often occluded in earlier narratives, such as the colonial histories inserted by Zadie Smith's *White Teeth*, the lesbian and pacifist characters revealed in Sarah Waters's *The Night Watch*, or the turn to Hiroshima and the Afghan wars in Kamila Shamsie's *Burnt Shadows*. In whatever way these novels try to recuperate the midcentury, whether belated repair or prophylactic action, they do so through a privileged vantage point only afforded by narrative structure.

However, these elaborate temporal schemes run the risk of reducing the "history" of historical fiction to mere, archetypical citations. Such a practice would fit Fredric Jameson's scathing diagnosis that the postmodern historical novel "can no longer set out to represent the historical past; it can only 'represent' our ideas and stereotypes about that past," making History with a capital "H" forever out of reach.[3] Or to turn to the language of György Lukács's *The Historical Novel* (1962), the century novel risks providing "only an abstract prehistory of ideas and not the concrete prehistory of the destiny of the people themselves," a failing Lukács saw in the humanist historical novels of his time, specifically the postwar German novel.[4] This failing was a

---

[2] An interesting and earlier counterpoint to this literary phenomena is described in Marina MacKay's account of the "metropolitan novel series," including C.P. Snow's "Strangers and Brothers" (1940–1970) and Anthony Powell's *A Dance to the Music of Time* (1951–1975), whose attention to political and public life "suggests a strong contemporary impulse to understand personal experience in long-range, fundamentally historical terms." "'Temporary Kings': The Metropolitan Novel Series and the Postwar Consensus," *MFS* 67.2 (Summer 2021), 322.

[3] Fredric Jameson, *Postmodernism, or, the Cultural Logic of Late Capitalism* (Durham: Duke University Press, 2003), 25.

[4] György Lukács, *The Historical Novel* (Lincoln: University of Nebraska Press, 1983), 337. In this way, the ethos of late Lukács in *The Historical Novel* is very much a postwar, or post-1945 logic, compared to his earlier *Theory of the Novel* (1916), a work deeply informed by the alienation of the First World War.

keen one, particularly in a postwar period where the German novel tradition was under special pressure to account for the rise of fascism. Lukács read this new charge of addressing the "great and urgent problems of the present" as paradoxically weakening the novel's ability to portray the present in all its depth and complexity.[5]

This diagnosis of the postwar historical novel resonates with the British novel tradition as well, particularly in its marked return to 1945 that this book has been tracking thus far. If the work of the historical novel is to track the felt expression of the age on the lives and problems of its characters, particularly through the dialectic between individual and nation, this relationship between the individual and the collective was strongly reactivated through the experience of the "People's War" and founding of the modern welfare state. At the same time, the democratic promises of war and postwar were always already limited, compromised by structures of imperialism, sexism, and racism that limited who, exactly, was imagined as inheriting postwar Britain. The chapters of Part II address works that attempt to limn these contradictory histories, which in doing so, reveal the contingencies of Britain's postwar promise while also investing in its narrative of social repair. Despite their limitations as a mode of approaching history, century novels still contend with its felt necessities. Their attempts should not be dismissed so easily, and are instructive even in their failures.

This chapter turns to the work of Alan Hollinghurst as one such century novelist, especially of the gay twentieth century. Though Hollinghurst has expressed a desire for critics to stop focusing on the identitarian politics of his writing, his *oeuvre* shows a marked dedication to gay male history.[6] His work is particularly animated by literary allusion and reverence for the gay literary and cultural canon, from Ronald Firbank's *The Flower Beneath the Foot* to Benjamin Britten's opera *Billy Budd*, as well as the study of gay lives through biographical writing or queer studies.[7] His novels make recognizable stops in or around certain epochs, such as the queerness of the

---

[5] Ibid., 338.
[6] Stephen Moss, "Alan Hollinghurst: Sex on the brain," *The Guardian*, June 17, 2011, http://www.theguardian.com/books/2011/jun/18/alan-hollinghurst-interview.
[7] This is in keeping with Hollinghurst's intellectual trajectory, which saw him earning a BA and MLitt in English from Oxford and the Newdigate Prize for poetry in 1974; lecturing at Oxford and University College London; and serving as the deputy editor of *The Times Literary Supplement* from 1985 to 1990, during which time he wrote his first novel, *The Swimming-Pool Library* (1988). His masters' thesis, entitled "The Creative Uses of Homosexuality in the Novels of E.M. Forster, Ronald Firbank and L.P. Hartley," can still be pulled from the shelves and read in Duke Humfrey's Library, Oxford, giving the reader not only the thrill of encountering handwritten edits, footnotes, and accent marks, but also a profound sense of familiarity, since his literary *oeuvre* has continued to inhabit these critical and theoretical commitments.

Great War male poets, the restrictive conservativism of the early 1950s, the eventual decriminalization of homosexuality in 1967, and the AIDS crisis of the 1980s and 1990s. Such a mode of history-telling might risk transforming these periods into Jameson's "pop history," if their citation turns gay history into something always already known and limits the stories that can be told. Yet his novels largely manage to avoid this pitfall, transforming historical landmarks into occasions for further examination. Their engagements with the past raise pressing questions over what it means to inherit a past marked by silence, hurt, and stigma.

One such novel is Hollinghurst's *The Line of Beauty* (2004), widely considered to be his best work, and winner of the Booker Prize. Its different sections, moving from 1983 to 1986 to 1987, squarely chart the rise of the AIDS crisis in Britain alongside Thatcher's neoliberalism, providing a history of the decade, keenly felt. Notwithstanding the acclaim this novel has received, this chapter proposes *The Swimming-Pool Library* as a more provocative case for thinking about the 1980s, due to its longer twentieth-century scope and complex structuring of queer history. A remarkable first novel, *The Swimming-Pool Library* deserves a closer look from literary critics, who have often passed it over in favor of Hollinghurst's later works.

Published in 1988, *The Swimming-Pool Library* shifts focus between its narrative present of 1983 and diaristic flashbacks that begin with the First World War and end in the 1950s. Through this longue durée, the novel presents Britain's Second World War in terms of its longer twentieth century. It shifts attention away from the London Home Front so that other epochs take on greater weight, including interwar Oxford and colonial Sudan, the long reach of the 1885 Labouchere Amendment before its 1956 repeal, and the period just before the AIDS crisis. As these historical signposts suggest, Hollinghurst's remapping of the twentieth century encourages the reader to see the Second World War and its aftermath alongside other social histories, including colonial and homophobic violence.

In this punctuated historicity, "post-1945" might become only one periodizing marker among others. Despite its sweep across the twentieth century, there is a curious temporal fold between the lives of its two protagonists, with the memoirs of one ending just before the birth of the other. As one character puts it: "Isn't there a kind of blind spot...for that period just before one was born? One knows about the Second World War, one knows about Suez, I suppose, but what people were actually getting up to in those years ... There's an empty, motiveless space until one appears on the scene."[8] However, it is the very encryption of the postwar period that leads to the novel's shattering epiphany. For hidden in the aftermath of the Second World War is a wound in need of repair—a wound that links the two protagonists, and which gains significance and power precisely from the spatialized and welfarist logic of postwar reparation. Through this narrative structure, Hollinghurst both questions and affirms the holding power of the postwar period on the ethical imagination, and asks to what extent we should carry responsibility for the middle of the century.

The Absent Center: Queer Narrative Temporality in *The Swimming-Pool Library*

Set in the summer of 1983, *The Swimming-Pool Library* tells the story of Will Beckwith, a young gay man and future peer enjoying "the last summer of its kind there was ever to be," "riding high on sex and self-esteem" in what he calls "my time, my belle époque."[9] The fantastic, suspended temporal space of this summer begins with Will having quit his job at the Cubitt *Dictionary of Architecture*, a gesture that echoes Charles Ryder's architectural painting work in Evelyn Waugh's *Brideshead Revisited* (1945) and anticipates the art magazine *Ogee* in Hollinghurst's *The Line of Beauty*. What lies on the other side of the summer is less than clear: at the beginning of the novel, the only hint given is a description of "a faint flicker of calamity, like flames around a photograph, something seen out of the corner of the eye."[10] The dedication of the novel to Nicholas Clark, a friend of Hollinghurst's from Oxford who died of AIDS in 1984, one of the first British victims of the epidemic, suggests the calamity to come. Will first meets Charles Nantwich, the second protagonist, while cottaging in the public lavatories of Kensington Gardens. After seeing Charles suffer a heart attack, Will administers CPR to the elderly peer and saves his life. When they randomly meet again at the swimming pool of the Corry gym, Charles asks Will to write his memoirs for him, giving him his diaries as a basis for the work. These papers are then interwoven with Will's narrative, and move chronologically from Charles's first schoolboy love in the First World War, to Oxford and colonial Sudan in the 1920s, wartime

---

[8] Alan Hollinghurst, *The Swimming-Pool Library* (New York: Random House, Inc., 1988), 279.
[9] Ibid., 3.
[10] Ibid.

London during the Blitz, and postwar incarceration for his homosexuality in 1954.

Through various structural and affective doublings between the two gay *Bildungsromane* of Charles and Will, Hollinghurst's novel primes us to see lines of connection and inheritance between their two generations. Charles's postwar arrest, for instance, finds new iteration in Will's best friend James and his present-day troubles with the police. Will's beating at the hands of a gang of neo-Nazi youth, an act both sexually and racially motivated, echoes the death of Taha, Charles's Sudanese servant whom he brings to London after a stint in colonial administration. And the swimming pool emerges as a shared site of meaning for the two men, from their shared dark laps in the Corry gym to the ancient Roman baths in Charles's London home, from the locker rooms of Will's schooldays to Charles's description of incarceration as underwater existence. These narrative and symbolic recurrences circle the challenge of grasping history, whether in terms of repetition, haunting return, progress, or even repair. Their resonances suggest one long history between two characters.

The question, however, is just how shared this history can be. The plot tests out this question through revelations of complex structures of personal connection, intergenerational trauma, and potential repair between the two men. Over the course of the novel, what eventually comes into view is the encrypted realization that Will's grandfather, Lord Denis Beckwith, played a major role in keeping homosexuality criminalized, in what Will later describes as the "gay pogrom" of the postwar period, and, furthermore, that their family owes their wealth and peerage to this unseemly political work. Through Charles's prison diaries, Will not only realizes the ugly truth about his family's past, but also comes to understand how much is riding on his writing Charles's biography. He imagines this biography as a political "campaign":

> If Charles had been orchestrating his campaign, as I sometimes believed he had, then he had brought it brilliantly and comprehensively to a head. The prison was the key. The one unspeakable thing that no one had been able to tell me threw light on everything else, and only left obscure the degrees of calculation and coincidence in Charles's offering me his biography to write—a task he must have known I could never, in the end, accept.[11]

---

[11] *Ibid.*, 263.

The reparative fantasy adhering to this "unspeakable thing" is that through writing the biography, Will would somehow not only mend the injury his grandfather had done to Charles, but also that as a gay man, his textual labor would have the added poignancy of sexual solidarity. His refusal to take on this intergenerational burden of biographical representation can be seen as abjuring both responsibility and the possibility of repair on an individual and collective level. This refusal is not merely empty negation, but rather a fraught negotiation with the demands of the postwar period.

If Charles had orchestrated a brilliant campaign, so too, of course, does Hollinghurst through his careful emplotment of the novel and his creation of empty space between the two main characters. The specificity of the novel's primary epiphany throws its historical situations into relief, transposing the energy of the post-1945 into post-1983. One of the few critics to study the postwar legacy of the novel is Alan Sinfield, who suggests that Hollinghurst "asserts subcultural history and responsibility, not only against Thatcherite selfishness, but against the consensus that failed to acknowledge gay men."[12] This comment recalls the sexual conservatism of the immediate postwar period, a time marked by a number of arrests, scandals, and studies that framed gay sexual practices as a social problem.[13] In some cases, public reports focused on the fame or elite status of their subjects, as in actor John Gielgud's 1953 arrest, and the 1954 trial of Lord Montagu of Beaulieu. In other cases, like that of Guy Burgess and Donald Maclean of the Cambridge Spy Ring, were cross-pollinated with Cold War paranoia, creating the fear that gay relations were a threat to national security. These "affairs" were indicative of a general atmosphere of heightened homophobia and sexual repression, qualities that tend to characterize the 1950s in histories of modern sexuality.[14] According to Sinfield, the novel's main function is to uncover this sexual conservatism and the ways discrimination belied the seemingly

---

[12] Alan Sinfield, "Culture, Consensus and Difference: Angus Wilson to Alan Hollinghurst," *British Culture of the Postwar*, ed. Alistair Davies and Alan Sinfield (New York: Routledge, 2000), 96.

[13] See for instance Frank Mort's *Capital Affairs: London and the Making of the Permissive Society* (New Haven: Yale University Press, 2010), which focuses on the "affair" as a defining element of 1950s and 60s metropolitan culture, particularly when it came to queer men; see also Matt Houlbrook's *Queer London: Perils and Pleasures in the Sexual Metropolis, 1918–1956* (Chicago: University of Chicago Press, 2005).

[14] As Heike Bauer and Matt Cook note, "long histories of modern sexuality have tended to give significance to the 1950s mostly in terms of repressive norms, against which the gay and women's liberation movements reacted in the decade that followed." *Queer 1950s: Rethinking Sexuality in the Postwar Years*, ed. Heike Bauer and Matt Cook (New York: Palgrave Macmillan, 2012), 2. Though Bauer and Cook's collection seeks to challenge this tendency, they are still careful not to discount the felt power of these norms on queer lives.

liberal postwar consensus. It does so by asserting gay subculture rather than reaffirming consensus, for as Sinfield reminds us, "In the 1980s, minorities must grab what space they can. After all, in Margaret Thatcher's view, society does not exist."[15]

Yet the ramifications of Hollinghurst's narrative palimpsest run deeper than the opposition between selfishness and society. For the 1980s marked another wave of social repression with the emergence of the AIDS crisis, a period marked by a resurgence of homophobia and public perception of the disease as the "gay plague" or "gay cancer." Its connection between the 1950s and 1980s charts a history of queer repression points, telling queer history in a way that focuses melancholically on pain as much as, if not more than, pleasure. Reminding the reader of the sexual conservatism of the 1950s can be seen as a pedagogical exercise on Hollinghurst's part: a touch from the past that might serve as a warning for the present, whether the narrative's 1983 or the publication year of 1988. To end on such a note raises the question of how Will will respond when he learns of his specific historical connection to Charles, and what it means to *feel historical*, or to be claimed by a specific history. It also raises the larger stakes of what it means to represent queer history, a history constituted by both stigma and pleasure.

My reading of the novel's narrative structure is thus informed by scholarship on queer temporality, a concept that, as Elizabeth Freeman puts it, "showcases the 'possibilities of a permeability and recursivity that is built into the field of queer studies at its best.'"[16] Building upon Bourdieu's concept of *habitus* and Judith Butler's theory of gender performativity, queer temporality challenges normal or "hetero-temporality" that manifests in the seemingly inevitable, natural sedimentation of gender, sexuality, and development of desires as mapped onto the experience of sequential time. Those who do not conform to these natural rhythms of a society are often seen as failures, queer in the sense of being premature, belated, or otherwise asynchronously developed. Work on queer temporality also engages time on a larger scale, moving beyond individual timelines to think about historicity. Heather Love, for instance, gives a powerful account of the negativity of queer history, one that cannot forget its foundations of "suffering, stigma, and loss," even as it engages in transformative politics or criticism.[17] Freeman, on the other hand, proposes a queer historiography formulated not in

---

[15] Sinfield, "Culture, consensus and difference," 95.
[16] Elizabeth Freeman, "Introduction," *GLQ* 13:2–3 (2007), 160.
[17] Heather Love, *Feeling Backward: Loss and the Politics of Queer History* (Cambridge: Harvard University Press, 2009), 1.

terms of loss and negativity, but in terms of a politics of pleasure. Calling this method "erotohistoriography," she asks: "How might queer practices of pleasure, specifically, the bodily enjoyments that travel under the sign of queer sex, be thought of as temporal practices, even as portals to historical thinking?"[18] *The Swimming-Pool Library* engages this question of the feeling of history, and more precisely, whether these portals to historical thinking are best felt as the inheritance of an injurious history, or the more idiosyncratic time of bodily pleasure.

These two modes find powerful synthesis, I argue, in the concepts of welfare and care, as they are manifested in the sense of queer collectivity. As a novel of development, *The Swimming-Pool Library* asks its characters to learn what it means to be responsible for the larger gay community, and to build networks of care that run parallel to those of the official welfare state. In asking Will to write the biography, Charles appeals to their shared status as members of a queer society, one defined not only by exclusion and injurious state power, but also, hopefully, communal care. We might think of this as a bid for an alternative consensus to that of 1945, an alternative history that would lead to a very different present. Claiming such a counter-consensus might underwrite a different present through insisting on an alternative basis for the welfare state. This imagined state of affairs was even more urgent at the height of the AIDS crisis in Thatcherite Britain, a period of gay history that demanded new forms of caretaking and thinking about the future. After all, as Jack Halberstam suggests, "queer time perhaps emerges most spectacularly, at the end of the twentieth century, from within those gay communities whose horizons of possibility have been severely diminished by the AIDS epidemic."[19] *The Swimming-Pool Library* is invested in the workings of those communities, whether in their erotic subcultures, alternative gay institutions such as gyms and movie theaters, or the project of writing itself.

---

[18] Freeman, "Time Binds, or, Erotohistoriography," *Social Text* 84–85, 23:3–4 (Fall-Winter 2005), 59.
[19] Jack Halberstam, *In a Queer Time and Place: Transgender Bodies, Subcultural Lives* (New York and London: NYU Press, 2005), 2. Other critics elaborate this idea. See Leo Bersani, "Is the Rectum a Grave?" *October* 43 (Winter 1987), 197–222, and Douglas Crimp, *Melancholia and Moralism: Essays on AIDS and Queer Politics* (Cambridge: MIT Press, 2002), particularly the essay "Mourning and Militancy," originally published in *October* 51 (Winter 1989), 3–18. For a more recent evaluation of AIDS and the time of mourning, see Dagmawi Woubset, *The Calendar of Loss: Race, Sexuality, and Mourning in the Early Era of AIDS* (Baltimore: John Hopkins University Press, 2015).

Bad Domesticity: Queering Wartime and Postwar Reconstruction

If Hollinghurst's novel is invested in exposing the discriminatory ethos of the postwar period, it does not do so by turning to political ideologies. While the two world wars, British imperialism, and the Falklands War are all described in the novel as clear and distinct historical moments, the postwar period registers primarily through reference to degraded spaces. These sites include the Blitzed ruins of wartime London, which become the houses bought up by Lord Beckwith and Charles; the church that Charles transforms into a Boys Club in 1955; the postwar housing towers, where Will is assaulted by the young neo-Nazis as he searches for Arthur; and of course, the prison where Charles is incarcerated. Criticism on Hollinghurst's engagement with the built environment mainly remarks on its representation as a tour of queer spaces or as symbolic of queer experience itself.[20] This chapter proposes a new historical register for understanding this literary investment, arguing that it indexes aspects of Britain's changing postwar landscape as it transitioned from a warfare to a welfare state and embarked on ambitious projects of architectural and social reconstruction. These elements also remind the reader of the sexual politics of reconstruction, which used the heterosexual, nuclear family home as a conceptual site for experimentation and repair: both as a repairing agent and as the thing to be repaired.

The state's new exertion of control over the domestic landscape had severe ramifications for Britain's gay population. For historians of modern sexuality, reconstruction's focus on the family home has become synonymous with the heightened conservatism of the 1950s.[21] As Richard Hornsey notes, the dark side of the reconstructive imagination was its desire to "offer the public a comforting framework for imagining a metropolis protected from

---

[20] Bart Eeckhout, for example, reads the epistemic gaps of *The Stranger's Child* as a queer narrative organization that ruptures both the traditional, continuous timelines of heteronormative family history and the history of these family's country homes. "English Architectural Landscapes and Metonymy in Hollinghurst's *The Stranger's Child*," *CLCWeb: Comparative Literature and Culture* 14.3 (2012), 1–11. Likewise, Allan Johnson reads *The Spell*'s structural motifs of the buried temple and the open plane as producing "considerable dismissal of any desire to seek permanence, or to seek immortality through the structures of a text or the structures around us," underscoring their transience and ultimately inhabitable nature. "Buried Temples and Open Planes: Alethea Hayter and the Architecture of Drug-Taking in Alan Hollinghurst's *The Spell*," *Textual Practice* 27:7 (2013), 1177–1195. See also Thomas Dukes, "Mappings of Secrecy and Disclosure," *Journal of Homosexuality* 31:3 (1996), 95–107.

[21] See Bauer and Cook, 2.

the possibility of conflict or trauma," which took the "insidious form of social management" of city spaces in which "malignant social practices would, quite literally, be unable to take place."[22] Through controlling social behavior through city planning and domestic design, the immediate postwar decades "witnessed a complex set of cultural contestations around the dynamics of metropolitan male same-sex desire, as certain practices became confirmed in their criminality, new forms of queer subjectivity took shape, and alternative modes of resistance emerged."[23] Frank Mort's work also highlights what he sees as the moral and ethical components of postwar urban planning, and their accompanying anxieties over areas such as the West End, the capital's sex trade center. Focusing on the visual pedagogy of *The County of London Plan*, Mort notes how Abercrombie and Forshaw projected a sanitized "civic monumentalism" for the city, as well as a strict vision of commercialism that would hopefully counter Soho's more unsavory reputation.[24] These assumptions—what might be called the biopolitics of reconstruction—contribute to what Leo Bersani calls the "redemptive reinvention of sex," or the wish for sex to be properly socialized or organized as productive of citizenship and capital.[25] Britain's postwar reconstruction and its structuring ethos did not make much room for queer people, and if it did at all, it divided the good queers from the bad along liberal lines of social citizenship, or those who fit securely into the plan and those who did not.

Given the narrative's twentieth-century structure, *The Swimming-Pool Library* provides an important case-study for examining these reconstructive structures of feeling. The labor of writing Charles's biography can be seen as itself a symbolic act of reconstruction, one that repairs the past ruins of his life in a socially conscious manner. Beyond these gestures, however, the novel engages with the very terms and assumptions of postwar reconstruction in a manner that doubles and displaces its coproduction of space and sexuality. This chapter's approach to the novel is thus also influenced by work in human geography and sexuality studies that examines

---

[22] Richard Hornsey, *The Spiv and the Architect: Unruly Life in Postwar London* (Minneapolis: University of Minnesota Press, 2010), 15.
[23] *Ibid.*, 3.
[24] Mort, *Capital Affairs*, 97 and 100.
[25] Bersani, "Is the Rectum a Grave?", 215. See also Part Four ("Politics") of Matt Houlbrook's *Queer London*, which gives an account of the "construction of the 'homosexual' as source of cultural danger and a threat to national stability and, hence, a suitable subject for criminal law" (15).

the intimate relationship between the production of space and sociality.[26] It is mindful of the ways formulations of queer space risk essentializing identity by mapping recognizable, visible, dissident practices of sexuality onto concrete, locatable spaces, and by overlooking more marginal, intersectional, or fluid sexualities. Even so, postwar reconstruction's priority of housing the white, nuclear heterosexual family invites a study of the relationship between sexuality and space. Hollinghurst's commitment to decenter such domestic spaces in favor of a map of the clubs, cinemas, schools, gyms that make up the social architectures of gay London also asks us to bring these categories together. Through exploring the way characters engage with these spaces, Hollinghurst asks whether one can experience intimacy without its institutionalization or domestic enclosure: the very inverse of postwar reconstruction's focus on organized, knowable, secure circuits of everyday life. As Hollinghurst's characters move through social spaces, they begin to outline a form of intimacy that, while still codified by institutional or public routines, is experienced as less coercive or stifling to its characters than that of the established home space as imagined by reconstruction.[27]

This refusal to fixate on the family estate as the primary site of inhabitation and institutionalization is one of the defining characteristics of *The Swimming-Pool Library*. As previous chapters have suggested, representations of the family home often reveal the limitations of reconstruction, its dreams of domestic stability shattered by multiple forms of bad domesticity. In *The Swimming-Pool Library*, the Beckwith's family estate is revealed to have shallow roots: "It was not until years later that I came to understand how recent and synthetic this nobility was—the house itself bought up cheap after the war, half ruined by use as an officers' training school, and then as

---

[26] See, for instance, *Mapping Desire*, ed. David Bell and Gill Valentine (New York: Routledge, 1995); Samuel Delaney's *Times Square Red, Times Square Blue* (New York: NYU Press, 1999); *Cities of Pleasure: Sex and the Urban Socialscape*, ed. Alan Collins (London, New York: Routledge, 2006); Natalie Oswin, "Critical Geographies and the Uses of Sexuality: Deconstructing Queer Space," *Progress in Human Geography* 32:1 (2008), 89–103; Halberstam's *In a Queer Time and Place*; Jasbir Puar, *Terrorist Assemblages: Homonationalism in Queer Times* (Durham: Duke University Press, 2007).

[27] Here, it might also be useful to juxtapose these two Hollinghurst novels with two by Sarah Waters, comparing *The Swimming-Pool Library* to *The Night Watch* (2006) and *The Stranger's Child* to *The Little Stranger* (2009). Unlike Hollinghurst's span of the twentieth-century and enfolding of the war/postwar period within them, Waters's novels are situated squarely in this period, with *The Night Watch* moving backwards in time from 1947 to 1944 to 1941 (and also featuring a prison space). *The Little Stranger* provides an even more direct comparison to *The Stranger's Child*, as both focus on a haunted family house.

a military hospital."[28] This degradation of a home by institutional use is a major form of dystopia for the postwar British novel, a tradition beginning with Waugh's *Brideshead Revisited* and finding purchase in works such as Muriel Spark's *Hothouse by the East River*, Ian McEwan's *Atonement*, Kazuo Ishiguro's *Never Let Me Go*, and Hollinghurst's own *The Stranger's Child*, which chronicles the transformation of the family home into a school for boys. That the Beckwiths buy their home "cheap" after the war is yet another twist to this melancholia for "the lost houses" of Britain, revealing how the spoils of private ownership—not just collective use—may be what ultimately completes the ruin of the home. In Hollinghurst's hands, of course, this critique of the family home gains extra charge as a specifically queer critique. For even more haunting than a history "bought up cheap," it turns out, is nobility shadily won: a peerage given to Will's grandfather over his role in the 1950s anti-gay pogrom, bestowed out of political embarrassment.

The novel's other form of bad domesticity turns away from the demise of the Big House to consider the rise of tower blocks, which as the Interlude suggested, comprises another dystopian horizon of postwar reconstruction. This architecture is brought into focus during Will's trip to visit his lover Arthur, who lives in a housing tower near the Victoria and Albert Docks (or as Will muses, "The Victoria and Albert *Docks*"). Will is attacked by a gang of skinheads who, after a protracted back-and-forth, label Will a "poof" and "n— - fucker" and beat him severely. Though these verbal attacks can be read as a traumatic return of Nazi violence and the Second World War, the way that Will recounts the assault underscores the mass institutionalization of domesticity and its erasure of individuality. After a detailed description of the prefab units, Will concludes: "The buildings, prefabricated units slotted and pinned together, showed a systematic disregard for comfort and relief, for anything the eye or heart might fix on as homely or decent. [...] I found myself sweating with gratitude that I did not live under such a tyranny, dispossessed in my own home by the insistent beat of rock or reggae."[29] Versions of this evaluative gaze haunt novels of reconstruction, from Stella's glimpse into the working-class home in Elizabeth Bowen's *The Heat of the Day*, to Samuel Selvon's reversal of the gaze in *The Lonely Londoners*. This iteration of the trope probes the limitations of Will's privileged subject-position, which shapes the paternalistic, often dismissive way he interacts with his

---

[28] Hollinghurst, *Library*, 4.
[29] Ibid., 169–170.

working-class and black boyfriends. These limits, in turn, determine the terms of his own sympathetic education, which depends not on individuation, but rather on understanding what it is like to belong to a marginalized or precarious group identity. While this episode is not given the status as the novel's final illumination, it certainly has a transformative, even epiphanic effect on the protagonist, challenging his fantasy of "absolute security."

In a passage reminiscent of Clarissa Dalloway's postwar London, Will is forced to confront these vulnerabilities:

> It was a bright, blowy tea-time. Already people were coming home, the traffic was building up at the lights. The pavements were normal, the passers-by had preoccupied, harmless expressions. Yet to me it was a glaring world, treacherous with lurking alarm. A universal violence had been disclosed to me, and I saw it everywhere—in the sudden scatter across the pavement of some quite small boys, in the brief mocking notice of me taken by a couple of telephone engineers in a parked van, in the dark glasses and cigarette-browned fingers of a man—German? Dutch?—who stopped us to ask directions. I understood for the first time the vulnerability of the old, unfortified by good luck or inexperience.[30]

The potential security of strangers is transformed into a profoundly treacherous relation. For the first time, Will assumes a paranoid position and interprets the movements and bodies of others as contributing to a structure of universal violence. At first, he describes this position as a personal revelation, discovering the tainted or spoiled nature of a previously anodyne, if not joyful world. This new self-positioning opens him to other subjects, including the precarious lives of the old, the ambiguous screams of children in either play or fear, and perhaps most notably, an imagined nameless "anyone": "If there were real screams, I found myself wondering, would it be possible to tell the difference, would anyone detect the timbre of tragedy? Or could an atrocity take place whose sonority was indistinguishable from the make-believe of youngsters, their boredom and scares?"[31] What began as a personal revelation has transformed into Will's fledgling registration of social vulnerability. His meditation also poses the problem of how one might distinguish injury and harm as distinct from normal life: a problem of listening and witnessing that he himself faces in his relationship with Charles.

[30] Ibid., 176–177.
[31] Ibid., 177.

Spatial Fantasies: Swimming-Pool Libraries, Colonial Homes

Hollinghurst's novels employ another heightened mode of spatial representation, one that plays with fantasies of remade and mediated spaces, exemplified in the titular "swimming-pool library" itself. The impact of Hollinghurst's dual *Bildungsroman* is most keenly felt through this doubling of spatial fantasies, which effects an eminently literary connection between characters. Both Will and Charles are drawn to an architecture of degraded homespaces and broken enclosures, sharing a predilection for shadows, slatted windows, whitewashed walls, and unfurnished or temporary rooms. These unfinished, even fantastic structures allow them to experience impossible forms of dwelling in conflict with both established, institutionalized forms of domesticity such as marriage and private home ownership, as well as London's sexual institutions affiliated with urban gay male subjectivity such as club, bathhouse, and cinema.

This spatial grammar is exemplified in Hollinghurst's introduction of the "swimming-pool library":

> I dream, once or month or so, of that changing-room, its slatted benches. In our retrogressive slang it was known as the Swimming-Pool Library and then simply as the Library, a notion fitting to the double lives we led. "I shall be in the library," I would announce, a prodigy of study. Sometimes I think that shadowy, doorless little shelter—which is all it was really, an empty, empty place—is where at heart I want to be. Beyond it was a wire fence and then a sloping, moonlit field of grass—"the Wilderness"— that whispered and sighed in the night breeze. Nipping into that library of uncatalogued pleasure was to step into the dark and halt. Then held breath was released, a cigarette glowed, its smoke was smelled, the substantial blackness moved, glimmered and touched. Friendly hands felt for the flies. There was never, or rarely, any kissing—no cloying, adult impurity in the lubricious innocence of what we did.[32]

While readers of the novel often contextualize this moment in light of the gay bathhouse, the "swimming-pool library" also critically exceeds this recognizable queer institution.[33] Its structural elements reflect the very shape of Will's desire, particularly his intimacy with strangers and his "irrational

---

[32] Ibid., 140–141.
[33] Dianne Chisholm offers an especially compelling reading of the recognizable queer institution of the gay bathhouse in Hollinghurst, arguing that Hollinghurst's literary representation

sense of absolute security that came from the conspiracy of sex with men I had never seen before and might never see again."[34] Its evocation thus invites the reader to imagine an architecture of sexuality away from enclosure, property, and the stasis of home, and toward distance, strangers, and the mobility of practices. Despite being an "empty, empty place," the swimming-pool library provides a form of shelter, perhaps even "absolute security": a vision of how to live securely in detachment and distance, in intimacy without domicile. Desire seems attached to the space itself as a site for sexual encounter, even more than to its subjects. This is not an entirely democratic vision: as Will notes, these "daring instincts were by no means infallible: their exhilaration was sharpened by the courted risk of rejection, misunderstanding, abuse."[35] Nor is it entirely antisocial; it does not quite belong to a politics of queer antirelationality, along the lines of Leo Bersani or Lee Edelman; it is neither the grave nor anti-communitarian.[36] As an imaginary space shot through with imminent danger and the possibility of collapse and destruction, it is an eminently unstable blueprint for a structure of queer sociality: which is to say, an eminently fictional one.

This specifically literary production of space recalls the "greenwood" of Forster's *Maurice*, one of literature's most powerful formulations of queer space. As described in *Maurice*'s "Terminal Note" written in September 1960, Forster was determined to let his protagonist and lover "fall in love and remain in it for the ever and ever that fiction allows, and in this sense Maurice and Alec still roam the greenwood."[37] Shifting to a more personal, reflective tone, Forster elaborates: "Our greenwood ended catastrophically and inevitably. Two great wars demanded and bequeathed regimentation which the public services adopted and extended, science lent her aid, and the wildness of our island, never extensive, was stamped upon and built over and patrolled in no time."[38] Hollinghurst was surely aware of the importance of the greenwood for both character and author, having written his MLitt

---

provides an alternative way of doing history and thinking historically to that practiced by social historians. "Love at Last Sight, or Walter Benjamin's Dialectics of Seeing in the Wake of the Gay Bathhouse," *Textual Practice* 13:2 (1999), 243–272. The introduction to her book also provides a good theoretical overview of queer space, which she delineates along the lines of the queer city, queer space, and her concept of "queer constellations." *Queer Constellations: Subcultural Space in the Wake of the City* (Minneapolis: University of Minnesota Press, 2005), 1–62.
[34] Hollinghurst, *Library*, 132.
[35] Ibid.
[36] See Lee Edelman, *No Future: Queer Theory and the Death Drive* (Durham: Duke University Press, 2004).
[37] Forster, *Maurice* (New York: W.W. Norton & Company, Inc., 1993), 250.
[38] Ibid., 254.

thesis on the "creative uses of homosexuality" in Forster's novels, as well as those of Ronald Firbank and L.P. Hartley. Indeed, the pre-AIDS structure and feel of *The Swimming-Pool Library* resonates deeply with that of *Maurice*'s own prewar setting of 1912, elegizing sexual innocence and anonymity. But Forster's elegy also has a postwar historical charge, even if vague. Written in the wake of two world wars, his language documents the loss of a gay past not only through wartime destruction, but also through a kind of institutional recognition instituted through and after war. Hollinghurst's novel shares that skepticism over postwar advancements in public service. As a utopian literary device, his "swimming-pool library" is responding to the specific historical situation of postwar reconstruction, and its top-down fantasies of how to contain and manage people.[39]

José Esteban Muñoz's distinction between "abstract" and "concrete" utopia provides a useful framework for understanding the swimming-pool library's historical relations. For Muñoz, drawing on Ernst Bloch's *The Principle of Hope*, an abstract utopia is "untethered from any historical consciousness," whereas a concrete one is "relational to historically situated struggles, a collectivity that is actualized or potential," though they can also be "daydreamlike" if their dream-life exists in "realm of educated hope."[40] Holding dream and reality in tension is crucial for theorizing a queer utopianism whose sociality is neither anti-relational nor strictly communitarian: a formulation that recalls Roland Barthes's concept of "idiorhythmy," and the search of a space that fosters both the singularity of individual desire and the ability to be a social being.[41] If, as Muñoz articulates, a queer aesthetic "frequently contains blueprints and schemata of a forward-dawning futurity," *The Swimming-Pool Library*'s aesthetic of place and space likewise gestures toward a queer dream-life of reconstruction, developing alongside but also critically outside of reconstruction's specific postwar history.[42]

Will's fantastic swimming pool gains historical resonance in relation to Charles's own spatial fantasies, which interrogate the colonial histories informing Britain's postwar reconstruction. Charles's first spatial imaginary takes the form of his home in colonial Sudan, where he lives with his servant

---

[39] We could also read the difference between "abstract" and "concrete" utopias as the difference between state planning of reconstruction and its lived reality (often literally in concrete, whether the squat postwar housing towers or Charles's prison cell), though that conceptualizes utopia rather differently.
[40] José Esteban Muñoz, *Cruising Utopia: The Then and There of Queer Futurity* (New York: NYU Press, 2009), 3.
[41] Ibid., 2–3. Interesting, too, to note that Ernst Bloch's work emerges from the wake of the Second World War.
[42] Ibid., 1.

or "houseboy," Taha. In his diaries from these days, Charles describes the house as an abstraction, one that does away with property, propriety, and specific geopolitical associations much like Will's swimming-pool library. For Charles, this utopian ideal of home reflects his professed unease with the trappings and formalities of colonial governmentality:

> There is something which charms me utterly about this house. It is whitewashed & square & has four rooms, each of the same size. It is a house reduced to its very elements, with empty holes for windows and doors, so that one looks from one room into the next—& through that to the outside, the surrounding shacks, the clustered peaks of the huts or the bald, enigmatic rocks. The house is a kind of frame for living in or discipline for thought—so that its few furnishings, the book-case, a rather hideous rug, the photograph of the king, seem unnecessary embarrassments.[43]

In its abstraction, the house seems less of a habitable environment and more of a blueprint or design for living; the observation that it is a "frame for living in" echoes Le Corbusier's famous dictum that "the house is a machine for living in," complete with its ethos of discipline or efficiency.[44] It is a form of the reconstructive imagination taken to its extreme, erasing the materiality of the house in favor of a Platonic ideal. This abstract space also enables Charles to imagine a form of intimacy with Taha, whom he finds "waiting, never snoozing or yawning, but squatting in perfect, illiterate silence. His beauty is enhanced by his watchfulness, which is never impertinent or burdensome; it is an almost abstract form of attention, a condition of life to him."[45] In effect, Charles does to Taha what he previously did to the home: abstracting, reducing, and dehistoricizing him into a pure form of relationality.

The home also allows Charles to engage in heteronormative, paternalistic fantasies. When Taha's life is endangered by a scorpion sting, Charles's new role as caretaker weaves together domestic space, political obligation, and queer kinship to produce a sense of responsibility. As he writes in his diary: "When I went back through the doorless aperture into the room where Taha was, asleep, unaware, & yet tormented, like some saint in ecstasy or martyrdom, I felt all my vague, ideal emotions about Africa & my wandering, autocratic life here take substance before my bleary eyes. [...] At once I

---

[43] Hollinghurst, *Library*, 206.
[44] Le Corbusier, *Towards an Architecture*, trans. Frederick Etchells (New York: Dover Publications, Inc., 1986), 4.
[45] Hollinghurst, *Library*, 206.

saw he was my responsibility made flesh: he was all the offspring I will never have, all my futurity."[46] Figured at once as child, lover, saint, and servant, Taha becomes a placeholder for the beloved in this spatial reverie, which inaugurates Charles's role as parent and benefactor. Even so, this revelation is not enough to transcend the power dynamics that structure their relationship. Though Charles manages to bring Taha back to London with him upon his return, it is as his domestic servant.

The postwar period catalyzes the second stage of Charles's sexualized spatial fantasies: his recurring dream of his entrapment and imprisonment under the Labouchere Amendment. Much as in his meditations on the colonial house, Charles describes and reiterates the scene in great spatial detail. Whereas the desert diaries begin with a description of the house and then become increasingly more literary and symbolic, the revelation about his imprisonment is inverted, beginning with fantasy and moving to the reality of his arrest. Charles's first dream begins with him walking with an undercover police officer to a cottage, which, in his dream-logic, transforms "into what is no longer simply the cottage but a light-filled space whose walls alter or roll away like ingenious stage machinery in a transformation scene. We make love in the drying-room at Winchester, or in a white-tiled institutional bathroom, or the white house at Talodi, bare of my scraps of furniture and revealed in all its harmonious vacancy: simple places whose very emptiness prompts desire."[47] This reverie is a gorgeous palimpsest of places, people, and parts, a beautiful writing of the no-place and every-place of queer utopia. Yet it cannot stay the fact of the arrest, told in a second iteration of the dream. Charles describes the event through a slow revelation: "There is a thumping silence, and the light of the one lamp across the wet tiled floor seems conscious that it will illuminate this and many other atrocities, just as it will go on shining through days and months of sudden speechless lusts, and all the intervening hours of silent emptiness."[48] Thus the aperture of possibility narrows. What was before a desirable emptiness has been degraded; the very structure of the dream-cottage becomes sentient of its new complicity in atrocity.

This transformation of Charles's spatial imagination is finally completed during his time in prison. While incarcerated, he hears news of Taha's racially motivated murder, which causes Charles to fall into a depressive

---

[46] *Ibid.*, 209–210.
[47] *Ibid.*, 251.
[48] *Ibid.*, 252.

state. This emotional retreat, however, does not last. Instead, prison catalyzes an education in collective thinking, as its subterranean world was "fuller than it ever had been with our people, as a direct result of the current brutal purges."[49] Describing how the prison "closed about me, offered me its pitiful comforts, and began to reveal its depths—now murky, now surprisingly coralline and clear," Charles is able to see its "structure of submerged bonds and loyalties."[50] Over time, he emerges as a full participant in this new social network and dedicates himself to "do something for others like myself, and for those more defenseless still."[51] Once released, Charles proves true to his word. Once released, he works to establish the Boys' Club and a boxing tournament in his name (the "Nantwich Cup"), and finds his fellow prisoner Bill a job "where his feeling for men and physical exercise can be fulfilled, rather than baulked and denied in some clerkly work." Space here becomes shelter rather than trap, expansive rather than criminalizing. In this way, Charles effects his own type of queer welfare, establishing institutions of care and employment for "his people" that directly counter the conservatism and homophobia of the postwar period.

While these spatial fantasies allow these protagonists a temporary escape from aspects of their personhood, enabling certain types of transgressive relationships along lines of race and sex, they are ultimately affirmed as just that: fantasies. Both Charles and Will discover the limits of imagination and desire in violence-based epiphanies which teach them, as Jameson put it, that "History is what hurts, it is what refuses desire and sets inexorable limits to individual as well as collective praxis."[52] As two upper-class white peers, both Charles and Will encounter the limits of their sympathy and understanding when it comes to black, working-class, colonial, or postcolonial subjects: men with whom both are troublingly infatuated, reflecting a protectionist or paternalist impulse mixed with colonial and postcolonial exoticism. Thus, when history returns to them, it often teaches them not only about their sexual precarity as gay men, but also their advantaged racial and economic backgrounds. Despite Charles's insistence that he is beyond the brute, racist civilizing mission of the "hard-hatted, heavy-handed empire-builder" and Will's seemingly unfettered mobility through the diverse sexual networks of London, the novel's epiphanies reveal not only the blindnesses that adhere to these characters, but also

---

[49] Ibid., 253.
[50] Ibid., 254 and 255.
[51] Ibid., 260.
[52] Fredric Jameson, *The Political Unconscious: Narrative as a Socially Symbolic Act* (Ithaca: Cornell University Press, 1981), 102.

the irony of their seeking an unlimited sexual freedom whose mobility and efficacy are predicated on personal privilege. Charles's prison writings and post-prison politics thus raise a challenge regarding Will's own transformation into an agent of social repair. Can Will reconstruct his previous, individuated spatial fantasy into a more socially aware formulation, as Charles has done before him? And how do we read the sublimation of this spatial work through Charles's request that Will write his biography, a textual form of this social reconstruction?

In this regard, *The Swimming-Pool Library* meets its ethical limit. For while the novel allows histories of racial and sexual violence to surface "as hurt," it privileges queer history as the hurt to be repaired at the expense of Britain's injurious history of colonialism and race relations. Though signaled, racial trauma remains on the margins, as the structure of generational transfer revolves around the injury of Charles's incarceration.

Epochs of Catastrophe, Moments of Desire

When Will finally learns that Charles's victimization by a "whole sort of gay pogrom" was orchestrated largely by his grandfather, who was then Director of Public Persecutions, it sets off a series of cascading crises that end only with the last lines of the novel. Will reads the diaries (the "digest of disasters"); goes to find solace with his lover, Phil, only to find him in bed with the much older Bill; has a truly comic-disastrous encounter with Gabriel, an Argentinian with a penchant for sex-shop accoutrements; and fails to retrieve the photos that would save his friend James. This realization is radically different in kind from Will's previous meditations on the nature of violence. Instead of generalizing the hurts of history to the "universal violence" lurking in every shop-goer, Will comes to terms with his blindness to his own past, and learns his life is not independent of history. Whether this realization has any ramifications for him as a protagonist is the central challenge posed by the text, one that has to be placed in relation to the novel's twentieth-century structure and layered spatial *Bildungsromane*. Critics are torn: some think Will learns nothing from Charles's object lesson, whereas others see it as a form of epiphany.

Will's reaction to these prison diaries is to fall into an ambiguous feeling of a "queer empty panic":

> I was so confused by this digest of disasters, I felt so stupid and so ashamed that I walked around the flat talking out loud, getting up and sitting down,

scratching my crew-cut head as if I had lice. It was impossible so quickly to formulate a plan, but I felt the important thing was to go to Charles, to say something or other to him. It took me ages to get a cab, and as at last it locked and braked its way through the West End closing-time crowds, I found all my ideas of what I might do rattling away, leaving me in a queer empty panic.[53]

This "queer empty panic" is worlds away from the generative emptiness of Charles's colonial house or Will's swimming-pool library. On the one hand, it evokes "gay panic," a legal defense that legitimates paranoid, homophobic violence, making it acceptable for individuals to use force against a person who is perceived to be making (homo)sexual advances toward them. Although Will has been called out and identified through Charles's sexual and textual request, Will is experiencing the opposite of legal paranoia; instead of reacting with violence against Charles, he seeks to connect and perhaps make amends; instead of projecting force outwards, he turns it inward through feelings of stupidity and shame. Nevertheless, the insertion of the word "empty" destabilizes its meaning, as does the word "queer." While "queer" recalls Will's description of the swimming-pool library and the original architecture of his sexuality, in this instance, queer as strangeness surfaces more strongly than previous references. After all, Will is hardly ever at a loss of what to do; his lack of mobility here underscores the shock and confusion of his realization.

However destabilizing, the phrase provides an apt description of the strangeness of Will's relationship to Charles Nantwich: one both kindred and non-kindred, once-removed and yet still terribly insinuating, and implying some form of debt and apology still owed even across generations. This queer empty panic is a structure of historical feeling that arises from this form of skewed relation, one that is uninhabitable more in the sense of Charles's postwar prison cell than the desirable, empty shelter of Will's swimming-pool library. Whereas Charles emerges from his imprisonment with a renewed sense of active commitment to other gay men, Will ultimately refuses to write Charles's memoirs for him. After all, as he says to Charles, the only writing that could come from this would be a "book about why I couldn't write the book"—perhaps the very book we now hold in our hands.[54]

---

[53] Hollinghurst, *Library*, 260.
[54] Ibid., 329.

As J. Stephen Murphy suggests, Will's refusal to write Nantwich's biography, like the novel's elision of AIDS itself, offers an "ethical responses to the catastrophe," a refusal to turn both into "objects of knowledge transparently available to narrative framing."[55] Rather than conceive history as catastrophe and historiography as a form of mourning—the dominant imperative of criticism ranging from deconstruction to trauma theory to Jameson's "history is what hurts"—Hollinghurst's novel employs irony, rather than memory, as a way to move beyond a calamitous history.[56] In this reading, the lesson from this refusal is that a focus on pain or catastrophe leads to a narrow, if not reductive conceptualization of history and group identity: a political viewpoint shared by the novel's protagonist.

I read Will's refusal as different type of ethical response to the catastrophe, one that sees the labor of writing the biography as too stifling a commitment or intimacy. Though having such an account written might be reparative for Charles, it is quite another matter to write on behalf of another person, especially under such conditions of responsibility, atonement, and paranoid revelation. For Will, serving as Charles's Swimming-Pool Librarian does not signify repair. Instead, it symbolizes yet another form of empty place, a hollow promise of fulfillment through historical reconstruction. To refuse this labor, then, is tantamount to refusing the reparative grammar of the state itself. Whereas Charles attempts to repair his imprisonment by building alternative institutions of queer welfare, Will opts out of this logic altogether, refusing to grant the reconstructive imagination power as the ultimate giver of epiphanies.

The full ramifications of Will's refusal are not felt until Will returns to the Corry gym. As he looks out over the group of gay men in the swimming pool, he muses:

> There were several old boys, one or two perhaps even of Charles's age, and doubtless all with their own story, strange and yet oddly comparable, to tell. And going into the showers I saw a suntanned young lad in pale blue trunks that I rather liked the look of.[57]

---

[55] J. Stephen Murphy, "Past Irony: Trauma and the Historical Turn in Fragments and The Swimming-Pool Library," *Literature & History* 13 (2004), 67.

[56] As Murphy writes: "Irony seems especially necessary now not only as a way to counter the excessive reverence in literary criticism for historical calamities—a reverence that sometimes seems to put the calamity above its victims and survivors—but also as a way, in fact, to honour the dead. It is precisely because Will Beckwith and Alan Hollinghurst refuse to respect history that they do it a service" ("Past Irony," 73).

[57] Hollinghurst, *Library*, 288.

This last sentence ends on an ultimately ironic and distancing move, one that eschews responsibility and a community based on injury and that instead celebrates individual desires and actions. However, the sentence that precedes it signals a key change in Will. Just as he newly understood the precarity of the elderly, young black men, and gay men, so too can he now see a deep, shared history of the "old boys." Connected by the additive conjunction "and" (rather than "but" or "yet"), these sentences show that Will can have it both ways: a double-consciousness he has earned over the course of the novel. Thus, even though the final lines of *The Swimming-Pool Library* end with the present, instantaneous pulse of sexual desire, its balancing of past and present reminds the reader of the rise of the AIDS crisis, which signifies both the endpoint of Will's halcyon summer and the novel's narrative arc. The novel asks not only what responsibility we have to a past we never experienced, but also, crucially, what responsibility we might owe to the future. Hollinghurst leaves us with these questions in order to encourage our own comparative historical consciousness. AIDS appears as the epoch we must contend with in our own moment, just as the postwar period is encrypted in Charles's diaries.

Yet this passage's ending also offers a warning to those readers who might privilege this burgeoning textuality over Will's now-familiar sexuality. It is tempting to read too much into Will's newfound appreciation of the old boys' stories as the ultimate outcome, even payoff, of the novel. This reading is especially inviting as the novel is presented as a quasi-*Bildungsroman* that documents Will's gay, and to a lesser degree, racial consciousness-raising. By turning our attention to the suntanned young man in the showers, Hollinghurst ensures that space and gay desire get the last word. This dual vision of queer history is *The Swimming-Pool Library*'s difficult reward. History may be what hurts, but the novel does not let it be what refuses desire, even (and especially) if the future attached to that desire looks dim.

Coda: The Attenuation of Postwar Feeling

This chapter closes with a consideration of Hollinghurst's later twentieth-century novels—*The Stranger's Child* (2011) and *The Sparsholt Affair* (2017)—asking how they measure against the vision of his first, and what, if any, historical argument they make about Britain's midcentury. Like *The Swimming-Pool Library*, *The Stranger's Child* is characterized by both the breadth and metahistorical nature of its timeline, though the emphasis on the postwar period is much weaker. Divided into five sections, the novel drops us squarely and unapologetically into the Edwardians' last hurrah of 1913, the interwar year 1926, gay history's watershed 1967 (and the decriminalization of homosexuality in England, here more a structure of feeling than explicitly foregrounded), the 1980s market for gay and lesbian biography, and finally 2008, characterized by the academic canonization of queer theory. *The Stranger's Child* is also a study of gay history's secrets and lies, desperate desires, dusty closets, and nested narratives, all focalized through the act of biography-writing. Its narrative describes the few brief days that Cecil Valance, a charming, poetic rogue, spends with the Sawle family in 1913. During that time, Cecil composes a poem in their daughter Daphne's autograph book that, in time, comes to seal his literary reputation. The secret that is revealed is that while the poem is given to Daphne, it is actually written about her brother, George ("And in their shadows lovers too / Might kiss and tell their secrets through"). Dying a war-hero's death in 1918, Cecil leaves the poem and its attendant shadows to take on lives of their own, which the novel charts through the winding, tortuous inheritance of his work and life across various generations.

Though it resembles *The Swimming-Pool Library* in its historical sweep, *The Stranger's Child* has different investments, focusing on what it means to academically institutionalize gay life rather than writing's own abilities to effect historical repair. Though *The Stranger's Child* charts gay history, it is primarily focused on the history of gay studies, twinned neatly with the family saga. Ultimately, it relies on readers' interest in academia itself, a novelistic premise with perhaps limited rewards. The question of the novel, then, is how to both move past but also recapture the very live, beating heart ensconced in its first eighty pages—the history that it spends the rest of its pages recovering, but also recovering from.

In some ways, this itinerary is deadening. As the novel progresses, Hollinghurst moves us from youthful woodland frolicking to the biographer's grubbing for scraps, from the laughing secrets of Cambridge men to the shifty-eyed competition of academics. Prewar parties become conferences, interviews, and funerals, and Hollinghurst's sharp social criticism transmutes into the less glamorous, but equally desperate terrain of biographical research. Perhaps Will was right to refuse the labor of writing Charles's life, thinks the reader of *The Swimming-Pool Library*. For the biographer's reward in *The Stranger's Child* lies somewhere between delusion and grandeur: described as the funny feeling of "a welcome from the literary family, of curtains held back, doors opening into half-seen rooms full of oddities and treasures that seemed virtually normal to the people who lived in them."[58] This hard-earned welcome may not seem like much of a payoff for the reader of *The Stranger's Child*, who has already been given full access to these hallowed halls in the earliest section of the novel. Our reward—if it is that—lies somewhere else, in the difficult witnessing of Hollinghurst's relentless narrative, with all the hauntings, misreadings, and disavowals that only time can tell. The lesson, when it comes, is a difficult one to swallow: history is made not only by those who show up, but also by the grudges and slow calcification of those who were there before, and the obsessive, ungainly intrusions of those who were not. Put differently—and to use the final lines of *The Swimming-Pool Library* as a kind of shorthand— by the end of *The Stranger's Child*, all we can see are the old boys with their odd and comparable stories. The suntanned young men of the world, alas, have all but disappeared.

In a way, *The Sparsholt Affair* (2017) can be read as a hybrid of *The Stranger's Child* and *The Swimming-Pool Library*, combining the former's forward march through the twentieth century with latter's historicization of postwar homophobia. Like both, it focuses on what it means to artistically capture a life, adding the medium of oil portraiture to that of textual biography that occupies the earlier two novels. It begins in Oxford during the Second World War, where it introduces David Sparsholt as an object of sexual desire among a group of undergraduates; shifts focus to David's son, Johnny, vacationing with his parents in a 1960s Cornwall beachtown and coming into his own gay sexuality; follows Johnny, now a painter, as he becomes acquainted with his father's Oxford friends and their "Memoir Club" in mid-1970s London; shifts to mid-1990s London after Johnny become a father himself, while he and his father awkwardly skirt the topic of David's sexuality; and finally ends in the 2010s after David's death.

As its title suggests, the propelling energy of these individual sections, both within themselves and between them, is the concept of the affair. By foregoing the metatextual, metafictional preoccupations of *The Stranger's Child*, *The Sparsholt Affair* reveals the possible contours of this theme over the course of the novel. The word is first used rather casually to describe a large oil painting done of David by one of the students at Oxford, and then another's triumphant sexual encounter with him. It subsequently takes on a scandalous connotation through a 1966 affair between David, a Tory MP, and other men that occupied the news cycle for a month or so, the year

---

[58] Hollinghurst, *The Stranger's Child* (New York: Alfred A. Knopf, 2011), 331.

before the decriminalization of homosexuality. Its final connotation is of a portrait done by Johnny, commissioned by an upper-class family, who jestingly call it "The Sparsholt Affair." First as tragedy, second as farce, always as stigma, queer history is driven both by the mainstream transformation of queerness as well as its abiding negativity—a combination that reaches its apex in the postwar period.

This historical structure might explain Hollinghurst's decision to begin *The Sparsholt Affair* during the Second World War, devoting its entire first section to the confluence of war and desire. While *The Swimming-Pool Library* and *The Stranger's Child* largely skip over the Second World War, *The Sparsholt Affair* grants this period more historical weight as the beautiful "before" period to the postwar's conservative "after." In this regard, *The Sparsholt Affair* represents a sexualized, intimate state of emergency, shot through with illicit sex and romance under the cover and chaos of the Blitz. From Elizabeth Bowen's *The Heat of the Day* and Graham Greene's *The End of the Affair* to contemporary novels such as Sarah Waters's *The Night Watch*, literature of the Second World War tends toward queerness—or if not queerness per se, then at least permissiveness and promiscuity that test the accepted boundaries of normative sexual practices. While *The Swimming-Pool Library* devotes surprisingly little time to these tropes of love and war, Hollinghurst's later novels are more willing to rehearse them, turning to them as sources of queer sexuality and enchantment. On this point, *The Sparsholt Affair* delivers beautifully, overlaying the secrecy and silences of gay desire on that of the wartime blackout. The first, momentary glimpse of David Sparsholt is revelatory of these possibilities: his body seen tantalizingly lit and framed by a window before the shutters close to block out the light ("a figure in a gleaming singlet, steadily lifting and lowering a pair of hand-weights...as if shaped from light himself").[59] The form of this glimpse, revealing and salacious, is repeated and reworked across the novel. It is later revealed as incriminating evidence: the "famous photo taken through a window" that confirms the novel's titular affair.[60] The window, and in particular the window frame, thus offers a sexual epistemology as both creating and surveilling desire: an ambivalent architecture that depends on the eye of the beholder.

In the world of the novel, the "Sparsholt Affair" carries another connotation, referring to a corruption case involving David's architectural firm. Mentioned only twice over the course of the novel, reviewers routinely

---

[59] Hollinghurst, *The Sparsholt Affair* (London: Picador, 2017), 5.
[60] Hollinghurst, *Sparsholt*, 193.

overlook this version of the "affair" for its more obvious sexual connotation. Yet this fictional event has a notable historical equivalent: a set of scandals in Britain's history of postwar planning, signaled by a minor character's remark ("It reminded me of the Poulson business, in a way").[61] John Poulson was an influential architect whose work spanned the prewar and postwar years. In the flurry of postwar building, his business grew immensely due to bribery and corruption, which helped him secure building contracts. After filing for bankruptcy in 1972, he was put on trial for corruption and sentenced to seven years in prison, implicating a vast range of people and organizations, including a number of MPs, council officials, and home secretary Reginald Maudling, who resigned due to the scandal. However fleeting, Hollinghurst's reference to the Poulson affair is a telling one. The event indexes a corruption that counters the democratic ideals of postwar reconstruction and urban planning, privileging private interest and profit over public duty. This affair has also been taken by historians as marking the beginning of British political decline, cited in the same breath as the Suez Crisis and Profumo Affair.[62] The betrayal Poulson represents is thus as severe a breaking of social consensus as that of Charles's imprisonment in *The Swimming-Pool Library*, or even the 1960s version of the Sparsholt Affair.

This brief reference suggests paying heightened attention to Hollinghurst's representation of architecture. In a way, reconstruction is more directly thematized in *The Sparsholt Affair* than in the other novels. Not only is David Sparsholt a postwar architect, but the grandfather of his eventual granddaughter, Peter Orban, is a prominent Hungarian modernist architect, whose brutalist, minimalist works are described as having risen to fame in the postwar period. His work, built and destroyed over the course of the novel, becomes a way of signaling the passage of time, as well as changing aesthetic and domestic tastes. In one telling episode, Johnny Sparsholt stops with his daughter to take in one of Orban's Corbusian modern homes:

"Why couldn't he make it the same as all the other houses?" she said.

"Well, sometimes, darling," said Johnny, holding her there just a little bit longer, "there's a point in being completely different and new."

---

[61] *Ibid.*, 404. That this comment is made by someone named "Alan" signals the potential weight of this reference.
[62] Peter Jones, "Re-Thinking Corruption in Post-1950 Urban Britain: The Poulson Affair, 1972–1976," *Urban History* 39:3 (2012), 512.

EMPTY PLACES: UNPROPERTIED INTIMACY, QUEER HISTORY   181

"Well, I think it's nasty," she said quietly, and turned her head to carry on down the street.

"A bomb knocked down the old house, you see, in the War," said Johnny, now rather on his mettle to defend the building. But talk of the war, which had coloured and conditioned so much of his own childhood, was meaningless to her.[63]

Unlike *The Swimming-Pool Library*'s privileging of quasi-public spaces of queer sociality over actual domestic structures, *The Sparsholt Affair* reinvests in the potential of queer domestic space, whether the rooms at Oxford, the beachtown bungalows, or the various living arrangements created by mixed, modern families. These spaces are no longer villainized nor metaphorized; instead, they emerge as livable, workable environments for their characters. The novel's utopian and reparative energies, previously attached to fantasies of space in *The Swimming-Pool Library*, have been relocated to the bonds of family. For in the end, this is a novel about parents and children, and about the open secrets they weave themselves so thoroughly into their lives that they scarcely know how to talk about them. The elder Sparsholt, famously button-lipped, is loathe to invite people into his private affairs, especially his son. Yet Johnny, also gay, craves the intimacy he imagines would come from discussing the affair with his father. In the end, he only accesses this vitality after his father's death, as he paints a portrait of his daughter: "He went back into the studio, capped the paint-tubes and peered with familiar yearning and dissatisfaction at the portrait, the eyes the blue-grey (he saw it at last) of her dead grandfather's, the lips, redone, still wet and workable."[64] Though this access is achieved only through an act of uninvited framing—which, as the novel has shown, can be an injurious act—here, it serves the purpose of capturing a life, however indirect the reconstruction.

---

[63] Hollinghurst, *Sparsholt*, 342.
[64] Ibid., 454.

5
Oasis Societies
Global Welfare and the Romance of Care

In 2018, The Booker Prize Foundation announced its intention to award "The Golden Man Booker Prize," a "best of" competition celebrating the Prize's fiftieth anniversary. Out of the fifty-one previous winners, five nominees were chosen—V.S. Naipaul's *In a Free State* (1971), Penelope Lively's *Moon Tiger* (1987), Ondaatje's *The English Patient* (1992), Hilary Mantel's *Wolf Hall* (2009), and George Saunders's *Lincoln in the Bardo* (2017)— one from each decade of the award's existence. Despite the haphazard and often scandalous nature of prize culture, this experiment revealed a marked esteem for the historical novel, whether Ondaatje's and Lively's Second World War, Mantel's early modern England, or Saunders's American Civil War. This taste for the historical characterizes much of the Booker's history, with more than half of prize winners written in the genre.[1] After these five nominees were chosen by individual judges, the public got to choose the overall winner, crowning *The English Patient* victorious in a kind of "People's Choice" Booker of Bookers. Of course, the novel's lush, romantic 1996 film adaptation may have had some influence here. Anthony Minghella's adaptation was critically acclaimed on its release, winning Best Picture at the Academy Awards, Best Drama at the Golden Globes, and Best Film at the BAFTA Awards, and it has remained popular viewing ever since.[2] However, it is possible that the Golden Booker Award recognized something more

---

[1] See, for instance, Matthew Eatough's assessment of the Booker Prize from the late twentieth century (the postcolonial historical novels of Ishiguro, Rushdie, Ondaatje) to the present day (emerging genres by Cusk, Mitchell, Oyeyemi): "Under this new dispensation, postmodern investigations into exclusionary historical records have seemingly diminished in importance at the same time as modernist-inflected experimentalism has experienced something of a renaissance, as witnessed in the work of McCarthy and Ali Smith." "'Are They Going to Say This Is Fantasy?': Kazuo Ishiguro, Untimely Genres, and the Making of Literary Prestige," *MFS* 67.1 (Spring 2021), 43.

[2] Ondaatje seemed to suggest as such in his brief acceptance speech for the Golden Booker, while also dismissing his novel, calling it "still cloudy, with errors in pacing." Golden Man Booker Speech, July 12, 2018, https://lithub.com/michael-ondaatjes-golden-man-booker-speech-is-really-great/.

than the thrill of Ralph Fiennes and Kristin Scott Thomas's desert affair. As this chapter suggests, part of the appeal of *The English Patient* is its test of the Second World War and 1945 as a threshold moment of social and historical possibility, particularly as a historical transition that tests the promise of Britain's postwar consensus against the violence of its colonial past. Though both novel and film eventually fail this test, Ondaatje's treatment of domestic space still holds out hope for the reparative power of connection and caretaking, even if these are only possible through literary means.

For Ondaatje, 1945 signals a historical crossroads, a particularly tender moment when the world today could have been otherwise. Set between V-E and V-J Day during the Second World War, *The English Patient* focuses on a group of strangers living together in an abandoned Italian villa, who seek to mend their physical and symbolic wounds. As its title suggests, the novel centers on the "English Patient," whose horrific burns seem to be irreparable, and whose storytelling drives the present narrative. Unlike the other works addressed in this book, *The English Patient* is considered part of a Global Anglophone canon, authored by a Sri Lankan-born Canadian writer. Yet its preoccupation with postwar Britishness and practices of postwar care indicates just how far the reach of Britain's 1945 extends as described in this project. Though the setting alternates between colonial Saharan Africa, wartime Italy and England, and finally postwar India and Canada—and though the Patient is not an Englishman, but rather a Hungarian count—the novel's eponymous Patient stands in for the questions of what, exactly, comprises the allegorical and geopolitical wound to England, and what will change when its empire falls.

With its international cast of characters, *The English Patient* conjures a very different vision of welfare and postwar reconstruction from the works described earlier in this book, even in comparison with Hollinghurst's *Swimming-Pool Library*. Ondaatje's de-emphasizing of the urban invites reconsideration of the imaginative space of reconstruction, which typically privileges London as the engine of its transformation. Yet as Raymond Williams has shown, the imperial metropole and colony cannot be thought separately. Both are underwritten by capitalist, and indeed, imperial modes of production, imperialism being "the story of the city and the country in its harshest form, and now on an unimaginably complex scale."[3] *The English Patient* can thus be read as an experiment in rescaling this story, shrinking it

---

[3] Raymond Williams, *The Country and the City* (Oxford: Oxford University Press, 1973), 283.

to the microcosmic international community of the villa. This social space becomes both the allegory and the site of direct interrogation of Britain's transition from warfare to welfare.

If Ondaatje describes his novel as "about very tentative healing among a group of people," this chapter reads this tentative healing as an experiment in nascent postwar geopolitics, or the possibility of international relations based not on old habits of war-making but instead on caretaking.[4] Despite the disruptive violence of Hiroshima and Nagasaki, *The English Patient* primes its reader to believe in the connective potential of communal living, insisting on the enchantment of postwar care over the disenchantment of war. Much of the criticism on the novel grapples with this mode of attachment and investment in literary enchantment, uncertain about Ondaatje's stylized treatment of war and violence.[5] For while his novels often make the case for the reparative value of language and imaginative fiction, their aesthetic bids are often undermined by their style and investment in metafiction. This is particularly the case with Ondaatje's war novels, whose aestheticization of violence can seem irresponsible, animated more by how to write a beautiful, moving work about war than in offering any substantive critique. Whether through the appeasing power of literature for their characters, or the masterful yet politically inconclusive tactic of bricolage, something about Ondaatje's style undoes any politically complex work his novels might have otherwise achieved.

This uneasy combination of aesthetics and geopolitics has made Ondaatje a polarizing figure, especially as an emblematic author of Global Anglophone or "World Literature." A telling indication of this position came in the responses to *n+1*'s polemical 2013 article "World Lite," which criticized the current market-determined state of "World Literature" as market-determined, calling instead for an international, potentially revolutionary form of literature. Among many responses, Poorva Rajaram and Michael Griffith were quick to point out that this charge puts the age-old burden of political representation on writers outside the USA and UK: "Why are these anaerobic literary litmus tests (Marxist or otherwise) mysteriously

---

[4] Eleanor Wachtel, "An Interview with Michael Ondaatje," *Essays on Canadian Writing* 53 (1994), 255–256.
[5] See J.U. Jacobs, "Michael Ondaatje's *The English Patient* (1992) and Postcolonial Impatience," *Journal of Literary Studies* 13.1-2 (1997), 92–112; Mike Marais, "Violence, Postcolonial Fiction, and the Limits of Sympathy," *Studies in the Novel* 43.1 (Spring 2011), 94–114; Vicki Visvis, "Traumatic Representation: The Power and Limitations of Storytelling as Talking Cure in Michael Ondaatje's *In the Skin of a Lion* and *The English Patient*," *ariel: A Review of International English Literature* 40.4 (2010), 89–108.

over-applied to Third World writers? And why refuse aesthetic considerations to these writers?"[6] The elements of this exchange recapitulate familiar debates around postcolonial writing, recalling in particular the Jameson–Ahmad exchange over Third World literature and national allegory.[7] What was peculiar to this back-and-forth, however, was its persistent turn to Michael Ondaatje as the litmus test for a good or bad world novelist. This debate began in the original *n+1* piece, which noted that "Michael Ondaatje, a Sri Lankan-born Canadian of Dutch ancestry and hero to many world litterateurs, has been exemplary in the worst way, with his sinuous capacity to suggest a political mind without betraying a real one."[8] In their response, Rajaram and Griffith came to his defense, arguing, "Michael Ondaatje crafts beautiful prose, not political pamphlets. Is Ondaatje (or any of the other writers the editors attack) required to do something that other writers are not?"[9] While conceding the political point, the final word went to *n+1,* who stood their ground on aesthetic judgment: "If we can't agree that Ondaatje is a terrible writer, we may, in fact, have to go our separate ways."[10] Though this gesture may seem like an olive branch, it still foregrounds and leaves open the question of Ondaatje's style and its relation, if any, to the political.

Turning specifically to *The English Patient*, this chapter proposes that what might feel like bad style can be read as an over-investment in the transformative potential of 1945. Ondaatje allegorizes this reconstructive ethos through the Italian villa, figuring it as a peculiarly reparative space for these wartime refugees. Though the villa anchors and gives structure to the itinerant, fragmentary narrative (as much as, say, the Patient's memories and commonplace book), little attention has been paid to the specific workings of this house other than as a convenient setting for a social experiment.

---

[6] Poorva Rajaram and Michael Griffith, "Why World Literature Looks Different From Brooklyn," *Tehelka.com*, August 16, 2013, https://web.archive.org/web/20150612225014/http://blog.tehelka.com/why-world-literature-looks-different-from-brooklyn/. In response, the editors of *n+1* noted that the opposite was true: "In fact, our preference, in 'first world' fiction, is often for the political. Our preference in non-first-world fiction—if we're to judge by the writers we've published—tends to be the opposite." Editors of *n+1*, "'The Rest is Indeed Horseshit,' Pt.6," *n+1*, August 23, 2013, https://nplusonemag.com/online-only/horseshit/the-rest-is-indeed-horseshit-pt-6/. This nonresponse is perhaps more symptomatic than any of the article's original implications, inverting rather than addressing the question at hand (i.e., the logical equivalent to "some of my best friends are...").

[7] Fredric Jameson, "Third World Literature in the Era of Multinational Capitalism," *Social Text* 15 (Autumn 1986), 65–88; Aijaz Ahmad, "Jameson's Rhetoric of Otherness and the 'National Allegory,'" *Social Text* 17 (Autumn, 1987), 3–25.

[8] Editors of *n+1*, "World Lite," *n+1*, Issue 17 (Fall 2013), https://nplusonemag.com/issue-17/the-intellectual-situation/world-lite/.

[9] Rajaram and Griffith, "Why World Literature Looks Different."

[10] Editors of *n+1*, "The Rest."

This chapter remedies this oversight, reading Ondaatje's engagement with domestic space in light of postwar changes: the urgency of care work, as well as the rise of heritage and imperial nostalgia.

In framing conversation around *The English Patient* in terms of domestic space and reconstruction, this chapter moves away from the mise-en-abyme risked by Linda Hutcheon's "historiographic metafiction," or the textual ambivalence Hilary Mantel finds so damning in her 1993 review.[11] Instead, I ask what critical purchase, if any, can be found in its metafiction when taken in relation to other forms of writing and knowledge-making discourse. With this, I join scholars such as Alice Brittan, Antoinette Burton, and Aarthi Vadde, who read Ondaatje's novels as engaging with practices of cryptology and the militarization of writing technologies; forensic science in the wake of wartime violence; and the archive's relation to national myth-making, respectively.[12] In particular, I examine Ondaatje's juxtaposition of the villa's romance of care with nostalgic reminiscences of colonial North Africa, a setting that hosted both the sexual romance between the Patient and Katharine Clifton and, more importantly, the Royal Geographic Society's geopolitical romance with the Sahara Desert. The novel's narrative present can be read as testing these past forms of romance, asking whether new forms of collectivity might supplant their dynamics of ownership and exploitation.

The English Patient's Two Romances

The previous chapter addressed how Britain's wartime history is inscribed in the structure of the century novel, a form of the historical novel that

---

[11] "Languid, exquisite, gently humorous, it seems to suggest that memory is not an individual possession, and that events do not exist in themselves, only as the sum of stories; it is a suggestion reinforced in *The English Patient*." Hilary Mantel, "Wraith's Progress," *New York Review of Books* (January 14, 1993).

[12] See Alice Brittan, "War and the Book: The Diarist, the Cryptographer, and *The English Patient*," *PMLA* 121.1 (2006), 200–213; Antoinette Burton, "Archive of Bones: Anil's Ghost and the Ends of History," *The Journal of Commonwealth Literature* 38.1 (2003), 39–56; and Aarthi Vadde's chapter 5, "Archival Legends: National Myth and Transnational Memory in the Works of Michael Ondaatje," in *Chimeras of Form: Modernist Internationalism Beyond Europe, 1914–2014* (New York: Columbia University Press, 2016), 149–181. To some degree, Ondaatje's own scholarship invites such readings, as indicated by his novels' acknowledgments. While these sections provide the typical credits for their in-text citations, they also index broader research in art history, archaeology, medicine, military history, and other scholarly discourses—a habit especially evident in his war novels. These references are by no means bibliographic in scope. Like his work, they are idiosyncratic, drawing on works from the well-known to the obscure, from general knowledge to paraphernalia.

encrypts the war and its postwar period as a source of present-day harm. This chapter considers another way of thinking about late twentieth-century historical fiction and the Second World War: that is, the rise of the heritage industry and imperial nostalgia, both of which sought to make an older, prewar Britishness loveable, or at least palatable, again. And as this book has shown through its emphasis on domestic space, it may come as no surprise that representations of the home were at the forefront of these movements, continuing to act as a symbol for the fate of the nation. The contemporary heritage lobby coalesced in the 1970s in the name of the country house, an institution threatened by the 1974 proposal of a "wealth tax" by the Labour government. That same year, the V&A mounted its popular exhibition "The Destruction of the Country House," which made a dramatic case for preserving these homes, followed in short order by the establishment of SAVE Britain's Heritage, a campaign group founded in 1975 by Marcus Binney.[13] By the mid-1980s, heritage was becoming a full-fledged industry, grounded by the 1980 and 1983 National Heritage Acts.

The rise of the British heritage industry proved a powerful, animating thematic for postmodern historiographic fiction of the 1980s and 1990s, as well as the more realist historical fiction of the 2000s and today. While some works directly engage this discourse, such as Julian Barnes's satirical *England, England* (1998), which describes the creation of a quintessentially English theme park on the Isle of Wight, Ondaatje's novels do so more obliquely, relying upon certain elements of heritage discourse as a shorthand for a certain kind of Britishness to produce both their plots and their appeal. In particular, the country house stands in as the archetypical site and impetus for cultural responses to heritage. Though concern over the Big House originated well before the late twentieth century, the site emerged as a clear and convenient synecdoche for British history in novels of the 1980s and 1990s, including Isabel Colegate's *The Shooting Party* (1980), Kazuo Ishiguro's *The Remains of the Day* (1989), and Elizabeth Jane Howard's *The Cazalet Chronicles* (1990–1995, 2013), continuing into the 2000s with Ian McEwan's *Atonement* (2001), Sarah Waters's *The Little Stranger* (2009), and Alan Hollinghurst's *The Stranger's Child* (2011), to name a few.[14]

---

[13] On this point, see Ruth Adams's "The V&A, The Destruction of the Country House and the Creation of 'English Heritage,'" *Museum & Society* 11.1 (March 2013), 6–7.

[14] Of course, concern over the fate of the country house originated well before the late twentieth century. Twentieth-century British fiction has revolved around the fate of the country home as national allegory, from E.M. Forster's *Howards End* (1910), Virginia Woolf's *Orlando* (1928) and *Between the Acts* (1941), Vita Sackville-West's *The Edwardians* (1930); wartime

In a sense, *The English Patient* asks whether an Italian villa might take on some of the associations of the old country house without its sociopolitical baggage. It rehearses one of the central fears expressed by the country-house genre: that the old, aristocratic Big House, after having served its wartime purpose as a military center, hospital, or haven for war orphans, would no longer be privately owned but rather continue as a space of group inhabitation such as a hotel or boarding-school—a fate that did indeed befell many. This tradition, as discussed in the previous chapter, figures the institutionalization of "the lost houses" of Britain as the postwar's inevitable conclusion and dystopian horizon: an organized living ultimately worse than the ruins of the Blitz.[15] Yet Ondaatje's *The English Patient* treats this transformation as a potential good. Though its Italian villa is turned into a place of temporary room and board, the novel also asks readers to consider the possibility that this might be more than a desperate or doomed halfway house, perhaps even a space that aids in the repair of its inhabitants. Crucially, this work does not require restoration, which would return the villa to its original function, or nostalgia for what the villa once was.[16] Instead, we glimpse new forms of domesticity and living together, whose imperfections not only match its impaired and disabled inhabitants, but also help them cope with their losses.

Ondaatje's engagement with postimperial nostalgia offers even more trenchant critique. This national feeling found purchase as cultural form in the films *Gandhi* (1982) and *Passage to India* (1984), as well as the televised mini-series, *The Far Pavilions* (1984) and *Jewel in the Crown* (1984). This nostalgia for lost empire is another side of the British heritage imagination, described by Salman Rushdie as "the fantasy that the British Empire represented something 'noble' or 'great' about Britain; that it was, in spite of all its flaws and meannesses and bigotries, fundamentally glamorous."[17] As

---

exercises in nostalgia including Evelyn Waugh's *Brideshead Revisited* (1945) and Dodie Smith's *I Capture the Castle* (1949), as more critical accounts such as Henry Green's *Loving* (1945). Midcentury also saw new genre permutations at midcentury, such as the drawing-room mystery (Agatha Christie; even J.B. Priestley's 1945 play *An Inspector Calls*) and the postcolonial novel (Jean Rhys's 1966 *Wide Sargasso Sea*; V.S. Naipaul's 1961 *A House for Mr. Biswas*). These works return to the country house with a difference: unveiling their complicity with past violence; unmasking their privilege; and calling their readers' nostalgia into question. Yet the later novels show a new degree of awareness vis-à-vis the emerging British heritage industry and what Evelyn Waugh called the "cult of the country house" in his 1959 preface to *Brideshead Revisited*.

[15] Bowen, "The Bend Back," 59.
[16] See Wachtel, "An Interview with Michael Ondaatje," 255–256.
[17] Salman Rushdie, "Outside the Whale," *Imaginary Homelands: Essays and Criticism 1981–1991* (New York: Penguin Books, 1992), 101.

discussed in Chapter 3, midcentury representations of Second World War often presented their own proleptic versions of the heritage imagination and imperial nostalgia through their postcolonial amnesia regarding empire's role in the war.[18] This chapter, however, engages a later moment when the whiteness of Britain's wartime past was solidified as cultural nostalgia, and is interested in the ways contemporary fiction engages that calcification in turn. Like Amitav Ghosh's *The Shadow Lines* (1988), Zadie Smith's *White Teeth* (2000), and Andrea Levy's *A Small Island* (2004), Ondaatje's *The English Patient* pushes back against these symptomatic erasures by bringing Britain's racial and geopolitical complexities back into view.

These works give an account of the war as marking the beginning of a modern, increasingly racially diverse Britain: a postwar Britain whose history cannot be thought separately from its colonies' participation in the war, nor their postwar independent movements. Combining the mythology of the war with the mythology of empire, these novels show that the work of distancing oneself from the whitewashed mythology of the Second World War carries with it distinctly anti-colonial potential. My aim in this chapter is thus not a comprehensive assessment of the heritage industry or imperial nostalgia, but rather to consider how Ondaatje engages tropes of national and imperial nostalgia only to dismantle them from within.

What distinguishes *The English Patient*, however, is the way it puts these industries and cultural formations in conversation with Britain's 1940s postwar, reconstructive imagination. While the discourse around heritage dates at least as far back as the National Trust's 1895 incorporation—an institution that acquired its first country house in 1907—it gained new urgency during the Second World War, whose damages activated a preservationist logic that found expression in the arts, architecture, and postwar planning. As Raphael Samuel argues, a "radical-patriotic version" of heritage coalesced during the war in "what a series of propaganda booklets called 'the spirit and framework of British institutions' and what in the handbooks and lectures of the Army Bureau for Current Affairs became 'the British Way.'"[19]

---

[18] This amnesia was recently exemplified by Christopher Nolan's 2017 film *Dunkirk* and the lack of representation of Indian soldiers. See, for instance, Yasmin Khan's "Dunkirk, the War and the Amnesia of the Empire," *NYTimes* August 2, 2017, https://www.nytimes.com/2017/08/02/opinion/dunkirk-indians-world-war.html.

[19] Raphael Samuel, *Theatres of Memory: Past and Present in Contemporary Culture* (London: Verso, 1994), 249. Samuel also asserts that the first cry of "heritage in danger" arose in response to the modernizations of 1950s including train dieselization, the building of motorways, and the rise of car ownership: a reading that still pits heritage in opposition to postwar reconstruction's modernizing, interventionist schemes. *Theatres of Memory*, 267.

These histories inform the 1980s revival of heritage discourse, which Patrick Wright diagnoses as "one of the Thatcher government's first (and perhaps less than fully conscious) attempts to revive the spirit of the Second World War and to set up its own patriotic measure against that long drawn-out betrayal known in more polite circles as the post-war settlement."[20] Measured against its contemporary moment, this 1980s version was narrower than the 1940s one, so much so that it can been seen as a reactionary alternative to Britain's postwar consensus. For this reason, the heritage industry has been often negatively characterized as form of illness—nostalgia, obsession, wish-fulfillment, hypnotism, fantasy, bell-jar—in which a retreat into the past stifles any critical or creative energies toward contemporary social and political change.[21]

One obvious way *The English Patient* imbricates the stakes of 1945 with the colonial interwar period is through the Patient's affair with Katharine, which develops amidst the backdrop of 1930s Cairo and the Sahara Desert. Their desert romance is the work's narrative mystery, teased out from the Patient under the influence of morphine and alcohol. It is also undoubtedly the focus of the 1996 film adaptation, whose iconic scene features Ralph Fiennes carrying Kristin Scott Thomas's shrouded body across a sweep of desert. Yet this singular, sexual romance is not the only foil to the Italian's villa's community of care. That distinction belongs instead to the London-based Geographical Society, which provides an important precursor for the villa's social experiment. Like the inhabitants of the villa, the Geographical Society's "men of all nations" make up "an oasis society," maintaining exceptional forms of intimacy created under duress.[22]

The focus on this group is in keeping with Ondaatje's established interest in stories at the margins of established national narratives, and in those that cross temporal and spatial boundaries. The characters that inhabit his narratives are likewise unorthodox in many ways; they form unlikely alliances and put their professional talents to eccentric uses. Above all, Ondaatje is

---

[20] Patrick Wright, *On Living in an Old Country: The National Past in Contemporary Britain* (Oxford: Oxford University Press, 2009), 41.

[21] The classic version of these accounts includes Robert Hewison's *The Heritage Industry: Britain in a Climate of Decline* (London: Methuen, 1987), Wright's *On Living in an Old Country* and later work *A Journey Through Ruins* (Oxford: Oxford University Press, 2009), which characterizes heritage as an "extraction of history...from a denigrated everyday life," in which "history seems to be purged of political tension" (69). See also Stuart Hall's "Un-settling 'The Heritage,' Re-imagining the Post-nation," which notes that heritage "is intended for those who 'belong'—a society which is imagined as, in broad terms, culturally homogeneous and unified" (*Third Text* 49, Winter 1999–2000, 6).

[22] Michael Ondaatje, *The English Patient* (New York: Vintage, 1993), 133, 136.

intrigued by the possibility of friendship between strangers brought together under unusual circumstances, often war or migration, which generate ties that bind and events that eventually sever. Whether the immigrants of *In the Skin of a Lion*, the unorthodox human rights experts of *Anil's Ghost*, the band of misfits in *The Cat's Table*, or the group of criminals in *Warlight*, these social groups can be read as experiments in a basic form of conviviality: that is, how people from diverse walks of life can live together, their differences making the intimacies they form all the more precious.

The English Patient's spokesperson for this sociality is the Patient himself, based on the historical László Almásy, and his search for the lost oasis of Zerzura. In the novel, Ondaatje's Almásy emerges as a romantic hero, partly due to his wooing of Katharine, but also, strikingly, in his belief in a world without maps:

> I believe in such cartography—to be marked by nature, not just to label ourselves on a map like the names of rich men and women on buildings. We are communal histories, communal books. We are not owned or monogamous in our taste or experiences. All I desired was to walk upon such an earth that had no maps.[23]

Unlike his fellow geographers, the Patient wishes to do away with such forms of compartmentalization, constructing a more radical vision of a world without borders or national sovereignty, what Deleuze and Guattari would call unstriated or smooth space. This desire challenges the violence of colonial order, what Frantz Fanon has described as producing "a world compartmentalized, Manichaean and petrified, a world of statues: the statue of the general who led the conquest, the statue of the engineer who built the bridge."[24] Instead, the Patient entertains the radical suggestion of allowing these spaces to keep their original names: "*Ain, Bir, Wadi, Foggara, Khottara, Shaduf.* I didn't want my name against such beautiful names. Erase the family name! Erase nations! I was taught such things by the desert."[25] The viability of this idea then gets retested in the villa as a possible mode of postwar reparation between colonizer and colonized, taking on renewed significance through the Patient's perceived Englishness.

---

[23] Ibid., 261.
[24] Frantz Fanon, *The Wretched of the Earth*, trans. Richard Philcox (New York: Grove Press, 2004), 15.
[25] Ondaatje, *Patient*, 139.

Yet there are limitations to this fantasy, even in the prewar period. Fundamentally, the Patient cannot do away with inherited compartmentalizations, maintaining an Orientalizing gaze that sexualizes, mythologizes, catalogs, and orders.[26] The novel keeps us attuned to this gaze, careful to temper Almásy's grand geopolitical statements with racialized objectifications: "There were rivers of desert tribes, the most beautiful humans I've met in my life. We were German, English, Hungarian, African—all of us insignificant to them. Gradually we became nationless. I came to hate nations. We are deformed by nation-states."[27] And despite his professed hatred of monogamy and ownership, Almásy's affair with Katharine is violently possessive. The sexual jealousy he feels toward her is then recapitulated by Clifton, Katharine's husband and British Intelligence officer, who divebombs the Patient with his plane in an attempt at murder-suicide. Between the two, Englishness resurfaces as a limiting, violent order, unable to let go of its impulse to name, own, and master.

Practices of Care, Processes of Disenchantment

Once the novel establishes this backstory, it poses the question of whether the social laboratory of the 1945 Italian villa might improve upon, even repair, that of 1930s Saharan Africa. Both spaces are characterized by degraded boundaries, newfound intimacies, and a general sense of worldedness produced by abolishing divisions along racial, national, and sexual lines. The villa's inhabitants are then the second iteration of the "men of all nations" or "desert Europeans" introduced through the Patient's backstory, but with a twist: they are neither all men nor all European, nor is their project one of empire building. Instead, *The English Patient* can be read as running an experiment in postwar governmentality, setting itself right at a historical moment where various forms of statehood were emerging and threatening to displace the older model of the British Empire. Speculating on the possibilities latent within this temporal shift, the novel asks whether the villa can successfully revise the desert's "oasis society," to the point of shedding its racial and sexual violences and compartmentalizations.

---

[26] The geographers' world is also clearly a male homosocial one, interrupted by the arrival of Katharine, who needs to be taught the desert's "sternness" (Ondaatje, *Patient*, 170).
[27] Ondaatje, *Patient*, 138.

The answer, at first, is that it can. As Ondaatje takes pains to remind us, what holds these characters together is neither nation, class, nor kinship, but instead, mutual care. This duty extends through and beyond the body through nursing and the defusing of bombs, as well as the sharing of small delights: peeled plums, cans of condensed milk, ampules of morphine, stray bottles of wine. Unlike Muriel Spark's Schiaparelli dress, these resources are available to all as sources of communal pleasure, health, and convalescence. The experiment in living together also entails forms of housekeeping, from gardening to bathing to cooking. Over time, the villa's characters also build tentative forms of friendship, exchanging stories, experiences, expertise. They adapt to each other's habits, finding ways to be together that still respect each other's individuality and idiosyncrasies, seeming to achieve the "idiorrhythmy" theorized in Roland Barthes's *How to Live Together*. This is the fantasy of *The English Patient*: that complete strangers can find ways to live with each other in a way that ultimately improves everyone. In a way, this sociability is largely due to wartime's state of emergency. Recalling representations of Blitz fellow-feeling, Ondaatje calls his characters "equal in darkness," made so by the near-blackout conditions of the devastated Italian countryside.

The novel underscores this mode of living together through its distribution of narrative voice, whose circulation expresses the shared community of its four central characters. Much like Elizabeth Bowen's limited imaginings of Louie Lewis in *The Heat of the Day*, Samuel Selvon's multifocal *The Lonely Londoners*, Muriel Spark's sociological gaze in *The Girls of Slender Means*, and Hollinghurst's moments of epiphanic collective vision in *The Swimming-Pool Library,* these narrative expansions test the boundaries of the individual by asking what we owe each other and how we are to live together. Of all these works, *The English Patient* offers the most intricate scheme of focalization, using frequent negotiations of point of view, voice, quoted speech, and medium to create a narrative system in which all voices seem to be equally accessible. This is especially the case for Hana and Almásy, whose dance of nurse and patient often results in moments where it is difficult to distinguish agency or focalization. Narrative technique and mutual care thus seem to reflect and enable one another, signaling the unique sociability of this wartime space.

Yet all is not equal in the villa. While the overall effect of this narrative trick may be the radical erasure of boundaries between characters, this shifting focalization does not entirely level the playing field for the four characters. Instead, Ondaatje's narrative style ultimately privileges the Patient's position, giving him a distinct brand of narrative focalization, as well as a unique claim on first-person narrative through the modes of oral storytelling and his writerly voice. Unmarked by quotations, interruptions by other characters, or any other signals of reported speech—narrative devices used in every other section to signpost who is talking—the Patient's speech becomes a metanarrative within the narrative diegesis. This authority is reinforced by the second narrative mode unique to the Patient: an 1890 copy of Herodotus's *The Histories*, which the Patient has turned into a commonplace book filled with handwritten notes, maps, drawings, and clippings from other texts. As the Patient's one surviving possession that came through the fire with him, *The Histories* promises insight into the mystery of his past, as well as to the events happening around them.[28]

Much of the Patient's authority within the story comes from this command over narrative. As a gifted storyteller, the Patient promises wisdom and enchantment in the face of wartime brutality. He also drives the plot of *The English Patient*, his identity being the central mystery of the novel. For Hana, listening to stories is part of her caretaking labor, signaled in the opening description of the Patient's "dragging the listening heart of the young nurse beside him to wherever his mind is, into that well of memory he kept plunging into during those months before he died."[29] Kip, too, is taken by the Patient's stories and memories, but with an awareness of their imperial background: "Your fragile white island that with customs and manners and books and prefects and reason somehow converted the rest of the world. [...] Was it just ships that gave you such power? Was it, as my brother said, because you had the histories and printing presses?"[30] Thus the novel's experiments with forms of postwar collective living revolve around the question of how to disenchant those imperial forms of power and persuasion that posit Englishness both as the thing to be cared for and the master key of interpretation.

The novel thematizes this question of care through young characters from the British Commonwealth—Hana, a Canadian nurse, and Kip, an Indian

---

[28] Though Hana also starts writing in random books in the villa's library, perhaps inspired by the Patient's Herodotus, her entries are more simply worded and shallowly focused on her present moment. Compared to his, hers read more like a young woman's diaries, either through descriptions of the other men in the villa or as a conduit for other's stories. And while the Patient's Herodotus is treated as a treasured object, saved even through his ordeal by fire, Hana's writing is more ephemeral and occasional, with the books returned to their random spot on the library shelf, never to be seen again.
[29] Ondaatje, *Patient*, 4.
[30] Ibid., 283.

sapper—asking, rather baldly, what allegiance is owed to the waning imperial order at midcentury. Both labor on behalf of England, whether Hana's tending to the Patient, or Kip's defusing of bombs for the Allies. There is also something excessive about both their work, some residual trauma that they are trying to heal through it. In this regard, they are differentiated from the novel's other notable model of care: the group of nomad Bedouin who tend to the Patient after he falls, burning, from the sky. The scenes between them are as lyrical and intimate as those with Hana. The Bedouin anoint him with oil, feed him dates softened with their saliva, and breathe upon him as they unwrap his bandages. Yet in the end, their labors are strictly utilitarian. Once their patient is healed, they task him with identifying a series of European guns, matching bullets to weaponry for their use. In the villa, then, the question becomes whether his care can decouple from the demands of war, its practice fully demilitarized.

As a Sikh working for England's war effort, Kip's relationship to Englishness is particularly fraught. His backstory draws on the historical participation of Sikhs in the two world wars, detailing his training as a sapper in England. There, he apprentices himself to the jovial Lord Suffolk ("the best of the English, he later told Hana"), whom he eventually deems both teacher, family, and friend.[31] Drawn into the group of sappers that declare themselves a "family," he learns to love the English. After Lord Suffolk dies trying to defuse a bomb, Kip becomes his symbolic next-of-kin, inheriting and carrying his specialist knowledge forward into his work for the Allies in Italy. For Kip, the question is whether the Patient might become another father-substitute, or whether he can detach from being made a "son" of empire yet again.

For Hana, on the other hand, the care she provides is distinctly demilitarized. After action ends in Italy, the other nurses at the villa demand that she continue her service for the greater good: "The war is not over everywhere, she was told. The war is over. This war is over. The war here. She was told it would be like desertion. This is not desertion. I will stay here."[32] Hana's refusal to divest from her caretaking labor holds out the possibility that individuals might come up with their own form of repair after the war, one detached from the grammar of state violence even as it tends to its wounds. In her work with the Patient, this healing goes beyond the demands

---

[31] Ibid., 185.
[32] Ibid., 41.

of his physical burned body to include the acts of reading aloud and bearing witness to his tales.

Eventually, Ondaatje's characters manage to disentangle themselves from their extreme, even perverse attachment to the Patient and all he represents. The clearest moment of severance in the novel comes when Kip hears the news of Hiroshima and Nagasaki, the shock of which catalyzes his flight from his sapper duties, the Allies, and Italy, and his subsequent repatriation in India. The event is imbued with irony: not only are the atomic bombs the weapons that no one can defuse, but they also re-stabilize the Englishness of *The English Patient*. As Kip notes,

> American, French, I don't care. When you start bombing the brown races of the world, you're an Englishman. You had King Leopold of Belgium and now you have fucking Harry Truman of the USA. You all learned it from the English.[33]

In a novel lauded for its lyricism and intricacies, this moment appears as sudden, total, and even flat-footed. (The 1996 film adaptation, for its part, sidesteps the atomic bombings altogether.) Rather than racial animus, what breaks the characters apart is news of V-E Day and the death of Kip's sapper-in-arms, a moment that reinscribes the West as the thing to be cared for most. However didactic, the novel's version of events does attempt to impress some anti-racist pedagogy on its readers. For Kip at least, 1945 appears as a moment of break or rupture that is also a historical corrective to England's imperial past. Yet the novel stops short of fully endorsing this vision of events, as Hana responds to Kip's scorching polemic with bewilderment. Given the heavily gendered burden of care placed upon her character throughout the novel, it is perhaps unsurprising, though disappointing, that it is difficult for her character to make such a radical break.

In this regard, *The English Patient* recapitulates a structural similarity with other novels studied in this project, which figure the climax of their novel as a breakage of social bonds that betray the novel's narrative welfare system: Louie's class disappointment with Stella in *The Heat of the Day*; Selina's theft of the communal Schiaparelli dress and Nicholas's horror in *The Girls of Slender Means*; and Will's turn away from gay solidarity as he refuses to write Charles's biography in *The Swimming-Pool Library*. In each of these novels,

[33] *Ibid.*, 286.

after the wounding of the social fabric or literary welfare system, characters are faced with the dilemma of redressing these seemingly irreparable moments. This dilemma results in moments of heightened contradiction, and often disappointment, in the novels' protracted *dénouements*. Bowen's Louie relaxes her class aspirations and becomes pregnant with an illegitimate child, rescued by the convenient news of her husband's death. Spark sets up a scene of potential mourning, returning Nicholas and Joanna's father to the ruins of the May of Teck Club, but ultimately refuses her reader significance or consolation. And while Hollinghurst's Will seems to reach an ideal synthesis of the novel's competing terms, able to recognize the importance gay history while also fulfilling his own sexual desire, this conclusion is thrown into disarray by the novel's setting in the halcyon summer before the AIDS crisis.

What distinguishes Ondaatje's work from these previous examples is its re-enchantment of the work of literature and the repair that it can afford. Ondaatje signals this investment through his engagement with domestic space, especially when the omniscient narrator interrupts the narrative to describe nuances of architecture and environment. Though there is no structural pattern to these lapses of descriptive omniscience, they tend to focus on the war's warping of specific locales (Italian fortress towns, the Libyan desert, Naples) in rich detail, attuning the reader to their alternating statuses of militarization and demilitarization. When this voice focuses on the Villa San Girolamo, it takes on a particular urgency: "From outside, the place seemed devastated. An outdoor staircase disappeared in midair, its railing hanging off. Their life was foraging and tentative safety."[34] These lines recall the striking opening of Spark's *The Girls of Slender Means*, whose description of 1945 London observes that "most of all of the staircases survived, like a new art-form, leading up and up to an unspecified destination that made unusual demands on the mind's eye."[35] But where Spark's new artform scathingly upends the myth of wartime community, Ondaatje's style reinvests in the possibility of a community born from war, and a postwar future based on practices of care.

This social imagination is aided by Ondaatje's heavy symbolizing of ruins. Empty rooms become aviaries. Missing walls admit starlight. A deserted hallway allows for long games of hopscotch. Bombed-out orchards provide

---

[34] *Ibid.*, 14.
[35] Spark, *Girls*, 7.

just enough to survive; a can of condensed milk becomes cause for celebration. In adapting to these makeshift living quarters, the villa's inhabitants exercise what Michel de Certeau would call tactical creativity, insinuating themselves into the abandoned space in surprising, even pleasurable ways. One such example comes in an early meditation on the villa's library. Like its war-torn environment, the library reflects the long half-life of injury and the labor required to repair it, recalling Kip's sapper work and Hana's nursing. Yet it also somehow "adapts itself" to its destruction, a magical reconstruction that admits a type of stark beauty, even agency to the site:

> Between the kitchen and the destroyed chapel a door led into an oval-shaped library. The space inside seemed safe except for a large hole at portrait level in the far wall, caused by mortar-shell attack on the villa two months earlier. The rest of the room had adapted itself to this wound, accepting the habits of weather, evening stars, the sound of birds. There was a sofa, a piano covered in a grey sheet, the head of a stuffed bear and the high walls of books. The shelves nearest the torn wall bowed with the rain, which had doubled the weight of the books. Lightning came into the room too, again and again, falling across the covered piano and carpet.[36]

This passage transforms war and reconstruction into a matter of textual and artistic representation. The wounding here is ultimately to the books, whose doubling in weight signifies both water damage and symbolic heft. Their residual damage raises a question about the role of art and repair in the postwar period. On the one hand, books are the ultimate casualty of the war, being at once beyond repair as well as unnecessary to postwar life: "The German army had mined many of the houses they retreated from, so most rooms not needed, like this one, had been sealed for safety, the doors hammered into their frames."[37] On the other, the narrator's suggestion that the library might adapt to its wounds opens the possibility that books might be participants and aids in reparation. As Hana cares for her Patient with reading material for his long days of rest, Ondaatje pushes against the specter of irreparability, revealing literature's healing capabilities.

The novel's conclusion relies on and even exploits these literary capabilities. In some unspecified future ("these years later"), Kip has returned to India and started a family. His new life symbolizes a post-Hiroshima and

---

[36] Ondaatje, *Patient*, 11.
[37] Ibid.

postcolonial work of repair effected through geographical and racial realignment: instead of working for the Allies, Kip is a doctor for his people; instead of loving the white Canadian Hana, he has a kitchen table where "all of their hands are brown."[38] Yet even amidst this picture of family harmony, Kip finds himself returning to memories of Hana, suggested by everyday events such as treating a burn patient or walking up a stone stairway. More than mere recollection. Ondaatje grants his character a magical ability, "a limited gift that he has somehow been given, as if a camera's film reveals her, but only her, in silence."[39] In this imaginative sweep across time and space, the novel reconnects the estranged Hana and Kip, granting them a textual intimacy that both recalls and differently re-iterates their sexual relationship.

This visionary gift is a reworking of the narrative epiphany, connecting characters across time and space. It is a form of coming together that is most poignant—and painful—in the novel's final lines:

> And so Hana moves and her face turns and in a regret she lowers her hair. Her shoulder touches the edge of a cupboard and a glass dislodges. Kirpal's left hand swoops down and catches the dropped fork an inch from the floor and gently passes it into the fingers of his daughter, a wrinkle at the edge of his eyes behind his spectacles.[40]

The breathtaking catch, the wrinkle of the eyes, and convenient happy ending are a powerful narrative effect, even if it might strain a reader's sympathy and immersion. Rather than a psychological act of imagined sympathy between characters, Ondaatje's form of epiphanic connection depends on a narratorial *deus ex machina* to effect this impossible reconciliation. In a way, this conclusion offers another layer of reparation as a rewriting of E.M. Forster's 1924 *A Passage to India*, another novelistic trial of colonial relationships. As readers may recall, Forster ends the work by breaking Fielding and Aziz's revolutionary friendship through similarly mystical means, as horses, earth, and sky all collude to drive them apart ("they said in their hundred voices, "No, not yet,' and the sky said, 'No, not there'").[41] Instead of concluding with delayed modernist potentiality, however, Ondaatje opts for instant gratification, trading Forster's environmental hostility for intercontinental hospitality. With this, *The English Patient* makes its final bid for the healing

---

[38] Ibid., 301.
[39] Ibid., 300.
[40] Ibid., 301–302.
[41] Forster, *A Passage to India* (New York: Harcourt, Brace and Company, 1924), 322.

power of literature: a statement offered despite its plot's arc towards disenchantment. Reiterating the belief that domestic space can rebuild broken social ties, Ondaatje imbricates the ethos of postwar reconstruction in the history of British colonialism, testing whether the former could ever repair the latter.

Coda: On Warlight

Like Hollinghurst's *The Sparsholt Affair* (2017), Ondaatje's *Warlight* (2018) proves that contemporary writers cannot let go of the Second World War as the motive of cultural production. In this more recent novel, Ondaatje draws yet again on the peculiar energies of the postwar, testing whether the bonds between strangers, forged through unconventional living arrangements, might come to repair the traumas of war. In some ways, *Warlight* brings *The English Patient*'s experiment of the Italian villa back to postwar London, making literal what was partly allegorical. Like *The English Patient*, *Warlight* is enamored by small collectives that approximate the family unit, both extending beyond its nuclear structure and, at the same time, never being enough to compensate for it. The novel tells the story of Nathaniel Williams, who along with his sister, is left by his parents during the war in the care of a curious collection of people, a "night zoo" with code names such as "The Moth" and "The Pimlico Darter."[42] To Nathaniel, the narrator, this social collective becomes the grammar of his childhood and then adulthood, whose rules can only be understood long after the war. As he comes to understand, this collective is held together by practices of inordinate care: strangers charged with protecting him and his sister, themselves collateral damage of their mother's wartime and postwar work.

However nascent or underdeveloped, the politics of this collective turns away from international community and cross-racial intimacy toward a more direct engagement with Britain's postwar domestic consensus. Ondaatje describes the group as "a little left of the new Labour Party—about three miles or so."[43] What kind of left they are, however, is not entirely clear: if anything, they seem to be to the left of the law, ferrying illegal greyhounds down the river, and possessing questionable skills in arson and anesthetics gained during the war. One potential political formation is buried within

---

[42] Ondaatje, *Warlight* (New York: Alfred A. Knopf, 2018), 46.
[43] Ibid., 35.

the mother's postwar work, which provided information that enabled the *foibe* massacres by Yugoslavian Communist Partisans. Characteristically, Ondaatje does not address the specific conditions of this violent historical episode, though his acknowledgments suggest that he has read at least one piece of scholarship about it.[44] Within the novel, the revelation of this historic violence has almost no impact on our first-person narrator, prompting neither discomfort nor reflection. Though it offers him a reason for his mother's murder, when Nathaniel reconstructs his history, he is only able to perceive a reductively crude scene of repair: "Quick and fatal. As if it was finally an ending of feuds, of a war. Perhaps allowing a redeeming. That is what I think now."[45]

As a promise of social collectivity, the novel turns out to be a more conservative version of *The English Patient*, limited by more traditional storylines of family and inheritance. Despite its description of alternative kinship possibilities, the novel revolves around the romance of the nuclear family: the mother and father off abroad doing unnamed political work; the children left in the care of strangers and acquaintances. From the beginning, Nathaniel attempts to piece together a coherent picture of those tumultuous years. He calls the "missing sequence" of his mother's life during and immediately after the war "the possibility of an inheritance."[46]

The full story of Nathaniel's family only comes into view halfway through the novel following his mother's murder, when he starts working in the archives of the Foreign Office. Through this job, he learns his mother was a radio operator in the last years of the war, and later she took part in a British counterinsurgency movement that—as is later revealed—had disastrous consequences. The last half of the novel is Nathaniel's recounting of his mother's story, a necessary, inevitable labor of love that recalls Roderick Rodney's speech about "being posterity" in Bowen's *The Heat of the Day*. Yet where Bowen's novel showed genuine confusion over how to narrate the events of the Second World War, resulting in fascinatingly tormented narrative form, the war in *Warlight* has a dull sense of inevitability.

Moreover, Ondaatje's metafictional treatment of this period overlaps war, memory, and history with a heavy hand that risks turning banal. If wartime is the unaccountable event, and a childhood during it is even more so,

---

[44] In particular, Ondaatje cites Gaia Baracetti's "*Foibe*: Nationalism, Revenge and Ideology in Venezia Giulia and Istria, 1943–5," *Journal of Contemporary History* 44.4 (October 2009), 657–674.
[45] Ondaatje, *Warlight*, 260.
[46] Ibid., 131.

the novel suggests the postwar deciphering of war is tantamount to a ritual of coming-of-age. As the novel's title suggests, war is and will always be the source of postwar knowledge, a thematic Ondaatje takes great pains to explain: "There are times these years later, as I write this all down, when I feel as if I do so by candlelight. As if I cannot see what is taking place in the dark beyond the movement of this pencil. These feel like moments without context...."[47]

Warlight's mechanism of revelation, however, is slightly more subtle than that of *The English Patient*. If *The English Patient* put its faith in the event of Hiroshima to deliver a form of uncontestable truth, *Wartime* uses the archive to throw the possibility of truth into question. As Nathaniel realizes through his job as a censor for the Foreign Office, "An unauthorized and still violent war had continued after the armistice, a time when the rules and negotiations were still half lit and acts of war continued beyond public hearing."[48] His work is "the silent correction," or the work of establishing an authorized history:

> And so for us, a generation later in the 1950s, the job was to unearth whatever evidence might still remain of actions that history might consider untoward, and which could still be found in stray reports and unofficial papers. In this post-war world twelve years later, it felt to some of us, our heads bent over the files brought to us daily, that it was no longer possible to see who held a correct moral position.[49]

With this last line, Ondaatje successfully completes a transition to moral relativism, evacuating any sense of critique that can accompany a narrative return to the Second World War. Though the work throws historical recordkeeping into question, it ultimately gives its reader a novel that privileges text over context, the stories we tell over the history we inherit. In doing so, it fully capitulates to the risk taken by *The English Patient*, whose faith in narrative enchantment critically limits the potential of its historiographic work.

---

[47] *Ibid.*, 32.
[48] *Ibid.*, 132.
[49] *Ibid.*, 133–134.

6
Institutional Life
Infrastructural Interiority as Postwar Feeling

If there was any doubt as to the post-millennial holding power of Britain's wartime promises of care, one need look no further than the 2012 London Olympics Opening Ceremony, which featured the postwar welfare state as a measure of Britain's contemporaneity and historical achievement. The ceremony announced this teleology as it began with England's unofficial anthem, "Jerusalem," associated with the rebuilding of the postwar world along the lines of the 1942 Beveridge Report. With lyrics taken from William Blake's 1808 poem "And did those feet in ancient times," the hymn details the apocryphal tale of Jesus's visit to England, and anticipates the Second Coming of Christ ("And did the Countenance Divine, / Shine forth upon our clouded hills? / And was Jerusalem builded here, / Among these dark Satanic Mills?"). The song famously ends:

> I will not cease from Mental Fight,
> Nor shall my Sword sleep in my hand:
> Till we have built Jerusalem,
> In England's green & pleasant Land

These words commenced the ceremony's historical pageantry, which moved from Britain's bucolic "green and pleasant lands" to the "dark satanic mills" of its industrial revolution, to various icons of the twentieth century: suffragettes, poppies, and the Empire Windrush. Still, none of these scenes provided the redemption promised by Jerusalem. For that, the audience had to wait for the contemporary portion of the pageant, a section that began with an homage to the National Health Service. As an EKG pulsed around the stadium, children bounced on trampoline hospital beds, and nurses and doctors danced around them, the broadcaster reminded the audience of the sentiment behind this postwar innovation, quoting the NHS creator, Aneurin Bevan: "No society can legitimately call itself civilised if a sick person is denied medical aid because of lack of means." The section ended by

204   STATES OF REPAIR

linking the midcentury welfare institution to the history of British children's literature. Menaced by the Queen of Hearts, Captain Hook, Cruella de Vil, and a giant Lord Voldemort, the child patients were saved by a veritable army of Mary Poppinses, who descended from the sky in a literal embodiment of the "nanny state." In this pageantry, it was welfare to the rescue, indeed.

What Jerusalem did postwar Britain build? In this book's first chapter, I closed with a discussion of Humphrey Jennings's *Diary for Timothy*, a work we might return to now to measure Britain's postwar world. Born September 3, 1944, the Timothys of Britain were in their golden years at the time of the Olympics Ceremony, and thanks to new opportunities in education, healthcare, and employment, were living longer and healthier lives than previous generations. Growing old with the welfare state, it seems, made a palpable difference (despite the actual Timothy's statistically premature death at 56).[1]

In other ways, of course, Jerusalem was still far away, its promises either broken, limited, betrayed, or still *in potentia*. Things may have gotten better, or in some ways more equal, since 1945, but is that enough?[2] As this book has endeavored to show, the symbolic, affective, and aspirational qualities of postwar reconstruction keep post-1945 British cultural production attached to this midcentury origin moment and its figured institutions of care. The Olympics Ceremony's fantasies are a reminder that above all, literature's reactivation of 1945 is a hopeful one. Perhaps it is not a bad thing that the promise of 1945 has yet to lose its potentiality, even in its limitations, diminutions, and decay.[3]

This chapter offers one final case study for this literary legacy: Kazuo Ishiguro's novel *Never Let Me Go* (2005), which provides this book's most

---

[1] Hugh Purcell calls Timothy the personification of Orwell's insular Englishman. "Whatever happened to Timothy?: The lost dream of 1945," *The New Statesman* (20 December 2013–9 January 2014), 59.

[2] See, for instance, the collection *Unequal Britain: Equalities in Britain Since 1945*, ed. Pat Thane (London: Continuum UK, 2010), which details the changes and persistent disadvantages certain groups have experienced since the Second World War, with essays by historians on topics of old age, race, religion, Gypsies and Travellers, gender and sexuality, and disability.

[3] These grand visions of Britain's postwar reconstruction are also akin to those needed to prepare an Olympic host city for the upcoming festivities. This is the subject of Iain Sinclair's *Ghost Milk*, in which he writes: "The trajectory from (Patrick) Abercrombie's reasoned proposal to the insidious CGI promos of the 2012 Olympic dream is inevitable. The long march towards a theme park without a theme." *Ghost Milk: Calling Time On the Grand Project* (London: Penguin, 2011), 11. Sinclair seeks to demystify the mythos around Olympic reconstructions in part by overlaying strata of the past (through history, memory, labor, documentary, and film footage) onto the site's CGI projections, and in part by describing their violences to the present landscape (through its ugliness, destruction, displacement, and personal harm).

extremely fictional test of the social aspirations of 1945. Much of Ishiguro's fiction is centered on the Second World War and its aftermath. As Ishiguro expressed in an 1989 interview, "I tend to be attracted to pre-war and post-war settings because I'm interested in this business of values and ideals being tested, and people having to face up to the notion that their ideals weren't quite what they thought they were before the test came."[4] Thus Etsuko of *A Pale View of Hills* (1982) reveals her guilt around her daughter's suicide in the difficult landscape of postwar Nagasaki; the retired artist Ono of *An Artist of the Floating World* (1986) looks back on his contributions to Japanese wartime propaganda; the butler Stevens of *The Remains of the Day* reflects on what it meant to give his personal and professional best to an employer with Nazi sympathies; and the detective Christopher of *When We Were Orphans* (2000) learns his inheritance came from his mother's service to a Chinese warlord. In each of these works, the postwar functions as proving grounds for characters, through often devastating realizations that disenchant them from their deeply held beliefs.

Never Let Me Go is both an exemplary and an exceptional case within Ishiguro's remarkably consistent *oeuvre*. Set in late-1990s England, the novel presents a world that remedies previously incurable diseases through the aid of a government program that harvests organs from human clones. The program has taken on the feel and function of a public utility, supplying goods that have become less like commodities and more like necessities, the government ensuring for the British public that "their own children, their spouses, their parents, their friends, did not die from cancer, motor neurone disease, heart disease."[5] The work is narrated by Kathy H., a clone about to begin "donating" her organs (per the program's euphemistic language) after tending to her fellow clones for eleven years. As her simple, even flat narrative style suggests, her subjectivity and perspective on these events is radically delimited by her status as a clone.

These dystopian valences make *Never Let Me Go* a defamiliarizing experience for readers of Ishiguro, departing from his typically locatable historical settings as well as his complexly rendered protagonists. The novel also provides an important test case for the novelistic tradition as a whole, whose

---

[4] Graham Swift, "Shorts: Kazuo Ishiguro," *Conversations with Kazuo Ishiguro*, ed. Brian W. Shaffer and Cynthia F. Wong (Jackson: University Press of Mississippi, 2008), 36. Of course, Ishiguro is also notoriously ambivalent and ambiguous about his fidelity to his own historical or geopolitical representation: see, for instance, Ishiguro and Kenzaburo Oe, "The Novelist in Today's World: A Conversation," *boundary 2* 18:3 (Autumn 1991), 109–122.
[5] Kazuo Ishiguro, *Never Let Me Go* (New York: Knopf), 263.

ideological core Nancy Armstrong has described as "the presupposition that novels think like individuals about the difficulties of fulfilling oneself as an individual under specific cultural historical conditions."[6] As many have suggested, *Never Let Me Go* forces us to contend with the disappearance of the individual and the emergence of the social aggregate—whether bureaucratic, statistical, or unoriginal—as well as the difficult, often alien emotions that arise from its dark biopolitical premise.[7] Yet the novel still maintains Ishiguro's trademark protagonist: a highly self-conscious character nostalgically, if ambivalently, orbiting around a lost past. In doing so, *Never Let Me Go* challenges what it means to feel historical—that is, to feel the postwar's pedagogical weight, so clear in his other works. For *Never Let Me Go*, in some ways Ishiguro's most domestically English novel, this historical feeling is deeply connected to the ethos of a welfare state.[8] As the reader eventually learns, the cloning program has a distinctly postwar provenance, proving an essential component of its counterfactual NHS. The program's development echoes those raised by developments in national infrastructure,

---

[6] Nancy Armstrong, *How Novels Think: The Limits of Individualism from 1719–1900* (New York: Columbia University Press, 2005), 9–10. Although Armstrong expresses doubt that novels can modify their ideological core, she also proposes that if the novel is to evolve, it must begin imagining a "genuine alternative to the individual, one that does not inspire phobia and yet is grounded in the world we now inhabit" (25).

[7] Lisa Fluet reads the novel as an experiment in class-consciousness. She wonders "what it might feel like to lose one's individual sense of 'me' in an impersonal, collective 'we'... with a bureaucratic, even actuarial eye to the exterior limits of human endeavor in the aggregate, rather than to the bottomless depths of strong, individual human feelings about those limits." "Immaterial Labors: Ishiguro, Class, and Affect," *Novel* 40.3 (2007), 285. Bruce Robbins approaches this in part through the problem of statistics, "[i]f only so as not to join the millions in thinking of myself as an improbably individual exception to the statistical rule." "Cruelty is Bad: Banality and Proximity in *Never Let Me Go*," *Novel* 40.3 (2007), 294. And while Rebecca Walkowitz suggests we consider the novel's networks of "unoriginal objects" (such as Kathy's lost cassette, the titular song, and even Kathy herself), her analysis still hinges on the fate of the individual. She interprets the novel's modes of comparison as helping us "recognize the large networks of approximation and comparison in which individuality functions." "Unimaginable Largeness: Kazuo Ishiguro, Translation, and the New World Literature," *Novel* 40.3 (2007), 226.

[8] Robbins also turns to *Never Let Me Go* as a case study in his literary history of the welfare state, whose narratives are best told through the genre of upward mobility. For Robbins, *Never Let Me Go* widens welfare's affective charge by admitting welfarist care as a vehicle for class anger, particularly through the figure of Miss Lucy. Though its historical project is different, this book is indebted to Robbins's study of how literature mediates welfare state contradictions and compromises (between welfare-state capitalism and socialism; political projects and historical realities; self-reliance and self-interest, to name a few). See Chapter 6 of Robbins's *Upward Mobility and the Common Good: Toward a Literary History of the Welfare State* (Princeton: Princeton University Press, 2007), 190–231.

whereby a previous luxury becomes more widely available (even, perhaps, an entitlement) through technological advancement.[9]

In ending with a discussion of *Never Let Me Go*, this book fulfills a trajectory of inversion that becomes evident in traversing twentieth-century cultural production: that is, works become motivated less by the fear of what happens when the private becomes public (i.e., institutionalized by the welfare state), and more by what happens when the public becomes private (i.e., privatized or corporatized on a business model). Indeed, Ishiguro's work can be read as engaging what David Harvey calls neoliberalism's "creative destructions," which in the name of freedom and individual liberty turned economic principles into common sense, political doxa, even a whole way of life.[10] Scholars have shown the complex ways literature indexes these creative destructions, whether through depictions of affect and financialization, or on a more sociological level, the deformations to the creative economy.[11] *Never Let Me Go*, however, mobilizes these neoliberal tenets largely through its science-fictional premise, through which a cloning program is maintained through remarkable feats of rationalization in the name of being a technical solution. The program maximizes the profits from its all-too-human resources by granting them only the minima of comfort during their foreshortened lives. It even obligates the clones to tend for each other at the end of their lives, reducing welfare expenditure on elder care in a disturbing update to "cradle to the grave" state care.

The novel's counterfactual setting in "England, late 1990s" also recalls the rise of New Labour and its historic win in the 1997 General Election. Promising to be "the party of welfare reform," New Labour's modernization relied on "welfare-to-work" programs, themselves prefigured by Conservative schemes such as Margaret Thatcher's "Restart" and John Major's "Community Action." This new emphasis on work found symbolic and actual

---

[9] The debates that shaped the course of Ishiguro's donations program closely echo those raised by developments in infrastructure, whereby a previous luxury becomes more widely available (even, perhaps, an entitlement) through technological advancement. See, for instance, Michael Rubenstein, *Public Works: Infrastructure, Irish Modernism, and the Postcolonial. Public Works* (Notre Dame: University of Notre Dame Press, 2010), 18.

[10] David Harvey, "Neoliberalism as Creative Destruction," *The ANNALS of the American Academy of Political and Social Science* 610 (2007), 24.

[11] See, for instance, Rachel Greenwald-Smith's *Affect and American Literature in the Age of Neoliberalism* (Cambridge: Cambridge University Press, 2015); Annie McClanahan's *Dead Pledges: Debt, Crisis, and Twenty-First-Century Culture* (Stanford: Stanford University Press, 2016); Jane Elliott's *The Microeconomic Mode: Political Subjectivity in Contemporary Popular Aesthetics* (New York: Columbia University Press, 2021); and Sarah Brouillette's *Literature and the Creative Economy* (Stanford: Stanford University Press, 2014).

capitulation in the 1996 renaming of Income Support (previously "National Assistance" and "Supplementary Benefit" in the postwar period) to "Jobseeker's Allowance," as well as the 2001 merger of the Benefits Agency and the Employment Service to become "Jobcentre Plus." With these reforms, the UK joined the USA in its neoliberal embrace of workfarism. Ishiguro's emphasis on work in this novel adds an unsettling valence to his trademark interest in his characters' professions as the measure of their lives' worth: an investment that reliably fails, or whose principles turn out to be utterly misguided. For no matter the skill or duration of the clones' labor, it will never afford them access to welfare benefits, nor exempt them from providing someone else's.

Despite its setting, this chapter reads *Never Let Me Go* less as a commentary on a historical late-1990s England than as a statement of attachment to Britain's postwar. It is the latter, I suggest, that is the novel's more urgent and productive counterfactual exercise. Ishiguro himself retains a deep appreciation for the welfare state and its postwar ethos, as he expressed in his autobiographical 2017 Nobel Prize Speech, "My Twentieth-Century Evening." Having migrated to England from Nagasaki in 1960 at the age of five, he states he was "amazed" at the degree of acceptance he and his family found there, especially as Japan and Britain had been at war not too long ago. In a characteristic look backward, Ishiguro attributes that generosity to Britain's postwar reconstruction: "The affection, respect and curiosity I retain to this day for that generation of Britons who came through the Second World War, and built a remarkable new welfare state in its aftermath, derive significantly from my personal experiences from those years."[12] Art, of course, does not always mimic life, and Ishiguro has been infamously reticent to label his work as "historical" at all. Still, these statements make it possible to return to *Never Let Me Go* with a renewed sense of what is at stake in its engagement with Britain's remarkable new welfare state. For as Kathy bears out, the novel tests welfare's limits while also—beyond reason, one might say—retaining a perverse affection, respect, and curiosity for its tenets.

What stops *Never Let Me Go* from being a fully paranoid rendering of the welfare state is its focus on the rise and fall of Hailsham, an experimental, privately funded institution in a larger cloning program that raises clones

---

[12] Ishiguro, "My Twentieth Century Evening—and Other Small Breakthroughs," *The Nobel Prize* 7 (December 2017), 5.

within a beautiful boarding-school environment. There, they are encouraged to produce art, in an attempt to convince the public that the clones "had souls at all." Within this national cloning infrastructure, Hailsham provides an important alternative to the program's typical "vast government homes," which, though never depicted, are implied to be host to horrific conditions. The boarding school also grants a special aura to its alumni, including Kathy H., the protagonist, who grows nostalgic for her time there.

Of course, Hailsham still feeds its charges back into the larger system. Its ideological "hailing" proves even more a sham than the program's euphemistic language of "carers," "donors," and "completion." Though these euphemisms help blunt the cold reality of the clones' lives, Hailsham's emphasis on a kind, beautiful environment plays an even stronger, more devastating role in its subjects' repression. *Never Let Me Go* thus emerges as a deliberation over the meaning-making potential of state infrastructures, and whether their promises of value actually sustain those whose lives are thoroughly instrumentalized. In doing so, it tests the foundational logic of postwar reconstruction, which promised a more equitable world for all through the establishment of caretaking institutions and, most prominently, through planned environments meant to foster community and a greater sense of responsibility to one's fellow neighbor.

Infrastructural Interiority

Although the legacy of welfare is unquestionably infrastructural, this chapter brings the language of infrastructure to bear on its analysis more overtly than other chapters.[13] For Ishiguro's *Never Let Me Go* presents an exceptional case study, expanding the parameters of welfare infrastructure to an extreme wherein humans have become utilities: the dark underside to its England's NHS. Recent work in the growing interdisciplinary field of infrastructure studies has moved past the classic definition of infrastructure as public works—physical systems such as roads, canals, and electrical networks that facilitate a state's development of capital—to include the roles

---

[13] This project thus joins the recent trend of studying literature and infrastructure, particularly infrastructures built in the name of the "public good," including Rubenstein's *Public Works*; Sophia Beal's *Brazil Under Construction: Fiction and Public Works* (New York: Palgrave, 2013); and Jessica Hurley's *Infrastructures of Apocalypse* (Minneapolis: University of Minnesota Press, 2020).

and contributions of human actors, activity, and affect.[14] Kathy's relation to infrastructure bears this relation between people and infrastructure to its extreme, as she herself an infrastructural element, what we might understand as sentient infrastructure. Her instrumentalized subjectivity recalls such theoretical concepts as Giorgio Agamben's bare life and *homo sacer*, or the speciation of human beings conceptualized within a Foucauldian notion of biopower. However, neither can sufficiently account for Kathy H.'s perspective as a clone, or the way that she directly mediates her crisis of self through the crisis of the institution. This chapter argues that innovative nature of *Never Let Me Go* lies precisely in the tension between Kathy's individual consciousness and infrastructuralized body, a dilemma that both relies upon and challenges Ishiguro's signature style.

Ishiguro gives us a glimpse of this tension in the opening lines to the novel, which begin to unfold the contours of the cloning program:

> My name is Kathy H. I'm thirty-one years old, and I've been a carer now for over eleven years. That sounds long enough, I know, but actually they want me to go on for another eight months, until the end of this year. That'll make it almost exactly twelve years. Now I know my being a carer so long isn't necessarily because they think I'm fantastic at what I do. There are some really good carers who've been told to stop after just two or three years. And I can think of one carer at least who went on for all of fourteen years despite being a complete waste of space. So I'm not trying to boast.[15]

While this passage introduces the euphemistic mechanisms of the donations program, as well as the dark, dystopian sense of an "I" versus a "them," what I want to draw attention to is Kathy's turn to her own figurative language—"a complete waste of space"—which she employs to describe a particularly unskilled carer. Her turn of phrase reveals the relationship between bodies, environment, utility, and waste that is central to the cloning program, and to clones' interactions with their environment. Though this description may seem merely idiomatic or officially euphemistic, it is significantly neither.

---

[14] See, for instance, AbdouMaliq Simone, "People as Infrastructure: Intersecting Fragments in Johannesburg," *Public Culture* 16:3 (2004), 407–429, or Lauren Berlant, "The Commons: Infrastructures for Troubling Times," *Environment and Planning D: Society and Space* 34.3 (2016), 393–419. This turn to the human is also the focus of the collection *The Aesthetics of Infrastructure: Race, Affect, Environment*, ed. Kelly Rich, Nicole Rizzuto, and Susan Zieger (Evanston: Northwestern University Press, 2022).

[15] Ishiguro, *Never*, 261.

Instead, even more chillingly, this language comes from Kathy herself, giving the reader a glimpse into her infrastructural interiority. Put differently, *Never Let Me Go* tracks Kathy's struggle to distinguish the self she cultivated at Hailsham from the self as the cloning program would have her: a self as mere infrastructure.

Though the link between organ donation and the welfare state may seem eminently fictional, it draws on and expands historic discussions about the possibilities of physically knitting bodies together in welfaristic community. One of welfare's greatest champions, Richard Titmuss, named blood donation as an exemplary litmus test for the values of society and its strength of social ties. As first Professor of Social Administration in the UK (LSE, 1950–1973), Titmuss was invested in studying the category of the "social" alongside the political and the economic, seeking a more capacious, even moral vision of state institutions. His 1970 *The Gift Relationship*, perhaps his most philosophical work, asks what happens when a social service like blood donation is treated as a commodity, governed by the logic of the marketplace. The consequences of doing so, he suggests, are dire.[16] Taking existing blood markets as case studies, Titmuss concludes that commercializing blood leads to the erosion of community, the lowering of scientific standards, increased hostility between patient and doctor, exploitation of the underclasses, and other outcomes. Worst of all, however, is the suppression of altruism, or the "moral choice to give in non-monetary forms to a stranger."[17] For Titmuss, altruism is a "social right," reminiscent of T.H. Marshall's concept of "social citizenship," and a crucial component of a welfare state. Rather than utilitarian, social services are instead "generators of moral conflict," which encourage individuals to think not only about themselves, but crucially, about others.[18] His work thus presses its reader to ask

---

[16] In sum: "From our study of the private market in blood in the United States, we have concluded that the commercialisation of blood and donor relationships represses the expression of altruism, erodes the sense of community, lowers scientific standards, limits both personal and professional freedoms, sanctions the making of profits in hospitals and clinical laboratories, legalises hostility between doctor and patient, subjects critical areas of medicine to the laws of the marketplace, places immense social costs on those least able to bear them – the poor, the sick and the inept – increases the danger of unethical behaviour in various sectors of medical science and practice, and results in situations in which proportionately more and more blood is supplied by the poor, the unskilled, the unemployed, Negroes and other low income groups and categories of exploited human populations of high blood yielders ... Moreover, on four testable non-ethical criteria, the commercialized blood market is bad." Richard Titmuss, *The Gift Relationship: From Human Blood to Social Policy* (Bristol: Bristol University Press: 2018), 210.
[17] *Ibid.*, 3.
[18] *Ibid.*

who is my stranger, widening toward its postwar reconstruction variant, *who is my neighbor, and what do I owe them?* For Titmuss, bodily donations prove exceptional test cases for describing social life and the ties that bind an individual to the collective. Ishiguro's novel, then, can be read as carrying these tests to their logical extremes.

Of course, blood donation is not the same as organ donation. Blood can be replenished, making it uniquely suited to be given freely as a gift, whereas organ harvesting requires more force and coercion. Titmuss and Ishiguro arrive at differing accounts of infrastructuralized interiors: for Titmuss, blood donation provides a public good as well as a moral choice to the public, both of which strengthen an individual's experience of the social contract. For Ishiguro, in contrast, this public good is foisted on the backs (or rather, organs) of a minority for the benefit of the majority, analogous to the international "blood proletariat" Titmuss feared would develop from commercializing medical care.[19] Since the 1970s, of course, this fear has since become realized in the global marketplace, whose patterns of organ trade, human trafficking, and "transplant tourism" reinforce inequalities between the developed and developing world.

Other scholars have addressed *Never Let Me Go*'s engagement with organ donation, whether in relation to the global organ market or the practice's implications for defining "quality of life."[20] This chapter, however, describes a different configuration of interiors and infrastructure: namely, the relationship between clones and their planned environment. For the novel's central problem—that of the disappearance of the individual amidst the social aggregate—is most keenly felt through its analogous concern over exceptional and nondescript places. As the clones pass through the program, the novel provides its reader an overabundance of information about the places they inhabit: the schools and cottages that they live in as young wards of the state; the bedsits, car parks, and highways they use as carers

---

[19] Ibid., 208.
[20] See Paul Narkunas's Chapter 8 in *Reified Life: Speculative Capital and the Ahuman Condition* (New York: Fordham University Press, 2018), which reads Ishiguro's "pre-individuation" of the human as "the key to thinking agency differently at the molecular level, to creating different combinations of collective forms of existence," including altruism and bioethics (230). See also Matthew Eatough's reading of affect and "quality of life" as key to understanding its narrative of development in "The Time that Remains: Organ Donation, Temporal Duration, and *Bildung* in Kazuo Ishiguro's *Never Let Me Go*," *Literature and Medicine* 29.1 (Spring 2011), 132–160. Narkunas's chapter specifically references Titmuss's *Gift Relationship* as an early, no longer viable model of altruistic organ donation, which depends on the NHS, welfare state, and empathy (Narkunas, *Reified Life*, 241).

for their fellow clones; the recovery centers that house them as donors; and the hospitals that harvest their organs until they die. The drama of *Never Let Me Go* comes precisely from this confluence of *Bildung* and environment: Kathy's narrative is occasioned not only by her transition from carer to donor, but also by the closure of Hailsham and other privately funded enterprises within this cloning program. The demise of these privately funded "privileged estates" signals an imminently bleak future, one stripped of all acculturating, humanizing structures and left with only the barest forms of housing, education, and care facilities. Despite this, the novel also refuses complete disenchantment from the promise of welfare infrastructures.

Hailsham's Paradoxical Infrastructure

As a privately funded estate within the cloning program, Hailsham's great illusion is obscuring its role in the cloning system: it shelters its clones from the outside world for as long as they remain under its care. It does so in part through the guardians' careful epistemological withholding when teaching their students about their place in the order of things: they cannily they let their students know only so much at a time. But deception is also built into Hailsham itself, with its provisions of education, its caretakers, and its beautiful surroundings designed to placate the clones among their otherwise bleak fate. The estate itself is large and immaculately groomed, with several rooms, halls, tranquil ponds, rhubarb patches, and sports pavilions that look like "those sweet little cottages people always had in picture books when we were young."[21] Its boarding-school atmosphere adds a level of intrigue to the students' lives, with its intimacies of dormitory living and attachments to favorite guardians. In this way, *Never Let Me Go* uncannily inhabits the novelistic infrastructure of British school fiction, disturbingly rendering education not as soul-producing, but rather organ harvesting.

By encouraging their creative development, Hailsham gives their students an intellectual superstructure of meaning-making values, practices, and places, either to forestall or to repress their knowledge of their infrastructural purpose. As Miss Emily puts it to Kathy, "Whatever else, we at least saw to it that all of you in our care, you grew up in wonderful surroundings. And we saw to it too, after you left us, you were kept away from the worst of

[21] Ishiguro, *Never*, 6.

those horrors. We were able to do that much for you at least."[22] The novel's consistent emphasis on environment draws on a long-standing belief in an environment's ameliorative effects on personal development, or as Douglas Mao puts it, the belief that exposure to beauty could "bring human beings to some kind of reconciliation with a world that otherwise seems alien, indifferent, fragmented, or oppressive."[23] Kathy appears to absorb this lesson: her narrative is predominantly spatial, and she is consummately in touch with her surroundings.[24]

Hailsham's environmental experiment is not a revolutionary turnover of the program; rather, it seeks to make the program more comfortable, and thus more acceptable, to its cloned subjects. The cultural attachments it offers to the clones are merely palliative, delivered in advance of the wounds administered by the state. Though privately funded, Hailsham nevertheless aids in maintaining and training its students to become healthy, willing organ donors, feeding them back into the larger system. While describing Hailsham, Kathy's narrative obliquely registers this chilling reality, giving us small reminders of its role as a clone factory. The reader learns, for instance, that the clones are sterile, and that they have been in Hailsham since their "Infants" stage. And while they are given lessons in literature, music, and geography, they are also subject to "Culture Briefings," role-playing sessions to help prepare them for the outside world, or at least the minimum level of social encounter they will need as carers. Though Kathy does not dwell in this paranoid space, she often uses these referents as a means of establishing common ground between her and her audience, such as this reference to her medical exams: "I don't know how it was where you were, but at Hailsham we had to have some form of medical almost every week—usually up in Room 18 at the very top of the house—with stern Nurse Trisha, or Crow Face, as we called her."[25] Through these asides, Kathy hails us as fellow

---

[22] Ibid., 261.
[23] Douglas Mao, *Fateful Beauty* (Princeton: Princeton University Press, 2008), 6–7.
[24] As Mao suggests, this relationship between the environment and its influence over personal development reached its apogee in the decades after the Second World War, as "revulsion at Nazi eugenic policies helped make inquiry into hereditary and even physiological influences on human development broadly unpalatable, which meant that in serious research (and in popular understandings growing out of the new science) environment had the field largely to itself" (15). *Never Let Me Go* provides a fascinating turn to this relationship, not only using this environmental hypothesis to alleviate (or provide consolation for) normalized practices of state violence against cloned subjects, but also by attributing Hailsham's closure to eugenic practices in creating superhuman clones.
[25] Ishiguro, *Never*, 13.

clones (perhaps even her donors), though the interpellation is never firmly established. Hailsham, however, cannot completely sustain its ideological illusions. Even though it tries to do away with the reality of its infrastructural purpose, the clones still have to come to terms with their status as infrastructure. As a result, they confront a series of psychic dilemmas regarding their utilitarian personhood and foreclosed futurity. For some, such as Kathy's friend Tommy, this manifests itself in forms of rebellion and moments of uncontrollable rage. For the most part, however, we see the students of Hailsham negotiating their clone status through compensatory mechanisms including particular forms of play, jokes, and fantasies that can help them make sense of their infrastructural status. The novel can be read as a series of these meaning-making experiments, one after another, up to the point their lives end.

These psychic dilemmas begin in their childhood years, as the young clones develop an uneasy relationship to their physical bodies as both their own and someone else's.[26] They register this ambivalence through imaginative play and figurative language, beginning with their concept of "unzipping." It starts as a cruel joke on Tommy. The students pretend that a wound on his elbow is at risk of unzipping like a bag, with "skin flopping about next to him 'like one of those long gloves in *My Fair Lady*.'"[27] Yet the idea of unzipping persists long after the joke ends. It finds new application as a way to conceptualize donations: "The idea was that when the time came, you'd be able just to unzip a bit of yourself, a kidney or something would slide out, and you'd hand it over."[28] Another example occurs during an English lesson with Miss Lucy, when the students discuss POW camps in the Second World War. As Kathy recalls, "One of the boys asked if the fences around the camps had been electrified, and then someone else had said how strange it must have been, living in a place like that, where you could commit suicide any time you liked just by touching a fence."[29] To Miss Lucy's horror (and ours), the students laugh and begin to impersonate "someone reaching out and getting electrocuted. For a moment things got

---

[26] An apt comparison might be made here to the epiphany in Ishiguro's *The Remains of the Day*, in which Stevens finally breaks down over the idea of "giving his best" to Lord Darlington (255).
[27] Ishiguro, *Never*, 86.
[28] Ibid., 88.
[29] Ibid., 78.

riotous, with everyone shouting and mimicking touching electric fences."[30] Part coping mechanism, part registration of the horror of their bounded, controlled lives, the clones' play is a metaphorization that reflects, but also does not quite fit, the reality they face. These moments of self-negation offer an exit from, even rebellion against, the clones' thoroughly instrumentalized lives. While there is no escape from being-as-infrastructure, the clones are still able to create a spectacle of violence, one that cuts through the subdued, euphemized atmosphere of the cloning program.[31]

While these early fantasies center on the materiality of the body, at the cottages they evolve into more complex questions about personhood and professionalism. For Kathy's friend Ruth, this takes the form of an excited search for her "possible," clonespeak for the person from whom each clone was modeled. As Kathy explains, the main idea behind the possibles was that if you caught a glimpse of your model, "you'd glimpse your future ... you'd get some insight into who you were deep down, and maybe too, you'd see something of what your life held in store."[32] Yet as Ruth's search unfolds, the importance of the possible becomes less about interior personhood and more about professional environment, her interest first piqued by the suggestion that her possible worked in an office in a distant seaside town. The fantasy does not take hold until Ruth sees an advertisement of a sparkling open office. Captivated by the ad's vision of professionalism ("Now *that* would be a *proper* place to work"), she uses the picture as the basis of her dream future, going into "all the details—the plans, the gleaming equipment, the chairs with their swivels and castors."[33] In a dark echo of New Labour's "welfare to work" ethos, Ruth's Hailsham-forged consciousness is drawn to beautiful managerial environments as the pinnacle of her personal development: the greatest possible future she as welfare infrastructure could have. When the clones take a field trip to search for Ruth's possible, however, the fantasy unravels, which leads to Ruth's bitter, abject catharsis: "We all know

---

[30] *Ibid.*
[31] The clones also favor the scene in *The Great Escape* when "the American jumps over the barbed wire on his bike," demanding that it be played again and again ("Rewind! Rewind!") (Ishiguro, *Never*, 99). This is the clearest, most potentially *redemptive* representation of freedom in the novel, a dramatic vision of escape with one's self intact. Of course, in the film, the American (the dashing Steve McQueen) is caught just seconds later, his body cruelly entangled in a second line of fencing. This captivity is closer to the world of *Never Let Me Go*, whose subjects continually vacillate between the body ensnared by the barbed wire and, as I suggest, the wire itself.
[32] Ishiguro, *Never*, 140.
[33] *Ibid.*, 144.

it. We're modelled from *trash*. Junkies, prostitutes, winos, tramps. Convicts, maybe, just as long as they aren't psychos."[34] The end of her tirade evacuates any sense of personhood: "If you want to look for possibles, if you want to do it properly, then you look in the gutter. You look in rubbish bins. Look down the toilet, that's where you'll find where we all come from."[35] In other words, look to the infrastructure. Not only has Ruth's vision of a fulfilling professionalism crumbled, her sense of viable personhood has disintegrated. In this moment, she is able to see herself as what she has been all along: an object circulating in the networks of society's refuse.

Poetics of Infrastructure: Searching for Hailsham

Despite the heightened emotions of the bitterly disillusioned Ruth, the ragefilled Tommy, or even the righteous guardian Miss Lucy, there is a reason why it is Kathy who narrates *Never Let Me Go*. For what worries Kathy the most is not the injustice or loathsome nature of her death, but rather the closure of her beloved alma mater and her increasing distance from her childhood life:

> "But what'll happen to all the students?" Roger obviously thought I'd meant the ones still there, the little ones dependent on their guardians, and he put on a troubled face and began speculating how they'd have to be transferred to other houses around the country, even though some of these would be a far cry from Hailsham. But of course, that wasn't what I'd meant. I'd meant *us*, all the students who'd grown up with me and were now spread across the country, carers and donors, all separated now but still somehow linked by the place we'd come from.[36]

To Kathy, the loss of Hailsham is not just institutional. She is not concerned about the physical relocation of the younger students, but rather the symbolic and psychic effects for the alumni.[37] Indicating its lingering influence as a place, Kathy points to what Gaston Bachelard calls a "poetics of

---
[34] *Ibid.*, 166.
[35] *Ibid.*
[36] *Ibid.*, 211.
[37] What's worse, Hailsham is not merely closing, but rather transforming: its house and grounds are being sold to a hotel chain, creating a new form of institutionalized domesticity uncannily related to Hailsham's original function. This grim course of reconstruction is a

the house" that has laid claim to her and her fellow students, one founded on Hailsham's environmental ideology.[38] If, as Bachelard suggests, writers "prove to us that the houses that were lost forever continue to live on in us; that they insist in us in order to live again, as though they expected us to give them a supplement of living," Kathy's narrative follows partially in suit, reanimating Hailsham just on the eve of its disappearance.[39] Yet where Bachelard finds the practice of nostalgia ultimately reparative ("How much better we should live in the old house today!"), Kathy's reflections are more conflicted.[40] While she does not fully jettison Hailsham's poetics of space in her post-Hailsham life, neither does she wholeheartedly reproduce it. Instead, she finds herself drawn to an archive of degraded spaces, such as fields and open roads, marshlands and ruins. In doing so, she builds her own poetics of infrastructure, which testify to, but also bear a fraught relationship with, Hailsham's institutional legacy.

In contrast to Ruth's looking down toilets and gutters, Kathy's poetics of infrastructure reflects a more mobile search, catalyzed by her travels through the English countryside. This leitmotif of the novel will be familiar to readers of Ishiguro, whose fixation on transportation is unmistakable: from the trams and trains in *An Artist of the Floating World* and *A Pale View of Hills*, to Stevens's country motoring in *The Remains of the Day*, Ishiguro's novels are both minutely located and vastly networked. Stevens provides the closest analog to Kathy, as their mobility across the English countryside contrasts with the situated accounts of Darlington Hall and Hailsham. Driving across the countryside provides a framing structure for both novels, catalyzing flashbacks to their respective pasts. But where *The Remains of the Day* gives us a tour of a mythical "Great" Britain ("as though the land knows of its own beauty, of its own greatness, and feel no need to shout it"), *Never Let Me Go* travels England's darker, uglier backroads, following the more banal, nondescript infrastructure that shapes its landscape.[41] And while Stevens's travels represent a rare moment of leisure for him, Kathy's driving is sponsored by the donations program, and characterized by a dreary fatigue from long commutes on the road from donor to donor. For Kathy and her fellow

---

ubiquitous specter in the postwar British novel, beginning with Evelyn Waugh's *Brideshead Revisited*, which finds the estate turned into military barracks. Regarding Ishiguro, see John J. Su's "Refiguring National Character."
[38] Gaston Bachelard, *The Poetics of Space*, trans. Maria Jolas (Boston: Beacon, 1994), xxxvi.
[39] Ibid., 56.
[40] Ibid.
[41] Ishiguro, *The Remains of the Day* (New York: Vintage, 1993), 29.

clones, the car is ultimately a symbol of their instrumentalized beings, rather than (as we might hope) a vehicle of escape.

For Kathy, driving allows an active way to continue searching for Hailsham:

> Driving around the country now, I still see things that will remind me of Hailsham. I might pass the corner of a misty field, or see part of a large house in the distance as I come down the side of a valley, even a particular arrangement of poplar trees up on a hillside, and I'll think: "Maybe that's it! I've found it! This actually *is* Hailsham!" Then I see it's impossible and I go on driving, my thoughts drifting on elsewhere. In particular, there are those pavilions... If I drive past one I keep looking over to it for as long as possible, and one day I'll crash the car like that, but I keep doing it.[42]

Kathy's driving is no carefree cruise down memory lane; its escapism suggests a deep ambivalence about what it means to search for Hailsham. Though the last sentence merely gestures to a potential car crash, Kathy's disregard for her own safety is nevertheless disturbing, especially in contrast to her careful professionalism. This specter of vehicular death raises two potential types of closure: either Kathy will metaphorically crash into reality (i.e., Ishiguro's trademark epiphany), or die before required to become a donor. In some sense, this episode recalls the Hailsham children's jokes about the POW camp, and the disruptive potentiality of the students' suicidal urges. Yet as before, while Ishiguro inserts the question of resistance into the novel, he does so only in a shadowy, underdeveloped form. *Never Let Me Go* is not interested in outward acts of rebellion, heroic attempts at escape, or even abject acknowledgments of one's fate, but rather in the limited ways clones fantasize themselves out of being infrastructure, limitations that come from their status *as* infrastructure. Even if Kathy does deliberately crash her car, the novel seems to suggest, she may end up fulfilling her infrastructural role after all: the idea itself seems intended to invoke, however, ironically, our own associations of organ donation with driver's license applications. There is little room for resistance, or even meaningful choice, in the world of *Never Let Me Go*.

Though Kathy never manages to find Hailsham, there is something about the empty, gray quality of England's landscape and roadways that is peculiarly conducive to remembering it. In her reminiscences, Kathy uniformly

---

[42] Ishiguro, *Never*, 6.

begins by describing the long, expansive nature of her commutes, whether "past fields on a long afternoon, or maybe drinking my coffee in front of a huge window in a motorway service station" or "past rows of furrowed fields, the sky big and grey and never changing mile after mile," each of which instigates a memory of Hailsham.[43] Like Proust's madeleine, these memories seem involuntary. No particular object or sensory pleasure prompts them. They come from the absence of direct stimulation, growing from a space where "thoughts have nowhere special to go."[44] It might seem counterintuitive that these bleak, empty infrastructures remind Kathy of Hailsham, especially in relationship to its beautiful, cultivated environment. And yet the unremarkable, utilitarian nature of these roads and service stations are closer to the true nature of being a clone—more than any well-meaning attempt to reform the lived experience of the donations program. Roads and motorway service stations reveal Hailsham's own true nature as a transient, unliveable infrastructure no different from any other vast government home. In this sense, Kathy's driving meditations can be read as akin to Tommy's excessive rage, or Ruth's bitter insistence that they are modeled from trash. They are her way of expressing resistance to, or at least awareness of, her thoroughly infrastructural being.

While this specter of potential violence haunts every clone, Kathy's nostalgia grants her an incisive double-vision that allows her to see both the beauty of past places and the bleakness of present ones. While her traveling provides the most immediate catalyst for entering this nostalgic mode, it is also activated by representations of past places, such as an old photograph of the Kingsfield, Tommy's recovery center. Taken in the late 1950s or early 1960s, this image shows Kingsfield when it was still a "holiday camp for ordinary families," before it had been converted into a center for ailing clones. The photograph shows a cheerful, sunny place, centering on a swimming pool with "all these happy people—children, parents—splashing about having a great time."[45] The only evidence left of this past structure during Tommy's time there is the metal frame supporting the pool's highdive, a remainder that exemplifies the current center's shoddy, unkempt nature. Looking at the photograph, Kathy muses, "It was only when I saw the photo it occurred to me what the frame was and why it was there, and today, each time I see it, I can't help picturing a swimmer taking a dive off

---

[43] Ishiguro, *Never*, 45 and 115.
[44] *Ibid.*, 55.
[45] *Ibid.*, 219.

the top only to crash into the cement."[46] This grim vision once again recalls the children's jokes about self-harm and Kathy's vision of a car crash. In this instance, though, Kathy's imagination doubles the point, as this bleak scene symbolizes not only the clones' entrapment, but also the slow leaching of care from the cloning program, as institutions like Hailsham crumble into bleak governmental facilities.

The novel's most poignant moment of infrastructural poetics appears in a scene when Kathy, Ruth, and Tommy travel out to a beached boat in the middle of a marshland. For the donors, the boat has been a peculiar legend, prompting their desire to encounter its physical features and see what mythical revelation it might hold. The trip is not easy, especially for ailing donors like Ruth. Eventually, the clones happen upon an eerie, bleached landscape of water and woods:

> The pale sky looked vast and you could see it reflected every so often in the patches of water breaking up the land. Not so long ago, the woods must have extended further, because you could see here and there ghostly dead trunks poking out of the soil, most of them broken off only a few feet up. And beyond the dead trunks, maybe sixty yards away, was the boat, sitting beached in the marshes under the weak sun.[47]

The boat, too, is just as bleached and decayed, with cracking paint, crumbling frames, and fading sky-blue color. What the clones see in all this degradation and disrepair, however, is Hailsham, or at least a version of it. As Tommy offers, "I always see Hailsham being like this now. No logic to it. In fact, this is pretty close to the picture in my head. Except there's no boat, of course. It wouldn't be so bad, if it's like this now."[48] And while Ruth at first refuses to see the likeness between the two structures, she then connects the scene to a dream she had about being back at Hailsham, where the school was flooded like a lake full of rubbish. Unlike her earlier tirade about being modeled on trash, Ruth finds her vision "nice and tranquil, just like it is here. I knew I wasn't in any danger, that it was only like that because it had closed down."[49] The boat thus offers Ruth and Tommy a compensatory aesthetic vision of their own ruinous status, whose stakes are heightened due to their status as active donors. To them, this dystopian wasteland provides a

---

[46] Ibid.
[47] Ibid., 224.
[48] Ibid., 225.
[49] Ibid.

form of sanctuary: a compellingly peaceful end for an object created, used, and eventually discarded. Finding Hailsham entails accepting its status as a ruined experiment, an abandoned structure, or in Ruth's dream, a giant lake of trash. For Kathy, however, who has yet to become a carer at this point in time, the boat offers no revelation. Her self-realization waits until the end of the novel, and takes shape in her own mythic landscape of rubbish, emptiness, and infrastructural remains.

Revising the Historical Epiphany

The epiphany arrived at the end of *Never Let Me Go* is distinct within Ishiguro's *oeuvre*, in part because the conditions of Ishiguro's typical narrative epiphany are simply not available to Kathy's subjectivity. For Ishiguro, epiphanies usually follow a narrative pattern, beginning with a protagonist reflecting on the remains of his or her day in a manner that suggests a concealing of, or a willful blindness toward, certain traumatic episodes. In recounting their past, the protagonist might express a pride about their status and social position, especially with regards to their consummate professionalism; however, this self-satisfaction becomes untenable as they come to terms with their complicity in a violent order of things, through a crisis that reveals what they needed to ignore, forget, or injure to continue their work.[50] As noted in this chapter's introduction, Ishiguro's plots are often historically and politically oriented around war, with characters playing out their ethical dilemmas against the backdrop of historical events and wartime referents. The clones, however, are not allowed such access to this historical consciousness. Their engagement with the outside world is as radically delimited as their short life spans and their ability to understand the system in which they live is as carefully monitored as their health. Thus, the real challenge posed by the novel is how, if at all, a clone might experience a

---

[50] The exception to this remarkably consistent oeuvre is *The Unconsoled* (1995), which is a more dream-like, surreal meditation on memory loss that is not immediately locatable in any specific historical moment. It was largely lambasted by literary critics, who were flummoxed as much by its departure from the typical Ishiguro novel as its length and experimental style. However, Ishiguro's short story collection *Nocturnes: Five Stories of Music and Nightfall* (2009) also obliquely follows this pattern, with each protagonist reflecting on the twilight of their days. See Walkowitz's chapter on Ishiguro's "treason" for another take on these consistencies to his oeuvre. *Cosmopolitan Style: Modernism Beyond the Nation* (New York: Columbia University Press, 2006), 109–130. See also Chris Holmes and Kelly Mee Rich, "On Rereading Kazuo Ishiguro," *Modern Fiction Studies* 67, no. 1 (Spring 2021), 1–19.

postwar epiphany in relation to a historical or social context that lies beyond their purview.

How, then, does historical epiphany fail in *Never Let Me Go*, and what emerges in its stead? The novel's attempted historical revelation occurs during Kathy and Tommy's visit to the home of her former Hailsham guardians, Madame and Miss Emily. At this point in the novel, Kathy is acting as carer for Tommy. The two make the pilgrimage to the house together, hoping that on the basis of their love, Tommy might be granted a deferral from his donations. Of course, this fantasy no more than another clone myth, and Madame and Miss Emily confirm the cruelty of the cloning program. This contrived encounter, recalling a *deus ex machina*, is often passed over in critical assessments of the novel. It is also unnecessarily didactic: the reader needs no further confirmation that cloning is bad, and this episode belabors the point.[51] However, the failure of this denouement takes on particular resonance when considered in relation to Ishiguro's other novelistic epiphanies.

A part of the peculiar function of this scene in this novel is to provide the historical background that the clones, with their limited consciousness, had been unable to provide up until this point in the story. As we learn, the clone program had its origins in the immediate postwar period, when scientific developments in cloning led to the eradication of previously incurable diseases. In the 1950s and 1960s, Hailsham and other estates were created as an experimental counter the general way the program was being run; these establishments reached the height of their influence in the late 1970s, when Hailsham's creators organized exhibitions of clone art to gather support for the compassionate treatment of clones. By the 1980s and throughout the 1990s, public support for Hailsham was lost through the Morningdale scandal, an experiment in genetic engineering aiming to create superhumans rather than clones. At the time of the novel's present day, Hailsham and the other planned environments are gone. Translated from the novel's world to our own, it would seem that this story simply traces the historical arc of the welfare state. Understood in this way, the novel would offer a damning indictment. Shattering the view of welfare as putatively caring, it envisages

---

[51] The episode thus confirms Robbins's characterization of Ishiguro's work as seeming to be "committed to making only the most banal and uncontroversial ethical statements," like "cruelty is bad" (Robbins, "Cruelty is Bad," 301). James Wood's reading also finds the novel "weakened by a didactic ending, in which the spirit of Wells or Huxley bests the spirit of Borges" ("The Human Difference," *The New Republic*, May 16, 2005, 38, https://newrepublic.com/article/68200/the-human-difference).

an exceptionally violent system, one that even trains the dead to bury their dead.

Yet this historical account cannot be the full story, not only because it is presented in such ungainly didactic terms, but also because it is ultimately illegibile for the clones themselves. After years of strategically being "told and not told" about their place in the world, the historical explanation they finally receive is foreign, even unrecognizable.[52] Here Lauren Berlant's concept of the *juxtapolitical* offers a productive way to think about history in *Never Let Me Go*. As a near or nearly political register, the juxtapolitical "flourish[es] in proximity to the political because the political is deemed an elsewhere managed by elites who are interested in reproducing the conditions of their objective superiority, not in the well-being of ordinary people or life-worlds."[53] Often emerging in marginalized collectivities, the juxtapolitical allows subjects relief from the political through "adaptation, adjustment, improvisation, and developing wiles for surviving, thriving, and transcending the world as it presents itself."[54] This is an apt way to describe Hailsham's *habitus*: with power so obviously managed elsewhere, the program creates its own intimate public that must, to make life livable, find ways to relieve its students of their thoroughly utilitarian subjecthood. We might likewise call Hailsham's project *juxtahistorical*, fighting back the bad history of the donations program. When Miss Emily admonishes, "From your perspective today, Kathy, your bemusement is perfectly reasonable. But you must try and see it historically,"[55] the reader knows the clones can never do so: unlike in Ishiguro's other novels, history is not what hurts them.

What the clones can register, even in limited terms, is the emergent historical and infrastructural tension between public utilities and their privatization. Faced with a reality of "vast government 'homes'" (which, Miss Emily assures, are so unspeakably awful that "you'd not sleep for days if you saw what still goes on in some of those places"), the former guardians of Hailsham retreat to a domestic interior, sequestered away from the world.[56] Though this is the first private domestic setting seen in the novel, it does not come as a relief. Instead, the clones find the house to be dark and dank,

---

[52] Ishiguro, *Never*, 81.
[53] Lauren Berlant, *The Female Complaint: The Unfinished Business of Sentimentality in American Culture* (Durham: Duke University Press, 2008), 3.
[54] Ibid., 2.
[55] Ishiguro, *Never*, 262.
[56] Ibid., 265.

with narrow hallways, a sealed-off fireplace, odious Victorian furniture, and an atmosphere as though "a servant of some sort had got the place ready for the night-time, then left."[57] As these women prided themselves on Hailsham's orderly, well-designed, and disciplined environment, their home's disrepair comes as a surprise. As Miss Emily notes, this decrepit domesticity is intimately tied to Hailsham's closure and the loss of their life's work:

> And as for Marie-Claude and me, here we are, we've retreated to this house, and upstairs we have a mountain of your work. That's what we have to remind us of what we did. And a mountain of debt too, though that's not nearly so welcome. And the memories, I suppose, of all of you. And the knowledge that we've given you better lives than you would have had otherwise.[58]

Having failed to save their young charges from the misery of growing up, the guardians retired from the outside world, with only their cobwebbed memories and relics to keep them company.[59] Like Misses Havisham of Hailsham, the clones encounter their guardians in a scene recalling Dickens's *Great Expectations*, though Miss Emily affirms what she has done rather than begging for forgiveness. The women have transformed their previous caretaking duties into both the stewardship of the Hailsham Gallery—an unruly, unmanageable mountain of clone artwork and debt—and the mundane labors of housekeeping and interior decorating.

Though Miss Emily implies that they are happy to house her former students' artwork (in comparison to her debt, "not nearly so welcome"), her next statement implies an uncertainty as to whether she wants to remember the clones themselves ("and the memories, I suppose, of all of you.") Work, debt, and memory are mingled together, as reminders of what she and Madame did all threaten to slide into a bad infinity, turning a proud accomplishment with lingering financial obligations into an uncertain trauma with lingering responsibility and guilt. Thus conflicted, her

---

[57] Ibid., 249.
[58] Ibid., 269.
[59] Though some critics compare *Never Let Me Go* to Shelley's *Frankenstein* (see especially Gabriele Griffen, Keith McDonald, and Tiffany Tsao), it is also fruitful to read it as a return to and reworking of the Victorian novel, whether in relation to Dickens's concern over orphans and marginal progenitor figures (for example, *Great Expectations*' Abel Magwitch as Pip's benefactor, which Ishiguro rewrites in *When We Were Orphans*), the doubling of "Kathy" as a protagonist name (as in *Wuthering Heights*, which also foregrounds her experience of wild, open spaces), or even Kathy's research project on Victorian novels. This is more evidence of Ishiguro's canny, parasitical inhabitation of the British novelistic tradition.

narrative can only find closure by restating the consolatory fiction—now "the knowledge"—that Hailsham had given the clones better lives than they would have otherwise had. This rhetorical transaction shifts the burden of blame and responsibility away from her and Madame and onto Kathy and Tommy, now in the peculiar position of needing to thank Miss Emily for not making them live the lives of typical clones.

The speech also belies the perverse, infinite nature of their caretaking duties, as they have made their own home the archive of Hailsham's hopes and dreams. Though perhaps a humanizing gesture that tries to close the gap between the human and the inhuman, their labor is ultimately doomed to fail, not only because they no longer have the clones under their care, but also because they cannot empathize with the clones, or connect the clones' artwork and memories with a legible, desirable personhood. In fact, their interactions with the clones are marked by revulsion, fear, or pity. Earlier in the novel, Kathy had remarked upon Madame's disgust for the students, a theory she and her friends test during their childhood days, and which causes her a mild existential crisis. This current encounter shows that Miss Emily, too, had suffered a similar dread, as she confesses, "There were times I'd look down at you all from my study window and I'd feel such revulsion... But I was determined not to let such feelings stop me doing what was right. I fought those feelings and I won."[60] In this rewriting of the modernist window scene, the window yet again dramatizes exceptional, humanizing acts of sympathy, though with terrible limitations.

Ishiguro's version of the window scene perversely reshapes the transformative potential of this symbolic threshold. During Hailsham's tenure, winning for Miss Emily meant not giving into one's personal, ugly feelings; after its closure, winning is similarly ambivalent insofar as she retreats into an infinite labor of bad domesticity. She transforms her previous management of the school and her students' interior design into a management of housework and interior decoration, her revulsion for the clones into a petty annoyance at various service workers who come to help with the home ("Oh dear, is that the men come for the cabinet?" "It's that awful man from the decoration company again").[61] Ultimately, it is these men who close their conversation with Tommy and Kathy, marking the end of their appeal and any hope they may have had for a deferral:

[60] Ishiguro, *Never*, 269.
[61] *Ibid.*, 259.

"This time it must be the men," Miss Emily said. "I shall have to get ready. But you can stay a little longer. The men have to bring the thing down two flights of stairs. Marie-Claude will see they don't damage it." Tommy and I couldn't quite believe that was the end of it.[62]

This interruption is an almost comic, if also devastating, moment of realism. This scene is not just simply some cinematic revelation about the history of Hailsham, nor even a devastating revelation that there are no deferrals, but also an ordinary day in the lives of the two women. Though severing Kathy and Tommy's drama with a reminder of mundane housework and movers, it is also not simply a random interruption. With this shadowy intrusion into domestic life, the reader is reminded that no home is a full retreat from the outside world.

Though the two women's domestic arrangement could be read as a generous gesture to rehouse the institutions of Hailsham, their labor is also clearly ambivalent, caught somewhere between gift and obligation, hospitality and hostility, guilt and self-righteous reconstruction. If the house does stand in some way for Hailsham, it cannot offer a satisfying memorial to the clones, only an obsolete archive of their work that substitutes furniture for bodies in an infinite labor of attempted repair. In its concern with Hailsham's substitution, the novel re-animates the novelistic trope of the obsolete, antiquated Big House, whose post-1945 fate is one of disrepair, repurposing, or transfomation as discussed in the previous chapter. In *Never Let Me Go*, the protracted afterlife of Hailsham represents one of the two possible ends of the Hailsham experiment: either total instrumentalization or total privatization, both bleak futures of the state's cloning program.

Somewhere, Wherever

Despite the postwar provenance of the cloning program, Kathy's self-awareness cannot take the form of a historical consciousness, nor can her epiphany be politically oriented through the welfarist ideology of Hailsham. What then, might it look like? This chapter has described how clones deploy verbal play, metaphors, and fantasies as compensatory mechanisms. For Kathy, there is one particularly powerful spatial fantasy that recurs throughout the novel and returns at its end as a means of epiphany: Norfolk. Unlike the unzipping, the search for a possible, or the archive of degraded spaces,

---

[62] Ibid., 265.

Kathy's Norfolk fantasy provides an alternative space of shelter that cannot be taken away or otherwise disillusioned. The clones learn of the existence of this county during a geography lesson with Miss Emily, who describes Norfolk as peaceful, but also as "something of a lost corner."[63] After this, the clones begin to associate the lost corner of Norfolk with Hailsham's lost and found, also called the "Lost Corner," and soon start imagining Norfolk as a place "where all the lost property found in the country ended up."[64] As Ruth reflects, it was important to them that "when we lost something precious, and we'd looked and looked and still couldn't find it, then we didn't have to be completely heartbroken. We still had that last bit of comfort, thinking one day, when we were grown up, and we were free to travel around the country, we could always go and find it again in Norfolk."[65] In a brief moment of magic later in the novel, Kathy seems to confirm her childhood fantasy when she finds a copy of her lost, beloved Judy Bridgewater tape in a Norfolk Woolworth's.

Unlike the tape, however, Hailsham is a loss that Kathy cannot recover. At the end of the novel, Kathy's solution is to internalize Hailsham wholesale, in the ultimate form of spatial fantasy: "Once I'm able to have a quieter life, in whichever centre they send me to, I'll have Hailsham with me, safely in my head, and that'll be something no one can take away."[66] As her language suggests, Kathy thinks of this internalization as a small act of defiance against the larger cloning system, a way to preserve the kind old world of her youth. At the same time, her solution follows the novel's arc of disenchantment, and its slow divestment of meaning from state infrastructure. For though this internalization preserves Hailsham's fiction of shelter, Kathy's language also exposes Hailsham's great lie, pitting its mythology against the reality of the external world. In these final moments of the book, then, Kathy has finally embraced the paranoid logic Hailsham leaves in its wake: a myth that good, caring state spaces can mitigate the harm wreaked by bad, harmful ones.

While this solution finally brings us up to the date of Kathy's narrative present, it is not the last word of *Never Let Me Go*. Having affirming Hailsham as something no one can take away, Kathy recounts one last return to Norfolk, a coda that interrupts any simple dichotomy of good and bad. As she tells us, "The only indulgent thing I did, just once, was a couple of weeks after I heard Tommy had completed, when I drove up to

---

[63] Ibid., 65.
[64] Ibid., 66.
[65] Ibid.
[66] Ibid., 286–287.

Norfolk, even though I had no real need to."[67] After driving through "field after flat, featureless field, with virtually no change," she finds herself in the now familiarly abject setting of an empty field surrounded by barbed wire, where "all along the fence, especially along the lower line of wire, all sorts of rubbish had caught and tangled."[68] Unlike Ruth's boat epiphany, however, Kathy does not fixate on the rubbish as a terminus to her thoughts. Instead, she starts to imagine what she describes as "just a little fantasy thing, because this was Norfolk after all, and it was only a couple of weeks since I'd lost him."[69] This exceptional acknowledgment of her personal loss and grief is followed an equally exceptional meditation:

> I was thinking about the rubbish, the flapping plastic in the branches, the shore-line of odd stuff caught along the fencing, and I half-closed my eyes and imagined this was the spot where everything I'd ever lost since my childhood had washed up, and I was now standing here in front of it, and if I waited long enough, a tiny figure would appear on the horizon across the field, and gradually get larger until I'd see it was Tommy, and he'd wave, maybe even call. The fantasy never got beyond that—I didn't let it—and though the tears rolled down my face, I wasn't sobbing or out of control. I just waited a bit, then turned back to the car, to drive off to wherever it was I was supposed to be.[70]

This scene is the last moment of enchantment in the novel, one final attempt at realizing humanity and meaning against the destructive infrastructures of the state. Turning away from her search for Hailsham, Kathy orients us toward a different space—registered through the figurative and the subjunctive—where Tommy can be brought back, closer and more recognizable the longer she waits. In this version of the Norfolk fantasy, we peer deeply into Kathy's spatial imaginary, with its insistence on the consolations of environment that it also troubles: a setting that recalls Hailsham but is also defined by liminality, waste, and uncultivated space.

After imagining this world and summoning the lost figure of the dead, Kathy stops herself, able to name the moment for what it is: a fantasy. The novel could end in this moment, or even after "I just waited a bit, then turned

---

[67] Ibid., 287.
[68] Ibid.
[69] Ibid.
[70] Ibid., 288.

back to the car." Such a scene of closure would recapitulate Ishiguro's typical endings, in which shattered protagonists recommit to living out their lives under conditions that are now abhorrent, trying to make them more bearable, even pleasurable. However, *Never Let Me Go* relieves Kathy from such an unliveable responsibility. Unlike Stevens's recommitment to bantering in *The Remains of the Day*, or Christopher's reinvestment in London in *When We Were Orphans*, Kathy does not convince herself of the necessity of returning to the professionalism or places of her present life, even in an ironic way. After Kathy turns back to the car, Ishiguro adds this final, enigmatic dependent clause: "to wherever it was I was supposed to be." With these words, he signals that while Kathy will return to her fate as a clone, it is merely a return, not a recommitment. As she turns back to the car, she leaves the fantastical "somewhere" of Norfolk for all the "wherevers" of the cloning program. Whatever this indefinite place might be, it is emptied of Hailsham's attachments, a place where she can finally let herself go.

While this moment offers disenchantment from the spaces of the cloning system, it does not completely hollow out the significance of enchantment for Kathy herself. Indeed, the novel itself is the ultimate enactment of Kathy's Norfolk fantasy, as it archives all the washed-up experiences of the clones' lost lives. Perhaps, as Kathy suggests, the only way to create meaning in such a totalizing system is through a registration of its loss. Read this way, *Never Let Me Go* mirrors this Norfolk fantasy. Documenting the clones' various attempts to rehabilitate themselves, the novel archives the detritus of all their attempts at becoming people, and finding belonging, in the face of utilitarian instrumentalization.

This concluding scene thus provides one more turn to literature's activation of Britain's postwar promises of repair: perhaps the most heartbreaking one described in this whole project. By extending the postwar fantasy of repair to its extreme, *Never Let Me Go* offers a cold picture of the welfare state's endgame, in which the individual becomes indistinguishable from—indeed, makes up—the infrastructure of the welfare state. The novel shatters the view of welfare as repair, revealing an exceptionally violent system, one that even trains the dead to bury their dead. But even within this world, Ishiguro does not simply repudiate the notion of a state that cares—as other dystopian novels have done, such as George Orwell's *1984* or J.G. Ballard's *High-Rise*. Instead, Ishiguro uses his clone protagonist to explore the reparative promises made by welfare services, and the hold they have even on a character as thoroughly instrumentalized and subject to state violence as Kathy H. Ishiguro is able to negotiate this seemingly impossible task by re-activating the promises of post-1945, and specifically, the spatial hypothesis that the built environment will create a better life for all its inhabitants. What results is an astonishing combination of critique and salvage, a demonstration of just how hard it is to let go of the belief that welfare provisions might create real institutions of care.

Coda

A Hostile Environment

On June 8, 2017, artist Grayson Perry presented *The Most Popular Art Exhibition Ever!*, a major exhibition of new work at the Serpentine Galleries. Opening the same day as the UK general election, many works spoke directly to the political *Zeitgeist*, engaging the spectrum of post-referendum feeling with vivid evocations of Britain's nation-state. Most *au courant* was "Matching Pair," a set of two large vases set on opposite sides of a room, adorned with imagery crowdsourced from "Leave" voters, on the one hand, and "Remain" voters, on the other. Equally striking, however, was Perry's "Battle of Britain." Hanging on the wall across from "Matching Pair," the 10 × 23 feet landscape tapestry depicts Britain in various states of disrepair, with row houses displaying "Vote Leave" on one side, and tents occupying a highway underpass on the other. Graffitied slogans of "Class War," "Toffs out," and "UKIP" reveal a Britain already in conflict, divided along lines of class, culture, and political ideology. And holding it all together is a vibrant rainbow, drawing the viewer's eye to the tapestry's center and distant horizon: its covenantal arc begging the question of what, exactly, has been promised to this contemporary audience.

This book has endeavored to show how Britain continues to be captivated by the promises and intimations of its imagined postwar reconstruction. The fight for Britain continued well beyond wartime into the postwar period: a period whose promises of the good life have yet to be made good, and that continues to shape contemporary desires and fantasies. This cultural dynamic is visible in Perry's citation of Paul Nash's "Battle of Britain" (1941), a large oil painting of the famous wartime campaign. If, as Perry notes, he only realized he was "unconsciously drawing a transcription" of Nash's work halfway through his own, perhaps it is because the "Battle of Britain" continues apace, only along different lines today.[1] While Nash presses the

---

[1] Perry, Grayson, and Sandi Toksvig, *The Most Popular Art Exhibition Ever!*, exh. cat. Serpentine Gallery, London, June 8–September 10, 2017 (London: Particular Books, 2017), 60–61. Quoted in https://www.victoria-miro.com/artworks/24323/.

viewer to see planes' smoke and fire as a terrifyingly new artform, signs unfurling against the blue sky and cloud formations, Perry's "Battle of Britain" brings us back to earth, inverting Nash's midair focus to allow details of Britain's landscape to come into view. Instead of Nash's abstract patches of gold and brown earth, Perry provides precise details, drawing the eye to different scenes and tableaux of the Britain in question. Nash's painting was finished in a year when British victory was anything but guaranteed, despite its success in the Battle of Britain. Perry's tapestry, too, debuted in a tumultuous time, with the fate of Britain hanging in the balance after the Brexit referendum. Yoking these two times together, this contemporary "Battle of Britain" shows that the question of "postwar order" is not only a perennial one, but a compounded one. Reconstruction continues unevenly apace, under a rainbow arc that always threatens to recede.

Today, these welfarist promises seem ever more distant. Britain's austerity program slashed welfare spending for those most in need, while the national response to the global migration crisis revealed the limits of state care for those seeking asylum. In a way, these phenomena recall Britain's own immediate postwar period, characterized by both an age of austerity as well as unprecedented numbers of displaced people. But whereas post-1945 saw a renewed commitment to social equality through the establishment of the modern welfare state, no such renewal is at hand today. Instead, welfare measures have atrophied, as has the sense of who deserves state benefits.

In responses to recent national crises, the prevailing logic has been to retract state support from those in need, rather than to extend or reimagine it. A driving force behind Brexit, this impetus has also shaped political since the late 1990s, a period that saw a rise in asylum applications to the UK and numbers of net migration. The calls to fix the country's "weak" immigration system that followed confirm Alison Mountz's observation that during perceived national crises, nation-states assume the contradictory postures of both the vulnerable state in need of production, as well as the strong state able to enforce its borders: a position that leads to increasing restrictions on migration.[2] The logic of self-protection has often been expressed as a fear that migrants will put an unbearable strain on the welfare state, making excessive claims for benefits that will somehow injure UK citizens.

This logic found renewed and direct expression through the 2012 Home Office "hostile environment" policies: a series of measures meant to make life extremely difficult, if not unbearable, for migrants in the UK. The term

[2] Alison Mountz, *Seeking Asylum: Human Smuggling and Bureaucracy at the Border* (Minneapolis: University of Minnesota Press, 2010), xvi.

originated with Theresa May, then Home Secretary, who in an interview with the *Telegraph* expressed that "the aim is to create here in Britain a really hostile environment for illegal migration," with the hope that people without "leave to remain" would voluntarily leave.[3] Critiques of these policies reached an apex in the 2018 Windrush Scandal, during which several citizens from the Windrush Generation were wrongfully detained and deported. Yet these policies should have been scandalous for all: they asked nothing less than that doctor should turn against patient, employer against employee, teacher against student, and neighbor against neighbor.

The creation of such a "hostile" environment was established through social welfare changes, including new limitations to benefits such as housing, healthcare and employment through increased ID checks and surveillance. One such scheme was "Right to Rent," introduced in England through the 2016 Immigration Act. "Right to Rent" required landlords to check their tenants' immigration statuses, making it illegal to rent to those unable to provide proof of their legal status. Its effect was one of delays, refusals, increased homelessness, and the implementation of systematic racial discrimination. The High Court eventually determined this policy to be a breach of human rights law, which stopped its rollout in Scotland, Wales, and Northern Ireland. This decision confirmed the necessary overlap between welfare and human rights, demonstrating the international implications of domestic policy.[4]

This book has shown that to talk about welfare, especially in its postwar formulations, has always meant to grapple with the rights of others, or what we owe those beyond our immediate vision. The rights of others can refer to cross-class friendship, queer desire, and the personhood of clones. It can signify physical safety for all bodies, not just the slenderest, or access to metropolitan pleasures and spaces, regardless of race or national origin. And as this project has suggested, literature mobilizes these rights through depicting situations of living together in domestic space, which I take as a proxy for larger welfare infrastructures. In this conclusion, I will consider a final form of living together: infrastructures of migration, whose physical structures include airports, prisons, and specifically, immigration removal centers that hold migrants for unspecified lengths of time upon their entry

---

[3] James Kirkup and Robert Winnett, "Theresa May interview: 'We're going to give illegal migrants a really hostile reception," *The Daily Telegraph*, May 25, 2012, https://www.telegraph.co.uk/news/0/theresa-may-interview-going-give-illegal-migrants-really-hostile/.

[4] "'Right to Rent' Checks Breach Human Rights—High Court," *BBC.com*, March 1, 2019, https://www.bbc.com/news/-47415383.

into the UK. These structures demonstrate just how far the obligations of British hospitality extend, and test the furthest reaching claims of Britain's postwar imagination and politics of repair.

Immigration Removal Structures: Contemporary Iterations

As a structural genre, immigration removal centers bear a complex relationship to the refugee camp, replacing and updating this former structure to reflect the evolving reality of Britain as a security state.[5] They take a few forms: Short Term Holding Facilities (STHFs), which hold people for up to seven days; Immigration Removal Centres (IRCs), which can hold people indefinitely, as the UK is the only European country to refuse limits on detention; and non-residential STHFs, which provide additional, temporary holding rooms in ports of entry to the UK. As of 2023, there are seven working IRCs in the UK (Brook House, Colnbrook, Derwentside, Dungavel, Harmondsworth, Tinsley House, and Yarl's Wood) along with three STHFs (Larne House, Manchester, and Swinderby). Taken together, they comprise a large network of centers to detain immigrants: one of the largest of its kind in Europe, including Europe's largest facility, Harmondsworth, which holds up to 676 detainees.

These centers are the opposite of what Marc Augé calls "non-places": structures of supermodernity such as bus stations, hotels, and supermarkets that are anonymizing, asocial, evacuated of history.[6] Instead, detention facilities are intentionally isolating and tactically hostile, inflicting harm through lack of information about immigration status; lack of access to mental health services; poor treatment at the hands of center staff, including torture; and degraded living conditions.[7] That they are often called "estates" or "houses," as if residence were voluntary, is more than a convenient euphemism.[8] As the

---

[5] Jordanna Bailkin, *Unsettled: Refugee Camps and the Making of Multicultural Britain* (New York: Oxford University Press, 2018), 208–210.
[6] Marc Augé, *Non-Places: Introduction to an Anthropology of Supermodernity*, 2nd ed. (London: Verso, 2008).
[7] See, for instance, Catherine Blanchard's "Never Truly Free," https://www.redcross.org.uk/-/media/documents/about-us/research-publications/refugee-support/never-truly-free-march-2018.pdf, or Amnesty International's "A Matter of Routine" (December 2017), https://www.amnesty.org.uk/resources/matter-routine-use-immigration-detention-uk-0.
[8] Additionally, Larne House STHF is located on "Hope Street," a twisted irony if there ever was one.

2016 Shaw report into "the welfare in detention of vulnerable persons" concluded, immigration detention is being used far too routinely, and estates should be smaller and more "strategically planned."[9] Morevoer, these structures deploy transnational enforcement strategies to prevent asylum seekers from making claims on sovereign territories. To preempt these claims, states manipulate their own geographies: creatively moving borders, ports of entry, and processing zones so as to redefine their territory and the services they are required to offer.[10] Exceeding traditional definitions of the state as sovereign territory that contains people, places, and things, removal centers prove their ambit to be beyond that of the nation.

Representations of removal centers are an important signal of the contemporary in today's cultural production.[11] Such representations call on and update the perennial concerns of postcolonial fiction including exile, dispossession, and geopolitical violence. Two representative examples are Abdulrazak Gurnah's *By the Sea* (2002) and Caryl Phillips's *A Distant Shore* (2005), whose present-day English plots are seeded by backstories of escape and exile from characters' native countries, whether Gurnah's Zanzibar or Phillips's unnamed African country. In these novels, detention figures as a part of longer, more complex chains of migration, which also include haphazard travels by boat, truck, train, and plane; in conversations with lawyers and negotiations with the state; and through stories of risk and desire long in the making. For both novels, the representation of immigration detention is fitted to overall style. Phillips's novel, the more allegorical and in ways extreme of the two, begins its flashback with protagonist Solomon wiping blood from the eyes of a fellow inmate, while a night warder watches television in the other room. While Gurnah's approach is more tempered and realist, focusing on the social organization of the removal center, he still communicates the structure's discomfort and dehumanization: "the sheds that accommodated us could once just as easily have contained sacks of cereals or bags of cement or some other valuable commodity that needed to be

---

[9] Stephen Shaw, "Review into the Welfare in Detention of Vulnerable Persons," Home Office Cm 9186, January 14, 2016, https://www.gov.uk/government/publications/review-into-the-welfare-in-detention-of-vulnerable-persons.

[10] See, for example, Mountz, *Seeking Asylum*.

[11] See, for instance, Matthew Hart's "Representing Immigration Detention and Removal," *English Language Notes* 49.1 (Summer 2011), 29–50, which turns to Chris Cleave's novel *Little Bee* (2008) and Melanie Friend's multimedia *Border Country* (2007) as examples of the kinds of contradiction these structures pose with regard to the nation-state. See also Hart's *Extraterritorial: A Political Geography of Contemporary Fiction* (New York: Columbia University Press, 2020) for a wider treatment of the type of political space the removal center represents.

kept secure and out of the rain. Now they contained us, a casual and valueless nuisance that had to be kept in restraint."[12]

Both novels figure detention as the shadow life of housing in Britain. They link their asylum seekers' experience of imprisonment and detention to their uneasy inhabitation of the spaces that follow. *By the Sea*'s protagonist Saleh is shuttled to a bed-and-breakfast, a temporary situation for refugees that proves almost more claustrophobic and oppressive than the removal center. Lorded over by the bullying, self-congratulatory Celia, Saleh finds himself desperately wanting to flee "that oppressive room and its duplicities and dissemblings, its smells, its atmosphere of neglect and cruelty, its paltriness."[13] Even when installed in his permanent apartment, he describes his existence as "the half-life of a stranger, glimpsing interiors through the television screen and guessing at the tireless alarms which afflict people I see in my strolls."[14] Though he has technically been taken in by the UK, granted social security and a home, he lives as though a ghost, excluded from the lives of his neighbors.

The corollary between detention center and domestic space is bluntly articulated in the opening lines of *A Distant Shore*: "England has changed. These days it's difficult to tell who's from around here and who's not. Who belongs and who's a stranger. It's disturbing. It doesn't feel right."[15] These social tensions are explored against the backdrop of Stoneleigh, a new development in Weston that proves a deadly proving-ground of belonging. As we discover, English insularity, characterized by nationalism, xenophobia, and racism, is dramatized largely through the ethos of neighborliness and through claims of inhabitation: who has lived there longest; whose doors are open; who is the subject of village talk; who are the right and wrong kinds of people. In this setting, the Second World War surfaces yet again as the horizon of the contemporary, inscribed in architectural aspirations of living together. As protagonist Dorothy notes, "In the estate agent's bumf about 'Stoneleigh' it says that during the Second World War the German town was bombed flat by the RAF, and the French village used to be full of Jews who were all rounded up and sent to the camps. I can't help feeling that it makes Weston seem a bit tame by comparison. Apparently, the biggest thing that had ever happened in Weston was Mrs. Thatcher closing the pits, and

---

[12] Abdulrazak Gurnah, *By the Sea* (London: Bloomsbury, 2002), 43.
[13] Ibid., 53.
[14] Caryl Phillips, *A Distant Shore* (New York: Vintage International, 2005), 2.
[15] Ibid., 3.

that was over twenty years ago."[16] The question the novel poses is whether this neighborhood will right its sister towns' histories and afford Solomon, the second protagonist and only person of color in Stoneleigh, a space to live. Weston, however, turns out to be a most untame town, one capable of "communal gawping," hate letters, and eventually, Solomon's murder.[17] That Solomon serves as Stoneleigh's caretaker adds a further element of pathos to his death. Try as he might to fix the bungalows' shoddy construction, the development proves rotten to its core.

These novels embed immigration detention in a richly symbolic narrative web, using them as a means of commenting on British hospitality to outsiders. Yet these structures signify something beyond themselves; they operate as suspiciously pure synecdoches of otherness in the contemporary novel. It is precisely this conceptual framework that informs Lisa Halliday's *Asymmetry* (2018). Like the previously described works, the narrative divides its focalization, this time into three parts. The first, "Folly," details the blossoming relationship between two writers in New York: a young woman named Mary-Alice Dodge and a Philip Roth character named Ezra Blazer, a famous author many decades her senior. The second part, "Madness," sharply diverges from the first by presenting the life story of Amar Jaafari, an Iraqi American economist being detained at Heathrow on the way to visit his brother in Kurdistan. The last part, "Ezra Blazer's Desert Island Discs," returns to Ezra as a guest on the long-running BBC program, where he reveals that Alice is the author of Part II. She has written a "surprising little novel" on the "extent to which we're able to penetrate the looking-glass and imagine a life, indeed a consciousness, that goes some way to reduce the blind spots in our own."[18] Given the attention paid to various social and geopolitical asymmetries in this novel, this wager of cutting through them is most serious; it is the premise the entire book is built upon, and one that Halliday needs Ezra Blazer to declare has succeeded in order to affirm the achievement of her work.

The conceit of this novel would be more felicitous were Part II not so limited in scope: a clear distinction between *Asymmetry* and the previously described novels by Gurnah and Phillips. If this is Alice imagining a life, it is not, to borrow E.M. Forster's distinction, a particularly round one: that is, a character whose life extends in all directions, and, crucially, who is

---

[16] *Ibid.*, 4.
[17] *Ibid.*, 55.
[18] Lisa Halliday, *Asymmetry* (New York: Simon & Schuster, 2018), 261.

able to surprise. Instead, Amar is flatly rendered. Stylistically, his section feels heavy with geographical and political references, dutifully presented, a far cry from the lightness of Alice's and Ezra's sections. Like *A Distant Shore* and *By the Sea*, Part II alternates between Amar's recounting of his life story, told through flashbacks, and the narrative present of his detention at Heathrow. This airport infrastructure physically and symbolically contains Amar, forming a cage around him. Its spaces are unsympathetically rendered, vaguely Kafkaesque in its combination of bureaucracy and violence, with rotating staff and strangers, undefined wait times, and maze-like appearance. Detention also delimits Amar's narrative arc. Unlike the cliffhanger granted to Alice, who at the end of Part I, is deciding whether to leave Ezra or not, Amar's arc ends by revealing the purpose of his trip as a search for his brother, kidnapped by terrorists. This revelation only returns to the reader to the beginning of Part II and the scene of Amar being questioned by airport security. Unlike Alice's moment of freedom and development as a writer, Amar is fated to run on a feedback loop, defined only by his racial identity and geopolitical situation. *Asymmetry*, then, critically fails the narrative mission it sets out to accomplish. Instead of penetrating the looking-glass through writerly imagination, it can only offer a one-way mirror: a structure better suited for surveillance than empathy.

Perhaps this typing is why a novel like Mohsin Hamid's *Exit West* (2017) chooses to forego the representation of traditional migration infrastructures: what one could argue is the novel's most magically real decision. Instead, Hamid offers the device of the portal, or door, which admits the passage of bodies from one location to another nearly instantaneously. These portals open and close at random, and lead to a worldwide transformation of how people move across national borders. While some readers have critiqued the universalizing nature of this device, calling it an uncritical fable, its usage does not completely free the novel of the various real-life asymmetries that shape global migration.[19] As the novel progresses, the portals become increasingly conditional and regulated. While at first migrants are able to move unseen, surveillance technologies eventually increase, as security cameras, drones, and mobile phones capture footage that curtail freedom upon emergence. Movement also is largely from impoverished or conflict-ridden areas to global cities such as Sydney, Tokyo, Dubai, and London, or to countries such as Germany and the USA. This asymmetry

---

[19] See Yogita Goyal's "'We Are All Migrants'": The Refugee Novel and the Claims of Universalism," *MFS* 66.2 (Summer 2020), 239–259 for an exemplum of this critique.

leads to restrictions of access, refugee camps, migrant ghettos, rioting, protests, and eventually the threat of war between nativist extremists, state military, and police forces on the one hand, and migrants and their supporters on the other. Hamid's move away from typical infrastructures of migration opens up what counts as its space or setting: a move that extends the felt reach of migration and refuge, even as it eschews locating its subjects in specific histories.

Taken together, this group of authors offers a choice between representations of removal centers as dark reality and as a symbol of contemporary racial difference. The works of Ali Smith navigate a middle ground between these possibilities. Smith's prolific, innovative *oeuvre* is the site of important political challenges to our moment, from her defense of public institutions in *Public Library and Other Stories* to her recently completed "Seasonal Quartet," a series of four novels that have come to be known as the "first great Brexit novels."[20] Published at a rapid pace, *Autumn* (2016), *Winter* (2017), *Spring* (2019), and *Summer* (2020) engage the UK's fraught political scene and coeval current events such as the migrant crisis, global warming, Grenfell Tower, the Windrush scandal, and the presidency of Donald Trump. The worlds of her quartet are full of modern-day *anomie*: the frustration of automated helplines and screens standing in for service; libraries labeled as "Ideas Stores"; places that look public but are actually privately owned; parkland turned to luxury flats and office spaces. But they also have their pulse on more sinister realities: the numberless homeless; migrant bodies washed ashore; racist graffiti; misogynist epithets hurled at a female MP; the murder of George Floyd. Representing this world is the fictional "SA4A," a shadowy corporation that surfaces across all four novels with dealings in copyright consolidation, private security, and immigration removal centers, and which despite its name—"safer"—bristles with menace.

That Smith's quartet concerns the current plight of refugees is not surprising: she is dedicated to working for their justice outside the pages of her novels as well. Along with Gurnah, Smith is a patron of "Refugee Tales," an organization working since 2015 in solidarity with refugees, asylum seekers, and those who have been held in immigration removal centers. Their organization follows the work of the Gatwick Detainees Welfare Group, a charity that began in 1995 to connect with and advocate for detainees. Taking

---

[20] See, for instance, Sarah Lyall's "From Ali Smith, It's the First Great Brexit Novel," *New York Times*, February 17, 2017, https://www.nytimes.com/2017/02/17/books/review/autumn-ali-smith.html.

inspiration from Chaucer's *Canterbury Tales*, Refugee Tales organizes a three-day walk across the UK, structured by readings, music, stories, and talks. The group has also published three anthologies of stories from those with lived experience of detention. From "The Migrant's Tale" to "The Interpreter's Tale," "The Friend's Tale" to the "Appellant's Tale," they offer a vast social tapestry of migration's social infrastructure.

From the start, these anthologies identify their work as that of hospitality, with Volume 1's "Prologue" declaring that "This prologue is not a poem / It is an act of welcome." This language resonates with Smith's own prologue to the Refugee Tales' website:

> The telling of stories is an act of profound hospitality. It always has been; story is an ancient form of generosity, an ancient form that will tell us everything we need to know about the contemporary world. Story has always been a welcoming-in, is always one way or another a hospitable meeting of the needs of others, and a porous artform where sympathy and empathy are only the beginning of things. The individual selves we all are meet and transform in the telling into something open and communal.[21]

The connections are clear: storytelling, hospitality, and community-making must overlap in their ethical imperatives for a better future.

Ali Smith's own contribution to *Refugee Tales* is "The Detainee's Tale." It recounts her meeting with a young man from Ghana, who, after a harrowing journey to the UK, has been given indefinite leave to remain as a victim of human trafficking. The tale, though, is only partly his; it is also Smith's. For unlike those of Chaucer's pilgrims, these are largely retellings "as told to" various contributors. Indeed, style is what distinguishes this collection from purer forms of nonfiction, with contributors recounting the Tales in their own style. Some choose to close the representational distance between themselves and their interviewee, collapsing into a single "I." Others use direct speech to distinguish between voice and story, maintaining an aura of verisimilitude as well as distance between themselves and their subject. Smith, eschewing quoted speech, maintains a middle ground between herself and the Detainee, whose story she tells using the second person. ("You make some friends at the church. You tell them about your life. They tell you there are things that can be done to make this better."[22]) This

---

[21] Ali Smith, "A welcome from our patron," refugeetales.org/about.
[22] Smith, "The Detainee's Tale," *Refugee Tales*, ed. David Herd and Anna Pincus (Manchester: Comma Press, 2016), loc. 815 of 2127, Kindle.

stylistic decision forces an uneasy intimacy between subject and listener, with occasional reminders of difference ("Cocoa, you explain to me, has to be dried twice"[23]). Yet the final lines crucially reaffirm the distance between detainee and narrator:

> But when I came to this place, when I came to your country, you say.
> I sit forward. I'm listening.
> You shake your head.
> I thought you would help me, you say.[24]

The insertion of the "I" risks presenting Smith as a do-gooder, leaning forward in a performance of exaggerated sympathy. Yet that is not the persona of Smith in the tale, who appears with equal parts outrage and self-reflection, observation and reportage. She is not one to sentimentalize the ugly realities of detention, which, she duly notes, can only be experienced at a remove: "What I'll go and visit is only what it's like to visit a detainee."[25] Smith gives not only the final word to the Detainee, but also the final emotion, prefacing this exchange by acknowledging the Detainee's "only flash of anger" that accompanies the last line. Powerfully, this ending forces Smith into alignment with a deeply inhospitable country, even as it dares the reader to act differently.

If the "Detainee's Tale" ends with a profound moment of disconnect, Smith's Seasonal Quartet allows her to explore types of social connection only available in fiction. In her modified version of E.M. Forster's "only connect," the novels feature odd, serendipitous relationships among strangers, such as the long neighborly friendship between an old man and young woman in *Autumn*, or the hiring of a stranger to pose as an ex-girlfriend during the Christmas season in *Winter*. Each relationship offers its own test of hospitality and draws explicit parallels between welcoming strangers into one's home and welcoming migrants into one's national borders. Part of the pleasure of these texts is watching these relationships unfold, and seeing how their hold is tested over the course of each novel and, eventually, the whole quartet. By the end, the novels have created a world where everything is interconnected, plotted along implausible vectors that converge in the last volume, *Summer*.

---

[23] *Ibid.*, loc. 768 of 2127, Kindle.
[24] *Ibid.*, loc. 942 of 2127, Kindle.
[25] *Ibid.*, loc. 845 of 2127, Kindle.

Though the novels all reference immigration removal centers, *Spring* brings us directly inside one—"Spring House"—and showcases its inhumane living conditions as a space without privacy, care, or comfort. One telling metaphor for these conditions is the window. In the IRC, these are made of Perspex, not glass, and imitate rather than perform their function: "Why can't we open window in this prison? He said. Open *a* window, she said. And this isn't a prison, it's a purpose-built Immigration Removal Centre with a prison design."[26] With its inclusion of such scenes, *Spring* has been hailed as Smith's most expressly political novel.

Spring's characters are drawn together and connected through the *wunderkind* Florence. Through her very presence and naivete, she succeeds in getting impossible tasks done, such as the cleaning of the toilets in an IRC, or the freeing of underage girls from a "really nasty sex house in Woolwich."[27] Florence's power lies in her ability to cross boundaries others cannot, and once across, her success in appealing to the better nature of pimps, guards, and prison management. In a moment verging on hagiography, she heals an IRC detainee prone to self-harm, who "found the girl in his room just standing there like a vision like the fucking Virgin Mary."[28] Departing from the model of the ending of "The Detainee's Tale," Smith grants these characters a transformative exchange: "The Eritrean self-harmer had said to her, this place they are keeping me in is like living in hopelessness, so why would I live? Only pain is keeping me alive. Then the schoolgirl'd said something back to him, though he wouldn't tell anyone what, and now he was like a new man."[29] As powerful as this conversation may be, it is hard to imagine the author of "The Detainee's Tale" wants us to buy fully into this model of repair. The scene includes an element of playfulness here, even mild skepticism toward the events it narrates. Yet the novel never fully disavows the power of Florence's enchantment, maintaining its potential as a social force.

Thankfully, *Spring*'s version of politics—effected only through the very young, and the purely good—is not the only one available in the world of the quartet. More rewarding, I would argue, is another mode of politics that appears in moments when the novel calls on past histories to make sense of its present moment. In casting its net toward other times, the Quartet mixes different literary styles and genre conventions, references and epigraphs, character histories and plotlines. The common denominator, and the history

---

[26] Smith, *Spring: A Novel* (New York: Pantheon Books, 2019), 160.
[27] Ibid., 188.
[28] Ibid., 137.
[29] Ibid.

that returns in fullest force, is that of the Second World War, which comes to figure as the quartet's immediate history. In *Autumn,* Daniel Gluck, who is English, chooses to spend the war interned with his German father on the Isle of Man. *Summer* then returns to Daniel's internment and the lost history of his sister, Hannah, a Resistance fighter. If Ali Smith's quartet is meant to be a commentary on the passage of time—whether cyclical like the seasons, or as she suggests in an interview, diachronous—what work is the Second World War supposed to be doing for the reader?

A part of the novel's investment in the Second World War is the point of comparison the conflict provides for the current refugee crisis, which, as the novel reminds us, is the largest of its kind since the war. This structure informs the opening of the Quartet, which begins with the elderly Daniel hallucinating that he has been washed ashore on a beach: a citation of the horrific, contemporary image of the migrant body washed ashore, dying in pursuit of a better, more secure life. That Daniel's life in turn has been defined by his wartime experience and German Jewish heritage brings the contemporary into close relation with the midcentury.

The figure of the camp, whether of wartime internment or of contemporary migrants seeking UK entrance in Calais, likewise brings these historical moments together.[30] The focus on the internment camp throughout the Quartet forces the reader to reckon with Britain's history of hostility toward its internal others as well as its external others. It offers a historical test to be corrected, out of time, in the present. This mode of temporal repair is explicitly suggested by Daniel's father, who was also interned during the First World War. Despite this personal history, he is convinced that things will be better the second time around, as England's "better self has come to the fore," and that "they know about fairness now, and why to go to war, and what happens when you do."[31] Though this moment could be read as one of false optimism, Smith has echoed this sentiment herself, noting that her research on wartime internment induced a sense of real, unexpected hope "that things can change—and above all that they'll change for the better, when we wise up to what's really at stake."[32]

---

[30] As Bailkin reminds us, the camp serves as an important index of British identity and its various unsettlements, especially as they often housed citizens as well as refugees: "The presence of citizens within the camps was perhaps one of the most volatile and troubling parts of the story. Their existence transforms the history of refuge from one of British aid to foreigners into a narrative of failed aid for citizens. Ironically, the refugee camp is where the unsettled nature of Britons themselves became visible" (*Unsettled*, 207).
[31] Smith, *Summer: A Novel* (New York: Pantheon Books, 2020), 165 and 166.
[32] "The Waterstones Interview: Ali Smith," August 25, 2020, https://www.waterstones.com/blog/the-waterstones-interview-ali-smith.

Smith's Quartet ends on just such a hopeful note. Like its sister novels, *Summer* begins with a pronouncement: "Everybody said: *so?* As in *so what?*"[33] As in the earlier novels, Smith draws a line from Dickens to apply to the present moment: *Autumn*'s "It was the worst of times, it was the worst of times," which summoned *A Tale of Two Cities* to comment on Brexit Britain; *Winter*'s "God was dead: to begin with," whose recall of "A Christmas Carol" headed a litany of dead things waiting for renewal; and *Spring*'s "Now what we don't want is Facts. What we want is bewilderment," which applied *Hard Times* to a public capable of electing Donald Trump.[34] *Summer*'s opening comes from Dickens's Christmas fancy "The Haunted Man and the Ghost's Bargain," its *"so what"* deployed to capture the sheer exhaustion of its present moment.

Unlike Smith's earlier citations from Dickens, however, the opening of *Summer* offers an additional historical moment to mediate relations between past and present. It appears as a restorative to the exhausted contemporary *Zeitgeist*:

So.
Instead, here's something I once saw.
It's an image from a film made in the UK roughly seventy years ago, not long after the end of the Second World War.
The film was made in London by a young artist who arrived in the city from Italy when London was one of the many places having to re-build themselves in those years nearly a lifetime ago, after the tens of millions of people of all ages across the world had died before their time.[35]

The reference in this passage is to artist Lorenza Mazzetti, another figure in the Quartet's leitmotif of female artists including Pauline Boty, Barbara Hepworth, and Tacita Dean. In turning to Mazzetti's first work, *K* (1954), a short film after Kafka's *Metamorphosis*, Smith invokes postwar Britain to recall its project of rebuilding, asking what a corollary might be for our present moment.

In holding out the possibility of the image the text is about to present, Smith's novel asks us to return to a time without today's *so what*, and charges the reader to ask, quite seriously, *what is next*. But first we are presented with the astonishing image of a man, painter Michael Andrews ("grave, slim,

---

[33] Smith, *Summer*, 3.
[34] Smith, *Autumn* (New York: Anchor Books, 2017), 3; *Winter* (New York: Anchor Books, 2018), 3; *Spring*, 3.
[35] Smith, *Summer*, 5.

preoccupied, terribly keen") dancing across the scarred rooftops of war-torn London with two suitcases in his hands. The narrator stops to force us to wonder:

> How can he be going so fast and not fall off the edge of the building? How can what he's doing be so wild and still so graceful, so urgent and blithe both at once?
> How can he be swinging those cases around in the air like that and still keep his balance? How can he be moving at such speed next to the sheer drop?
> Why is he risking everything?[36]

Smith asks us to ponder his impossible balance, his kinetic beauty, his talent and grace. His is a lone figure of aesthetic compensation against a destroyed landscape, a reinvestment in the human individual. His feat is all the more significant due to the suitcases he's carrying, which attach a certain labor or responsibility to his movements. They also make him a traveler of sorts, which, in Smith's Quartet, we might associate with the figure of the migrant. If so, *K*'s dancing figure is worlds away from that of the contemporary detainee, though both, arguably, are "risking everything" as, to quote Warsan Shire, "home is the mouth of a shark."[37]

Though it focuses on this redemptive and hopeful moment of promise, Smith's reference to Mazzetti is haunted by the starker, more difficult depictions of Mazzetti's second film, *Together* (1956). Following the lives of two dockworkers living together in London's East End after the war, *Together* paints a much bleaker picture of human existence. The men, brilliantly portrayed by sculptor Eduardo Paolozzi and a reprisal by Andrews, are both deaf and mute. Objects of curiosity and scorn, they sustain the suspicion of their neighbors, the glowering of their landlady, and the taunts of the children following them like rats after the Pied Piper. Their world is dark and dank, pitted with unreconstructed bombsites and jagged brick walls; even their apartment feels treacherous, with a low ceiling and dark wallpaper that seems to compress them. *K*'s earlier kinetic joy, so marveled in *Summer*, is nowhere to be found. Instead, in a macabre twist, Andrews is pushed to his death off a bridge by a gang of neighborhood children, a dark recall of his character's rooftop dancing in *K*. And as Paolozzi goes to meet his

---

[36] Ibid., 6.
[37] Warsan Shire, *Teaching My Mother How to Give Birth* (UK: Flipped Eye Publishing, 2011), 27.

absent friend, the graffitied slogan "BAN-JAP-GOOD'S" comes into view, along with fascist iconography. *Together*, then, reveals a world without care for one's neighbor: a New Jerusalem whose inheritors—the "Timothys" for whom the war was fought and a better future imagined—may have already lost the battle for their moral souls. Taken together, these films pose an urgent question for the reader. Which world would you like to occupy? And what can we do to ensure its existence?

Smith's Quartet ends with an expression of hope, with the words of a migrant—recalling the end of the "Detainee's Tale," but with the difference that this speaker is unexpectedly, at least temporarily free. Released from the Immigration Removal Center with fifteen other detainees, he has been welcomed into the home of Charlotte and her Aunt Iris, two of the Quartet's central characters. This narrative gesture echoes the release of 350 people from immigration detention during the COVID-19 pandemic, a process that has proved uneven and chaotic, with detainees unable to access legal help and in many cases, deported. *Summer*'s alternative, however fictional, offers a corrective to this bleak reality. Moreover, Smith characteristically adds one final flourish that ties this narrative magical thinking together: a detail about the migrant's name, "ANH KIET," which in Vietnamese, he tells us, "is like a picture of a figure with wide shoulders, or a house with two wide strong roofs, with one roof placed on top of the other roof."[38] This architectural feature, of course, recalls the war-torn rooftops in Lorenza Mazzetti's *K*, except this time, the wonder comes not from Anh's ability to dance upon them, but rather, shelter underneath them. Though this shelter may be temporary, it offers a powerful final image of what it could mean to extend care, share space, and, ultimately, live together.

---

[38] Smith, *Summer*, 378.

Bibliography

Abrams, Mark. *The Teenage Consumer*. London: London Press Exchange Limited, 1959.

Adams, Ruth. "The V&A, The Destruction of the Country House and the Creation of 'English Heritage.'" *Museum and Society* 11, no. 1 (2013), 1–18.

Addison, Paul. *The Road to 1945: British Politics and the Second World War*. London: Cape, 1975.

Adorno, Theodor W. *Prisms*. 1st MIT Press ed. Cambridge: MIT Press, 1981.

Ahmad, Aijaz. "Jameson's Rhetoric of Otherness and the 'National Allegory.'" *Social Text* 17, no. 17 (1987), 3–25.

Amnesty International United Kingdom Section. "A Matter of Routine: The Use of Immigration Detention in the UK." December 2017. https://www.amnesty.org.uk/resources/matter-routine-use-immigration-detention-uk-0.

Anker, Elizabeth S. *Fictions of Dignity: Embodying Human Rights in World Literature*. Ithaca: Cornell University Press, 2012.

Anonymous. "A London Caravanserai." *Saturday Review of Politics, Literature, Science and Art* 47, no. 1232 (1879), 702–703.

Anonymous. *Planning for Reconstruction*. London: Knapp, Drewett & Sons Ltd, 1944.

Appiah, Kwame Anthony. "Is the Post- in Postmodernism the Post- in Postcolonial?" *Critical Inquiry* 17, no. 2 (1991), 336–357.

Arendt, Hannah. *Between Past and Future: Eight Exercises in Political Thought*. New York: Penguin Books, 1977.

Armstrong, Nancy. *How Novels Think: The Limits of British Individualism from 1719–1900*. New York: Columbia University Press, 2005.

Attewell, Nadine. *Better Britons: Reproduction, National Identity, and the Afterlife of Empire*. Toronto: University of Toronto Press, 2014.

Attfield, Judy. "Good Design by Law: Adapting Utility Furniture to Peacetime Production: Domestic Furniture in the Reconstruction Period 1946–56." In *Design and Cultural Politics in Postwar Britain: The Britain Can Make It Exhibition of 1946*, edited by Patrick Maguire and Jonathan Woodham, 99–109. London and Washington: Leicester University Press, 1997.

Augé, Marc. *Non-Places: Introduction to an Anthropology of Supermodernity*. 2nd ed. London: Verso, 2008.

Bachelard, Gaston. *The Poetics of Space*. Boston: Beacon Press, 1994.

Bailkin, Jordanna. *The Afterlife of Empire*. Berkeley and Los Angeles: University of California Press, 2012.

Bailkin, Jordanna. *Unsettled: Refugee Camps and the Making of Multicultural Britain*. Oxford: Oxford University Press, 2018.

Ballard, J.G. "A Handful of Dust." *The Guardian*, March 20, 2006. https://www.theguardian.com/artanddesign/2006/mar/20/architecture.communities.

Ballard, J.G. *High-Rise*. New York: Liveright Pub., 2012.

Barthes, Roland. *How to Live Together: Novelistic Simulations of Some Everyday Spaces*. New York: Columbia University Press, 2012.

Barthes, Roland. *Mythologies*. Translated by A. Lavers. New York: Hill and Wang, 1972.

BIBLIOGRAPHY 249

Bauer, Heike, and Matt Cook, eds. *Queer 1950s: Rethinking Sexuality in the Postwar Years*. 1st ed. Genders and Sexualities in History. London: Palgrave Macmillan, 2012.
BBC News. "'Right to Rent' Checks Breach Human Rights - High Court," March 1, 2019, sec. UK. https://www.bbc.com/news/uk-47415383.
Beal, S. *Brazil under Construction: Fiction and Public Works. Brazil under Construction.* New Directions in Latino American Cultures. New York: Palgrave Macmillan US, 2013.
Benhabib, Seyla. *The Rights of Others: Aliens, Residents and Citizens*. John Robert Seeley Lectures 5. Cambridge: Cambridge University Press, 2004.
Benjamin, Walter. *Illuminations*. New York: Harcourt, Brace & World, 1968.
Bennett, Louise. "Colonization in Reverse." Rt. Hon. Dr. Louise Bennett Coverley. http://louisebennett.com/colonization-in-reverse/.
Berlant, Lauren Gail. *Cruel Optimism*. Durham: Duke University Press, 2011.
Berlant, Lauren Gail. "The Commons: Infrastructures for Troubling Times." *Environment and Planning. D, Society & Space* 34, no. 3 (2016), 393–419.
Berlant, Lauren Gail. *The Female Complaint: The Unfinished Business of Sentimentality in American Culture*. Durham: Duke University Press, 2008.
Bersani, Leo. "Is the Rectum a Grave?" *October* 43 (1987), 197–222.
Beveridge, Sir William. *Social Insurance and Allied Services*. London: His Majesty's Stationery Office, 1942.
Bhabha, Homi K. *Nation and Narration*. London: Routledge, 1990.
Bhabha, Homi K. *The Location of Culture*. London: Routledge, 2004.
Blanchard, Catherine. "Never Truly Free: The Humanitarian Impact of the UK Immigration Detention System." British Red Cross, 2018. https://www.redcross.org.uk/-/media/documents/about-us/research-publications/refugee-support/never-truly-free-march-2018.pdf.
Bogdanor, Vernon, and Robert Skidelsky. *The Age of Affluence 1951–1964*. London: Macmillan, 1970.
Born, Daniel. "Private Gardens, Public Swamps: 'Howards End' and the Revaluation of Liberal Guilt." *Novel: A Forum on Fiction* 25, no. 2 (1992), 141–159.
Bowen, Elizabeth. "A Passage to E.M. Forster." In *Aspects of E.M. Forster*, edited by Oliver Stallybrass, 1–12. London: Edward Arnold, 1969.
Bowen, Elizabeth. *Bowen's Court*. New York: Alfred A. Knopf, 1942.
Bowen, Elizabeth. Elizabeth Bowen to Charles Ritchie, November 19, 1945. In *Love's Civil War: Elizabeth Bowen and Charles Ritchie*, edited by Victoria Glendinning and Judith Robertson, 73–77. Toronto: McClelland and Stewart, 2008.
Bowen, Elizabeth. Elizabeth Bowen to Virginia Woolf, January 5, 1941. Monks House Papers, University of Sussex Special Collections.
Bowen, Elizabeth. Elizabeth Bowen to Virginia Woolf, July 1, 1940. Monks House Papers, University of Sussex Special Collections.
Bowen, Elizabeth. "London, 1940." In *The Mulberry Tree: Writings of Elizabeth Bowen*, edited by Hermione Lee, 21–24. London: Virago Press, 1986.
Bowen, Elizabeth. "Postscript By the Author." In *The Demon Lover and Other Stories*, 2nd ed. 216–224. London: Jonathan Cape, 1952.
Bowen, Elizabeth. "The Bend Back." In *The Mulberry Tree: Writings of Elizabeth Bowen*, edited by Hermione Lee, 54–60. London: Virago Press, 1986.
Bowen, Elizabeth. *The Heat of the Day*. New York: Anchor Books, 2002.
Bradley, Kate. "Becoming Delinquent in the Post-War Welfare State: England and Wales, 1945–1965." In *Juvenile Delinquency and the Limits of Western Influence, 1850–2000*, edited by

Heather Ellis, 227–247. Palgrave Studies in the History of Childhood. London: Palgrave Macmillan UK, 2014.
Brandt, Bill, and Alan Pryce-Jones. "An Odd Lot." *Lilliput* 25, no. 5 (November 1949), 49–56.
Briggs, Asa. "The Welfare State in Historical Perspective." *Archives Européennes de Sociologie. European Journal of Sociology.* 2, no. 2 (1961), 221–258.
British Institute of Public Opinion. "The Beveridge Report and the Public." London: H. Clarke & Co. Ltd, 1942.
British Pathé. "Stepney 1946," May 12, 1946. https://www.britishpathe.com/video/pathe-front-page-stepney.
British Pathé. "Pathé Reporter Meets—," June 1948. https://www.britishpathe.com/video/pathe-reporter-meets.
Brittan, Alice. "War and the Book: The Diarist, the Cryptographer, and '*The English Patient*.'" *PMLA: Publications of the Modern Language Association of America* 121, no. 1 (2006), 200–213.
Brouillette, Sarah. *Literature and the Creative Economy.* Stanford: Stanford University Press, 2014.
Brown, J. Dillon. *Migrant Modernism: Postwar London and the West Indian Novel.* Charlottesville: University of Virginia Press, 2013.
Brown, J. Dillon, and Leah Reade Rosenberg, eds. *Beyond Windrush: Rethinking Postwar Anglophone Caribbean Literature.* Jackson: University Press of Mississippi, 2015.
Brown, Wendy. *Walled States, Waning Sovereignty.* 2nd paperback ed. Cambridge: MIT Press, 2017.
Burton, Antoinette M. "Archive of Bones: Anil's Ghost and the Ends of History." *Journal of Commonwealth Literature* 38, no. 1 (2003), 39–56.
Burton, Antoinette M. *At the Heart of the Empire: Indians and the Colonial Encounter in Late-Victorian Britain.* Reprint 2020. Berkeley: University of California Press, 1998.
Calder, Angus. *The Myth of the Blitz.* London: Cape, 1991.
Calder, Angus. *The People's War: Britain 1939–45.* London: Cape, 1969.
Chapman, James. *A New History of British Documentary.* Basingstoke: Palgrave Macmillan, 2015.
Cheng, Anne Anlin. *The Melancholy of Race: Psychoanalysis, Assimilation and Hidden Grief.* Race and American Culture. Oxford: Oxford University Press, 2000.
Chihaya, Sarah, Joshua Kotin, and Kinohi Nishikawa. "'The Contemporary' by the Numbers." *Post45: Contemporaries*, February 29, 2016. https://post45.research.yale.edu/2016/02/the-contemporary-by-the-numbers/.
Chisholm, Dianne. "Love at Last Sight, or Walter Benjamin's Dialectics of Seeing in the Wake of the Gay Bathhouse." *Textual Practice* 13, no. 2 (1999), 243–272.
Chisholm, Dianne. *Queer Constellations: Subcultural Space in the Wake of the City.* Queer Constellations. New ed. Minneapolis: University of Minnesota Press, 2004.
Churchill, Winston. *The War Speeches of Winston Churchill.* Vol. 2. London: Cassel & Company LTD, 1965.
Clausewitz, Carl von. *On War.* Princeton Shorts. Princeton: Princeton University Press, 2008.
Claybaugh, Amanda. "Government Is Good." *The Minnesota Review* 2008, no. 70 (2008), 161–166.
Cohen, Deborah. *The War Come Home: Disabled Veterans in Britain and Germany, 1914–1939.* Berkeley: University of California Press, 2001.
Cole, Sarah. *At the Violet Hour: Modernism and Violence in England and Ireland.* Oxford: Oxford University Press, 2012.

Cole, Sarah. "Enchantment, Disenchantment, War, Literature." *PMLA: Publications of the Modern Language Association of America* 124, no. 5 (2009), 1632–1647.

Colombino, Laura. *Spatial Politics in Contemporary London Literature: Writing Architecture and the Body.* New York: Routledge, 2013.

Corbyn, Jeremy. "Speech given 26 September 2018." September 26, 2018. https://blogs.spectator.co.uk/2018/09/full-text-jeremy-corbyns-labour-conference-speech/.

Corcoran, Neil. *Elizabeth Bowen: The Enforced Return.* Oxford: Clarendon Press, 2004.

Craggs, Ruth. "The Commonwealth Institute and the Commonwealth Arts Festival: Architecture, Performance and Multiculturalism in Late-Imperial London." *London Journal* 36, no. 3 (2011), 247–268.

Crimp, Douglas. *Melancholia and Moralism: Essays on AIDS and Queer Politics.* Cambridge: MIT Press, 2002.

Crinson, Mark. "Imperial Story-Lands: Architecture and Display at the Imperial and Commonwealth Institutes." *Art History* 22, no. 1 (1999), 99–123.

Darling, Elizabeth. *Re-Forming Britain: Narratives of Modernity before Reconstruction.* London: Routledge, 2007.

Davis, Thomas. *The Extinct Scene: Late Modernism and Everyday Life.* New York: Columbia University Press, 2015.

Dawson, Ashley. *Mongrel Nation: Diasporic Culture and the Making of Postcolonial Britain.* Ann Arbor: University of Michigan Press, 2007.

De Boever, Arne. *Narrative Care: Biopolitics and the Novel.* New York and London: Bloomsbury Academic, 2013.

De Certeau, Michel. *The Practice of Everyday Life.* 2nd ed. Translated by Steven F. Rendall. Berkeley and Los Angeles: University of California Press, 1988.

Deer, Patrick. *Culture in Camouflage: War, Empire, and Modern British Literature.* Oxford: Oxford University Press, 2009.

Deleuze, Gilles. *A Thousand Plateaus: Capitalism and Schizophrenia.* Minneapolis: University of Minnesota Press, 1987.

Derdiger, Paula. *Reconstruction Fiction: Housing and Realist Literature in Postwar Britain.* Columbus: The Ohio State University Press, 2020.

Derrida, Jacques. "Hostipitality." *Angelaki: Journal of Theoretical Humanities* 5, no. 3 (2000), 3–18.

D'hoker, Elke. "The Poetics of House and Home in the Short Stories of Elizabeth Bowen." *Orbis Litterarum* 67, no. 4 (2012), 267–289.

Dinis, Edmund. "Nation: Who's Who at the Kennedy Inquest." *Time*, September 5, 1969. https://content.time.com/time/subscriber/article/0,33009,901341,00.html.

Donnell, Alison. *Twentieth-Century Caribbean Literature: Critical Moments in Anglophone Literary History.* London: Routledge, 2006.

Douglas, Lawrence. *The Memory of Judgment: Making Law and History in the Trials of the Holocaust.* New Haven: Yale University Press, 2001.

Dudziak, Mary L. *War Time: An Idea, Its History, Its Consequences. War Time.* Oxford: Oxford University Press, 2012.

Dukes, Thomas. "'Mappings of Secrecy and Disclosure': 'The Swimming Pool Library,' the Closet, and the Empire." *Journal of Homosexuality* 31, no. 3 (1996), 95–107.

Eatough, Matthew. "'Are They Going to Say This Is Fantasy?': Kazuo Ishiguro, Untimely Genres, and the Making of Literary Prestige." *Modern Fiction Studies* 67, no. 1 (2021), 40–66.

Eatough, Matthew. "The Time That Remains: Organ Donation, Temporal Duration, and Bildung in Kazuo Ishiguro's *Never Let Me Go*." *Literature and Medicine* 29, no. 1 (2011), 132–160.

Edelman, Lee. *No Future: Queer Theory and the Death Drive.* Durham: Duke University Press, 2004.

Edgerton, David. "War, Reconstruction, and the Nationalization of Britain, 1939-1951." *Past & Present* 210, no. 1 (2011), 29.

Edmunds, Susan. *Grotesque Relations: Modernist Domestic Fiction and the U.S. Welfare State*. Oxford; New York: Oxford University Press, 2008.

Eeckhout, Bart. "English Architectural Landscapes and Metonymy in Hollinghurst's *The Stranger's Child*." *CLCWeb: Comparative Literature and Culture* 14, no. 3 (2012), 1-11.

Elliott, Jane. "Suffering Agency: Imagining Neoliberal Personhood in North America and Britain." *Social Text* 31, no. 2 (2013), 83-101.

Elliott, Jane. *The Microeconomic Mode: Political Subjectivity in Contemporary Popular Aesthetics*. New York, NY: Columbia University Press, 2018.

Emecheta, Buchi. *In the Ditch*. African Writers Series. Oxford: Heinemann, 1994.

Enfield, Harry. Lyrics to "Loadsamoney (Doin' Up the House)." London: Guerilla Studios. https://genius.com/Harry-enfield-loadsamoney-doin-up-the-house-lyrics.

English, James F, ed. *A Concise Companion to Contemporary British Fiction*. Oxford: Blackwell Publishing, 2006.

Engster, Daniel. *Justice, Care and the Welfare State*. Oxford: Oxford University Press, 2015.

Engster, Daniel and Maurice Hamington, eds. *Care Ethics and Political Theory*. Oxford: Oxford University Press, 2015.

Esping-Andersen, Gøsta. *The Three Worlds of Welfare Capitalism*. Princeton: Princeton University Press, 1990.

Esty, Joshua. *A Shrinking Island: Modernism and National Culture in England*. Princeton: Princeton University Press, 2003.

Fanon, Frantz. *The Wretched of the Earth*. New York: Grove Press, 2021.

Feigel, Lara. *The Love-Charm of Bombs: Restless Lives in the Second World War*. London: Bloomsbury, 2013.

Felman, Shoshana. *The Juridical Unconscious: Trials and Traumas in the Twentieth Century*. Cambridge: Harvard University Press, 2002.

Fielding, Steven. "What Did 'the People' Want?: The Meaning of the 1945 General Election." *The Historical Journal* 35, no. 3 (1992), 623-639.

Fisher, Berenice, and Joan Tronto. "Toward a Feminist Theory of Caring." In *Circles of Care: Work and Identity in Women's Lives*, edited by Emily K. Abel and Margaret K. Nelson, 36-54. Albany: State University of New York Press, 1990.

Flatley, Jonathan. *Affective Mapping: Melancholia and the Politics of Modernism*. Cambridge: Harvard University Press, 2008.

Fluet, Lisa. "Immaterial Labors: Ishiguro, Class, and Affect." *Novel: A Forum on Fiction* 40, no. 3 (2007), 265-288.

Forshaw, John Henry, and Patrick Abercrombie. *County of London Plan*. London: Macmillan and Co. Limited, 1943.

Forster, E.M. *A Passage to India*. New York: Harcourt, Brace and Company, 1924.

Forster, E.M. *Howards End*. New York: Penguin Books, 2000.

Forster, E.M. *Maurice*. New York: W.W. Norton & Company, Inc., 1993.

Forster, E.M. *Selected Letters of E.M. Forster*, Vol. 2: 1921-1970, edited by P.N. Furbank and Mary Lago. Cambridge: Belknap Press, 1985.

Foucault, Michel. *"Society Must Be Defended": Lectures at the Collège de France, 1975-76*. 1st ed. Translated by D. Macey. New York: Picador, 2003.

Foucault, Michel. *The Hermeneutics of the Subject: Lectures at the Collège de France, 1981-82*. Translated by G. Burchell. New York: Palgrave Macmillan, 2005.

Fraser, Derek. *The Evolution of the British Welfare State: A History of Social Policy since the Industrial Revolution*. 3rd ed. Houndmills: Palgrave Macmillan, 2003.

Freeman, Elizabeth. "Introduction." *GLQ* 13, no. 2-3 (2007), 159-176.

Freeman, Elizabeth. "Time Binds, or, Erotohistoriography." *Social Text* 23, no. 3-4 (2005), 57-68.
Freeman, Elizabeth. *Time Binds: Queer Temporalities, Queer Histories*. Durham: Duke University Press, 2010.
Freud, Sigmund. *Beyond the Pleasure Principle*. New York: Norton, 1989.
Fryer, Peter. *Staying Power: The History of Black People in Britain*. London: Pluto Press, 1984.
Fussell, Paul. *The Great War and Modern Memory*. New York: Oxford University Press, 2013.
Galbraith, John Kenneth. *The Affluent Society*. 40th anniversary ed. Boston: Houghton Mifflin, 1998.
Games, Abram. *Your Britain - Fight for It Now (Health Centre)*. 1943. Art.IWM PST 2911. Imperial War Museum. https://www.iwm.org.uk/collections/item/object/10300.
Games, Abram. *Your Britain—Fight for It Now (Housing)*. 1942. Art.IWM PST 2909. Imperial War Museum. https://www.iwm.org.uk/collections/item/object/10300.
Gardiner, Michael. "Spark versus *Homo economicus*." *Textual Practice* 32, no. 9 (2018), 1513-1528.
Gilmour, Rachael, and Bill Schwarz, eds. *End of Empire and the English Novel since 1945*. Manchester: Manchester University Press, 2011.
Gilroy, Paul. *Postcolonial Melancholia*. Wellek Library Lectures at the University of California, Irvine. New York: Columbia University Press, 2005.
Gladstone, Jason, Andrew Hoberek, and Daniel Worden, eds. *Postmodern/Postwar and After: Rethinking American Literature*. Iowa City: University of Iowa Press, 2016.
Glendinning, Miles. *Tower Block: Modern Public Housing in England, Scotland, Wales, and Northern Ireland*. New Haven: Published for the Paul Mellon Centre for Studies in British Art by Yale University Press, 1994.
Glendinning, Victoria. *Elizabeth Bowen: Portrait of a Writer*. New York: Alfred A. Knopf, 1977.
Goffman, Erving. *Asylums*. Garden City: Anchor Books, 1961.
Goldman, Mark. "Virginia Woolf and E. M. Forster: A Critical Dialogue." *Texas Studies in Literature and Language* 7, no. 4 (1966), 387-400.
Goyal, Yogita. "'We Are All Migrants': The Refugee Novel and the Claims of Universalism." *Modern Fiction Studies* 66, no. 2 (2020), 239-259.
Greene, Graham, Elizabeth Bowen, and V.S. Pritchett. "The Artist in Society." In *From the Third Programme: A Ten-Years' Anthology*, edited by John Morris, 97-112. London: Nonesuch Press, 1956.
Gurnah, Abdulrazak. *By the Sea*. London: Bloomsbury, 2001.
Halberstam, Judith. *In a Queer Time and Place: Transgender Bodies, Subcultural Lives*. New York: New York University Press, 2005.
Hall, Catherine, and Sonya Rose, eds. *At Home with the Empire: Metropolitan Culture and the Imperial World*. Cambridge: Cambridge University Press, 2006.
Hall, Stuart. *Familiar Stranger: A Life Between Two Islands*. London: Allen Lane, an imprint of Penguin Books, 2017.
Hall, Stuart. "Reconstruction Work." *Ten.8* 16 (1984), 2-9.
Hall, Stuart. *The Hard Road to Renewal: Thatcherism and the Crisis of the Left*. London: Verso, 1988.
Hall, Stuart. "Whose Heritage?: Un-Settling 'The Heritage,' Re-Imagining the Post-Nation." *Third Text* 13, no. 49 (1999), 3.
Hall, Stuart, and Tony Jefferson, eds. *Resistance through Rituals: Youth Subcultures in Post-War Britain*. 2nd ed. London: Routledge, 2006.
Halliday, Lisa. *Asymmetry*. New York: Simon & Schuster, 2018.
Hanley, Lynsey. *Estates: An Intimate History*. London: Granta Books, 2007.

Hansen, Jim, and Matthew Hart. "Contemporary Literature and the State." *Contemporary Literature* 49, no. 4 (2008), 491–513.
Harris, Alexandra. *Romantic Moderns: English Writers, Artists and the Imagination from Virginia Woolf to John Piper*. London: Thames & Hudson, 2010.
Harris, Bernard. *The Origins of the British Welfare State: Society, State and Social Welfare in England and Wales, 1800–1945*. New York: Palgrave Macmillan, 2004.
Harris, Jose. "Society and the state in twentieth-century Britain." In *Endings*, edited by F.M.L. Thompson, 63–117. Vol. 3 of *The Cambridge Social History of Britain, 1750–1950*. Cambridge: Cambridge University Press, 1990.
Harris, Jose. "War and Social History: Britain and the Home Front during the Second World War." *Contemporary European History* 1, no. 1 (1992), 17–35.
Harris, Jose. *William Beveridge: A Biography*. Oxford: Oxford University Press, 1997.
Harris, Neil. *Capital Culture: J. Carter Brown, the National Gallery of Art, and the Reinvention of the Museum Experience*. Chicago: University of Chicago Press, 2013.
Hart, Matthew. *Extraterritorial: A Political Geography of Contemporary Fiction*. New York, NY: Columbia University Press, 2020.
Hartley, Jenny. *Millions like Us: British Women's Fiction of the Second World War*. London: Virago Press, 1997.
Harvey, David. "Neoliberalism as Creative Destruction." *The Annals of the American Academy of Political and Social Science* 610, no. 1 (2007), 22–44.
Hatherley, Owen. *The Ministry of Nostalgia*. London: Verso, 2016.
Hayek, Friedrich A. *The Road to Serfdom; with, The Intellectuals and Socialism*. London: Institute of Economic Affairs, 2005.
Hazan, Pierre. *Judging War, Judging History: Behind Truth and Reconciliation*. Stanford: Stanford University Press, 2010.
Head, Dominic. *The Cambridge Introduction to Modern British Fiction, 1950–2000*. Cambridge: Cambridge University Press, 2002.
Hepburn, Allan. *A Grain of Faith: Religion in Mid-Century British Literature*. Oxford: Oxford University Press, 2018.
Hepburn, Allan. "Memento Mori and Gerontography." *Textual Practice* 32, no. 9 (2018), 1495–1511.
Hepburn, Allan. "Trials and Errors: The Heat of the Day and Postwar Culpability." In *Intermodernism: Literary Culture in Mid-Twentieth-Century Britain*, edited by K. Bluemel, 131–149. Edinburgh: Edinburgh University Press, 2022.
Hepburn, Allan, ed. *Around 1945: Literature, Citizenship, Rights*. Montreal & Kingston: McGill-Queen's University Press, 2016.
Herd, David, and Anna Pincus, eds. *Refugee Tales*. Vol. II, 2. Manchester: Comma Press, 2016. Kindle.
Herman, David. "'A Salutary Scar': Muriel Spark's Desegregated Art in the Twenty-First Century - Introduction." *Modern Fiction Studies* 54, no. 3 (2008), 473–486.
Hewison, Robert. *The Heritage Industry: Britain in a Climate of Decline*. London: Methuen London, 1987.
Hill, Amelia. "'Hostile Environment': The Hardline Home Office Policy Tearing Families Apart." 11/ 28/2017. The Guardian. https://www.theguardian.com/uk-news/2017/nov/28/hostile-environment-the-hardline-home-office-policy-tearing-families-apart.
Ho, Janice. *Nation and Citizenship in the Twentieth-Century British Novel*. New York, NY: Cambridge University Press, 2015.
Hodgkins, Hope Howell. "Stylish Spinsters: Spark, Pym, and the Postwar Comedy of the Object." *Modern Fiction Studies* 54, no. 3 (2008), 523–543.

BIBLIOGRAPHY 255

Hoff, Molly. *Virginia Woolf's Mrs. Dalloway: Invisible Presences.* Clemson: Clemson University Press, 2009.
Hoggart, Richard. *The Uses of Literacy.* New Brunswick: Transaction Publishers, 1998.
Hollinghurst, Alan. *The Line of Beauty.* New York: Bloomsbury, 2005.
Hollinghurst, Alan. *The Sparsholt Affair.* London: Picador, 2017.
Hollinghurst, Alan. *The Spell.* New York: Penguin Books, 2000.
Hollinghurst, Alan. *The Stranger's Child.* New York: Alfred A. Knopf, 2011.
Hollinghurst, Alan. *The Swimming Pool Library.* New York, NY: Random House, 1988.
Holman, Valerie. *Print for Victory: Book Publishing in England 1939–1945.* London: British Library, 2008.
Holme, Christopher. "BBC Radio Script by Christopher Holme, with Letter, 1965, of Christopher Holme," 1965. Acc. 10989/97. Muriel Spark Archive, National Library of Scotland.
Holmes, Chris and Kelly Mee Rich. "Rereading Kazuo Ishiguro." *Modern Fiction Studies* 67 no. 1 (Spring 2021), 1–19.
Hopkins, Owen. *Lost Futures: The Disappearing Architecture of Post-War Britain.* London: Royal Academy of Arts, 2017.
Hornsey, Richard and Quentin Donald. *The Spiv and the Architect: Unruly Life in Postwar London.* Minneapolis: University of Minnesota Press, 2010.
Houlbrook, Matt. *Queer London: Perils and Pleasures in the Sexual Metropolis, 1918–1957.* Chicago: University of Chicago Press, 2005.
Hubble, Nick, John McLeod, and Philip Tew, eds. *The 1970s: A Decade of Contemporary British Fiction.* London: Bloomsbury Academic, 2014.
Hungerford, Amy. "On the Period Formerly Known as Contemporary." *American Literary History* 20, no. 1–2 (2008), 410–419.
Hurley, Jessica. *Infrastructures of Apocalypse: American Literature and the Nuclear Complex.* Minneapolis: University of Minnesota Press, 2020.
Hutcheon, Linda. *A Poetics of Postmodernism: History, Theory, Fiction.* New York: Routledge, 1988.
Irving, Henry. "Keep Calm and Carry On – The Compromise Behind the Slogan." GOV.UK, June 27, 2014. https://history.blog.gov.uk/2014/06/27/keep-calm-and-carry-on-the-compromise-behind-the-slogan/.
Ishiguro, Kazuo. *My Twentieth Century Evening and Other Small Breakthroughs: The Nobel Lecture.* New York: Alfred A. Knopf, 2017.
Ishiguro, Kazuo. *Never Let Me Go.* New York: Knopf, 2005.
Ishiguro, Kazuo. *The Remains of the Day.* Vintage international ed. Vintage International. New York: Vintage Books, 1993.
Ishiguro, Kazuo, and Oe Kenzaburo. "The Novelist in Today's World: A Conversation." *Boundary 2* 18, no. 3 (1991), 109–122.
Jacobs, Jane M., and Loretta Lees. "Defensible Space on the Move: Revisiting the Urban Geography of Alice Coleman." *International Journal of Urban and Regional Research* 37, no. 5 (2013), 1559–1583.
Jacobs, J.U. "Michael Ondaatje's *The English Patient* (1992) and Postcolonial Impatience." *Journal of Literary Studies (Pretoria, South Africa)* 13, no. 1–2 (1997), 92–112.
James, David. "Wounded Realism." *Contemporary Literature* 54, no. 1 (2013), 204–214.
Jameson, Fredric. *Postmodernism, or, The Cultural Logic of Late Capitalism.* Durham: Duke University Press, 1991.
Jameson, Fredric. *The Political Unconscious: Narrative as a Socially Symbolic Act.* Ithaca: Cornell University Press, 1981.

Jameson, Fredric. "Third-World Literature in the Era of Multinational Capitalism." *Social Text* 15, no. 15 (1986), 65–88.
Jencks, Charles. *The Language of Post-Modern Architecture*. New York: Rizzoli, 1977.
Jephcott, Agnes Pearl. *A Troubled Area; Notes on Notting Hill*. London: Faber and Faber, 1964.
Johnson, Allan. "Buried Temples and Open Planes: Alethea Hayter and the Architecture of Drug-Taking in Alan Hollinghurst's *The Spell*." *Textual Practice* 27, no. 7 (2013), 1177–1195.
Jones, Colin. *The Black House*. New York: Prestel, 2006.
Jones, Peter. "Re-Thinking Corruption in Post-1950 Urban Britain: The Poulson Affair, 1972–1976." *Urban History* 39, no. 3 (2012), 510–528.
Jordan, Heather Bryant. *How Will the Heart Endure?: Elizabeth Bowen and the Landscape of War*. Ann Arbor: University of Michigan Press, 1992.
Kalliney, Peter J. *Cities of Affluence and Anger: A Literary Geography of Modern Englishness*. Charlottesville: University of Virginia Press, 2007.
Kalliney, Peter J. *Commonwealth of Letters: British Literary Culture and the Emergence of Postcolonial Aesthetics*. New York: Oxford University Press, 2013.
Kefford, Alistair. "Housing the Citizen-Consumer in Post-War Britain: The Parker Morris Report, Affluence and the Even Briefer Life of Social Democracy." *20th Century British History* 29, no. 2 (2018), 225–258.
Khan, Yasmin. "Dunkirk, the War and the Amnesia of the Empire." *The New York Times*, February 8, 2017. https://www.nytimes.com/2017/08/02/opinion/dunkirk-indians-world-war.html.
Kinnock, Neil. "Leader's Speech, Blackpool." 1988. http://www.britishpoliticalspeech.org/speech-archive.htm?speech=194.
Klein, Melanie, and Joan Riviere. *Love, Hate and Reparation*. New York: Norton, 1964.
Kynaston, David. *Austerity Britain, 1945–51*. London: Bloomsbury, 2007.
Langhamer, Claire. "The Meanings of Home in Postwar Britain." *Journal of Contemporary History* 40, no. 2 (2005), 341–362.
Larkham, Peter J. *Planning the "City of Tomorrow": British Reconstruction Planning, 1939–1952; an Annotated Bibliography*. Pickering: Inch's Books, 2001.
Larkin, Brian. "Promising Forms: The Political Aesthetics of Infrastructure." In *The Promise of Infrastructure*, edited by Nikhil Anand, Akhil Gupta, and Hannah Appel, 175–202. Durham: Duke University Press, 2018. 177.
Le Corbusier. *Towards a New Architecture*. Translated by F. Etchells. New York: Dover Publications, Inc., 1986.
Lee, Hermione. *Virginia Woolf*. New York: Alfred A. Knopf, 1997.
Light, Alison. *Forever England: Femininity, Literature, and Conservatism between the Wars*. London: Routledge, 1991.
Little, Kenneth Lindsay. *Negroes in Britain: A Study of Racial Relations in English Society*. London: K. Paul, Trench, Trubner, 1948.
Lloyd, David. *Culture and the State*. New York: Routledge, 1998.
Loach, Ken. *The Spirit of '45*. Documentary, History. Fly Film Company, Sixteen Films, Film4, 2013.
Loh, Lucienne. *The Postcolonial Country in Contemporary Literature*. New York: Palgrave Macmillan, 2013.
Love, Heather. *Feeling Backward: Loss and the Politics of Queer History*. Cambridge, MA: Harvard University Press, 2007.
Lowe, Rodney. "The Second World War: Consensus and the Foundation of the British Welfare State." *Twentieth Century British History* 1.2 (1990), 152–182.

Lowe, Rodney. *The Welfare State in Britain since 1945*. 3rd ed. Houndmills: Palgrave Macmillan, 2005.
Lukács, György. *The Historical Novel*. Lincoln: University of Nebraska Press, 1983.
Lyall, Sarah. "From Ali Smith, It's the First Great Brexit Novel." *The New York Times*, February 17, 2017. https://www.nytimes.com/2017/02/17/books/review/autumn-ali-smith.html.
MacDonald, Sally, and Julia Porter. *Putting on the Style: Setting up Home in the 1950s. Putting on the Style*. London: The Geffrye Museum, 1990.
MacKay, Marina. "'Is Your Journey Really Necessary?': Going Nowhere in Late Modernist London." *PMLA: Publications of the Modern Language Association of America* 124, no. 5 (2009), 1600–1613.
MacKay, Marina. *Modernism and World War II*. Cambridge: Cambridge University Press, 2007.
MacKay, Marina. "Muriel Spark and Self-Help." *Textual Practice* 32, no. 9 (2018), 1563–1576.
MacKay, Marina. "'Temporary Kings': The Metropolitan Novel Series and the Postwar Consensus," *MFS* 67.2 (Summer 2021), 320–341.
MacKay, Marina. "The Wartime Rise of The Rise of the Novel." *Representations* no. 119 (2012), 119–143.
MacKay, Marina, and Lyndsey Stonebridge, eds. *British Fiction After Modernism: The Novel at Mid-Century*. London: Palgrave Macmillan UK, 2007.
Macmillan, Harold. "Speech, July 20, 1957." *BBC News*, n.d. http://news.bbc.co.uk/onthisday/hi/dates/stories/july/20/newsid_3728000/3728225.stm.
MacPhee, Graham. *Postwar British Literature and Postcolonial Studies*. Postcolonial Literary Studies. Edinburgh: Edinburgh University Press, 2011.
Maher, Ashley. *Reconstructing Modernism: British Literature, Modern Architecture, and the State*. Oxford: Oxford University Press, 2020.
Maher, Ashley. "Swastika Arms of Passage Leading to Nothing: Late Modernism and the 'New' Britain." *ELH* 80, no. 1 (2013), 251–285.
Malpass, Peter. "Housing and the New Welfare State: Wobbly Pillar or Cornerstone?" *Housing Studies* 23, no. 1 (2008), 1–19.
Malpass, Peter. *Housing and the Welfare State: The Development of Housing Policy in Britain*. Basingstoke: Palgrave Macmillan, 2005.
Malpass, Peter. *Housing Policy and Practice*. 5th ed. London: Macmillan, 1999.
Mantel, Hilary. *An Experiment in Love*. London: Viking, 1995.
Mantel, Hilary. "An Interview with Hilary Mantel." *Atlantis* 20, no. 2 (December 1998).
Mantel, Hilary. *Giving up the Ghost: A Memoir. Giving up the Ghost*. New York: Picador, 2004.
Mao, Douglas. *Fateful Beauty: Aesthetic Environments, Juvenile Development, and Literature 1860–1960*. Princeton: Princeton University Press, 2008.
Marais, Mike. "Violence, Postcolonial Fiction, and the Limits of Sympathy." *Studies in the Novel* 43, no. 1 (2011), 94–114.
Marcus, Laura. "The Legacies of Modernism." In *The Cambridge Companion to the Modernist Novel*, edited by Morag Shiach, 82–98. Cambridge Companions to Literature. Cambridge: Cambridge University Press, 2014.
Marshall, T.H. "Citizenship and Social Class." In *Inequality and Society: Social Science Perspectives on Social Stratification*, edited by Jeff Manza and Michael Sauder, 148–154. New York: W. W. Norton and Co., 2009.
Martin, Theodore. *Contemporary Drift: Genre, Historicism, and the Problem of the Present*. New York, NY: Columbia University Press, 2017.
Marx, John. "Literature and Governmentality." *Literature Compass* 8, no. 1 (2011), 66–79.
Mass-Observation. *Enquiry into People's Homes: A Report Prepared by Mass-Observation for the Advertising Service Guild*. London: Advertising Service Guild, 1943.
Matera, Marc. *Black London: The Imperial Metropolis and Decolonization in the Twentieth Century*. Oakland: University of California Press, 2015.

May, Theresa. "Theresa May Interview: 'We're Going to Give Illegal Migrants a Really Hostile Reception'." *The Telegraph*, May 25, 2012. https://www.telegraph.co.uk/news/0/theresa-may-interview-going-give-illegal-migrants-really-hostile/.

Mcbride, Lorraine. "Charlie Higson: 'We Created Loadsamoney, Harry Enfield Cashed in'." *The Telegraph*, January 31, 2016. https://www.telegraph.co.uk/finance/personalfinance/fameandfortune/12127643/Charlie-Higson-We-created-Loadsamoney-Harry-Enfield-cashed-in.html.

McCarthy, Helen. "Gender Equality." In *Unequal Britain: Equalities in Britain since 1945*, edited by Pat Thane, 105–124. London: Continuum, 2010.

McCarthy, Helen. "Social Science and Married Women's Employment in Post-War Britain." *Past & Present* 233, no. 233 (2016), 269–305.

McClanahan, Annie. *Dead Pledges: Debt, Crisis, and Twenty-First-Century Culture*. Stanford: Stanford University Press, 2020.

McDonald, Keith. "Days of Past Futures: Kazuo Ishiguro's *Never Let Me Go* as 'Speculative Memoir'." *Biography (Honolulu)* 30, no. 1 (2007), 74–83.

McLeod, John. *Postcolonial London: Rewriting the Metropolis*. London: Routledge, 2004.

Meek, James. "Where Will We Live?" *London Review of Books* 36, no. 1 (January 9, 2014).

Mellor, David, Gill Saunders, and P. Wright, eds. *Recording Britain: A Pictorial Domesday of Pre-War Britain*. London: David & Charles in association with the Victoria and Albert Museum, 1990.

Mellor, Leo. *Reading the Ruins: Modernism, Bombsites and British Culture*. Cambridge: Cambridge University Press, 2011.

Miller, K.A. "'Even a Shelter's Not Safe': The Blitz on Homes in Elizabeth Bowen's Wartime Writing." *Twentieth Century Literature* 45, no. 2 (1999), 138–158.

Ministry of Health. *Housing for Special Purposes: Supplement to the Housing Manual, 1949*. London: His Majesty's Stationery Office, 1951.

Ministry of Health. *Housing Manual, 1944*. London: His Majesty's Stationery Office, 1944.

Ministry of Health. *Housing Manual, 1949*. London: His Majesty's Stationery Office, 1949.

Ministry of Housing and Local Government. *Houses 1952; Second Supplement to the Housing Manual, 1949*. London: His Majesty's Stationery Office, 1952.

Ministry of Information. *Keep Calm and Carry On*. 1939. http://www.wartimeposters.co.uk/.

Ministry of Information. *"TOGETHER."* Her Majesty's Stationery Office, Lowe & Brydone Printers, 1939.

Minow, Martha. *Between Vengeance and Forgiveness: Facing History after Genocide and Mass Violence*. Boston: Beacon Press, 1998.

Mitchell, Timothy. *Colonising Egypt*. Berkeley: University of California Press, 1991.

Moran, Joe. "Imagining the Street in Post-War Britain." *Urban History* 39, no. 1 (2012), 166–186.

Moretti, Franco. *The Way of the World: The Bildungsroman in European Culture*. London: Verso, 2000.

Morgan, Kenneth. *Britain Since 1945: The People's Peace*. 3rd ed. Oxford: Oxford University Press, 2001.

Mort, Frank. *Capital Affairs: London and the Making of the Permissive Society*. New Haven: Yale University Press, 2010.

Moss, Stephen. "Interview: Alan Hollinghurst: Sex on the Brain." June 17, 2011. *The Guardian*. https://www.theguardian.com/books/2011/jun/18/alan-hollinghurst-interview.

Mountz, Alison. *Seeking Asylum: Human Smuggling and Bureaucracy at the Border*. Minneapolis: University of Minnesota Press, 2010.

BIBLIOGRAPHY 259

Muñoz, Jose Esteban. *Cruising Utopia: The Then and There of Queer Futurity*. New York: New York University Press, 2009.

Murphy, J. Stephen. "Past Irony: Trauma and the Historical Turn in Fragments and *The Swimming-Pool Library*." *Literature and History* 13, no. 1 (2004), 58–75.

N+1 Editors. "World Lite," July 25, 2013. https://www.nplusonemag.com/issue-17/the-intellectual-situation/world-lite/.

N+1 Editors. "'The Rest Is Indeed Horseshit,' Pt. 6." *N+1* (blog), August 23, 2013. https://www.nplusonemag.com/online-only/horseshit/the-rest-is-indeed-horseshit-pt-6/.

Nairn, Tom. *The Break-up of Britain: Crisis and Neo-Nationalism*. London: NLB, 1977.

Narkunas, J. Paul. *Reified Life: Speculative Capital and the Ahuman Condition*. New York: Fordham University Press, 2018.

Noble, Virginia A. *Inside the Welfare State: Foundations of Policy and Practice in Post-War Britain*. New York: Routledge, 2009.

Novick, Peter. *The Holocaust in American Life*. Boston: Houghton Mifflin, 1999.

Olusoga, David. *Black and British: A Forgotten History*. London: Macmillan an imprint of Pan Macmillan, 2016.

Ondaatje, Michael. *Anil's Ghost*. New York: Vintage International, 2001.

Ondaatje, Michael. *In the Skin of a Lion*. In the Skin of a Lion. New York: Penguin Books, 1988.

Ondaatje, Michael. "Michael Ondaatje's Golden Man Booker Speech." *Literary Hub* (blog), July 12, 2018. https://lithub.com/michael-ondaatjes-golden-man-booker-speech-is-really-great/.

Ondaatje, Michael. *Running in the Family*. New York: Vintage, 1993.

Ondaatje, Michael. *The English Patient*. New York: Vintage Books, 1993.

Ondaatje, Michael. *Warlight*. New York: Alfred A. Knopf, 2018.

Orwell, George. *1984*. New York: Penguin Books Ltd, 1985.

Orwell, George. "London Letter to *Partisan Review*." (Early May? 1946). In *The Collected Essays, Journalism and Letters of George Orwell*, edited by Sonia Orwell and Ian Angus, Vol. 4. London: Secker & Warburg, 1968. 184–186.

Orwell, George. *The Road to Wigan Pier*. New York: Mariner Books, 1972.

Osborne, John. *Look Back in Anger*. Penguin Plays. New York: Penguin, 1982.

Panayi, Panikos. *Migrant City: A New History of London*. New Haven: Yale University Press, 2020.

Patterson, Sheila. *Dark Strangers; A Sociological Study of the Absorption of a Recent West Indian Migrant Group in Brixton, South London*. London: Tavistock Publications, 1963.

Paul, Kathleen. *Whitewashing Britain: Race and Citizenship in the Postwar Era*. Ithaca: Cornell University Press, 2018.

Pedersen, Susan. *Family, Dependence, and the Origins of the Welfare State: Britain and France, 1914–1945*. Cambridge: Cambridge University Press, 1993.

Perry, Kennetta Hammond. *London Is the Place for Me: Black Britons, Citizenship, and the Politics of Race*. New York: Oxford University Press, 2015.

Phillips, Caryl. *A Distant Shore*. New York: Vintage Books, 2005.

Picture Post. *A Plan for Britain*, edited by Tom Hopkinson. 1st ed. Vol. 10. London: Hulton Press, Ltd, 1941.

Pierson, Paul. "The New Politics of the Welfare State," *World Politics* 48, no. 2 (1996), 143–179.

Piette, Adam. *Imagination at War: British Fiction and Poetry, 1939–1945*. London: Papermac, 1995.

Plain, Gill, ed. *British Literature in Transition, 1940–1960: Postwar.* Cambridge: Cambridge University Press, 2019.

Plain, Gill. *Literature of the 1940s: War, Postwar and "Peace."* Edinburgh: Edinburgh University Press, 2013.

Pleydell-Bouverie, Millicent Frances. *Daily Mail Book of Post-War Homes, Based on the Ideas and Opinions of the Women of Britain and Specially Compiled for The Daily Mail.* London: Daily Mail, 1944.

Pong, Beryl. *British Literature and Culture in Second World Wartime: For the Duration. British Literature and Culture in Second World Wartime.* Oxford Mid-Century Studies. Oxford: Oxford University Press, 2020.

Powell, Enoch. "The Enemy Within: Speech during 1970 General Election Campaign." Birmingham, June 13, 1970.

Procter, James. *Dwelling Places: Postwar Black British Writing.* Manchester: Manchester University Press, 2003.

Procter, James, ed. *Writing Black Britain, 1948–1998: An Interdisciplinary Anthology.* Manchester: Manchester University Press, 2000.

Purcell, Hugh. "What Ever Happened to Timothy: The Lost Dream of 1945." *New Statesman* 142, no. 5189–5191 (2013).

Rajaram, Poorva, and Michael Griffith. "Why World Literature Looks Different From Brooklyn." *Tehelka.Com* (blog), August 16, 2013. https://web.archive.org/web/20150612225014/http://blog.tehelka.com/why-world-literature-looks-different-from-brooklyn/.

Rau, Petra. "The Common Frontier: Fictions of Alterity in Elizabeth Bowen's *The Heat of the Day* and Graham Greene's *The Ministry of Fear.*" *Literature and History* 14, no. 1 (2005), 31–55.

Ravetz, Alison. *Council Housing and Culture: The History of a Social Experiment.* New York: Routledge, 2001.

Rawlinson, Kevin, Nadeem Badshah, and Matthew Weaver. "Windrush Scandal: Timeline of Key Events." *The Guardian*, March 31, 2022, sec. UK news. https://www.theguardian.com/uk-news/2018/apr/16/windrush-era-citizens-row-timeline-of-key-events.

Rawlinson, Mark. *British Writing of the Second World War.* Oxford English Monographs British Writing of the Second World War. Oxford: Clarendon, 2000.

Reichman, Ravit Pe'er-Lamo. *The Affective Life of Law: Legal Modernism and the Literary Imagination.* Stanford: Stanford University Press, 2009.

Rich, Kelly Mee, Nicole Rizzuto, and Susan Zieger, eds. *The Aesthetics of Infrastructure: Race, Affect, Environment.* Evanston: Northwestern University Press, 2022.

Robbins, Bruce. "Cruelty Is Bad: Banality and Proximity in *Never Let Me Go.*" *Novel: A Forum on Fiction* 40, no. 3 (2007), 289–302.

Robbins, Bruce. "Orange Juice and Agent Orange." *Occasion: Interdisciplinary Studies in the Humanities* 2 (December 20, 2010). https://arcade.stanford.edu/occasion/orange-juice-and-agent-orange.

Robbins, Bruce. *Upward Mobility and the Common Good: Toward a Literary History of the Welfare State.* Princeton: Princeton University Press, 2007.

Rogers, Asha. *State Sponsored Literature: Britain and Cultural Diversity after 1945. State Sponsored Literature.* Oxford: Oxford University Press, 2020.

Romanek, Mark, Alex Garland, Andrew Macdonald, Allon Reich, Kazuo Ishiguro, Tessa Ross, Carey Mulligan, et al. *Never Let Me Go.* Beverly Hills: Twentieth Century Fox Film Corporation, 2010.

Rose, Jacqueline. *Why War?– Psychoanalysis, Politics, and the Return to Melanie Klein.* Oxford: B. Blackwell, 1993.

Rose, Sonya O. *Which People's War?: National Identity and Citizenship in Britain, 1939–1945*. Oxford: Oxford University Press, 2003.
Rosner, Victoria. *Modernism and the Architecture of Private Life*. New York: Columbia University Press, 2005.
Royal Institute of British Architects. *Rebuilding Britain*. London: Percy Lund, Humphries and Co. Ltd, 1943.
Royal Institute of British Architects. *Towards a New Britain*. London: Knapp, Drewett & Sons Ltd, 1944.
Rubenstein, Michael. *Public Works: Infrastructure, Irish Modernism, and the Postcolonial. Public Works*. Notre Dame: University of Notre Dame Press, 2010.
Rumbarger, Lee. "Housekeeping: Women Modernists' Writings on War and Home." *Women's Studies* 35, no. 1 (2006), 1–15.
Rushdie, Salman. "Outside the Whale." In *Imaginary Homelands: Essays and Criticism, 1981–1991*, 87–101. New York: Penguin Books, 1992.
Saint-Amour, Paul K. *Tense Future: Modernism, Total War, Encyclopedic Form*. New York: Oxford University Press, 2015.
Salter, Joseph. *The Asiatic in England: Sketches of Sixteen Year's Work among Orientals*. Seeley, Jackson & Halliday, 1873.
Samuel, Raphael. *Theatres of Memory: Past and Present in Contemporary Culture*. London: Verso, 2012.
Sanders, Mark. *Ambiguities of Witnessing: Law and Literature in the Time of a Truth Commission*. Meridian (Stanford, California). Stanford: Stanford University Press, 2007.
Sayers, Janet, and John Forrester. "The Autobiography of Melanie Klein." *Psychoanalysis and History* 15, no. 2 (2013), 127–163.
Seiler, Claire. *Midcentury Suspension: Literature and Feeling in the Wake of World War II*. New York: Columbia University Press, 2020.
Selvon, Samuel. *Moses Ascending*. Heinemann Caribbean Writers Series. Oxford: Heinemann Educational Books Ltd, 1984.
Selvon, Samuel. *The Housing Lark*. Washington DC: Three Continents Press, 1990.
Selvon, Samuel. *The Lonely Londoners*. Longman Caribbean Writers Series. New York: Longman Publishing Group, 2001.
Shaw, Stephen. "Review into the Welfare in Detention of Vulnerable Persons," January 14, 2016. GOV.UK. https://www.gov.uk/government/publications/review-into-the-welfare-in-detention-of-vulnerable-persons.
Sherry, Vincent B. *The Great War and the Language of Modernism*. Oxford: Oxford University Press, 2003.
Schaffer, Talia. *Communities of Care: The Social Ethics of Victorian Fiction*. Princeton: Princeton University Press, 2021.
Shih, Shu-mei. "Is the Post in Postsocialism the Post in Posthumanism?" *Social Text* 30, no. 1 (2012), 27–50.
Shire, Warsan. *Teaching My Mother How to Give Birth*. London: Flipped Eye Publishing, 2011.
Sillitoe, Alan. *Saturday Night and Sunday Morning*. New York: Vintage International, 2010.
Simone, AbdouMaliq. "People as Infrastructure: Intersecting Fragments in Johannesburg." *Public Culture* 16, no. 3 (2004), 407–429.
Simpson, Julian M., Aneez Esmail, Virinder S. Kalra, and Stephanie J. Snow. "Writing Migrants Back into NHS History: Addressing a 'Collective Amnesia' and Its Policy Implications." *Journal of the Royal Society of Medicine* 103, no. 10 (2010), 392–396.
Sinclair, Iain. *Ghost Milk: Calling Time on the Grand Project*. London: Penguin, 2011.

Sinfield, Alan. "Culture, consensus and difference: Angus Wilson to Alan Hollinghurst." In *British Culture of the Postwar*, edited by A. Davies and A. Sinfield. New York: Routledge, 2000, 83–102.
Sinfield, Alan. *Literature, Politics, and Culture in Postwar Britain*, 2nd ed. London and New York: Continuum Press, 2004.
Slaughter, Joseph R. *Human Rights, Inc: The World Novel, Narrative Form, and International Law*. New York: Fordham University Press, 2007.
Smith, Ali. "About." Refugee Tales. https://www.refugeetales.org/about.
Smith, Ali. *Autumn*. New York: Anchor Books, 2017.
Smith, Ali. *Spring, A Novel*. New York: Pantheon Books, 2019.
Smith, Ali. *Summer, A Novel*. New York: Pantheon Books, 2020.
Smith, Ali. The Waterstones Interview: Ali Smith. Interview by A. Orhanen, August 25, 2020. Waterstones. https://www.waterstones.com/blog/the-waterstones-interview-ali-smith.
Smith, Ali. *Winter*. New York: Anchor Books, 2018.
Smith, Rachel Greenwald. *Affect and American Literature in the Age of Neoliberalism*. New York: Cambridge University Press, 2015.
Smith, Zadie. *NW*. New York: Penguin Press, 2012.
Spark, Muriel. *Curriculum Vitae: A Volume of Autobiography*. New York: New Directions, 2011.
Spark, Muriel. *The Girls of Slender Means*. New Directions Classics. New York: New Directions Pub., 1998.
Spark, Muriel. *The Hothouse by the East River*. New York: Penguin Books, 1977. Kindle.
Spark, Muriel. *The Informed Air: Essays*, edited by Penelope Jardine. New York: A New Directions Book, 2014.
Spark, Muriel. *The Prime of Miss Jean Brodie*. New York: Harper Perennial Modern Classics, 2009.
Steedman, Carolyn. *Landscape for a Good Woman: A Story of Two Lives*. New Brunswick: Rutgers University Press, 1987.
Stewart, Victoria. *The Second World War in Contemporary British Fiction: Secret Histories*. Edinburgh: Edinburgh University Press, 2011.
Stonebridge, Lyndsey. "Hearing Them Speak: Voices in Wilfred Bion, Muriel Spark and Penelope Fitzgerald." *Textual Practice* 19, no. 4 (2005), 445–465.
Stonebridge, Lyndsey. *The Judicial Imagination: Writing After Nuremberg*. Edinburgh: Edinburgh University Press, 2011.
Su, John J. "Refiguring National Character: The Remains of the British Estate Novel." *Modern Fiction Studies* 48, no. 3 (2002), 552–580.
Suh, Judy. "The Familiar Attractions of Fascism in Muriel Spark's 'The Prime of Miss Jean Brodie.'" *Journal of Modern Literature* 30, no. 2 (2007), 86–102.
Swenarton, Mark, Tom Avermaete, and Dirk van den Heuvel, eds. *Architecture and the Welfare State*. London: Routledge, Taylor & Francis Group, 2015.
Swift, Graham. "Shorts: Kazuo Ishiguro." In *Conversations with Kazuo Ishiguro*, edited by Brian W. Shaffer and Cynthia F. Wong, 35–41. Literary Conversations Series. Jackson: University Press of Mississippi, 2008.
Symons, Julian. Review of *The Myth of the Blitz*, by Angus Calder. *London Review of Books*, September 12, 1991. https://www.lrb.co.uk/the-paper/v13/n17/julian-symons/the-brief-possibility-of-a-different-kind-of-history.
Szalay, Michael. *New Deal Modernism: American Literature and the Invention of the Welfare State*. Durham: Duke University Press, 2000.

BIBLIOGRAPHY 263

Taunton, Matthew. *Fictions of the City: Class, Culture and Mass Housing in London and Paris.* New York: Palgrave Macmillan, 2009.
Taylor, Fred. *"Rehabilitation: It Takes Time."* London Transport, 1945. Art.IWM PST 15256. Imperial War Museum.
Taylor, Ken. "BBC Television Rehearsal Script by Ken Taylor, 1975," 1975. Acc. 10989/98–100. Muriel Spark Archive, National Library of Scotland.
Teekell, Anna. *Emergency Writing: Irish Literature, Neutrality, and the Second World War.* Evanston: Northwestern University Press, 2018.
Tew, Philip. *The Contemporary British Novel.* London: Continuum, 2004.
Thane, Pat. *Foundations of the Welfare State. The Foundations of the Welfare State.* Social Policy in Modern Britain. London: Longman, 1982.
Thane, Pat, and Liza Filby, eds. *Unequal Britain: Equalities in Britain since 1945.* London: Continuum, 2010.
Thatcher, Margaret. Interview for *Woman's Own* ("no such thing as society"). Interview by Douglas Keay, October 31, 1987. Thatcher Archive. https://www.margaretthatcher.org/document/106689.
Thatcher, Margaret. *The Downing Street Years.* 1st ed. New York: HarperCollins, 1993.
"The West India Docks: Offices, Works and Housing." In *Survey of London: Volumes 43 and 44, Poplar, Blackwall and Isle of Dogs*, edited by Hermione Hobhouse, 313–326. British History Online. London: London County Council, 1994. https://www.british-history.ac.uk/survey-london/vols43-4/ pp 313–326.
Timmins, Nicholas. *The Five Giants: A Biography of the Welfare State.* New ed. London: Harper Collins Publishers, 2001.
Titmuss, Richard. *Problems of Social Policy.* London: His Majesty's Stationery Office, 1950.
Titmuss, Richard. *The Gift Relationship From Human Blood to Social Policy.* 3rd ed. Bristol: Policy Press, 2018.
Torgersen, Ulf. "Housing: the Wobbly Pillar under the Welfare State." *Scandinavian Housing and Planning Research* 4 (1987), 116–126.
Torgovnick, Marianna. *The War Complex: World War II in Our Time.* Chicago: University of Chicago Press, 2005.
Trilling, Lionel. *E.M. Forster.* Norfolk: New Directions Books, 1943.
Tsao, Tiffany. "The Tyranny of Purpose: Religion and Biotechnology in Ishiguro's 'Never Let Me Go'." *Literature & Theology* 26, no. 2 (2012), 214–232.
Vadde, Aarthi. *Chimeras of Form: Modernist Internationalism Beyond Europe, 1914–2016.* New York: Columbia University Press, 2016.
Vernon, James. *Hunger: A Modern History.* Cambridge: The Belknap Press of Harvard University Press, 2007.
Vernon, James. "Hunger, the Social, and States of Welfare in Modern Imperial Britain." *Occasion* 2 (December 20, 2010), 7–8.
Vidler, Anthony. "Bodies in Space/Subjects in the City: Psychopathologies of Modern Urbanism." *differences (Bloomington, Ind.)* 5, no. 3 (1993), 31–51.
Visram, Rozina. *Asians in Britain: 400 Years of History.* London: Pluto Press, 2002.
Visvis, Vikki. "Traumatic Representation: The Power and Limitations of Storytelling as 'Talking Cure' in Michael Ondaatje's *In the Skin of a Lion* and *The English Patient*." *ariel: A Review of International English Literature* 40, no. 4 (2009), 89–108.
Wachtel, Eleanor. "An Interview with Michael Ondaatje." *Essays on Canadian Writing* 53 (1999), 250.
Walkowitz, Rebecca L. *Cosmopolitan Style: Modernism beyond the Nation.* New York: Columbia University Press, 2006.

Walkowitz, Rebecca L. "Unimaginable Largeness: Kazuo Ishiguro, Translation, and the New World Literature." *Novel: A Forum on Fiction* 40, no. 3 (2007), 216.
Waugh, Evelyn. "Preface." In *Brideshead Revisited*. New York: Little, Brown and Co., 2012.
Webster, Wendy. *Englishness and Empire, 1939–1965*. Oxford: Oxford University Press, 2007.
Webster, Wendy. *Mixing It: Diversity in World War Two Britain*. Oxford: Oxford University Press, 2018.
Wetherell, Sam. *Foundations: How the Built Environment Made Twentieth-Century Britain*. Princeton: Princeton University Press, 2020.
White, Leslie. "Vital Disconnection in *Howards End*." *Twentieth Century Literature* 51, no. 1 (2005), 43–63.
Whittall, Daniel. "Creating Black Places in Imperial London: The League of Coloured Peoples and Aggrey House, 1931–1943." *London Journal* 36, no. 3 (2011), 225–246.
Williams, Raymond. *Culture and Society, 1780–1950*. New York: Columbia University Press, 1983.
Williams, Raymond. *The Country and the City*. New York: Oxford University Press, 1973.
Williams, Raymond. *The Long Revolution*. Cardigan: Parthian, 2011. https://www.parthianbooks.com/products/the-long-revolution.
Wilson, Nicola. *Home in British Working-Class Fiction*. Farnham: Ashgate, 2015.
Winter, J.M. *Sites of Memory, Sites of Mourning: The Great War in European Cultural History*. Cambridge: Cambridge University Press, 1995.
Wollaeger, Mark A. *Modernism, Media, and Propaganda: British Narrative from 1900 to 1945*. Course Book. Princeton: Princeton University Press, 2007.
Wood, James. "The Human Difference." *The New Republic*, May 16, 2005. https://newrepublic.com/article/68200/the-human-difference.
Woolf, Virginia. "A Sketch of the Past." In *Moments of Being: Unpublished Autobiographical Writings*, edited by Jeanne Schulkind, 1st American ed. 64–149. New York: Harcourt Brace Jovanovich, 1976.
Woolf, Virginia. *Jacob's Room*. Collins Classics. New York: Harcourt, Inc., 1950.
Woolf, Virginia. "Mr. Bennett and Mrs. Brown." In *Essentials of the Theory of Fiction*, edited by Michael J. Hoffman and Patrick D. Murphy, 21–34. Durham: Duke University Press, 2020.
Woolf, Virginia. *Mrs. Dalloway*. New York: Harcourt, Inc., 1981.
Woolf, Virginia. *To the Lighthouse*. New York: Harcourt, Inc., 1927.
Woubshet, Dagmawi. *The Calendar of Loss: Race, Sexuality, and Mourning in the Early Era of AIDS. The Calendar of Loss*. Baltimore: Johns Hopkins University Press, 2015.
Wright, Patrick. *A Journey Through Ruins: The Last Days of London*. Oxford: Oxford University Press, 2009.
Wright, Patrick. *On Living in an Old Country: The National Past in Contemporary Britain*. Oxford: Oxford University Press, 2009.
Yelling, Jim. "The Incidence of Slum Clearance in England and Wales, 1955–85." *Urban History* 27, no. 2 (2000), 234–254.
Zaretsky, Eli. *Political Freud: A History*. New York: Columbia University Press, 2015.

Index

For the benefit of digital users, indexed terms that span two pages (e.g., 52–53) may, on occasion, appear on only one of those pages.

Figures are indicated by an italic *f* following the page number.

Abercrombie, Patrick, 19–20, 56–57, 162–163
affairs, 178–181
affect, 15–16, 75
affluence, 74–75
Agamben, Giorgio, 209–210
Aggrey House, 123
Ahmad, Aijaz, 184–185
AIDS crisis, 155–158, 160, 161, 175, 176, 196–197
altruism, 211–212
Amercanization, 74–75
Angry Young Men, 75–76
Angry Young Women, 33–34, 76–77, 89
antisociality, 167–168
  See also sociality
apartment buildings, 165–166
  See also homes and housing
Appiah, Kwame Anthony, 107–108
architecture, 31–32 n.65, 55, 142, 143–145, 154, 167–168
archives, 130–131
Arendt, Hannah, 13, 30–31
Armstrong, Nancy, 205–207
art and artists, 62–64, 208, 225–226, 232, 245
  See also painting; photography
Asymmetry (Halliday), 238–239
Atkinson, Kate, 154
atmosphere (Bowen), 46–47
Atonement (McEwan), 164–165
Attlee, Clement, 35, 137–138

audience (addresses to), 114–115
Augé, Marc, 235–236

Bachelard, Gaston, 217–218
Bailkin, Jordanna, 244 n.30
Ballard, J.G., 35, 143–145, 230–231
Barnes, Julian, *England, England*, 187
Barthes, Roland, 12, 24–25, 169, 193
bathhouses, 167–168
Bennett, Louise, 106
Berlant, Lauren, 224
Bersani, Leo, 162–163, 162–163 n.25, 167–168
Between Past and Future (Arendt), 30–31
Bevan, Aneurin, 25–26, 203–204
Beveridge Report (1942), 8–11, 13, 79, 101, 203
Beveridge, William, 8–11, 17–18
Bhabha, Homi, 109
Bildungsroman, 87–88, 158, 167, 173, 212–213
Binney, Marcus, 186–187
biography, 158–159, 163–164, 175, 177–178
  See also life writings
biopolitics, 102–104
biopower, 209–210
Black as political signifier, 125–126
Black British people, 104–105 n.8, 106–107
Black Cultural Archives, 128–129
Blackness (construed) as primitive, 128–129

Black Power Movement, 123–126, 134
Blake, William, 203
Blitz, the, 1–2, 12, 41–42, 56–57, 125
Bloch, Ernst, 169
blood donation, 211–212
Bloomsbury coterie, 28
bodies, 102–104, 234–235
Booker Prize, 182–183
books, 198
Bourdieu, Pierre, 160–161
Bowen, Elizabeth
  biographical details, 42–43
  Britain in, 3
  domestic space in, 45–46
  influences on, 44, 66–67
  interior vs. exterior life, 29
  modernism and, 44
  photographs of, 41–42*f*
  on postwar reconstruction, 46
  reception of work, 49–50, 65
  syntax, 60–62
  Woolf and, 43–44
  Bowen's Court, 61–62
  The Demon Lover, 47–48
  See also *Heat of the Day, The*
Brandt, Bill, 41, 42*f*
Brideshead Revisited (Waugh), 157–158, 164–165, 217–218 n.37
  See also Waugh, Evelyn
Briggs, Asa, 16 n.34
Britain Can Make It No. 12, 21, 24*f*, 69–70
Britishness, 124–125, 195
Britten, Benjamin, 155–156
brutalism, 180
  See also architecture
Builders (Jackson, documentary), 69–70
Butler, Judith, 160–161
By the Sea (Gurnah), 236–237

Calder, Angus, 1–2, 13 n.23, 80 n.17
camp, as figure, 244
care
  as term, 15–16

  architectures of, 18
  fantasies of, 26, 36–37
  lack of, 246–247
  political theory and, 14–15 n.31
  practices of, 192
  studies of, 14–15
  urgency for, 185–186
  Foucault on, 14–15 n.31
  in *The English Patient*, 194–196
  in *The Swimming-Pool Library*, 161
Catholicism, 77–78, 89–90, 96–97
characters, flat renderings of, 238–239
children (future as entrusted to), 69–70
Churchill, Winston, 31–32 n.63, 56–57
citizenship, 211–212
class differences, 29, 53, 121
class relations, 172–173
Clausewitz, Carl von, 17–18
Cold War paranoia, 159–160
Coleman, Alice, 142–143
collective consciousness, 129–130
collective living
  idealizations of, 33–34
  "lost houses," 188
  midcentury legacy of, 131–132
  representations of, 24–26, 137, 143–144
  See also homes and housing; Spark, Muriel
collective, the and collectivity
  the individual vs., 3–4, 133
  ownership, 126
  politics of the, 200–201
  responsibility, 13–14
  social, 201
  space, 118
  in *The Housing Lark*, 126
  in *The Lonely Londoners*, 114–115
colonialism
  language and, 111
  postwar reconstruction histories under, 169–170
  in reverse, 112
  Windrush generation and, 105–106
comedy, 139–140

Commonwealth Immigrants Act
  1962, 124–126
Commonwealth Immigrants Act
  1968, 124–125
Commonwealth Institute, 125–126
Communism, 200–201
community, 123–125
Compton-Burnett, Ivy, 41
Conservative Manifesto, 138 n.8
contemporary, the, 1, 128–129,
  237–238
country houses, 187 n.14
County of London Plan (Forshaw,
  Abercrombie), 19–20f, 23f, 56–57,
  162–163
COVID-19 pandemic, 247
cryptology, 186
cultural production, 236–237
cultural studies, 59–60, 88, 120–121
Curriculum Vitae (Spark), 94–96

death and dying, 97–98, 229–230
de Certeau, Michel, 27, 120–121
decolonization, 112–113, 147–148
  See also colonialism
Defensible Space (Newman), 142–143
Deleuze, Gilles, 191
democratization, 29, 52–53
Demon Lover, The (Bowen), 47–48
  See also Bowen, Elizabeth
Derrida, Jacques, 109–110
detention, 237–238, 247
Diary for Timothy, A (Forster), 69–72f
diets, 79
disease, 8–10, 205
disenchantment, 192
Distant Shore, A (Phillips), 236–238
documentary aesthetics, 59–60
domesticity
  communal (dreams of), 34
  femininity and, 122
  idealizations of, 76
  immigrants and, 112–113
  as private, 122
  uncanniness and, 45–46
  in *Never Let Me Go*, 227

domestic space
  decentering of, 163–164
  novelistic representations of, 18–19,
    45, 80–81
  queer, 181
  as (not always) welcoming, 118
  in *A Distant Shore*, 237–238
  in *The English Patient*, 186–187
  in *The Lonely Londoners*, 117–118,
    120, 123
  See also space
Drinkwater, John, 92–93, 96
dystopia, 75 n.8, 143–144, 164–166,
  205–207, 210–211, 230–231

eating disorders, 97–98
Edelman, Lee, 167–168
Edmundson, Helen, 130–131
Emecheta, Buchi, *In the Ditch*, 35,
  143–148
enchantment, 184, 197, 230
England, England (Barnes), 187
English at Home, The (Brandt), 41
English Patient, The (Ondaatje)
  appeal of, 182–183
  care in, 194–196
  heritage industry and reconstruction
    in, 36
  identity in, 191–192, 194
  narrative in, 199
  Ondaatje on, 184
  plot details, 183, 190, 194–197,
    199–200
  postwar imagination in, 189–190
  reception, 182–183, 186, 196
  romance in, 186
  sociality in, 191
  space and spatiality in, 186–188,
    191, 192, 197–198
  See also Ondaatje, Michael
equality and welfare state, 233
Esping-Andersen, Gøsta, 137 n.4
Esty, Jed, 91, 107–108, 120–121
ethics, 28–29, 173
everyday life, 49–50 n.19, 120–121, 134

268 INDEX

Exit West (Hamid), 239–240
Experiment in Love, An (Mantel), 96

family
  acts related to, 10–11
  alternative models to, 24–26,
    164–165, 200, 201
  conservatism associated
    with, 162–163
  as (normative) figure, 18 n.38, 21,
    86–87, 201
  inheritances, 61–62
  literature on, 14–15
  neighbors vs., 137–138
  nuclear, 25–26, 35–36, 77–78, 87–88,
    112–113, 119, 145–146, 162
  racial purity of, 119
  reconstruction and, 162–163
  the state and, 86–87
  war as forming, 52–53
  See also Swimming-Pool Library, The
Fanon, Frantz, 191
feeling (structures of), 163–164
femininity (domesticity as), 122
Firbank, Ronald, 155–156
form, 47–48, 141
Forshaw, John, 19–20, 56–57, 162–163
Forster, E.M.
  Bowen and, 66–67
  communal life for, 28–29
  photographs of, 41
  reception of work, 44, 131–132
  World War II (support for), 42–43
  A Passage to India, 199–200
  Maurice, 168–169
  See also Diary for Timothy, A;
    Howards End; place-feeling
Foucault, Michel, 14–15 n.31, 102–104,
  209–210
"from the cradle to the grave," 31–32
  n.63, 137, 207
Fussell, Paul, 4–5 n.6

Gatwick Detainees Welfare
  Group, 240–241

gay men and sexuality, 155–156,
  159–161, 177
gender, 21–24, 86–87, 160–161
Gielgud, John, 159–160
Gilligan, Carol, 14–15
Gilroy, Paul, 108–110
Girls of Slender Means, The (Spark)
  gender in, 86–87
  good and evil in, 90
  language (use of), 93
  1945 in, 88–89
  opening, 197
  other works compared to, 147–148
  parody of social ideals, 26–27, 80
  plot details, 79, 84–86, 89–92
  quotation in, 96
  reception, 91–92 n.47, 96–97
  social differentiation in, 83–84
  sociality in, 86
  structure, 84–85
  subculture in, 88
  warfare and, 33–34, 77–78
  windows in, 81
  See also Experiment in Love, An;
    Spark, Muriel
Goffman, Erving, 26
Golden Man Booker Prize, 182–183
Goldfinger, Ernő, 20–21, 22f
G-plan (furniture company), 119–120
Graves, Robert, 41
Greene, Graham, 41–43, 47–48
Green, Henry, 42–43
Greenwood, Arthur, 8–10
grief and grievance, 15–16 n.33
Group, The (McCarthy), 88–89
Guattari, Felix, 191
Gurnah, Abdulrazak, *By the
  Sea*, 236–237

habitus (Bourdieu), 160–161, 224
Halliday, Lisa, *Asymmetry*, 238–239
Hall, Stuart, 13, 102–104, 128–131,
  134, 136, 189–190 n.21
Hamid, Mohsin, *Exit West*, 239–240
Hanley, Lynsey, 138 n.10, 139
Harris, Jose, 2–3

INDEX 269

Harrow Road (neighborhood), 120
Harvey, David, 207
haunting, 148, 177–178
healthcare, 203–204
Heat of the Day, The (Bowen)
  England in, 68–69
  literary influences, 66–67
  plot details, 48–55, 64–65
  reception, 49–50
  reconstructive imagination in, 47
  spaces in, 47, 55, 57–59
  syntax, 60–61
  war in, 33, 42–43
  working class in, 121
  See also Bowen, Elizabeth
Held, Virginia, 14–15
Hepburn, Allan, 49–50 n.22, 68–69
heritage industry, 187, 189–190
hermeneutics of suspicion
  (Ricoeur), 16
Herodotus, 193–194
heterogeneity, 27
high-density council estate, 142
  See also homes and housing
High-Rise (Ballard), 35
Hiroshima, 202
historical fiction, 141
historical novels, 153–155
historical time, as term, 1
historic preservation, 62–63
historiographic fiction, 186–187
historiography, 36, 105–106, 141,
  160–161
Hoggart, Richard, 13, 59–60
Hollinghurst, Alan
  overview, 155–156
  architecture in work, 180
  clubs and gyms in, 29
  education, 168–169
  1945 in work, 3
  reception of work, 159–160
  spatial representation in work, 167
  The Line of Beauty, 156–158
  The Sparsholt Affair, 35–36,
    176–178, 180–181

The Stranger's Child, 164–165,
  176–178
  See also The Swimming-Pool Library
homes and housing
  as concept, 112–113, 169–170
  country houses, 187 n.14
  destruction of, 93–94
  England (as metonym for), 66–67
  ideas around, 43–44
  identity politics and, 127–128
  images of, 21, 22f, 122
  institutional use as
    degrading, 164–165
  literature on, 56, 59–60
  London as, 106–107
  militarized home front, 3, 43–44,
    69–70
  ownership, 123–124, 127–128,
    164–165
  photographs of, 58f
  poetics of (Bachelard), 217–218
  postwar repair and, 18, 29
  representation and, 3–4, 143–144
  "Right to Rent," 234
  as social service, 35
  as space of social experiment, 28
  styles of, 55, 56 n.41, 142–143,
    145–146, 165–166
  utopian ideals of, 169–170
  in *The Heat of the Day*, 55
  in *The Swimming-Pool
    Library*, 169–171
Homes for the People (Mander), 69–70
homosexuality, (de)criminalization
  of, 158, 176–179
hospitality, 109–110, 132–133, 241, 242
hostels, 123, 148–149
"hostile environment"
  policies, 233–234
hostility, 109–110
Hothouse by the East River, The
  (Spark), 93–94, 164–165
Housing Lark, The (Selvon), 120–121,
  126–128
housing policies, 25–26

Housing Subsidy Act, 142
Howards End (Forster), 66–69
Hutcheon, Linda, 153–154 n.1, 186

identity, 126–128, 165–166, 191–192, 194
idiorhythmy (Barthes), 169, 193
idleness, 8–10
ignorance, 8–10
illness, heritage industry as, 189–190
imagination (reconstructive), 41, 47
immigrants and immigration
  contributions of, 112
  domesticity and, 112–113
  fears over, 125
  hostility towards, 109–110
  legal acts around, 124–125
  motivations of, 111
  politics against, 233–234
  removal structures, 235
Immigration from the Commonwealth (White Paper), 124–125
Immigration Removal Centre, 37
imperialism, 183–184
individuality, 193, 205–207
individual, the vs. the collective, 3–4, 133
individuation, 212–213 n.20
industrial revolution, 203–204
infrastructure
  humanizing abilities of, 29
  interiority and, 209
  literature on, 209–210
  as meaning-making, 209
  of migration, 234–235
  paradoxical, 213
  poetics of, 217
  in *Never Let Me Go*, 228
inheritances, 61–62, 66–69, 158, 164–165
innovation, 141
institutionalization, 177
institutional spaces, 26–27, 36–37
interiority, 29, 44, 52, 81–82, 209
interwar period, memory of, 46–47
In the Ditch (Emecheta), 35, 143–148

intimacy, 24–25
  girlish, 33–34
  personal forms of, 3–4
  queer, 35–36
  social, 77
Ishiguro, Kazuo
  biographical details, 208
  cloning structures in, 29
  1945 in work, 3
  welfare state and, 208
  works by, 204–205, 218–219, 222–223 n.50
  World War II in work, 204–205
  See also Never Let Me Go

Jameson, Fredric, 21–24, 154–155, 184–185
Jennings, Humphrey, 42–43, 204
Jephcott, Pearl, 112–113 n.28
Jerusalem (Blake, Parry), 203
Jones, Claudia, 125–126
Joyce, James, 131–132
juxtapolitical (Berlant), 224

Kafka, Franz, 30–31, 245
Kalliney, Peter, 75
"Keep Calm and Carry On," 7–8f, 95–96
Kinnock, Neil, 139–140 n.16
Kitchener, Lord. *See* Roberts, Aldwyn
Klein, Melanie, 16

labor, 55, 86–87
Labour government, 186–187, 207–208
Labour Government, 11–12
Labour Party, 200–201
landlords, 123–124, 126
landscape, 218–220
Landscape for a Good Woman (Steedman), 60–61
language
  colonialism and, 111
  figurative, 215–216
  as repair, 184
  in *The Swimming-Pool Library*, 176
Larkin, Brian, 29–30

INDEX 271

Le Corbusier, 144–145, 170
Levy, Andrea, *Small Island*, 34, 130–131
Liberal government, 13 n.21
Life after Life (Atkinson), 154
life writings, 80–81, 94–95, 155–156
  See also biography
Little, Kenneth, 113–114
Lloyd George, David, 5, 56
Loadsamoney, 139–141
London
  Black London, 116
  as privileged, 106–107
  ruins of, 162
loneliness, 126, 133
Lonely Londoners, The (Selvon)
  overview, 114–115
  domesticity in, 34, 106–107
  evaluative gaze in, 165–166
  homes in, 122
  immigration in, 24–25, 114–116
  literature on, 117–118
  loneliness in, 115–116
  as a pedagogical novel, 116
  place in, 116–118
  space in, 120, 123
  welfare and, 118
Look Back in Anger (Osborne), 75–76
Love, Heather, 160–161
Lowe, Rodney, 18–19
Lukács, György, 154–155

MacKay, Marina, 4–5 n.6, 42–43, 71, 77–78 n.14, 88 n.40, 91, 107–108, 143–144, 154 n.2
MacMillan, Harold, 73
Maher, Ashley, 143–144
"make it new"/"make it anew," 49–50
mansions, 145–146
  See also homes and housing
Mantel, Hilary, 186
  See also Experiment in Love, An
Mao, Douglas, 213–214
maps, 20f
Marcus, Laura, 81–82
Marshall, T.H., 13, 211–212

Matera, Marc, 123
materiality, 216–217
May, Theresa, 233–234
Mazzetti, Lorenza, 245–247
McCarthy, Mary, *The Group*, 88–89
mediation, 134
memory, 4–5 n.6, 46–47, 54
mid-century, as term, 107–108 n.13
Midcentury Modern, 119–120
migration, 234–235
Minghella, Anthony, 182–183
modernism
  in architecture, 31–32 n.65
  ethics in, 28–29
  interiority and, 44
  "make it new"/"make it *anew*," 49–50
  place-feeling and, 117–118
  postwar, 28, 49–50
  potentiality and, 199–200
  progressive and radical politico-aesthetics of, 4–5
  techniques, 131–132
  World War I and, 4–5, 83–84
  Ballard on, 145
  Bowen and, 44
  in Smith's work, 133
  Spark's work as, 78–79
modernization, 189–190 n.19
morality and relativism, 202
Mort, Frank, 162–163
Moses Ascending (Selvon), 114–115, 123–124, 126
Moses Migrating (Selvon), 123–124
Most Popular Art Exhibition Ever! (exhibit), 232
  See also art and artists
Mountz, Alison, 233
mourning, 4–5 n.6, 55
Mrs. Dalloway (Woolf), 28–29, 78–79, 82–83, 147–148
  See also Woolf, Virginia
multiculturalism, 120–121
Muñoz, José Esteban, 169
Murphy, J. Stephen, 175
myth, 12, 33–34, 59–60

names, 247
narration, 92, 217
narrative
   about 1945, 108–109
   in *The English Patient*, 199
   national, 190–191
   patterns, 222–223
   of postwar reconstruction, 110–111
   social world (distance from), 114–115
   technique, 193–194
Nash, Paul, 232–233
National Gallery, 20–21, 62–63
National Health Service, 203–204
nationhood, 102–104, 190–191
Naziism, 165–166
negativity (of queer history), 160–161
neighborhood, 121
neighbourliness, 148
neoliberalism, 207–208
"never had it so good," 73–75
Never Let Me Go (Ishiguro)
   about, 204–205
   as allegory of postwar Britain, 36–37
   dystopia in, 205–207
   family (representations of) in, 164–165
   history in, 224
   infrastructure in, 209–210, 228
   narration in, 217
   plot details, 205, 208–209, 212–220, 223–229
   political aspects, 207
   reception of work, 225 n.59
   reconstruction fantasies of care, 26
   space and spatiality in, 221–222, 224–225, 227–229
   welfare state in, 230–231
   windows in, 225–226
   work in, 207–208
   See also Ishiguro, Kazuo
New Brutalism, 142
New Labour, 207–208
Newman, Oscar, *Defensible Space*, 142–143

newness, 13
1984 (Orwell), 26–27, 50–51, 230–231
   See also Orwell, George
1945
   the contemporary and, 1
   cultural legacy of, 36
   historical reception of, 11–12
   narratives about, 108–109
   the novel as returning to, 3
   "post," 156–157
   representation in literature, 204
   temporality of, 31–32
   in *The Girls of Slender Means*, 88–89
   for Ondaatje, 183, 196
Noddings, Nel, 14–15
Norris, Rufus, 130–131
nostalgia, 36
"Notes from the year 1920" (Kafka), 30–31
novels
   century, 35–36, 153–155, 186–187
   climaxes of, 100
   as form, 47–48, 84–85
   modernist (types of), 45
   1945 and, 3
   pedagogical, 116
   reconstructive discourse and, 24–25
   sociality and genre of, 47–48
   of World War II, 179

objects and objecthood, 43–44, 85–86
"Odd Lot: A Gallery of Literary Portraits, An" (Brandt), 41
Olympics Opening Ceremony, 203–204
Ondaatje, Michael
   heritage discourse in work, 187
   narrative style, 193–194
   1945 in work, 3
   reception of work, 184–185
   re-enchantment in work, 197
   villas in, 29
   works by, 190–191
   on *The English Patient*, 184
   Warlight, 36, 190–191, 200
   See also English Patient, The

organ donation, 211–215, 219
Orwell, George, 11–12, 42–43
  See also 1984
Osborne, John, *Look Back in Anger*, 75–76

painting, 62–64
  See also art and artists; photography
Paolozzi, Eduardo, 246–247
Patterson, Sheila, 113–114
Paul, Kathleen, 124–125
peace, 2–3, 62, 94
performativity of gender, 160–161
periodicals, 101
Perry, Grayson, 232
Phillips, Caryl, *A Distant Shore*, 236–238
photography, 128–131, 133–135, 220–221
Picture Post (magazine), 101, 102*f*, 102–104, 128–129
Piette, Adam, 6–7
place
  as term, 116
  longing for, 115–116
  no places, 117–118, 235–236
  in Selvon's work, 106–107
  specificity of, 229–230
  in Windrush literature, 114
place-feeling, 44, 66–67, 80–81, 116, 117–118
"Planning Your Neighbourhood: for home, for work, for play" (exhibition), 20–21
poetics of house (Bachelard), 217–218
political identity, 126
politics
  art about, 232
  bio-, 102–104
  of reconstruction, 232–233
  of resistance (Black), 129–130
  in Smith's Seasonal Quartet, 243–244
Poor Law reforms, 13 n.21, 56, 59–60
postcolonialialism, 32–34, 106, 107–109, 236–237
posterity, 66

postmodernism, 107–108
postness, 31, 34, 107–108
postwar
  as term, 107–108
  the contemporary and, 128–129
  defining chronology of, 6, 31
  diffusion of, 12
  literature, 141 n.17
  policies, 25–26
  postcolonial vs., 106, 109
  social transformations of, 11–12
postwar modernism, 49–50
postwar reconstruction. *See* reconstruction
potentiality, 19, 199–200, 220–221
Poulson, John, 179–180
poverty, 139
Powell, Anthony, 154 n.2
Powell, Enoch, 125
power, 123–124
preservation of history, 62–63
Pritchard, V.S., 47–48
private, the
  domesticity as, 122
  beyond family home, 26
  postwar novel and, 3–4
  the public vs., 3–4, 21–24, 83–84, 207
  space, 117–118
prizes, 182–183
Proctor, James, 106–107 n.8
propaganda, 42–43, 103*f*, 101
Pryce-Jones, Alan, 41–42
public good, 1–2
public health, 205–207
public housing
  discourse around, 137–138
  plurality from, 137–138
  postwar reconstruction and, 142–143
  postwar sociality and, 142
  quality of life in, 74–75
  rise and fall of, 35
  Thatcher's attack on, 138

public, the
  private vs., 3–4, 21–24, 83–84
  the private vs., 207
public works, 14–15 n.28

queer
  as term, 174
  "empty panic" (*Swimming-Pool Library*), 173–174
  history, 160
  intimacy, 35–36
  space, 167–169, 181
  studies, 155–156
  subjectivity, 162–163
  temporality, 160–161
  utopia, 171
  welfare, 171–172, 175
quotation, 92–93, 96, 245

Race Relations Act, 124–125
racial difference, 240
racial discrimination, 234
racial diversity, 189
racialization
  of bodies, 102–104
  of home buying, 127–128
  objectification, 192
racism, 119, 129–130
readers and reading, 16, 20–21, 134
realism, 76, 78–79, 227
Rebuilding Britain (Royal Institute for British Architects, booklet), 57
"Rebuilding Britain" (exhibition), 20–21
reception theory, 128–129
reconstruction
  appeal of, 232–233
  Bowen on, 46
  Britain's obsession with, 3
  British discourses of, 102–104
  collectivity and, 25–26
  colonial histories of, 169–170
  corruption and, 179–180
  cultural history as, 128–129
  cultural imaginary of, 106–107
  family and, 162–163
  in film, 69–70
  housing and, 3–4
  inward turn of, 91
  literatures of, 7
  logic of, 3
  narratives of, 110–111
  new art-form of, 90
  politics of, 232–233
  potentiality of, 128
  privilege through, 163–164
  publications about, 101
  public housing and, 142–143
  queering, 162
  racial imaginary of, 32–33
  reader's role in, 20–21
  repair of, 109
  sexual politics of, 162
  timeline of, 8–10
  as untimely, 5
  utopic aspects, 15–16
  whiteness of, 108–109
  in *The Girls of Slender Means*, 90
"Recording Britain" project, 62–64
Redgrave, Michael, 70
Refugee Tales (organization), 240–242
rehabilitation, 7–8, 9*f*
reinscription, 28
repair
  fictionality of, 16–17
  of interior space (potential), 126
  language as, 184
  of postwar reconstruction, 109
  potentiality of, 68
  promise of, 15–16
  in *Never Let Me Go*, 230–231
reparative turn, 16
representation
  in biography, 159
  of British welfare state, 136
  of collective living, 143–144
  of communal living, 137
  of the "I," 241–242
  of reconstruction, 198
  spatial (in Hollinghurst's work), 167
  of World War II, 188–189

rhythm, 24–25, 27, 169, 193
Ricoeur, Paul, 16
"Right to Buy" policy, 138–139
"Right to Rent," 234
Robbins, Bruce, 14–15 n.28, 205–207 n.8, 223 n.51
Roberts, Aldwyn, 111–112, 114
Robinson, Fiona, 14–15
Rosner, Victoria, 28, 44, 81–82, 143–144
Ruddick, Sara, 14–15
ruins, 91–93, 162, 197–198
Rushdie, Salman, 131–132, 188–189

Salter, Joseph, 148–149
Samuel, Raphael, 189–190
sanitization, 162–163
Saturday Night and Sunday Morning (Sillitoe), 75–76
Schaffer, Talia, 14–15 n.30
Schwarz, Bill, 107–108 n.13
Sedgwick, Eve Kosofsky, 16
Seiler, Claire, 29–30 n.59, 49–50, 49–50 n.21
selfishness, 160
self, the, 210–211, 233
Selvon, Samuel
  Britain in, 3
  communal domesticity (dreams of), 34
  literary politics of place in, 106–107
  neighborliness, 29
  reception of work, 133–134
  Moses Ascending, 114–115, 123–124, 126
  Moses Migrating, 123–124
  The Housing Lark, 120–121, 126–128
  See also *Lonely Londoners, The*
sensitivity, 55
Serpentine Galleries, 232
sexual conservatism, 88–89
sexuality, architecture of, 167–168
Sherry, Vincent, 4–5 n.6
signs, 120
Sillitoe, Alan, 75–76

simulacra, 58–59
Sinfield, Alan, 75 n.6, 159–160
skepticism, 33
Small Island (Levy), 34, 130–131
Smith, Ali, 3, 240–247
Smith, Zadie, 34, 107, 131–135, 149
social change, allegories for, 87–88
social citizenship, 211–212
social collectivity, 201
social connection, 242
social insurance, 13
sociality, 132, 167–168, 191
"Social Security and Its Allied Services" (White Paper), 8–10, 13
social spaces, 43–44
social theory, 100
social welfare, 2–3, 13, 53–54
social world, 114–115
society, 137, 159–160
sociology, 59–60, 86–87, 98–99
Solanke, Ladipo, 123
space and spatiality
  abandoned, 197–198
  abstract, 170
  collective, 118
  domestic, 117–118
  empty, 159–160
  in *The English Patient*, 188
  fantasies of, 167
  institutional, 83–84
  literary production of, 168–169
  private, 117–118
  queer, 163–164, 167–169
  smooth/unstriated (Deleuze and Guattari), 191
  social organization of, 26–27
  in Windrush literature, 114
  in *Never Let Me Go*, 221–222, 224–225, 227–229
  in *The English Patient*, 191–192, 197–198
Spark, Muriel
  as an "angry young woman," 76–77
  Britain in, 3
  influences on, 80–81

Spark, Muriel (*Continued*)
  language in work, 95–96
  literary modernism in, 78–79
  reception of work, 96
  ruins, 29
  social intimacy in work, 77
  women (groups of) in, 86–89
  See also Curriculum Vitae; *Girls of Slender Means, The*; *Hothouse by the East River, The*
squalor, 8–10
state, as term, 235–236
Steedman, Carolyn, 60–61, 98–99 n.69
Stonebridge, Lyndsey, 49–50 n.22, 107–108 n.13
Strangers' Home, 148–149
subjectivity, 162–163, 166
suburban encroachment, 68–69
surveillance, 49–51
Swimming-Pool Library, The (Hollinghurst)
  overview, 156
  collective care in, 161
  family estate in, 164–165
  fantasies in, 171–173
  history (feeling of), 160–161
  narrative temporality in, 157
  plot details, 157–158, 173, 174
  as a quasi-*Bildungsroman*, 176
  spatiality in, 167, 171–173
  subjectivity of paranoia in, 166
  trauma in, 35–36
  use of language in, 176
  windows in, 167
Szalay, Michael, 14–15 n.28

temporality
  postness, 31
  of postwar condition, 30–31
  of wartime, 29–30, 73
  windows and, 81–82
  in *Summer* (Seasonal Quartet, Smith), 245
  in *The Swimming-Pool Library*, 157
  See also queer: temporality

Thatcherism, 31–33, 207–208
Thatcher, Margaret, 35, 98 n.65, 136, 138, 189–190
thick description, 120–121
Titmuss, Richard, 10–11, 13, 211–212
togetherness, 2–3, 105–106
"TOGETHER" war propaganda poster, 101, 103*f*, 110
Torgersen, Ulf, 18–19
Tory government, 98, 178–179
translation, 30–31 n.61
trauma, 154
Trilling, Lionel, 28
Tronto, Joan, 14–15
True Glory, The (documentary), 102–104 n.3
truth, 202

urban, 183–184
utopia
  abstract vs. concrete, 169
  as failed, 136
  homes (ideals of), 169–170
  liteary devices of, 168–169
  queer, 168–169, 171
  space as, 123
  thought, 24–25

violence, 91, 173, 174, 184, 195–196, 200–201, 220–221

Waiting for Godot (Beckett), 49–50 n.21
Walkowitz, Rebecca, 205–207 n.7
wallpaper, 127
warfare
  alternative forms of, 33–34
  anti-colonial potential of, 189
  history beyond, 65
  as over, 195–196
  propaganda, 101, 103*f*
  support for, 94–95
  temporality of, 29–30, 73
  transnational, 36
  welfare vs., 17–18, 79
  in *Warlight*, 201–202

Warlight (Ondaatje), 36, 190–191, 200
  See also Ondaatje, Michael
Waters, Sarah, 163–164 n.27
Waugh, Evelyn, 41–43, 157–158, 164–165, 217–218 n.37
  See also *Brideshead Revisited*
"we," 98–99, 110
wealth tax, 186–187
Webster, Wendy, 102–104 n.3
welfare and welfare state
  as term, 16 n.34, 30–31
  as citizens' reward, 16–17
  consolidation of, 35
  creation of, 10–11
  decolonization and, 112–113
  equality and, 233
  "from the cradle to the grave," 31–32 n.63
  housing as lived modality of, 18–19
  infrastructural legacy of, 209–210
  Ishiguro and, 208
  literary representations of, 14–15, 99–100
  loneliness of, 118
  queer, 171–172, 175
  reforms of, 136
  warfare vs., 17–18, 79
  in *Never Let Me Go*, 230–231
welfare provisions, 2–3
West African Students' Union (WASU) House, 123
West India House, 149
White, Leslie, 68 n.77
whiteness of postwar reconstruction, 108–109
Williams, Raymond, 13, 16 n.34, 59–60, 183–184
Willmott, Peter, 59–60
Wilson, Nicola, 56 n.41
windows, 81
  in *Girls of Slender Means*, 84–86
  in *The Heat of the Day*, 50–51, 54–55
  in *The Lonely Londoners*, 121
  in *Mrs. Dalloway*, 81–83
  in *Never Let Me Go*, 225–226
  in *The Sparsholt Affair*, 179
  in *Spring* (Seasonal Quartet, Smith), 243
  in *Swimming-Pool Library*, 167
Windrush generation
  about, 104–105
  contemporary iterations of, 107
  legacy of, 130–131
  literature on, 105–106
  postwar, 107
  reconstructing, 128
  space/place in literature, 114
  2018 Scandal, 233–234
  women, 86–87, 245
Woolf, Virginia
  domesticity in, 80–81 n.18
  letter from Bowen, 43–44
  on other writers, 45
  Mrs. Dalloway, 28–29, 78–79, 82–83, 147–148
working class, 55–57, 121
world literature, 184–185
World War I, 4–5 n.6, 83–84
World War II
  the contemporary and, 1, 237–238
  cultural production and, 200
  diversity and, 102–104
  economic boom after, 73
  in Ishiguro's fiction, 204–205
  labor and, 86–87
  literature about, 73
  modernism and, 4–5
  narrative conflict of, 154
  novels of, 179
  as "people's war," 1–2, 7, 80, 93, 102–104, 155
  refugee crisis of present vs., 244
  representations of, 188–189
  spatial lexicon of, 19
  support from artists, 42–43

World War II (*Continued*)
  trauma of, 165–166
  whiteness and, 108–109
  in Smith's Seasonal Quartet, 244
  See also Hollinghurst, Alan: *The Sparsholt Affair*

Wright, Patrick, 189–190
writer, role of the, 47–48

YMCA Indian Students' Union and Hostel, 123
Young, Michael, 59–60
youth, 87–88